Russia's Rulers:
THE
KHRUSHCHEV
PERIOD

INTERIM
HISTORY

Russia's Rulers:
THE
KHRUSHCHEV
PERIOD

Edited by Lester A. Sobel

FACTS ON FILE, INC.   NEW YORK

Russia's Rulers:
THE
KHRUSHCHEV
PERIOD

© Copyright, 1971, by Facts on File, Inc.

Library of Congress Catalog Card Number: 73-115036

ISBN 0-87196-175-X

9 8 7 6 5 4 3 2 1

CONTENTS

1957

1958

1959

1960

1961

1962

1963

1964

FOREWORD

THIS BOOK ATTEMPTS TO SUPPLY the main facts that helped determine who would rule Russia during the first dozen years after the death of Joseph V. Stalin. It is largely a record of the actions and policies of the Soviet Communist Party and government during the period dominated by Nikita S. Khrushchev.

Khrushchev was the 3d man—after Lenin and Stalin—who could be described with any accuracy as the ruler of the Soviet Union. The role of ruler, according to some observers of the Soviet system, appears to be indispensable in the complicated Soviet scheme. Leonard Shapiro, political science professor at the London School of Economics & Political Science, touched on this view Apr. 16, 1970 in a statement before the National Security & International Operations Subcommittee of the U.S. Senate. "Experience suggests," Shapiro said, "that it is the nature of the Soviet political system, whichever personalities may be active at any one period, for it to be led and, to a greater or lesser extent, dominated by one man. Periods of so-called 'collective leadership'... are transitional to the one-man rule, which alone the nature of the system makes workable."

The history of despotic rule in Russia, of course, long predates the Soviet era. According to tradition, the Russian state was founded in 862 when East Slavic and Finnish tribes in northwestern Russia invited Rurik, leader of Varangian (Viking) tribesmen, to rule them. Rurik reigned in Novgorod, where he established the house of Rurikids, the first of Russia's 2 ruling dynasties. Rurik's successor, Oleg, moved south and founded a 2d Russian state in Kiev in 878. The 2 states gradually merged, and members of the house of Rurikids ultimately ruled all of Russia.

Russia was invaded by the Mongols (Tatars, or Tartars) in 1237 and remained part of the Mongol empire until 1480.

1

Ivan III, or Ivan the Great, the first Russian ruler to use the title *tsar* (czar, or Caesar), ascended the throne in 1462 and extended the Russian domain to the Urals as the Mongol empire receded. Ivan IV, or Ivan the Terrible, who became *tsar* in 1533 at the age of 3, also expanded Russian rule eastward. Known for his cruelty and as the originator of tsarist absolutism, Ivan IV was crowned at 17 as "*tsar* and autocrat," the title used by all succeeding *tsars*. It was under Ivan IV that the Russian secret police came into existence.

Ivan IV's excesses were at least partly responsible for the period of civil wars, known as "the time of troubles," that followed his death in 1584. During this period the Poles seized Moscow, the Swedes took Novgorod and the Turks invaded the Crimea. Russia's feudal nobles (the *boyars*) finally drove the Poles out of Moscow, and in 1613 Ivan IV's grandnephew Michael Romanov, then 17, was elected as *tsar* by the Assembly of the Land. The house of Romanov thereafter supplied Russia with its *tsars* until the overthrow of the Russian empire in 1917.

The Romanov *tsar* Peter I, or Peter the Great, who reigned from 1689 to 1725, started Russia on the road to modern statehood. He reorganized the army, started a navy and merchant marine, subordinated the clergy to the monarchy, reformed the government and civil service and promulgated a law authorizing the *tsar* to name his own successor. But Peter I, who in 1721 was proclaimed the first "emperor of all Russia," was also capable of extreme cruelties. He had his son Aleksei tortured to death and ordered the mass execution of 12,000 members of his imperial guard (the *streltzi*).

Prussian-born Catherine II, or Catherine the Great, married the future Peter III in 1745 and succeeded him to the throne in 1762 after she presumably arranged his murder. This lady of many lovers, it was reported, considered herself an enlightened despot, but she increased the privileges of the nobility at the expense of the peasants.

Following Russia's defeat in the Crimean war, Alexander II liberated the serfs in 1861 and made many reforms. But Alexander II was assassinated in 1881, and his son, Alexander III, renewed tsarist oppression.

Nicholas II, the last *tsar,* survived a revolt in 1905, but he was overthrown in 1917 in the February Revolution and was later executed.

The Bolsheviks (Communists), led by Nikolai Lenin (born Vladimir Ilyich Ulyanov), were a minority among Russia's revolutionary groups and played virtually no role in the February Revolution. In fact, Lenin was in Switzerland in exile when it took place. Under Lenin's guidance, however, the Bolsheviks seized the government in the October Revolution.

Lenin then ruled as a dictator through his leadership of the Bolshevik party (which became the Communist Party in 1919) and through his post as premier (chairman of the Council of People's Commissars).

The Leninist government suppressed opposition, nationalized land and set about trying to make communism work in Russia. The Russian economy, however, was battered by war and mismanagement. Recognizing this, Lenin in 1921 instituted a New Economic Policy (NEP), which permitted some private enterprise in commerce and farming. The NEP, which helped restore the Russian economy, lasted until 1927.

Lenin's death in 1924 led to a power struggle in which Joseph Vissarionovich Stalin (born Iosif V. Djugashvili) emerged as victor in 1926 over Leon Trotsky (Lev Davidovich Bronstein). Stalin became the undisputed ruler of the Union of Soviet Socialist Republics (the name adopted in 1922 as more descriptive of the Soviet federation), while Trotsky was expelled from the Soviet Union in 1929 and murdered in Mexico by a Stalinist agent in 1940.

Under Stalin, a series of 5-year plans was started in 1928 in a move to develop the economy. The program called for speedy industrialization and for collectivizing farmland. Many *kulaks* (wealthy peasants) resisted collectivization, and Stalin retaliated with various measures, including police and military action, seizures of crops and farm property and deportations. The struggle produced an "artificial famine" in 1932-3, and perhaps 5 million peasants died—many as a result of starvation—before the collectivization program was completed.

During his 30-year rule, Stalin consolidated his power by purges of opponents, of colleagues who might develop into opponents and of many innocent bystanders. 4 massive purges during 1934-8 sent thousands of victims to prison or to the executioners for alleged treason. Such trials as took place were regarded as farces in which confessions, if given, were presumed to have been forced. Most freedoms considered normal in the

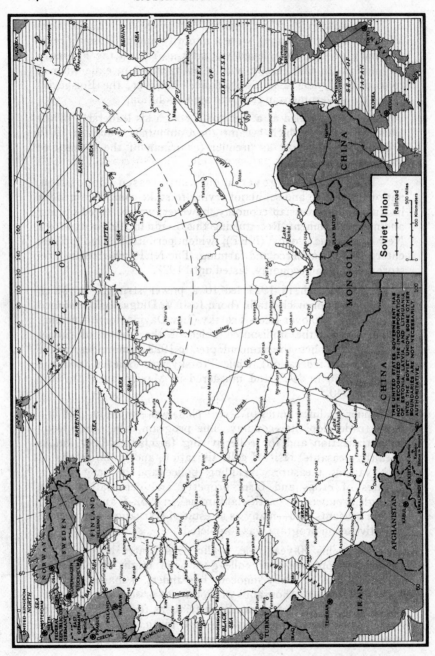

West—freedom of speech, of assembly and of the press—were denied in the USSR.

Stalin took active command of Soviet forces during World War II, and he also took most of the credit for victory over the Nazis. During the war (but before the USSR entered the war), Stalin annexed the independent Baltic states of Estonia, Latvia and Lithuania. Following the war, Soviet-occupied territories of Eastern Europe were turned into Communist-run satellites of the USSR. Only Yugoslavia, under a Communist government headed by the former partisan leader Tito, successfully retained its full independence.

During Stalin's declining years Western observers indulged in what might be described as a guessing game in which they tried to determine how Stalin's dictatorship would end and who would succeed Stalin. Within 2 years after Stalin's death, Nikita Sergeyevich Khrushchev had emerged as the undoubted ruler of the USSR.

The people ruled by Khrushchev were divided into more than 170 separate ethnic groups and totaled some 229 million by the time Khrushchev was deposed. The East Slavs comprised about 3/4 of the population. 2/3 of the East Slavs were Russians and Byelorussians living in the southwestern and western part of the USSR, and the remaining 1/3 of the East Slavs were Ukrainians.

Soviet territory stretches from the Baltic Sea across the northern Eurasian landmass to the Bering Strait, where an island belonging to the Soviet Union lies only 3 miles from an island that is part of Alaska. Its total area is more than 8.5 million square miles, or almost 2-1/2 times that of the U.S. Most of the USSR is above 50 degrees north latitude. The latitude of Moscow is the same as that of southern Alaska. In the west, from the Pripet Marshes near the Polish border to the Ural Mountains, Soviet territory stretches over a broad plain broken by occasional low hills. Crossing this plain to the south are a number of rivers, of which the most important are the Dnieper, which empties into the Black Sea, and the Volga, which empties into the Caspian Sea. Between the Black and Caspian Seas lie the Caucasus Mountains. The low Urals mark the traditional division between European and Asiatic Russia. To the east are the vast Siberian lowlands and the deserts of Central Asia. Beyond are the barren Siberian highlands and the mountain ranges of the

Soviet Far East. Numerous large rivers flow north through Siberia to the Arctic Ocean. Farther to the east, and south of the deserts of Central Asia, lie higher mountain ranges, including the Pamirs, Altai, and Tien Shan. The climate of the Soviet Union is varied, but for the most part it is characterized by long, cold winters and brief summers. The variations are reflected in the vegetation zones, which extend east and west. The marshy tundra in the north is marked by cold winters, sparse rainfall and an absence of forest vegetation. In parts of the eastern Siberian tundra, temperatures of —90 degrees F. have been recorded, and the January average is about —60 degrees F. South of the tundra is the large forest belt occupying more than half the country. South of the forests are the steppes (prairies), where the soil is rich and dark and rainfall is abundant. The steppes make up 12% of the area of the USSR and contain 2/3 of the arable land.

In the Soviet system ultimate power is exercised by the leaders of the Communist Party. The most powerful policy-making organ in the Communist Party is the Politburo of the party's Central Committee. The Secretariat of the Central Committee provides day-to-day executive and administrative direction for the entire party machine. Together the Politburo and Secretariat constitute the real seat of power in the Soviet Union. In theory the Politburo and Secretariat are accountable to the Central Committee. In fact, however, the Central Committee is only a forum for presenting party policy to the most important party members. Normally, it gives party policies unanimous, automatic approval. It is not in a position to initiate policy, although on rare occasions the Central Committee has been called on to mediate when a serious deadlock has developed within the Politburo. According to party statutes, the Central Committee should meet twice a year. It met rarely in Stalin's time but more frequently under Khrushchev. The party Congress is, in theory, the highest authority of the party, but its real role is to approve policies set by the party leaders. The party operates through a government apparatus that has no independent authority. The legislative organ is the Supreme Soviet, which is, in theory, the highest authority in the Soviet Union. It has 2 coequal houses— the Soviet of the Union, elected on the basis of population, and the Soviet of Nationalities, elected on the basis of territorial units. Elections are called for every 4 years. Usually only one deputy, approved by the party, runs from each constituency.

Between the brief and infrequent sessions of the Supreme Soviet, formal power is vested in the Presidium of the Supreme Soviet. The Supreme Soviet periodically appoints the highest executive organ of the government apparatus, the Council of Ministers, or cabinet. The Council is the most important part of the government structure. Under Communist Party direction, it supervises the work of the ministries and other governmental bodies, executes the national economic plan, conducts foreign affairs, and directs the armed forces. Party and government organizations in each of the union republics are patterned after the central party and government organizations and are subject to the policies and administrative direction of the all-union organizations.

This book, based largely on material from FACTS ON FILE plus Soviet, U.S. State Department and other official sources, covers the 12 years (1953-64) of the Khrushchev period—from Stalin's death to Khrushchev's downfall. It is a journalistic narration that describes the activities, policies and personalities involved in a struggle for control of the biggest and 3d-most-populous country in the world.

1953

Stalin's death in Mar. 1953 ended the one-man dictatorship that had held the USSR in its grip for nearly 30 years. Georgi M. Malenkov quickly succeeded Stalin as Premier, and Nikita S. Khrushchev soon rose to occupy the top party post. Although Western-style freedoms remained alien to the Soviet Union, a liberalization of Soviet policy accompanied the successor regime. Secret service chief Lavrenti P. Beria, accused of wholesale atrocities and brutality, was convicted and executed on treason charges. Many prisoners were released from jail, including 9 physicians (6 of them Jews) accused in the "doctors' plot" of planning the deaths of Soviet leaders. The government and party ordered increases in consumer-goods production.

Dictator Dies of Cerebral Hemorrhage

Soviet Premier Joseph Vissarionovich Stalin, 73, died at 9:50 p.m. (Moscow time) Mar. 5 in his apartment in the Kremlin. His death was announced by Moscow radio at 4:07 a.m. Mar. 6. A reorganization of the Soviet government with Georgi Maximilianovich Malenkov, 51, succeeding to the premiership was announced late Mar. 6. Stalin's body was interred beside the body of Nikolai Lenin in the Lenin mausoleum in Red Square Mar. 9 after one of the most elaborate funerals in Soviet history.

Stalin had been reported unconscious and sinking since he was stricken by cerebral hemorrhage in the late evening of Mar. 1. He succumbed despite the ministrations of 10 doctors working under the jurisdiction of Public Health Min. Andrei F. Tretyakov and I. Kuperin, chief of the Kremlin medical board. The doctors presumably were cleared of any suspicion that they had mishandled Stalin's case. An announcement several hours after Stalin's death said their treatment had been approved after an autopsy.

Stalin had ruled the USSR since Lenin's death in 1924, having emerged as strong man through the use of his position as secretary general of the All-Union (USSR) Communist Party Central Committee. He had become premier May 6, 1941.

Stalin's illness had been disclosed Mar. 4 by Moscow radio. The broadcast revealed that Stalin's duties had been taken over by the CP (Communist Party) Central Committee and the USSR Council of Ministers (cabinet). The Central Committee and Council of Ministers said in a joint announcement Mar. 4 that "the great misfortune which has befallen our party and our people—the grave illness of Comrade J. V. Stalin"—had caused his "temporary withdrawal...from leading state and party activity." They disclosed that 9 doctors were treating Stalin. They told the "party and whole Soviet people" to "display the greatest unity and cohesion, staunchness of spirit and vigilance" and "redouble their energies in building communism in our country." American correspondents reported from Moscow that the public appeared stunned, many grief-stricken by news of Stalin's illness. Russian Orthodox churches were reported crowded Mar. 5 in response to a call by Patriarch Alexis for

10

prayers for Stalin. The rabbi of the Moscow Synagogue also declared Mar. 6 a "Jewish fasting day for the great Stalin." U.S. Pres. Dwight D. Eisenhower and many other anti-Communist leaders issued expressions of personal sympathy for the Russians and Stalin Mar. 4. Meanwhile Western governments went into consultation on the questions of who might succeed Stalin and what effect his death might have on Soviet policy. 3 Soviet deputy prime ministers figured most prominently in the speculation: Malenkov, once Stalin's personal secretary and regarded as 2d only to Stalin in the CP Secretariat; Vyacheslav M. Molotov, 62, chief deputy in foreign affairs and said to be acting as cabinet chairman during Stalin's illness; Lavrenti Pavlovich Beria, 53, overseer of police agencies and atomic energy projects. Marshal Nikolai A. Bulganin, 57, believed to rank next to Stalin in the armed forces, was rated 4th among contenders for the succession.

The announcement of Stalin's death was made jointly Mar. 6 by the CP Central Committee, the USSR Council of Ministers and the Presidium of the Supreme Soviet (Parliament). It coupled lavish eulogies of Stalin with a call for "steel-like unity and monolithic unity of the ranks of the party" and a rallying of "all peoples of our country" behind the regime as power passed from Stalin to his successors. Excerpts from the announcement:

"The heart of the comrade and inspired continuer of Lenin's will, the wise leader and teacher of the Communist Party and the Soviet people—Joseph Vissarionovich Stalin—has stopped beating. Stalin's name is boundlessly dear to our party, to the Soviet people, to the workers of the whole world." Lenin and Stalin had molded the USSR into a "great fraternal family under the tested leadership of the Communist Party." The party and government would continue to show "particular solicitude" for the "constantly growing material and cultural needs of the entire society." The CP and government were "constantly raising our [armed] preparedness for a decisive rebuff to any aggressor." Soviet foreign policy "always is the policy of maintaining peace, the struggle against preparation and unleashing of another war, the policy of international collaboration and the development of businesslike relations with all countries..., fraternal friendship with the great Chinese people, with the workers of all the countries of the people's democracy, friendly relations with workers of the capitalist and colonial countries fighting for the cause of peace, democracy and socialism." The Soviet CP must

Joseph V. Stalin

educate "all Communists and workers in the spirit of high political vigilance, irreconcilability and stalwartness in the struggle against internal and external foes."

International Tributes to Stalin

Public tributes to Stalin began Mar. 6 throughout the USSR. Black-draped portraits of the late premier were raised in public centers, and his coffin was moved from the Kremlin to the House of Trade Unions, a former tsarist noblemen's club 2 blocks off Red Square known as the Hall of Columns. From 4 p.m. Mar. 6 until 2 a.m. Mar. 9 a constant procession of Soviet citizens said in Moscow dispatches to have numbered "millions" filed past 8 abreast as the body lay in state. High-ranking associates of Stalin's maintained a vigil at the bier. The line of people waiting in sub-zero cold to view the body was said to have stretched several miles from the hall. Soviet broadcasts concentrated on classical funeral music, tributes to Stalin and appeals for the party and citizenry to carry on his programs. Communist leaders from all parts of the USSR, its satellites and some Western countries converged on Moscow for his funeral. The government announced Mar. 6 that Stalin had been embalmed by the same process as Lenin so that his body could be preserved permanently on public view. It said that he would be buried temporarily in Lenin's tomb but that a new "monumental building—pantheon"—would be erected as a burial place for Lenin, Stalin and other Soviet leaders then buried in the Kremlin wall.

The East German Communist regime staged a parade in East Berlin Mar. 9 to coincide with Stalin's funeral in Moscow. 5,000 Iranian leftists staged a peaceful demonstration in memory of Stalin in Teheran Mar. 9. Communist workers in Italy stopped work for 20 minutes Mar. 9, but other workers rejected an "invitation" to take part in the demonstration. The French Army and Navy flew flags at half staff Mar. 6, 7 and 9, reportedly on orders from Acting Defense Min. Edouard Bonnefous and despite protests by many anti-Communists. Pres. Juan Peron of Argentina cabled to Moscow his "sincere condolences on the loss of the eminent statesman."

An estimated 50,000 persons witnessed Stalin's funeral in Red Square at 10 a.m. Mar. 9 and heard Malenkov, Beria and Molotov deliver funeral orations. Although state-approved churches had joined in the general tributes to Stalin, there were no references to religion in his last rites.

Malenkov said he indorsed a Lenin-Stalin doctrine that the Socialist and capitalist countries could live peacefully in "co-existence and competition." Neither he, Beria nor Molotov mentioned the U.S. directly, but Malenkov declared that the USSR would "go forward without hesitation, and if anyone dares stand in our way [or] hinder our work, he will be destroyed by the people." "No force exists in the world to arrest our advance to communism," he warned. Malenkov praised the Korean and Chinese Communists and Indo-Chinese rebels. Beria said: "Our enemies think our loss will bring disorder to our ranks. They will be disappointed." Molotov said Stalin had "led the USSR from a backward position to leadership of the peace camp."

Red Army cannon fired 30 salvos as cabinet and CP Central Committee members, Lt. Gen. Vasily Stalin (Stalin's son) and other military commanders bore Stalin's coffin to the Lenin mausoleum. Among representatives of Soviet bloc countries at the funeral: Pres. Klement Gottwald of Czechoslovakia (who died of pneumonia 5 days later in Prague); Premiers Chou En-lai of Communist China, Yumzhagin Tsedenbal of Outer Mongolia, Otto Grotewohl of East Germany, Vulko Chervenkov of Bulgaria, Matyas Rakosi of Hungary, Boleslaw Bierut of Poland, Gheorghe Gheorghiu-Dej of Rumania. CP leaders Harry Pollitt of England, Palmiro Togliatti of Italy and Jacques Duclos of France attended. Premier Urho Kekkonen represented Finland. Western countries were represented by members of their Moscow diplomatic missions (the U.S. by Charge d'Affaires Jacob D. Beam).

Pres. Dwight D. Eisenhower instructed the U.S. State Department late Mar. 5 (EST) to transmit to Moscow a message offering the U.S.'s "official condolences" to the Soviet government. It omitted any expression of sympathy or tribute to Stalin. State Secy. John Foster Dulles said Mar. 9 in a news conference at UN headquarters in New York that a 10-year period during which "the world has been dominated by the malignant power of Stalin" had ended with the dictator's death. "The Eisenhower era begins as the Stalin era ends," Dulles observed. He said the President enjoyed "a prestige unmatched in history." He expressed hope that the "new era" would establish a world order of "liberty, not enslavement," and that "human relations will be those of fraternity, not one-man domination."

A Voice of America broadcast to Eastern Europe Mar. 6 said Malenkov's selection "by no means signifies that the great problem of Soviet succession has been permanently solved." It said there might be a "prolonged struggle among topmost personalities" in the Kremlin for supremacy. Democratic Party leader Adlai E. Stevenson warned in Honolulu Mar. 7 that it would be "dangerous" to assume either that things "are going to be better or will disintegrate" in the USSR.

The British government announced Mar. 7 it had sent Russia only the expression of sympathy "required under normal diplomatic procedure." The Vatican newspaper *l'Osservatore Romano* said Mar. 6 that Stalin's name "remains forever bound to the great and silent suffering of the Church."

All UN delegations in New York sent representatives to call at the Russian delegation headquarters when it opened Mar. 7-8 to receive messages of condolence. UN Secy. Gen. Trygve Lie said on hearing of Stalin's death that he was "one of the outstanding statesmen of our time." UN General Assembly Pres. Lester B. Pearson of Canada recalled that Stalin was "one of the founders" of the UN and an "indomitable leader in the common struggle against Nazi aggression" in World War II. Indian Prime Min. Jawaharlal Nehru commented Mar. 6 that Stalin's "weight and influence had been in favor of peace," but he was "ruthless in the pursuit of his objectives."

The U.S. Communist Party Mar. 7 issued a statement calling Stalin's death "an historic loss," denouncing "war-mad Wall St. monopolists" and postponing publication of a new draft party program pending "the most rounded and thoroughgoing discussion by the entire party."

Stalin's illness prompted world Jewish leaders Mar. 5 to postpone indefinitely a scheduled conference in Zurich on recent Soviet anti-Jewish measures, among them the arrest of prominent Russian-Jewish physicians on charges of a "Zionist" plot to murder leading members of the Soviet hierarchy. Although the USSR had severed diplomatic relations with Israel Feb. 12, Tel Aviv sent condolences Mar. 8 on Stalin's death by way of the Netherlands, which was looking after Israeli interests in Moscow.

PARTY & GOVERNMENT

Cabinet & Central Committee Revised

Uncertainty over Stalin's successor was cut short with the announcement at 11:30 p.m. Mar. 6 that the cabinet and CP Central Committee had been revamped under the apparent control of Malenkov, who inherited Stalin's offices, and 9 other veteran followers of Stalin.

A new 5-member Presidium (executive group) of the Council of Ministers consisted of Premier (Chairman) Malenkov and his chief rivals for the succession to Stalin: Deputy Premiers Lavrenti P. Beria, 54; Vyacheslav M. Molotov, 62; Marshal Nikolai A. Bulganin, 57; and Stalin's brother-in-law Lazar M. Kaganovich, 59 (order of importance as indicated in published listings and lineup of officials at public functions). The 3 top-ranking deputies, who had been deputy premiers under Stalin also took back cabinet portfolios they had held previously:

●Beria became internal affairs minister in a consolidation of the State Security and Internal Affairs Ministries.

●Molotov reassumed direction of the Foreign Affairs Ministry from Andrei Y. Vishinsky. Vishinsky was made a first deputy foreign minister (as was Jacob A. Malik) and assigned to the UN as permanent Soviet representative.

●Bulganin became war minister. His first deputies: ex-Acting War Min. Aleksandr M. Vasilevsky and Marshal Georgi K. Zhukov, top Soviet field commander during World War II but often reported in disfavor since 1945.

Kaganovich, an economic specialist and the only Jew in the Soviet CP Presidium, did not receive a specific ministry.

These major consolidations of economic ministries were announced Mar. 6: the Foreign and Internal Trade Ministries were merged under Anastas I. Mikoyan, 58; the Ministries of the Auto & Tractor Industry, Machine & Instrument Building, Agricultural Machine Building and Machine Tool Building merged as the Ministry of Machine Building under Maxim Z. Saburov; the Ministries of Transport, Shipbuilding, Heavy Machine & Construction and Road Machine Industry merged as the Ministry of

Transport & Heavy Machine Building under Vyacheslav A. Malyshev; a Ministry of Electrical Power Stations & Industries, created from 3 previous ministries, was assigned to Mikhail G. Pervukhin.

G. P. Kosychenko was named Economic Planning Commission chairman. Nikolai M. Shvernik, previously president of the Presidium of the Supreme Soviet—equivalent to president of the USSR—became chairman of the All-Union Central Committee of Trade Unions. (Shvernik's successor in the presidency: Marshal Kliment Y. Voroshilov, 72.) Vasily V. Kuznetsov, deputy foreign minister in the new cabinet, was appointed ambassador to Communist China Mar. 10 to replace Aleksandr S. Panyushkin. (Communist Chinese Pres. Mao Tse-tung promised Mar. 7 that the USSR would continue to have his government's confidence and support.)

The CP Central Committee Presidium, formed in Oct. 1952 with 25 full members to replace the old Soviet Politburo, was reduced to 10 members: Malenkov, Beria, Molotov, Voroshilov, Nikita S. Khrushchev, Bulganin, Kaganovich, Mikoyan, Saburov, Pervukhin. (Shvernik, Panteleimon K. Ponomarenko, L. G. Melnikov and M. D. Bagirov were named alternate members.) The party Secretariat, in which Stalin had ranked first and Malenkov 2d among 10 members, was reduced to 8: Malenkov, Khrushchev, Mikhail A. Suslov, Nicolai A. Mikhailov, A. B. Aristov, Semyon Diesovich Ignatiev, Petr N. Pospelov, Nikolai N. Shatalin.

The announcement of the new appointments, issued jointly by the Central Committee, cabinet and Parliamentary Presidium, said firm steps had been taken for the "prevention of any kind of disarray and panic" in the wake of Stalin's death. *Pravda,* the Communist Party newspaper, said Mar. 7 that "the cause of Lenin and Stalin is in reliable and strong hands."

The reorganization of the Soviet cabinet under Malenkov was completed and indorsed unanimously Mar. 15 by the 1,200-member Supreme Soviet. The Supreme Soviet also formally elected Marshal Voroshilov as its president and heard Malenkov's inaugural speech as premier. The newly designated ministers: Finance—Arseny G. Zverev; Agriculture (the former Ministries of Agriculture, State Farms, Cotton, Procurement, Forestry)—Aleksei Ivanovich Koslov; Culture (Higher Education, Labor Reserves, Cinema, Committees on Arts, Radio and Polygraphic

Arts)—Panteleimon K. Ponomarenko; Light & Food Industry (Light Industry, Food Industry, Meat & Milk Products, Fish)— Aleksei Nikolayevich Kosygin; Coal Industry—Aleksandr F. Zasyadko; Metallurgy (Heavy and Light Metallurgy)—Ivan T. Tevosyan; Oil Industry—Nikolai K. Baibakov; Chemical Industry—Sergei Tikhomirov; Defense Industry (including Aircraft)— Dmitri F. Ustinov; Construction Materials—Pavel A. Yudin; Timber & Paper (combined)—Georgi M. Orlov; Heavy-Industry & Machine-Building Plants Construction—Nikolai A. Dygai; River & Sea Transport (including Northern Sea Administration)—Zosim A. Shashkov; Transport (including Railroads, Auto Transport)—Boris P. Beshchev; Communications—Nikolai D. Psurtzev; Public Health—Andrei F. Tretyakov; Justice— Konstantin P. Gorshenin; State Control—Vsevolod N. Merkulov; State Committee for Construction (chairman)—Konstantin M. Sokolov.

The cabinet list announced by Malenkov Mar. 15 disclosed that the Soviet Navy Ministry had been abolished and that jurisdiction over the navy had been assigned to Defense (War) Min. Marshal Nikolai A. Bulganin. Interior Min. Lavrenti P. Beria, Foreign Min. Vyacheslav M. Molotov, Bulganin and Lazar M. Kaganovich were each given the title of first deputy premier. Foreign & Internal Trade Min. Anastas I. Mikoyan was designated a deputy premier.

(The Supreme Soviet adjourned Mar. 15 after approving Malenkov's appointments but without taking action on the annual USSR state budget, usually approved at a parliamentary meeting in March.)

The CP Central Committee announced Mar. 21 that Malenkov had voluntarily given up his post as CP secretary general but remained as first member of the CP Presidium. (Stalin had made the post of CP secretary general preeminent and had ruled the USSR from that office alone from the mid-1920s until 1939.) The party announced a new 5-member CP Secretariat consisting of Khrushchev, Suslov, Ignatiev, Pospelov and Shatalin.

(The Foreign Ministry May 1 listed 4 deputy foreign ministers. Among them Andrei Y. Vishinsky, permanent delegate to the UN, was accorded highest rank next to Foreign Min. Vyacheslav M. Molotov. Andrei A. Gromyko was designated as chief deputy foreign minister in Moscow, followed by Valerian A.

Zorin and Vasili V. Kuznetsov. Jacob A. Malik went to London May 5 to succeed Gromyko as ambassador to Britain. Ex-Agriculture Min. Ivan Benediktov was appointed ambassador to India Apr. 29 to succeed K. V. Novikov.)

(Moscow reports May 5 disclosed that a general reorganization and streamlining of Soviet state governments had been started after Stalin's death and had resulted in the abolition of many *oblast* and *okrug* [units on the regional and local levels] organizations. A year-old Communist Party purge in Georgia was nullified Apr. 16 as a frameup of "absolutely innocent" persons engineered by N. M. Rukhadze, former state security minister in Georgia. Rukhadze was arrested by the new Georgian regime of Premier V. M. Bakradze, a follower of Lavrenti P. Beria. A Latvian cabinet shakeup announced in Riga Apr. 21 resulted in the replacement of 6 Latvians in the state cabinet by Russians, including Nikolai Kusmich Kovalchuk as interior minister. The navy's newspaper *Red Fleet* was dropped Apr. 8 and the army's *Red Star* became the journal of the entire defense establishment. 3 agricultural dailies were combined as *Rural Economy,* and the newspaper *Soviet Art* was made the organ of the new Culture Ministry. *Kommunist,* CP Central Committee publication edited since Nov. 1952 by D. I. Chesnokov, listed S. M. Avalin as new chief editor beginning Apr. 21.)

Prisoners Freed, Doctors Cleared

The Soviet government Mar. 28 granted an amnesty releasing all prisoners serving terms of 5 years or less. All pregnant women, children 10 years or under, juvenile delinquents, men over 55, women over 50 and prisoners suffering from incurable diseases were freed regardless of length of sentence. The amnesty also granted a 50% reduction in sentences of persons imprisoned for more than 5 years—except those imprisoned for counterrevolutionary crimes, major thefts against the state and murder.

The new Internal Affairs Ministry announced Apr. 4 that 9 prominent physicians, 6 of them Jews, accused Jan. 13 of plotting the deaths of ailing Soviet leaders, had been freed because the charges against them had proven false. 6 other doctors implicated with the original 9 also were cleared. A former deputy cabinet minister was accused of faking the case, and a Communist Party secretary was dismissed for having let the ex-minister succeed with his scheme.

The exoneration of the doctors erased one of the principal reasons given for an anti-Zionist campaign in the USSR during the last weeks of Stalin's life. Israel, with which Russia had broken diplomatic relations Feb. 12, called on the new Soviet regime Apr. 4 to complete its "redress of injustice" by a "termination of the anti-Jewish campaign" and a resumption of "normal relations" with Israel. An Israeli communique said Moscow's release of the doctors refuted the Soviet charges, made at the time of their arrest, that Zionist groups and the Joint Distribution Committee (JDC), a Jewish relief agency, had carried on subversive activities in Eastern Europe for the U.S.

The accused doctors: Professors M. S. Vovsi, B. B. Kogan, A. I. Feldman, A. M. Grinstein and I. G. Etinger (charged as U.S. agents recruited through the JDC); Professors V. N. Vinogradov and M. B. Kogan and Dr. P. I. Yagorov (alleged "former agents of British intelligence"); Dr. G. I. Mayorov (or Mairov). All except Yagorov, Vinogradov and Mayorov were Jews.

The Moscow announcement said that confessions and other evidence against the doctors had been obtained through "the use of impermissible means of investigation which are strictly forbidden" under Soviet law. The Communist Party newspaper *Pravda* Apr. 6 singled out a deputy chief of the former State Security Ministry named Ryumin as instigator of the miscarriage of justice. It said he and several of his colleagues, who had sought to inflame "nationalist hostilities" in the USSR, had been arrested. *Pravda* reported Apr. 7 that Semyon D. Ignatiev had been dismissed from the new 5-man Communist Party Secretariat because, as state security minister when the doctors were arrested, he had been guilty of "political blindness and gullibility."

The doctors had been accused in January of having killed 2 Politburo members (Col. Gen. Alexander S. Shcherbakov in 1945 and Andrei A. Zhdanov in 1948) by diagnosing and treating their illnesses improperly, and of plotting to destroy other Soviet leaders by the same means. Solomon Mikhoels, late director of the Jewish State Theater, who had died in 1948, had been named as a link between the doctors and the JDC. *Pravda* Apr. 6 cleared Mikhoels as well as the doctors. It said Ryumin and his associates had concealed from an investigating commission certain facts about the medical treatment of Zhdanov and Shcherbakov. The paper promised every Soviet citizen that "his citizen's rights are under the reliable protection of Soviet Socialist legality," and each citizen's constitutional rights "will be sacredly observed and secured by the Soviet government."

An Apr. 7 UP dispatch cleared by Soviet censors relayed rumors in Moscow that Beria had intervened in the case personally after he became internal affairs minister. The dispatch said Beria's name was associated in Russia with "many judicial and internal security reforms" after his appointment as interior commissar in 1938. Western observers generally had associated Beria with the brutal methods practiced by Soviet police.

Beria's Downfall

Stalin's death was followed within months by the downfall of Soviet internal security chief Lavrenti P. Beria, who was convicted on treason charges and executed before the year had ended.

Beria's dismissal as chief of internal security was announced in Moscow July 10. It was the first known purge within the Kremlin's top hierarchy since Stalin's death. But Beria's downfall set off a series of actions against men associated with him, particularly in his native Georgian Republic (Stalin was also born in Georgia). Most of the Soviet republics were affected by the purge. Beria was accused of "criminal and anti-state activities" aimed at gaining personal power and converting the USSR to capitalism. A communique from the Soviet Communist Party Central Committee revealed his ouster as a first deputy premier and as internal affairs minister, his expulsion from the CP and his arrest to stand trial before the USSR Supreme Court.

People who had been in Moscow shortly before the announcement speculated July 11 that Beria's arrest actually had taken place June 27. They recalled that tanks and truckloads of soldiers inexplicably had appeared in the Soviet capital that day. In the evening, Beria had been the only absentee when top Soviet leaders attended the Bolshoi opera.

(Beria was succeeded as internal affairs minister by Col. Gen. Sergei N. Kruglov, his deputy minister since the cabinet consolidation following Stalin's death. Kruglov had served as deputy internal affairs commissar during World War II, and as internal affairs minister from Jan. 1946 until Mar. 1953.)

A *Pravda* editorial July 10 outlined the details of Beria's alleged "criminal venture" as a "people's enemy." It said, in part: "By various careerist machinations" Beria had "wormed himself into confidence and threaded his way to leadership." His "anti-party and anti-state activity" was at first "deeply concealed and masked, but lately—having become impudent and letting himself go—Beria started to disclose his real face." He tried to "put the USSR Ministry of Internal Affairs before the party and government" and pack it with people chosen for "personal loyalty to himself." He "impeded" urgent decisions on agriculture to create "difficulties in food supply." He sought "by various crafty schemes" to "undermine the friendship" of the various Soviet republics in a "multinational Socialist state." He "impeded" efforts to liquidate "some facts of lawlessness and arbitrary action." Beria finally "lost the face of a Communist and changed into a bourgeois renegade and became an agent of international imperialist forces. He hatched plans to grab the leadership of the party and country with the aim of actually destroying... the party by a capitulatory policy which would have brought about ultimately the restoration of capitalism."

The Soviet press July 12 printed editorials charging that Beria had sought to exploit nationalism among various Soviet races and spread disunity in the USSR. *Pravda* July 13 repeated another recent party theme: Marxist-Leninist theory called for collective leadership, not one-man rule. The government announced July 14 that the entire Supreme Soviet would meet July 28, presumably to approve cabinet changes resulting from Beria's ouster. (The removal of Vyacheslav A. Malyshev as minister for transport machinery and heavy machinery was announced July 14. His successor, Ivan Isidorovich Nosenko, denounced Beria. The expulsion from the Communist Party of Vladimir G. Dekanozov, recently installed by Beria as the Georgian Republic's internal affairs minister, was announced July 15. The replacement of Ivan Usenko by Walter Raudsalu as Estonian justice minister was reported the same day.)

Western observers disagreed on the meaning of the Beria purge. There was speculation that it represented victory (1) for Malenkov and his career CP faction, or (2) for Molotov and the "old guard" associates of Stalin or (3) for the Soviet military over the police. Observers could not agree on whether to expect a reversal or intensification of the "soft" policies on foreign affairs and Eastern Europe that the new Soviet leaders had instituted after Stalin's death. There had been no apparent letup in the "peace" and "leniency" program. A speech by ex-Premier Matyas Rakosi of Hungary July 11 indicated that new Communist policies would stand. Some thought Beria would be made scapegoat in a "show" trial for discontent, production lags and disorders in both the USSR and the East European satellite states.

U.S. State Secy. Dulles, speaking at a Western foreign ministers' meeting in Washington July 10, said: "A new convulsion is under way" in Russia, and the dictatorship's "inherent weakness is disclosed." The State Department said Amb.-to-Moscow Charles E. Bohlen had given it an advance tip to expect Beria's downfall. He was in Paris on a vacation trip when the news came, and he flew to Washington immediately. Sen. Alexander Wiley (R., Wis.), Senate Foreign Relations Committee chairman, predicted "the inevitable blood-bath" as Beria's rivals wiped out his "vast apparatus" throughout the USSR. Wiley said "this may be one of our greatest opportunities" to "exploit boiling tensions inside the Iron Curtain" and expose "the true hideous nature of the Soviet slaughterhouse."

Moscow radio announced Dec. 16 that Beria had confessed to "state crimes." The Soviet Procurator's office announced Dec. 24 that Beria and 6 co-defendants had been executed by firing squad as traitors after a secret trial before a special Judicial Commission of the USSR Supreme Court. The announcement said that the 6-day trial had taken place Dec. 18-23 and that the death sentences, not subject to appeal, had been carried out that day. Marshal Ivan S. Konev was chairman of the special court. Beria was said to have confessed to conspiring with foreign intelligence agents from 1919 until "the moment of his exposure and arrest" in 1953 to "seize power," "restore the rule of the bourgeoisie" and terrorize patriotic Soviet Communist leaders. He was charged with attempts to sabotage current agricultural programs in the USSR.

Executed with Beria were ex-State Security & State Control Min. V. N. Merkulov, ex-Deputy Internal Affairs Min. B. Z. Kobulov, ex-Georgian Internal Affairs Min. V. G. Dekanozov, ex-Ukrainian Internal Affairs Min. Pavel Y. Meshik, and Sergei A. Goglidze and L. E. Vlodzimirsky, former high-ranking police officials.

(John Fischer reported in the Mar. 1969 issue of *Harper's Magazine* that Khrushchev had claimed to have shot Beria. Fischer said that Khrushchev had told a Western diplomat that Beria had "made one silly mistake. Beria came into a conference room one day without his bodyguard. I [Khrushchev] shot him.")

Khrushchev Heads Party

Nikita Sergeyevich Khrushchev was elected first secretary of the Soviet Communist Party's Central Committee Sept. 13. He thus became 2d only to Premier Malenkov in the ruling Soviet hierarchy. The Central Committee also approved a broad agricultural reform program proposed by Khrushchev to increase farm production and the supply of consumer goods. Khrushchev, 59, had headed the Central Committee's 5-man Secretariat since Mar. 20, when a Moscow radio announcement disclosed that he had succeeded Malenkov as CP secretary general.

The election made Khrushchev the first formal successor to Stalin as leader of the Soviet party. In a report issued Aug. 20, 1952, Khrushchev had criticized "not a few party members [who] take a formal, passive attitude towards the carrying out of party decisions." Khrushchev said: "This [attitude] is a great evil against which the party must fight resolutely.... Members are obliged to be active fighters for the fulfilment of party decisions, and a passive attitude is incompatible with membership of the party. Another evil which exists in our party is that some Communists incorrectly consider that there are two party disciplines—one for the rank-and-file members and another for the leaders. The party cannot tolerate such a conception of discipline.... It must be pointed out that our party has one discipline for all Communists, irrespective of the positions they hold, and that violation of party and state discipline is incompatible with party membership.... No little harm is done by Communists who shout about their devotion to the party but do not permit criticism from below. The party has always attached tremendous importance to self-criticism, and particularly criticism from below, to uncovering shortcomings, and to the fight against complacency.... Suppression of criticism is a grievous evil, and he who stifles criticism, and who substitutes for it pompousness and bragging, has no place in the party. Neither can the fact be ignored that there have been fairly widespread manifestations of political carelessness and slackness, and cases of disclosure of party and state secrets.... Lastly, it must be admitted that in many party, Soviet, and economic organizations, a great evil is presented by an unhealthy approach to the selection of cadres, when this selection is made on the basis of friendly relations, personal attachment, and kinship.... The rules [of the CP] must indicate the duty of members strictly to fulfill the party's instructions concerning the correct selection of cadres in accordance with their political and professional qualifications, and must record that violation of these instructions is incompatible with party membership."

In a report at the Sept. 3-7 meeting of the Central Committee, Khrushchev, chief party spokesman on agricultural matters since 1950, had severely criticized past agricultural practices in the Soviet Union. His new plan, adopted by the Central Committee, nullified procedures set by Beria and emphasized the importance of the personal farm plots worked by peasant members of collectives. Under new measures he proposed to stimulate livestock output: procurement prices paid by the government were raised and a peasant's workday credits for labor on livestock or fodder production were increased by 10%.

As part of the program, these 6 new government ministries were created Sept. 15: Food Ministry, headed by Vassily P. Zotov, for fish, meat, milk and other food enterprises; Manufactured (Consumer) Goods, headed by Aleksei Nikolayevich Kosygin, to control light manufacturing; Domestic Trade, under Anastas I. Mikoyan; Foreign Trade, under Ivan Grigorievich Kabanov; State Farms, under Aleksei Ivanovich Kozlov; Agriculture Procurement, under ex-Amb.-to-India Ivan A. Benediktov, to handle procurements from collective farms.

The appointment of Vassili Yavoronkov as state control minister was announced Dec. 16. Yavoronkov replaced V. N. Merkulov, who later was convicted in the Beria trial and was executed.

Moscow radio Dec. 21 announced the Presidium's reappointment of 5 deputy premiers who had lost their posts in the Soviet government shakeup following Stalin's death: State Planning Commission Chrmn. Maxim Z. Saburov, Electric Power Min. Mikhail G. Pervukhin, Metallurgical Industry Min. Ivan T. Tevosyan, Manufactured Goods Min. Aleksei N. Kosygin and

Medium Machinery Min. Vyacheslav A. Malyshev (reputed successor to Beria as head of the Soviet atomic energy program). The AP reported Dec. 19 that *Pravda* had revealed the assignment of Averky B. Aristov to a high government post in the Khabarovsk area of the Far East. He had been dropped as a CP Central Committee secretary after Stalin's death.

(The establishment of a strict 8-hour workday in all Soviet ministries, departments and other government establishments in Moscow had been reported by *Pravda* Sept. 1. The order banned loafing, of which many officials were accused, and it required the discontinuation of irregular working habits, such as starting work in mid-day and continuing until late at night. Many Soviet officials were said to have followed Stalin's practice of doing their work at night.)

Soviet Policies Soften?

In another action viewed as an indication of a liberalization in Soviet attitudes, the Soviet government permitted 7 executives of newspapers and radio stations in smaller U.S. cities to visit Moscow after a tour of other points in Europe and the Middle East. This was the first such group admitted since 4 members of the American Society of Newspaper Editors visited the USSR in 1946. The group was given special visas by the Soviet embassy in London Mar. 28. It arrived in Moscow by special plane from Helsinki Mar. 31.

New principles and policies of the Soviet Communist Party de-emphasizing individual leadership and affirming "coexistence" with capitalism were published July 26 in a 7,500-word *History of 50 Years of the Communist Party of the Soviet Union, 1903-1953.* The names of only 2 leaders—Lenin and Stalin—were mentioned, with Lenin cited many times, Stalin only once. No current party leader signed the statement, nor were any quoted in it. According to the new *History:* (1) "Maximum satisfaction of the constantly growing demands of the Soviet people" was a major CP concern; (2) the USSR's chief foreign policy task was "to secure the peace and [bar] a new war"; (3) though communism would eventually win over capitalism, "our party proceeds from Lenin's statement about the possibility of the lengthy coexistence...of the 2 systems"; (4) fractionalism and individualism were against CP policy, and the "cult of individual leaders" was contrary to the Marxist principle of "collective leadership"; (5) capitalism had not been eradicated completely from the minds of Russians; careerists, "bourgeois degenerates and agents of international imperialism" had attempted to penetrate the CP for "hostile activity."

The *History* praised the July Central Committee meeting at which Beria had been charged with treason. Issued by the Party's Agitation & Propaganda Department and the Marx-Lenin-Engels-Stalin Institute, the *History* was produced to replace an earlier version, credited to Stalin and used since 1939. The institute used Stalin's name in its title for the first time in making the announcement.

A sharp increase in the production of consumer goods by the end of 1954 was ordered in decrees issued by the Soviet government Oct. 23 and by the CP Oct. 28. Among new goals (percentage of increase over 1950): meat 230% instead of the previous goal of 90%; butter 190% instead of 70%; furniture 400% instead of 300%; clothing 240% instead of 80%; sewing machines 510% instead of 240%; refrigerators, washing machines and vacuum cleaners 1,000%. Stores were ordered to reject poor-quality goods.

The government Dec. 2 repealed a 1947 decree that had forbidden Soviet citizens to marry foreigners.

1954

A new Supreme Soviet was elected in Mar. 1954, and 80% of the deputies chosen were new members. The Soviet cabinet was again reorganized. The USSR started Nikita Khrushchev's program for growing grain on millions of acres of "virgin lands" in Siberia and other undeveloped areas of the Soviet Union. In a continuation of the apparent easing of post-Stalin policies, the USSR made overtures to increase trade with the West, and steps were taken to make life more pleasant for Soviet citizens.

GOVERNMENT & POLICY

New Supreme Soviet Elected

The Soviet Electoral Commission reported Mar. 17 the results of national elections held Mar. 14 for the bicameral Supreme Soviet. The single lists of candidates presented by the Communist Party polled 120,479,249 votes (99.79%) in balloting for the Soviet of the Union and 120,539,860 votes (99.84%) for the Soviet of Nationalities. These were the highest popular and percentage votes in Russian history. 247,897 negative votes were cast and 680 ballots spoiled in voting for the Soviet of the Union; corresponding figures for the Soviet of Nationalities were 187,357 and 609. A total of 99.98% of those eligible to vote participated in the election.

The publication Mar. 18 of the names of deputies of the new Supreme Soviet (708 in the Soviet of the Union, 639 in the Soviet of Nationalities) showed that 80% were new members. The U.S. Information Service said Mar. 23 that 17 of the 125 full members and 6 of the 110 alternates named to the Soviet CP Central Committee in Oct. 1952 had been dropped from the new Supreme Soviet. Among those missing was Aleksandr N. Poskrebyshev, Stalin's personal aide.

Cabinet Changes

Soviet Health Min. Andrei F. Tretyakov, physician in charge of treating Stalin at the time of Stalin's death, was replaced in his cabinet post Mar. 2 by his deputy, Dr. Maria Dmitriyevna Kovrygina. Dr. Kovrygina became the USSR's first female member of the Council of Ministers (cabinet).

It was announced Mar. 7 that Nikita Semyonovich Ryzhov had succeeded Soviet Deputy Premier Aleksei N. Kosygin as consumer goods industry minister.

Georgi Fedorovich Aleksandrov, veteran CP ideologist, was named Soviet culture minister Mar. 16. He succeeded Panteleimon K. Ponomarenko, who became party chief in Kazakhstan.

Vyacheslav Petrovich Yelyutin was named Mar. 16 to head the new Higher Education Ministry.

The Supreme Soviet approved a reorganization of the Soviet Council of Ministers by Premier Georgi M. Malenkov Apr. 27. About 12 new ministries were created, and council membership was set at 55 (as against 73 under Stalin and 32 in March 1953, when the Malenkov government was first formed). State and internal security functions, combined in 1953 into a single Internal Affairs Ministry under the late Lavrenti Beria, were again separated. Matters involving state security (threats from abroad) were assigned to a cabinet-level Committee of State Security (KGB)—its formation was revealed Apr. 26—under the chairmanship of Col. Gen. Ivan A. Serov, veteran secret police official. Domestic security remained under Internal Affairs Min. Sergei N. Kruglov.

Other new ministers named: Radio Manufacture—Valery Dmitriyevich Kalmykov; Ferrous Metals—Anatoly Nikolayevich Kuzmin; Nonferrous Metals—Peter Faddeyevich Lomako; Meat & Milk Products—Sergei Fedorovich Antonov; Power Stations—Aleksei Sergeyevich Pavlenko; Electrical Goods—Ivan Skidanenko; Shipbuilding—Ivan Isidorovich Nosenko (ex-transport and heavy-machinery minister); Transport Machine Construction—Sergei Stepanov; Heavy Machinery Construction—Nikolai Kazakov; Building & Road Machinery—Yefim Stepanovich Novoselov; Autos, Tractors & Agricultural Machinery—Stepan Akopov; Machine Tools & Instruments—Peter Ivanovich Parshin; Timber—Georgi M. Orlov; Paper & Wood Products—Fedor Dmitriyevich Varaksin; Construction of Metal & Chemical Plants—David Yakovlevich Raizer; Building Industry—Nikolai A. Dygai; State Bank—Vasili Fedorovich Popov; Machine Tool & Toolmaking Industry—Anatoli Ivanovich Kostousov; Roads & Structures Construction Machinery—Yefim Novosyolov.

'Virgin Lands' Program

Early in 1954 the Soviet Communist Party began to put into operation the program proposed by CP First Secy. Nikita S. Khrushchev for opening up millions of acres of virgin lands for farming.

The Russian press reported Mar. 6 that 100,000 members of the Komsomols (Young Communist groups) were being sent to the Kazakhstan Urals and Siberia to help work on preparing 32,100,000 acres for grain crops.

The CP Central Committee and the Council of Ministers announced Aug. 17 that the sowing of virgin soil would be increased to 37,100,000 acres in 1955 and to 74,100,000 acres in 1956.

Additional workers were assigned to the virgin lands program under a decision announced Nov. 20 to shift thousands of office workers to farms and factory work from government bureaus that were said to be overstaffed and inefficient.

Easing of Soviet Policies

In what appeared to be a further softening of Soviet attitudes following the death of Stalin, the Soviet government offered Feb. 4 to buy more than $1 billion worth of British industrial products in 2 years. This was the biggest gesture so far in Russia's campaign to revive its trade with the West. The £400 million ($1.12 billion) cash-for-goods offer was made in Moscow by Soviet Foreign Trade Min. Ivan G. Kabanov to a delegation of 32 British businessmen. (In 1953 the USSR had bought about $34.5 million worth of British goods and had sold to Britain about $111. million worth, mostly grain and timber.)

But British Board of Trade Min. Derick Heathcoat Amory estimated Feb. 16 that more than half of Russia's trade offer related to strategic goods subject to embargo. He told Commons that £180 million ($504 million) worth of goods sought by Russia was free of controls and could be exported by British manufacturers; the remaining £220 million ($616 million) worth could not be delivered unless Allied restrictions on trade with Communist countries were modified or abolished. And J. B. Scott, leader of 33 British businessmen who sought contracts in Moscow, said Feb. 16 that the Russians seemed to "know a lot about" the secret list of goods withheld by the West from Iron Curtain nations. Scott reported that Russia had refused to buy British textiles or other consumer goods and insisted on heavy industrial equipment such as machine tools and diesel generators. (Soviet Amb.-to-Canada Dmitri S. Chuvakhin said in Ottawa Feb. 15 that Russia wished to increase its trade with Canada, particularly by buying ships, industrial equipment, wheat, meat, butter and rawhide.)

U.S. government officials Feb. 21 released confidential statistics on world trade to prove their contention that the USSR's much-publicized campaign to buy consumer goods from the free world was more propaganda than fact. These figures, from the U.S. Foreign Operations Administration and State and Defense Departments, estimated 1953's total Western exports to Russia at $325-$350 million, with less than half in consumer goods (1952 total: $481 million). They showed a 1/3 drop in total Soviet foreign trade in 1953, although consumer-goods buying rose.

(The UN Economic Commission for Asia & the Far East, in Colombo, Ceylon Feb. 17, rejected a Soviet motion asking member and associate nations to restore normal trade relations with all countries.)

Deputy Premier Maxim Z. Saburov, principal speaker at the annual CP meeting in the Bolshoi Theater in Moscow Nov. 6 on the eve of Revolution Day, issued an invitation to the estranged Communist government of Yugoslavia to resume "normal relations" and the "old friendship" with Russia. The first Soviet-Yugoslav trade accord since 1948 had been signed Oct. 1. It provided for the exchange of non-strategic goods.

Domestically, the USSR had taken another step to favor consumers by announcing Apr. 1 that it was reducing prices by 5%-44.5% on 71 categories of food and other consumer items.

Premier Malenkov Apr. 26 announced these production goals in 4 major fields for 1954: steel—41.2 million metric tons, an increase of 51% over 1950; coal—346 million metric tons, a 33% increase over 1950; electric power—147.2 billion kilowatt hours, a rise of 63% over 1950; cement—18.5 million metric tons, an 80% increase over 1950.

Prof. Trofim D. Lysenko, head of the Soviet Institute of Genetics and virtual dictator of Soviet biological sciences under Stalin, was sharply rebuked in the Moscow CP daily *Pravda* Mar. 26 for having accepted an allegedly unsatisfactory doctoral dissertation from V. C. Dmitriev. Dmitriev had been ousted in 1953 as agricultural planning chief of the State Planning Commission. Lysenko's controversial theory of the dominant effect of environment in the origin of species was attacked July 5 by the Soviet Academy of Sciences' *Journal of General Biology.* Under Stalin, the Lysenko theory had been made virtually an article of faith for biologists, and farm policy had required that it be followed in agricultural planning. But the *Journal of General Biology* denounced the theory as "unsubstantiated and essentially mistaken" and, in some instances, as "clearly falsified."

The CP Central Committee, in a Nov. 11 *Pravda* article signed by CP First Secy. Khrushchev, criticized anti-religious propaganda in the Soviet press as "overzealous and offensive." It said there must be gradual "liberation" of the Soviet people from "religious prejudice" without violating a Soviet Constitutional guarantee of "freedom to practice religion" as well as "to conduct anti-religious propaganda."

The Soviet government Dec. 24 announced the executions of these colleagues of the late Soviet secret police chief Lavrenti P. Beria on charges of falsely accusing and jailing Soviet citizens: ex-State Security Min. Viktor S. Abakumov, investigator A. G. Leonov and V. I. Komarov and M. T. Likhachev, ex-deputies to Leonov. I. A. Chernov was given a 25-year prison sentence, and Y. M. Broverman got a 15-year sentence.

1955

Georgi Malenkov was ousted as Soviet premier in Feb. 1955, not quite 2 years after he had succeeded the late Stalin to the post. It quickly became evident that Nikolai Bulganin, the new premier, would be 2d to Communist Party chief Nikita Khrushchev as the USSR's dominant figure. Khrushchev and Bulganin visited Yugoslavia in May in an effort to end the Soviet-Yugoslav rift and persuade the Yugoslavs to return to the Soviet fold. A 640,000-man reduction in USSR military strength was announced, but Soviet power apparently was strengthened by the Warsaw Treaty, which created an East European military alliance under a unified command. The Russians returned to Finland the Soviet air-naval base on the Porkkala Peninsula.

GOVERNMENT & PARTY

Malenkov Ousted as Premier

Georgi M. Malenkov was dismissed as Soviet premier Feb. 8. The government, in announcing his ouster, renounced Malenkov's stress on consumer goods production at the expense of heavy industrial output. It also warned the U.S. that American atomic weapons strength was "behind" the USSR's and demanded that the West abandon its "aggressive" plans to rearm West Germany.

Marshal Nikolai A. Bulganin, 59, defense minister under Malenkov, was named to replace him as premier. But there were rumors from Moscow that Nikita S. Khrushchev, first secretary of the Communist Party's Central Committee, had emerged as the USSR's strongest political figure. Marshal Georgi K. Zhukov, 59, previously first deputy defense minister, succeeded Bulganin as defense minister Feb. 9.

Malenkov, 59, resigned on the ground that his "inexperience" in dealing with local problems had caused his regime to fail in economic affairs. Malenkov was named a deputy premier Feb. 9 and was assigned the Ministry of Power Stations, which had charge of a major electrification program.

The leadership changes were announced and approved at a Moscow meeting of the USSR Supreme Soviet. They apparently took most members by surprise. Chairman Aleksandr Volkov of the Soviet of the Union (upper house) opened the session Feb. 8 by reading a statement by Malenkov in which the latter made his "request to be relieved from the post of chairman [premier] of the USSR Council of Ministers." Malenkov confessed his "guilt and responsibility" for "the unsatisfactory state of affairs which has arisen in agriculture." He attributed this to his "insufficient experience in local work [and] guidance of individual branches of national economy." He indorsed a newly approved CP plan for building up agriculture "on the only correct foundation: the further development by every means of heavy industry." This, he said, would "create the necessary conditions for a real upsurge in the production of all essential commodities for popular consumption." Malenkov predicted that "bourgeois hysterical viragos" would make "slanderous inventions" about his withdrawal as premier. He said he would remain in the government and "perform in the most conscientious manner" the new duties assigned him. He remained a member of the Presidium of the CP Central Committee. Malenkov's resignation was accepted without dissent by an immediate vote (show of hands) of the 1,300-member Supreme Soviet.

The Supreme Soviet then took a recess, after which CP First Secy. Khrushchev announced at a 2d session the same day that Defense Min. Bulganin was the unanimous choice of the CP Central Committee and cabinet to become premier. Bulganin's election was approved without dissent by a show-of-hands vote.

Khrushchev took first place in the order of entry and seating of Soviet leaders at the Supreme Soviet's meeting. He led their procession to the stage of the hall for the session at which Malenkov resigned. Malenkov was permitted to lead the participants and acknowledge applause at the later session for Bulganin's election as premier. But Khrushchev occupied the central front-row seat of leadership and received a long ovation when he nominated Bulganin for the post.

Premier Bulganin, in his inaugural address Feb. 9, told the Supreme Soviet that the U.S. was to blame for tension between the 2 countries. He said: "Those lunatics who are brandishing atomic weapons and calling for atomic war must be called to order"; "the Chinese people receive much support from our people"; the USSR must build up heavy industry as "the basis of all our economy." (The CP Central Committee had announced Feb. 2 that the Soviet government would place new emphasis on heavy industry to build up the "national economy" and "defense.") Bulganin nominated Zhukov as defense minister and Malenkov as deputy premier and power stations minister, and both were indorsed by the Supreme Soviet Feb. 9. Aleksei Sergeyevich Pavlenko was dismissed as power stations minister to make way for Malenkov.

West Sees Tougher Soviet Policy

The opinion most widely expressed by Western leaders about the change in Soviet leadership was that it indicated a new armaments production drive and a trend back to the "tough" policy practiced by Stalin after World War II. Among other opinions was speculation that the Russians actually were launching a new kind of "peace offensive" or that they were concerned primarily with internal economic difficulties, particularly a lag in agricultural production.

Pres. Eisenhower said at his news conference in Washington Feb. 9: The effect of the new Russian developments "won't be apparent for some time," and the U.S. must remain "watchful and alert"; it was possible but not necessarily true that the USSR would toughen its policy toward the U.S. Commenting on a Soviet claim that the USSR had gained superiority in hydrogen weapons, the President asserted: "Certainly there is no proof to that effect.... That would be rather a remarkable feat, but I believe it is not worthwhile speculating on." Mr. Eisenhower suggested that the Soviet government shakeup "does express dissatisfaction with what has been going on internally." He said there was hopeful speculation, although no actual evidence, that Russia's hold on Communist China and its East European satellites was weakening. The President confirmed at his news conference that he had, on instructions from the government, invited Zhukov to fly to the U.S. in the Eisenhower plane for a visit in 1946. He would not renew the invitation currently without consulting with his advisers, and it would be "a remarkable thing at the present state of affairs," Mr. Eisenhower told the reporters. He said he had found Zhukov an able military commander with whom he had succeeded in "getting along...on a number of local problems" when both were occupation commanders in Germany. (Zhukov, interviewed in Moscow Feb. 7 by U.S. publisher William Randolph Hearst Jr., had recalled the 1946 invitation from Mr. Eisenhower and had said the time was not right for him to accept a renewal of it.)

Other comment Feb. 8 on the USSR's change in premiers and policies: State Secy. Dulles—It confirmed his belief that there was internal trouble in the USSR. Defense Secy. Charles E. Wilson—It was "just another ripple" and would provoke no change in U.S. defense planning. Sen. Alexander Wiley (R., Wis.), Senate Foreign Relations Committee minority leader—It showed that the world "cannot rely on the so-called peaceful coexistence theme formerly emphasized" by Malenkov's regime. Ex-Amb.-to-Russia George F. Kennan—The premiership was not Russia's top office, and there was "no evidence that Khrushchev is not the top dog in the party." N.Y. Gov. W. Averill Harriman, ex-ambassador to Russia—"It now appears that the

Kremlin is returning to the Stalin policy of developing heavy industry and armament at the expense of consumer goods."

Diplomats and editorialists in London generally interpreted Malenkov's dismissal as meaning the end of the Soviet "coexistence" campaign. West German Chancellor Konrad Adenauer, who recalled Khrushchev's recent denial of a rift with Malenkov, said his ouster proved the futility of believing "what these people say."

Cabinet & Party Changes Continue

The Presidium of the Supreme Soviet announced several new cabinet changes Mar. 1. Trade specialist Anastas I. Mikoyan, fuels and power administrator Mikhail G. Peruvkin and economic planning expert Maxim Z. Saburov were raised to the rank of first deputy premiers. (Mikoyan, who had stressed consumer production, had been relieved as trade minister in January. His replacement, Dmitri V. Pavlov, advocated more heavy industrial production.) Production administrators V. A. Kucherenko, Pavel P. Lobanov, Col. Gen. A. P. Zavenyagin and Lt. Gen. Mikhail V. Khrunichev were made deputy premiers; Zavenyagin was designated also as medium machine building minister, believed responsible for atomic production. The replacement of State Farms Min. Aleksei Kozlov by Ivan A. Benediktov and Coal Industry Min. Aleksandr Fyodorovich Zasyadko by A. N. Zademidko was announced by Premier Bulganin Mar. 2.

Culture Min. Georgi F. Aleksandrov, chief World War II propagandist and friend of ex-Premier Malenkov, was dismissed from his post because he had "failed to assure the leadership" of his ministry, it was announced Mar. 21. No details of Aleksandrov's alleged failure were given. Amb.-to-Poland Nikolai A. Mikhailov was named to replace him. Deputy Foreign Min. Vasily V. Kuznetsov, 53, was raised Mar. 22 to the rank of first deputy foreign minister, a post held by the late Andrei Y. Vishinsky. Ex-Amb.-to-East Germany Vladimir S. Semyenov was named a deputy foreign minister, as was Nikolai T. Fedorenko, an Asian affairs specialist.

Aleksei I. Kirichenko, Ukrainian Communist Party first secretary, and Mikhail A. Suslov, a secretary of the Soviet CP Central Committee, were elected to the CP Presidium at the semi-annual meeting of the CP Central Committee in Moscow

July 4-11. They were the first new members named since the Presidium's membership was reduced after Stalin's death. Both had worked closely with CP First Secy. Khrushchev. The Central Committee also elected 3 new party secretaries: Dmitri T. Shepilov, *Pravda* editor; Nikolai I. Belyayev, a party secretary in the Altai territory; Averky B. Aristov, Khabarovsk territorial government chief. The Central Committee, at the July meeting, approved a decree submitted by Khrushchev to convene the 20th CP Congress in Moscow Feb. 14, 1956 to elect party leaders and approve the next (6th) Soviet 5-year plan. The Central Committee reported that the 5th 5-year plan had been fulfilled May 1, 8 months ahead of schedule.

Vladimir V. Matskevich was named agriculture minister Oct. 17. The post had been vacant since the former incumbent, Ivan Benediktov, was made state farms minister in 1954.

Molotov Retains Foreign Affairs Post

Soviet Foreign Min. Vyacheslav M. Molotov assured Canadian External Affairs Min. Lester B. Pearson and other officials attending a Moscow reception Oct. 10 that he would represent the USSR at a Big 4 foreign ministers' meeting scheduled to begin in Geneva Oct. 27. Molotov told newsmen at the reception that "no question of retirement arises" as the result of an ideological slip he had made in a speech before the Supreme Soviet Feb. 8.

In a letter dated Sept. 16 and published Oct. 8 in the Soviet CP magazine *Kommunist,* Molotov had admitted his "theoretically and politically dangerous" error. He said his Feb. 8 address had "incorrectly formulated the question of building a Socialist society in the USSR." Molotov explained: "In [my] report it was said: 'Together with the USSR, where the foundations of a Socialist society have already been built, there are also those people's democratic countries which have taken only the first but very important steps in the direction of socialism.' This mistaken formula leads to incorrect deductions that allegedly a Socialist society has still not been built in the USSR, that only the foundations of a Socialist society have been built—that is, the basis of a Socialist society—which does not correspond with reality and is at variance with repeated evaluations of the results of building socialism in the USSR given in party documents." Molotov said his "mistaken formula" was politically harmful because "it brings confusion into ideological questions and contradicts the decisions of the party." "It throws doubt on the presence of a Socialist society which has already been built in the main in our country," he said.

(*Pravda* Nov. 4 published the most comprehensive article on communism to be printed recently in the USSR. It criticized the views recanted by Molotov Sept. 16 and declared: "Communism is developing out of every facet of Socialist life and is becoming so real that no one can fail to notice and feel its approach." "Communism is not a dream for the far future.")

In remarks overheard at a reception Oct. 22 for visiting Burmese Premier U Nu, Molotov added to the speculation about his political future. Asked whether he intended to resign as foreign minister, Molotov was quoted as saying that "This will be made clear at Geneva"; "I'll answer that at Geneva." This was interpreted to mean that Molotov, who went to Geneva 3 days later, would announce whether he would quit, but Soviet journalists explained later that Molotov meant his presence at Geneva would show that he was still foreign minister.

POLICY CHANGES

Rapprochement with Yugoslavia

The post-Stalin Soviet leaders, in fulfillment of their promise to try to restore friendly relations with Yugoslavia's dissenting Communist regime, visited Yugoslavia and later negotiated a 3-year trade agreement with the Yugoslavs.

The Soviet government newspaper *Izvestia* had announced in bold-face type May 14 that Soviet CP First Secy. Khrushchev (listed first), Premier Bulganin, First Deputy Premier Mikoyan, Deputy Foreign Trade Min. Pavel Kumyikin and Deputy Foreign Min. Andrei A. Gromyko would confer with Marshal Tito, the Yugoslav president, in Belgrade at the end of May. The announcement said the visit was to be made "with the aim of further improvements in relations" with Tito, who had been expelled from the Soviet-led Cominform in 1948 because of "nationalistic" policies. (Both countries had withdrawn their ambassadors in Oct. 1949.) During a Kremlin conference on labor productivity May 18, Khrushchev said the Russians would visit Tito "with open hearts and pure souls" and firmly believed "that normal relations between states should be based on the principle of equal rights and mutual non-interference in each other's affairs." Khrushchev said "all the necessary conditions exist to insure full normalization of relations" with Yugoslavia. He denied foreign speculation that the USSR wanted to take over all Europe. He said "the main principle of Soviet foreign policy is the possibility and necessity of peaceful co-existence of different social systems."

The Soviet delegation arrived at Belgrade's Zemun Airport May 26. Tito listened impassively and made no reply to an 11-minute arrival speech read in Russian by Khrushchev. Khrushchev addressed himself to "dear Comrade Tito... dear comrades and citizens" and recalled the "ties of long brotherly friendship and the joint struggle against the [Nazi German] enemy." He said that "we sincerely regret" that "these good relations were destroyed" and that his group "resolutely" rejected the Kremlin-Tito rupture. He added: "We ascribe without hesitation the aggravations to the provocative role that Beria, Abakumov [both executed by the post-Stalin regime] and others—recently exposed enemies of the people—played in the relations between Yugoslavia and the USSR."

Khrushchev said: The Soviet leaders had "studied assiduously the materials on which had been based the serious accusations... against the leaders of Yugoslavia. The facts show that these materials were fabricated by imperialist enemies who by deceptive methods pushed their way into the ranks of our party.... We are profoundly convinced that this period of the deterioration of our relations has been left behind us. For our part we are ready to do everything necessary to eliminate all obstacles standing in the way of complete normalization of relations between our states." "The strongest ties" were created among those countries "where the leading forces are parties that base their activities on the teachings of Marxism-Leninism.... We would not be doing our duty to our peoples and to the working people of the whole world if we did not do everything possible to establish mutual understanding" between the Soviet and Yugoslav Communist parties. The USSR, "following the teachings of ... Lenin," based its relations with other countries "on principles of the peaceful co-existence of states, on principles of equality, non-intervention and respect for sovereignty and national independence, on principles of non-aggression and ... the impermissibility of some states' encroaching upon the territorial integrity of others." Khrushchev expressed hope that a strengthening of USSR-Yugoslav friendship "will contribute to improvement of relations among all countries" and "to consolidation of peace in general."

After 2 days of talks in Belgrade, Tito and Khrushchev led their respective delegations May 29 to Brioni Island, in the Adriatic Sea off Pula, where the talks continued at Tito's villa. Daily communiques gave no details of the discussions, except for references to talks about "future Soviet-Yugoslav relations." American press reports from Belgrade May 27-28 said Tito had resisted Khrushchev's efforts to get the Yugoslav CP to rejoin the Cominform and bring the country back to the Soviet political bloc. Tito was said to have (a) told the Russians that Yugoslavia must retain its current independence and (b) insisted on a settlement of economic questions, including Yugoslavia's contention that Russia owed $200 million for broken trade pacts.

In his first major speech since the Soviet visit, Tito said at a rally in Karlovac, Croatia July 27 that the USSR had canceled a debt of $90 million Yugoslavia owed for Russian goods exported to Yugoslavia before the Cominform dispute of 1948 disrupted Yugoslav-Soviet trade relations.

Soviet First Deputy Premier Mikoyan signed a 3-year trade agreement in Moscow Sept. 1 with a Yugoslav delegation headed by Gen. Svetozar Vukmanovic-Tempo, a vice president of the Federal Executive Council. The level of trade was fixed at $70 million a year—Yugoslavia to supply bauxite, lead, tobacco and hemp and receive Soviet coke, oil and cotton. Discussions in Jan. 1956 would cover the details of a 3-year Soviet credit of $54 million to Yugoslavia and a Soviet gold loan of $30 million, presumably for purchases outside the USSR. The loan terms—2% interest and repayable in 10 years—were said to be the same as those the USSR offered its European satellites.

Yugoslavia and the USSR also agreed Sept. 3 to set up direct airline service between Moscow and Belgrade. (Similar Soviet agreements with Poland and Czechoslovakia earlier in 1955 were the first to permit foreign airlines to make regular flights to Moscow since World War II.)

Military & Defense Policy

The post-Stalin regime took steps during 1955 to reduce the USSR's expensive military establishment—and thereby cut the defense budget. But it also bolstered Russia's military power by consolidating the armed might of the Soviet Union with the forces of its Eastern European allies under a single Warsaw Treaty command.

The Soviet news agency Tass announced Aug. 13 that the USSR would reduce its armed forces by 640,000 men by Dec. 15 to promote "relaxation of international tension and [establish] confidence among nations." Tass said "certain relaxation of tension" already had occurred following "recent developments and especially" the Big 4 summit meeting at Geneva. The government newspaper *Izvestia* said Aug. 14 that similar cuts by the Western powers would "strengthen the atmosphere of confidence... and have a favorable effect on the solution of the disarmament problem." U.S. State Secy. John Foster Dulles, at his news conference Aug. 16, said the U.S. "welcomed" this announcement of "the first significant reduction... in Soviet armed manpower in the last 8 years." But he noted that "the military significance of the Soviet reduction is not easy to judge" because "no official information has ever been provided" on Soviet armed forces, reserves and weapons. "Even after this reduction, however, Soviet standing forces will certainly still be much larger than those of the U.S.," Dulles said, since the USSR "maintains very large organized reserves... capable of being mobilized rapidly." Dulles recalled that modern weapons had enabled the U.S. to cut its armed manpower from 3,500,000 men to 2,900,000 in the past 2 years. He said "these factors indicated why full information regarding armed forces and effective inspection to verify the facts are necessary for any meaningful and intelligent approach to... international control and reduction of armament." (Estimates of Soviet armed manpower ranged from 3 million to 4.75 million men.) Moscow radio announced Dec. 12 that the 640,000-man reduction had been completed, with demobilized men "transferred to agriculture."

Marshal Ivan S. Konev, 57, Soviet deputy defense minister and 2d Ukranian Front commander in World War II, was named supreme commander of a unified military command to be set up in Moscow under a 20-year mutual defense treaty signed in Warsaw May 14 by the USSR, Albania, Bulgaria, Czechoslovakia, East Germany, Hungary, Poland and Rumania. The treaty signing was attended by Soviet Premier Bulganin, Foreign Min. Molotov and Defense Min. Zhukov. The treaty text said that the ratification of Western agreements authorizing a "remilitarized" West Germany "increases the danger of a new war and creates a threat to the national security of peace-loving states." A Warsaw Conference communique said East German participation "in measures regarding the armed forces of the unified command is to be examined later." Article I of the treaty said the 8 signatories "undertake, in accordance with the UN Charter, to abstain in their international relations from threats of violence or its use." The 11th (final) article said the treaty would lapse as soon as an East-West collective security treaty came into force. (The U.S. government estimated that 6 million men were in the Warsaw nations' armies—175-225 Soviet divisions and 80 satellite divisions.)

The Soviet Union's 1955 budget, adopted by the Supreme Soviet Feb. 7, provided for a 12% increase in military expenditures—to a total of 112.123 billion rubles (or $28 billion at the USSR's official rate of $1 to 4 rubles). But the Supreme Soviet Dec. 28 approved a 1956 national budget that cut defense items by 8.5% below the 1955 figure and brought them close to the 1954 level. 102.5 billion rubles were allocated for defense in 1956. In presenting the budget Dec. 26, Finance Min. Arseny G. Zverev had noted that the ruble's purchasing power had been increased by a cut in wholesale prices in 1955. Prices of heavy industrial products and freight shipments were reduced Apr. 1 for government agencies but not for private purchasers. Defense accounted for 18.2% of the budget, compared with 19.9% in 1955, 17.8% in 1954. Zverev said that money saved on defense would go to develop the national economy, particularly heavy industry, and to education. He said the lower defense figures meant that the USSR, "not only in words but in deeds, shows its concern for lessening world tension and insuring peace and international security."

Premier Bulganin announced Sept. 17 that the USSR would give up its air-naval base on the Porkkala Peninsula in Finland, and Defense Min. Zhukov said next day that the USSR had decided to liquidate all its military bases on foreign soil. The

Soviet decision to evacuate Porkkala within 3 months was incorporated into a renewal of the USSR-Finnish mutual defense alliance signed by Russian and Finnish officials in Moscow Sept. 19. Finnish Pres. Juho K. Paasikivi, Premier Urho K. Kekkonen and other Finnish officials had arrived in Moscow Sept. 15 to discuss the treaty. One delegation member said Sept. 17 that the USSR apparently had decided "well in advance" to give up Porkkala. "We didn't even have to ask," he said. (Finland had given Russia a 50-year lease on Porkkala in 1947. The Russians agreed to pay "rent" of about 5¢ per acre on the 152-square-mile area, which was about 12 miles from Helsinki.) The protocol signed Sept. 17 provided that the 10-year mutual defense treaty concluded in 1948 should be extended 20 years after ratification by the Finnish and Soviet Parliaments and after ratification instruments were exchanged. If neither country denounced the treaty one year before it expired, it would continue automatically for 5 more years and for 5-year periods after that unless denounced. At a Kremlin reception after the signing, Paasikivi said: "I am here in Moscow for the 7th time for negotiations..., but this is the first time that I return to our capital satisfied. Usually I have returned unsatisfied." (Soviet troops began leaving Porkkala Oct. 24.)

Zhukov's remarks about liquidation of all foreign military bases were made to newsmen at a reception Sept. 18. He said: "The sooner others follow our example the better it will be for peace in our opinion." Asked what "others" he had in mind, Zhukov replied: "For example, the U.S." "Talk of peace must be reinforced by actions, and that is what we are doing," Zhukov said. (U.S. State Department officials said they knew of no other Soviet-leased bases on foreign soil besides Porkkala and Port Arthur, returned to Communist China in May.)

These 10 Soviet army and air force generals were raised Mar. 11 to marshal's rank: (army) Vassili Ivanovich Chuikov, Ivan Khristoforovitch Bagramian, Sergei Semenovich Biryuzov, Aleksandr Ivanovich Yeremenko, Andrei Antonovich Grechko, Kiril Semenovich Moskalenko, Sergei Sergeevich Varentsov, Vassili Ivanovich Kasakov; (air force) Sergei Ignatyevich Rudenko, Vladimir Aleksandrovich Sudets. Aviation Marshal Pavel Fedorovich Zhigarev was made chief marshal.

Shifting Soviet Attitudes?

Domestic and foreign-policy developments involving the USSR were studied by foreign observers during 1955 as possible clues to changes in the Soviet regime's attitudes and policies.

Soviet collective farm leaders were given more authority to decide local agricultural policy under a decree issued Mar. 10 by Premier Bulganin and CP First Secy. Khrushchev. The decree criticized past centralized policy as being unrealistic, destroying initiative and causing loss of productivity.

The economics magazine *Voprosi Ekonomiki (Questions of Economics)* reappeared on Moscow newsstands Mar. 12 after a 2-month absence. The new issue apologized editorially for a Sept. 1954 article urging more production of consumer goods. This was called "a serious political and theoretical mistake."

Prof. J. Bartlet Brebner, Columbia University's representative to Moscow University's bicentenary celebration, said in Cambridge, England May 18, while en route home, that he had seen evidence of new intellectual freedom in the USSR. Soviet scholars, he said, seemed to know works not favored by the government.

Khrushchev Sept. 17 delivered an impromptu speech on the future of communism and capitalism. Speaking at a dinner for an East German delegation in Moscow, Khrushchev referred to Western speculation about the Russians "starting to smile." "That smile is genuine," Khrushchev said. "We wish to live in peace, tranquillity. But if anyone believes that our smiles involve abandonment of the teaching of Marx, Engels and Lenin, he deceives himself poorly. Those who wait for that must wait until a shrimp learns to whistle [an old Russian proverb]." "We honestly said to [West German Chancellor Konrad] Adenauer: 'Your star is waning. It is the star of capitalism. That of socialism is only beginning, but it will shine with a thousand fires.' "

A "worldwide victory for communism" in the 20th century was predicted by Soviet First Deputy Premier Lazar M. Kaganovich Nov. 6 in the keynote speech at the traditional gathering of Soviet leaders in Moscow's Bolshoi Theatre on the eve of the anniversary of the Bolshevik revolution. Those who said the USSR was exporting revolutionary ideas were either "fools or provocateurs" because communism cannot be imposed from without but must arise from within each country, Kaganovich declared. He said Communist ideas were spreading throughout the world "without visas and without fingerprints." "No one can break the close ties linking the Soviet people with the broad masses and working classes of all countries of the world," he said. "Revolutionary ideas know no frontiers."

West German Chancellor Konrad Adenauer and Soviet Premier Bulganin had agreed during talks in Moscow Sept. 9-13 to a normalization of bilateral relations and the resumption of diplomatic exchanges halted in 1941. Both countries' governments formally agreed to this by Sept. 25, and the Soviet Union thereupon began repatriating 9,626 German war prisoners—some to East Germany. (The Soviet regime Mar. 25, 1954 had unilaterally recognized East German sovereignty.) The USSR Sept. 18 announced an amnesty for Russians who had collaborated with the Germans during World War II. The amnesty provided for the immediate release of minor collaborators, reduction of sentences for major collaborators and the immediate liberation of persons convicted of serving in German military or police units. *Izvestia* said that one reason for the amnesty was the ending of the state of war with Germany.

A joint Soviet-Canadian communique, issued Oct. 12 after a week-long visit to Moscow by Canadian Foreign Min. Lester B. Pearson, said that Pearson and Soviet leaders had discussed the "possibility of concluding a trade pact on the most-favored-nation basis." Agreement was reached on the need to remove "obstacles to a freer exchange of information and views and to enlarge as much as possible the degree of cooperation between the 2 countries in the spheres of culture, science and technology." Pearson was the first Western foreign minister to pay an official visit to the USSR since the start of the Cold War. Pearson, at a meeting with Khrushchev at the latter's villa in the Crimea Oct. 12, commented on the vast reconstruction he had seen in Stalingrad and Sebastopol. Khrushchev replied that "it now appears that Canada, Britain and the U.S. are planning to wreak new destruction through NATO." Pearson repeated earlier explanations of NATO as a defensive alliance, but Khrushchev replied that it was not the first time in history that an "aggressive organization" was described as defensive. "The best advice I can give to Canada is to get out of NATO," he said.

6 British warships, headed by the carrier *Triumph,* flagship of the British Home Fleet, arrived in Leningrad harbor Oct. 12 for a 6-day goodwill visit. They were the first British Navy units at Leningrad since 1946. 6 Soviet warships, headed by the 12,000-ton cruiser *Sverdlov,* arrived at Portsmouth, England the same day in an exchange of visits. Although the British warships were open to all visitors, Soviet authorities said Oct. 14 that only Soviet citizens with special passes from factories, unions, etc. could visit the ships.

7 Soviet journalists made a month-long tour of the U.S. Oct. 17-Nov. 18. They told New York newsmen Oct. 20 that one reason for their visit was to show "we can fully express our opinions." They said that criticism of Soviet officials and agencies appeared in the Soviet press "regularly" and that there were as many differences of opinion among them as in any group of journalists.

Soviet deputies Dec. 25 approved Soviet participation in the Inter-Parliamentary Union and recommended more exchange visits among parliamentarians, particularly those from Asia and Africa. (The USSR Aug. 30 had become the first Soviet-bloc country to be elected to the Executive Committee of the Inter-Parliamentary Union. The election took place during the union's meeting in Helsinki.)

The U.S. embassy in Moscow announced Dec. 23 that the USSR had agreed to a U.S. suggestion of Sept. 9 again to allow the distribution of 50,000 copies a month of the Russian-language magazine *Amerika* (published by the U.S. State Department until 1952) starting next spring. The Soviet embassy in Washington was to be permitted to resume distribution of an information bulletin in the U.S.

An American production of *Porgy & Bess* opened in Leningrad Dec. 26. Company tour manager Anatole Heller said in Moscow Nov. 11 that the USSR had agreed to pay the travel expenses.

The executions of 5 officials of the Soviet Georgian Republic government for conspiring with the late Stalinist police chief Lavrenti P. Beria were announced on a Tiflis (Georgia) radio broadcast Nov. 22. Among those executed was ex-State Security Min. Nikolai M. Rukhadze. 2 others were jailed for life by a military tribunal, the broadcast said. The trials had taken place in September.

1956

In 1956 Nikita Khrushchev and his associates began an all-out attack on the late Stalin's policies and repressive regime. The anti-Stalin campaign took place as Stalin's heirs embarked on a program of modifying domestic and foreign policies, de-escalating the Cold War, seeking friendlier relations with Western nations, easing press restrictions, rehabilitating purge victims and making life easier for Soviet citizens. The Cominform was dissolved, Vyacheslav Molotov lost his job as foreign minister, and Trofim Lysenko was ousted as virtual dictator of biological/genetic science in the USSR. The Soviet rulers indicated that they were ending the harsh repression of political dissent in Russia. But they used military force to crush revolt in Hungary.

KHRUSHCHEV'S DENUNCIATION OF STALIN

Murders & 'Cult of Individual' Assailed

The 20th Congress of the Soviet Communist Party, held in Moscow Feb. 14-25, was climaxed Feb. 24-25 by a 26,000-word secret speech in which CP First Secy. Nikita S. Khrushchev denounced the long and tyrannical rule of the late Joseph V. Stalin. Khrushchev charged that with the assistance of the late Lavrenti P. Beria and other aides, Stalin had caused the execution of thousands of "honest Communists" and other innocent people during the repressions and purges of the 1930s and later years. According to Khrushchev, these victims were seized under false charges fabricated on Stalin's instigation and were convicted on the basis of false "confessions" exacted by torture. Khrushchev also denounced Stalin's "megalomania" and said that Stalin's penchant for self-glorification had led to a "cult of the individual."

The attack on Stalin's rule had been started Feb. 14 in Khruschev's 7-hour keynote speech at the congress. Khruschev asserted that the CP Central Committee had "vigorously condemned the cult of the individual as being alien to the spirit of Marxism-Leninism and making a particular leader the hero and miracle-worker." The "cult of the individual tended to minimize the role of collective leadership . . . and at times resulted in serious drawbacks" in the CP's work. The "working collective of leaders" set up since Stalin's death was based "on ideas and principles permitting neither mutual forgiveness nor personal antagonism." The Central Committee had sometimes "found it necessary to correct some people who introduced confusion in certain clear issues which the party had settled long before."

Khrushchev's attack on Stalin was amplified Feb. 16 by First Deputy Premier Anastas I. Mikoyan. Mikoyan's speech, containing the most detailed and lengthy indictment of Stalin's policies presented publicly to the congress, was not published until Feb. 18. Mikoyan assailed both Stalin's dictatorship and his writing of the USSR's early history. Mikoyan said:

● "The main feature which characterizes the work of the [CP] Central Committee and its Presidium during the past 3 years is the fact that, after a long interval, collective leadership has been created in our party." It had developed "a strongly welded leading collective whose strength lies not only in the fact that it consists of comrades who have become a team in the course of many years of revolutionary struggle.... The most important thing is that this collective, guided by Lenin's ideas and Lenin's principles of the structure of the party and party leadership, has within a short space of time achieved the restoration of Lenin's forms of party life, from top to bottom. The principle of collective leadership is elementary for the proletarian party... of the Lenin type." For "about 20 years we, in fact, had no collective leadership. The cult of personality, condemned already by Marx and... Lenin, flourished, and this, of course, could not but exert an extremely negative influence...." With collective leadership in "the past 3 years," the "entire fruitful influence of the Lenin methods of leadership can be felt." This has given "a fresh strength to our party."

● Current textbooks (prepared during Stalin's regime) on the USSR's early history must be revised thoroughly to correct their mistakes about "allegedly subversive activity of some former party leaders who many years after the events described were wrongly declared enemies of the people." The Ukrainians Vladimir Antonov-Ovsenyenko, a military leader under Lenin and a diplomat under Stalin, and Stanislav V. Kossior (Kossio), Ukrainian Bolshevik leader, had been falsely accused in the Stalinist purges in the 1930s. The Stalinist *Short Course of the History of the Party* no longer was adequate as a textbook on Soviet CP history because it offered no "accepted history of the party" for the past 20 years.

Other government leaders at the congress also discussed Stalin's rule. Deputy Premier Georgi M. Malenkov, in his first major speech since he had stepped down as premier in 1955, told the congress Feb. 17 that one-man rule had led to "arbitrary, irrevocable decisions," "high-handedness" and "serious abnormalities." Premier Nikolai A. Bulganin, in a Feb. 21 speech, also attacked the "cult of the individual" and lauded its replacement by collective leadership.

Khrushchev's secret Feb. 24-25 speech was made at a closed meeting of the 1,300 delegates. The Soviet press at first did not even hint at the content of the address, and it was not until Mar. 15 that U.S. diplomats and newsmen in Moscow reported that the speech had been devoted to a lengthy indictment of Stalin.

The U.S. State Department June 4 released a document that, it said, "purports to be a version" of Khrushchev's Feb. 24-25 secret speech denouncing Stalin. This version, "obtained from a confidential source," "is understood to have been prepared for the guidance of a party leadership of a Communist party outside of the USSR," the State Department said.

Text of the Khrushchev speech as released by the State Department:

Comrades! In the report of the Central Committee of the Party at the 20th Congress, in a number of speeches by delegates to the Congress, as also formerly during the plenary CC/CPSU [editor's note: Central Committee/Communist Party of the Soviet Union] sessions, quite a lot has been said about the cult of the individual and about its harmful consequences.

After Stalin's death the Central Committee of the Party began to implement a policy of explaining concisely and consistently that it is impermissible and foreign to the spirit of Marxism-Leninism to elevate one person, to transform him into a superman possessing supernatural characteristics akin to those of a god. Such a man supposedly knows everything, sees everything, thinks for everyone, can do anything, is infallible in his behavior.

Such a belief about a man, and specifically about Stalin, was cultivated among us for many years.

The objective of the present report is not a thorough evaluation of Stalin's life and activity. Concerning Stalin's merits, an entirely sufficient number of books, pamphlets and studies had already been written in his lifetime. The role of Stalin in the preparation and execution of the Socialist Revolution, in the Civil War, and in the fight for the construction of socialism in our country is universally known. Everyone knows this well. At the present we are concerned with a question which has immense importance for the party now and for the future—[we are concerned] with how the cult of the person of Stalin has been gradually growing, the cult which became at a certain specific stage the source of a whole series of exceedingly serious and grave perversions of party principles, of party democracy, of revolutionary legality.

Because of the fact that not all as yet realize fully the practical consequences resulting from the cult of the individual, the great harm caused by the violation of the principle of collective direction of the party and because of the accumulation of immense and limitless power in the hands of one person—the Central Committee of the Party considers it absolutely necessary to make the material pertaining to this matter available to the 20th Congress of the Communist Party of the Soviet Union.

Allow me first of all to remind you how severely the classics of Marxism-Leninism denounced every manifestation of the cult of the individual. In a letter to the German political worker Wilhelm Bloss, Marx stated: "From my antipathy to any cult of the individual, I never made public during the existence of the International the numerous addresses from various countries which recognized my merits and which annoyed me. I did not even reply to them, except sometimes to rebuke their authors. Engels and I first joined the secret society of Communists on the condition that everything making for superstitious worship of authority would be deleted from its statute. Lassalle subsequently did quite the opposite."

Sometime later Engels wrote: "Both Marx and I have always been against any public manifestation with regard to individuals, with the exception of cases when it had an important purpose; and we most strongly opposed such manifestations which during our lifetime concerned us personally."

The great modesty of the genius of the revolution, Vladimir Ilyich Lenin, is known. Lenin had always stressed the role of the people as the creator of history, the directing and organizational role of the party as a living and creative organism, and also the role of the Central Committee.

Marxism does not negate the role of the leaders of the workers' class in directing the revolutionary liberation movement.

While ascribing great importance to the role of the leaders and organizers of the masses, Lenin at the same time mercilessly stigmatized every manifestation of the cult of the individual, inexorably combated the foreign-to-Marxism views about a "hero" and a "crowd" and countered all efforts to oppose a "hero" to the masses and to the people.

Lenin taught that the party's strength depends on its indissoluble unity with the masses, on the fact that behind the party follow the people—workers, peasants and intelligentsia. "Only he will win and retain the power," said Lenin, "who believes in the people, who submerges himself in the fountain of the living creativeness of the people."

Lenin spoke with pride about the Bolshevik Communist Party as the leader and teacher of the people; he called for the presentation of all the most important questions before the opinion of knowledgeable workers, before the opinion of their party; he said: "We believe in it, we see in it the wisdom, the honor, and the conscience of our epoch."

Lenin resolutely stood against every attempt aimed at belittling or weakening the directing role of the party in the structure of the Soviet state. He worked out Bolshevik principles of party direction and norms of party life, stressing that the guiding principle of party leadership is its collegiality. Already during the pre-revolutionary years Lenin called the Central Committee of the Party a collective of leaders and the guardian and interpreter of party principles. "During the period between congresses," pointed out Lenin, "the Central Committee guards and interprets the principles of the party."

Underlining the role of the Central Committee of the Party and its authority, Vladimir Ilyich [Lenin] pointed out: "Our Central Committee constituted itself as a closely centralized and highly authoritative group...."

During Lenin's life the Central Committee of the Party was a real expression of collective leadership of the party and of the nation. Being a militant Marxist-revolutionist, always unyielding in matters of principle, Lenin never imposed by force his views upon his co-workers. He tried to convince; he patiently explained his opinions to others. Lenin always diligently observed that the norms of party life were realized, that the party statute was enforced, that the party congresses and the plenary sessions of the Central Committee took place at the proper intervals.

In addition to the great accomplishments of V. I. Lenin for the victory of the working class and of the working peasants, for the victory of our party and for the application of the ideas of scientific communism to life, his acute mind expressed itself also in this: that he detected in Stalin in time those negative characteristics which resulted later in grave consequences. Fearing the future fate of the party and of the Soviet nation, V. I. Lenin made a completely correct characterization of Stalin, pointing out that it was necessary to consider the question of transferring Stalin from the position of the secretary general because of the fact that Stalin is excessively rude, that he does not have a proper attitude toward his comrades, that he is capricious and abuses his power.

In Dec. 1922 in a letter to the Party Congress Vladimir Ilyich [Lenin] wrote: "After taking over the position of secretary general Comrade Stalin accumulated in his hands immeasurable power, and I am not certain whether he will be always able to use this power with the required care."

This letter—a political document of tremendous importance, known in the party history as Lenin's "testament"—was distributed among the delegates to the 20th Party Congress. You have read it, and will undoubtedly read it again more than once. You might reflect on Lenin's plain words, in which expression is given to Vladimir Ilyich's anxiety concerning the party, the people, the state, and the future direction of party policy.

Vladimir Ilyich said: "Stalin is excessively rude, and this defect, which can be freely tolerated in our midst and in contacts among us Communists, becomes a defect which cannot be tolerated in one holding the position of the secretary general. Because of this, I propose that the comrades consider the method by which Stalin would be removed from this position and by which another man would be selected for it, a man, who above all, would differ from Stalin in only one quality, namely, greater tolerance, greater loyalty, greater kindness and more considerate attitude toward the comrades, a less capricious temper, etc."

This document of Lenin's was made known to the delegates at the 13th Party Congress, who discussed the question of transferring Stalin from the position of secretary general. The delegates declared themselves in favor of retaining Stalin in this post, hoping that he would heed the critical remarks of Vladimir Ilyich and would be able to overcome the defects which caused Lenin serious anxiety.

Comrades! The Party Congress should become acquainted with two new documents, which confirm Stalin's character as already outlined by Vladimir Ilyich Lenin in his "testament." These documents are a letter from Nadezhda Konstantinovna Krupskaya to [Lev Borisovich] Kamenev, who was at that time head of the Political Bureau, and a personal letter from Vladimir Ilyich Lenin to Stalin.

1. I will now read these documents:

"Lev Borisovich!

"Because of a short letter which I had written in words dictated to me by Vladimir Ilyich by permission of the doctors, Stalin allowed himself yesterday an unusually rude outburst directed at me. This is not my first day in the party. During all these 30 years I have never heard from any comrade one word of rudeness. The business of the party and of Ilyich are not less dear to me than to Stalin. I need at present the maximum of self-control. What one can and what one cannot discuss with Ilyich—I know better than any doctor, because I know what makes him nervous and what does not; in any case, I know better than Stalin. I am turning to you and to Grigory as to much closer comrades of V. I. and I beg you to protect me from rude interference with my private life and from vile invectives and threats. I have no doubt as to what will be the unanimous decision of the Control Commission, with which Stalin sees fit to threaten me; however, I have neither the strength nor the time to waste on this foolish quarrel. And I am a living person and my nerves are strained to the utmost.

N. Krupskaya"

Nadezhda Konstantinovna wrote this letter on 23 Dec. 1922. After 2 1/2 months, in Mar. 1923, Vladimir Ilyich Lenin sent Stalin the following letter:

2. *The letter of V. I. Lenin*

"To Comrade Stalin:

"Copies for: Kamenev and [Grigori Evseyevich] Zinoviev.

"Dear Comrade Stalin!

"You permitted yourself a rude summons of my wife to the telephone and a rude reprimand of her. Despite the fact that she told you that she agreed to forget what was said, nevertheless Zinoviev and Kamenev heard about it from her. I have no intention to forget so easily that which is being done against me, and I need not stress here that I consider as directed against me that which is being done against my wife. I ask you, therefore, that you weigh carefully whether you are agreeable to retracting your words and apologizing or whether you prefer the severance of relations between us. [Commotion in the hall]

"Sincerely: Lenin

"5 Mar. 1923"

Comrades! I will not comment on these documents. They speak eloquently for themselves. Since Stalin could behave in this manner during Lenin's life, could thus behave toward Nadezhda Konstantinovna Krupskaya, whom the party knows well and values highly as a loyal friend of Lenin and as an active fighter for the cause of the party since its creation—we can easily imagine how Stalin treated other people. These negative characteristics of his developed steadily and during the last years acquired an absolutely insufferable character.

As later events have proven, Lenin's anxiety was justified: in the first period after Lenin's death Stalin still paid attention to his [*i.e.,* Lenin's] advice, but later he began to disregard the serious admonitions of Vladimir Ilyich.

When we analyze the practice of Stalin in regard to the direction of the party and of the country, when we pause to consider everything which Stalin perpetrated, we must be convinced that Lenin's fears were justified. The negative characteristics of Stalin, which, in Lenin's time, were only incipient, transformed themselves during the last years into a grave abuse of power by Stalin, which caused untold harm to our party.

We have to consider seriously and analyze correctly this matter in order that we may preclude any possibility of a repetition in any form whatever of what took place during the life of Stalin, who absolutely did not tolerate collegiality in leadership and in work, and who practiced brutal violence, not only toward everything which opposed him, but also toward that which seemed, to his capricious and despotic character, contrary to his concepts.

Stalin acted not through persuasion, explanation and patient co-operation with people, but by imposing his concepts and demanding absolute submission to his opinion. Whoever opposed this concept or tried to prove his viewpoint, and the correctness of his position—was doomed to removal from the leading collective and to subsequent moral and physical annihilation. This was especially true during the period following the 17th Party Congress, when many prominent party leaders and rank-and-file party workers, honest and dedicated to the cause of communism, fell victim to Stalin's despotism.

We must affirm that the party had fought a serious fight against the Trotskyites, rightists and bourgeois nationalists, and that it disarmed ideologically all the enemies of Leninism. This ideological fight was carried on successfully, as a result of which the party became strengthened and tempered. Here Stalin played a positive role.

The party led a great political-ideological struggle against those in its own ranks who proposed anti-Leninist theses, who represented a political line hostile to the party and to the cause of socialism. This was a stubborn and a difficult fight but a necessary one, because the political line of both the Trotskyite-Zinovievite bloc and of the Bukharinites led actually toward the restoration of capitalism and capitulation to the world bourgeoisie. Let us consider for a moment what would have happened if in 1928-1929 the political line of right deviation had prevailed among us, or orientation toward "cotton-dress industrialization," or toward the *kulak,* etc. We would not now have a powerful heavy industry, we would not have the kolkhozes, we would find ourselves disarmed and weak in a capitalist encirclement.

It was for this reason that the party led an inexorable ideological fight and explained to all party members and to the non-party masses the harm and the danger of the anti-Leninist proposals of the Trotskyite opposition and the rightist opportunists. And this great work of explaining the party line bore fruit; both the Trotskyites and the rightist opportunists were politically isolated; the overwhelming party majority supported the Leninist line, and the party was able to awaken and organize the working masses to apply the Leninist party line and to build socialism.

Worth noting is the fact that even during the progress of the furious ideological fight against the Trotskyites, the Zinovievites, the Bukharinites and others—extreme repressive measures were not used against them. The fight was on ideological grounds. But some years later, when socialism in our country was fundamentally constructed, when the exploiting classes were generally liquidated, when the Soviet social structure had radically changed, when the social basis for political movements and groups hostile to the party had violently contracted, when the ideological opponents of the party were long since defeated politically— then the repression directed against them began.

It was precisely during this period (1935-1937-1938) that the practice of mass repression through the government apparatus was born [and used], first against the enemies of Leninism—Trotskyites, Zinovievites, Bukharinites, long since politically defeated by the party—and subsequently also against many honest Communists, against those party cadres who had borne the heavy load of the Civil War and the first and most difficult years of industrialization and collectivization, who actively fought against the Trotskyites and the rightists for the Leninist party line.

Stalin originated the concept "enemy of the people." This term automatically rendered it unnecessary that the ideological errors of a man or men engaged in a controversy be proven; this term made possible the usage of the most cruel repression, violating all norms of revolutionary legality, against anyone who in any way disagreed with Stalin, against those who were only suspected of hostile intent, against those who had bad reputations. This concept, "enemy of the people," actually eliminated the possibility of any kind of ideological fight or the making of one's views known on this or that issue, even those of a practical character. In the main, and in actuality, the only proof of guilt used, against all norms of current legal science, was the "confession" of the accused himself; and, as subsequent probing proved, "confessions" were acquired through physical pressures against the accused.

This led to glaring violations of revolutionary legality and to the fact that many entirely innocent persons, who in the past had defended the party line, became victims.

We must assert that in regard to those persons who in their time had opposed the party line, there were often no sufficiently serious reasons for their physical annihilation. The formula "enemy of the people" was specifically introduced for the purpose of physically annihilating such individuals.

It is a fact that many persons who were later annihilated as enemies of the party and people had worked with Lenin during his life. Some of these persons had made errors during Lenin's life, but, despite this, Lenin benefited by their work, he corrected them, and he did everything possible to retain them in the ranks of the party; he induced them to follow him.

In this connection the delegates to the Party Congress should familiarize themselves with an unpublished note by V. I. Lenin directed to the Central Committee's Political Bureau in Oct. 1920. Outlining the duties of the Control Commission, Lenin wrote that the commission should be transformed into a real "organ of party and proletarian conscience." "As a special duty of the Control Commission there is recommended a deep, individualized relationship with, and sometimes even a type of therapy for, the representatives of the so-called opposition—those who have experienced a psychological crisis because of failure in their Soviet or party career. An effort should be made to quiet them, to explain the matter to them in a way used among comrades, to find for them (avoiding the method of issuing orders) a task for which they are psychologically fitted. Advice and rules relating to this matter are to be formulated by the Central Committee's Organizational Bureau, etc."

Everyone knows how irreconcilable Lenin was with the ideological enemies of Marxism, with those who deviated from the correct party line. At the same time, however, Lenin, as is evident from the given document, in his practice of directing the party demanded the most intimate party contact with people who had shown indecision or temporary nonconformity with the party line but whom it was possible to return to the party path. Lenin advised that such people should be patiently educated without the application of extreme methods.

Lenin's wisdom in dealing with people was evident in his work with cadres.

An entirely different relationship with people characterized Stalin. Lenin's traits—patient work with people; stubborn and painstaking education of them; the ability to induce people to follow him without using compulsion, but rather through the ideological influence on them of the whole collective—were entirely foreign to Stalin. He [Stalin] discarded the Leninist method of convincing and educating; he abandoned the method of ideological struggle for that of administrative violence, mass repressions and terror. He acted on an increasingly larger scale and more stubbornly through punitive organs, at the same time often violating all existing norms of morality and of Soviet laws.

Arbitrary behavior by one person encouraged and permitted arbitrariness in others. Mass arrests and deportations of many thousands of people, execution without trial and without normal investigation created conditions of insecurity, fear and even desperation.

This, of course, did not contribute toward unity of the party ranks and of all strata of working people but on the contrary brought about annihilation and the expulsion from the party of workers who were loyal but inconvenient to Stalin.

Our party fought for the implementation of Lenin's plans for the construction of socialism. This was an ideological fight. Had Leninist principles been observed during the course of this fight, had the party's devotion to principles been skillfully combined with a keen and solicitous concern for people, had they not been repelled and wasted but rather drawn to our side—we certainly would not have had such a brutal violation of revolutionary legality, and many thousands of people would not have fallen victim of the method of terror. Extraordinary methods would then have been resorted to only against those people who had in fact committed criminal acts against the Soviet system.

Let us recall some historical facts:

In the days before the October Revolution 2 members of the Central Committee of the Bolshevik Party—Kamenev and Zinoviev—declared themselves against Lenin's plan for an armed uprising. In addition, on 18 October they published in the Menshevik newspaper *Novaya Zhizn* a statement declaring that the Bolsheviks were making preparations for an uprising and that they considered it adventuristic. Kamenev and Zinoviev thus disclosed to the enemy the decision of the Central Committee to stage the uprising and that the uprising had been organized to take place within the very near future.

This was treason against the party and against the revolution. In this connection, V. I. Lenin wrote: "Kamenev and Zinoviev revealed the decision of the Central Committee of their party on the armed uprising to Rodzyanko and Kerensky...." He put before the Central Committee the question of Zinoviev's and Kamenev's expulsion from the party.

However, after the Great Socialist October Revolution, as is known, Zinoviev and Kamenev were given leading positions. Lenin put them in positions in which they carried out most responsible party tasks and participated actively in the work of the leading party and Soviet organs. It is known that Zinoviev and Kamenev committed a number of other serious errors during Lenin's life. In his "testament" Lenin warned that Zinoviev's and Kamenev's October episode was of course not an accident. But Lenin did not pose the question of their arrest and certainly not their shooting.

Or let us take the example of the Trotskyites. At present, after a sufficiently long historical period, we can speak about the fight with the Trotskyites with complete calm and can analyze this matter with sufficient objectivity. After all, around Trotsky were people whose origin cannot by any means be traced to bourgeois society. Part of them belonged to the party intelligentsia, and a certain part were recruited from among the workers. We can name many individuals who in their time joined the Trotskyites; however, these same individuals took an active part in the workers' movement before the revolution, during the Socialist October Revolution itself, and also in the consolidation of the victory of this greatest of revolutions. Many of them broke with Trotskyism and returned to Leninist positions. Was it necessary to annihilate such people? We are deeply convinced that had Lenin lived such an extreme method would not have been used against many of them.

Such are only a few historical facts. But can it be said that Lenin did not decide to use even the most severe means against enemies of the revolution when this was actually necessary? No, no one can say this. Vladimir Ilyich demanded uncompromising dealings with the enemies of the revolution and of the working class and when necessary resorted ruthlessly to such methods. You will recall only V. I. Lenin's fight with the Socialist Revolutionary organizers of the anti-Soviet uprising, with the counter-revolutionary *kulaks* in 1918 and with others, when Lenin without hesitation used the most extreme methods against the enemies. Lenin used such methods, however, only against actual class enemies and not against those who blunder, who err, and whom it was possible to lead through ideological influence, and even retain in the leadership.

Lenin used severe methods only in the most necessary cases, when the exploiting classes were still in existence and were vigorously opposing the revolution, when the struggle for survival was decidedly assuming the sharpest forms, even including a civil war.

Stalin, on the other hand, used extreme methods and mass repressions at a time when the revolution was already victorious, when the Soviet state was strengthened, when the exploiting classes were already liquidated and Socialist relations were rooted solidly in all phases of national economy, when our party was politically consolidated and had strengthened itself both numerically and ideologically. It is clear that here Stalin showed in a whole series of cases his intolerance, his brutality and his abuse of power. Instead of proving his political correctness and mobilizing the masses, he often chose the path of repression and physical annihilation, not only against actual enemies, but also against individuals who had not committed any crimes against the party and the Soviet government. Here we see no wisdom but only a demonstration of the brutal force which had once so alarmed V. I. Lenin.

Lately, especially after the unmasking of the Beria gang, the Central Committee looked into a series of matters fabricated by this gang. This revealed a very ugly picture of brutal willfulness connected with the incorrect behavior of Stalin. As facts prove, Stalin, using his unlimited power, allowed himself many abuses, acting in the name of the Central Committee, not asking for the opinion of the committee members nor even of the members of the Central Committee's Political Bureau; often he did not inform them about his personal decisions concerning very important party and government matters.

Considering the question of the cult of an individual we must first of all show everyone what harm this caused to the interests of our party.

Vladimir Ilyich Lenin had always stressed the party's role and significance in the direction of the Socialist government of workers and peasants; he saw in this the chief precondition for a successful building of socialism in our country. Pointing to the great responsibility of the Bolshevik Party, as a ruling party in the Soviet state, Lenin called for the most meticulous observance of all norms of party life; he called for the realization of the principles of collegiality in the direction of the party and the state.

Collegiality of leadership flows from the very nature of our party, a party built on the principles of democratic centralism. "This means," said Lenin, "that all party matters are accomplished by all party members—directly or through representatives—who without any exceptions are subject to the same rules; in addition, all administrative members, all directing collegia, all holders of party positions are elective, they must account for their activities and are recallable."

It is known that Lenin himself offered an example of the most careful observance of these principles. There was no matter so important that Lenin himself decided it without asking for advice and approval of the majority of the Central Committee members or of the members of the Central Committee's Political Bureau.

In the most difficult period for our party and our country, Lenin considered it necessary regularly to convoke congresses, party conferences and plenary sessions of the Central Committee, at which all the most important questions were discussed and where resolutions, carefully worked out by the collective of leaders, were approved.

We can recall, for an example, the year 1918 when the country was threatened by the attack of the imperialistic interventionists. In this situation the 7th Party Congress was convened in order to discuss a vitally important matter which could not be postponed—the matter of peace. In 1919, while the Civil War was raging, the 8th Party Congress convened, which adopted a new party program, decided such important matters as the relationship with the peasant masses, the organization of the Red Army, the leading role of the party in the work of the Soviets, the correction of the social composition of the party, and other matters. In 1920 the 9th Party Congress was convened, which laid down guiding principles pertaining to the party's work in the sphere of economic construction. In 1921, the 10th Party Congress accepted Lenin's New Economic Policy and the historical resolution called "About Party Unity."

During Lenin's life party congresses were convened regularly; always, when a radical turn in the development of the party and the country took place, Lenin considered it absolutely necessary that the party discuss at length all the basic matters pertaining to internal and foreign policy and to questions bearing on the development of party and government.

It is very characteristic that Lenin addressed to the Party Congress, as the highest party organ, his last articles, letters and remarks. During the period between congresses the Central Committee of the Party, acting as the most authoritative leading collective, meticulously observed the principles of the party and carried out its policy.

So it was during Lenin's life.

Were our party's holy Leninist principles observed after the death of Vladimir Ilyich?

Whereas during the first few years after Lenin's death party congresses and Central Committee plenums took place more or less regularly, later, when Stalin began increasingly to abuse his power, these principles were brutally violated. This was especially evident during the last 15 years of his life. Was it a normal situation when over 13 years elapsed between the 18th and 19th Party Congresses, years during which our party and our country had experienced so many important events? These events demanded categorically that the party should have passed resolutions pertaining to the country's defense during the Patriotic War and to peacetime construction after the war. Even after the end of the war a congress was not convened for over 7 years.

Central Committee plenums were hardly ever called. It should be sufficient to mention that during all the years of the Patriotic War not a single Central Committee plenum took place. It is true that there was an attempt to call a Central Committee plenum in Oct. 1941, when Central Committee members from the whole country were called to Moscow. They waited two days for the opening of the plenum, but in vain. Stalin did not even want to meet and to talk to the Central Committee members. This fact shows how demoralized Stalin was in the first months of the war and how haughtily and disdainfully he treated the Central Committee members.

In practice Stalin ignored the norms of party life and trampled on the Leninist principle of collective party leadership.

Stalin's willfulness vis-a-vis the party and its Central Committee became fully evident after the 17th Party Congress, which took place in 1934.

Having at its disposal numerous data showing brutal willfulness toward party cadres, the Central Committee has created a party commission under the control of the Central Committee Presidium; it was charged with investigating what made possible the mass repressions against the majority of the Central Committee members and candidates elected at the 17th Congress of the All-Union Communist Party (Bolsheviks). The commission has become acquainted with a large quantity of materials in the NKVD archives and with other documents and has established many facts pertaining to the fabrication of cases against Communists, to false accusations, to glaring abuses of Socialist legality—which resulted in the death of innocent people. It became apparent that many party, Soviet and economic activists, who were branded in 1937-1938 as "enemies," were actually never enemies, spies, wreckers, etc., but were always honest Communists; they were only so stigmatized and often, no longer able to bear barbaric tortures, they charged themselves (at the order of the investigative judges—falsifiers) with all kinds of grave and unlikely crimes. The commission has presented to the Central Committee Presidium lengthy and documented materials pertaining to mass repressions against the delegates to the 17th Party Congress and against members of the Central Committee elected at that Congress. These materials have been studied by the Presidium of the Central Committee.

It was determined that of the 139 members and candidates of the Party's Central Committee who were elected at the 17th Congress, 98 persons, *i.e.,* 70%, were arrested and shot (mostly in 1937-1938). [Indignation in the hall.]

What was the composition of the delegates to the 17th Congress? It is known that 80% of the voting participants of the 17th Congress joined the party during the years of conspiracy before the Revolution and during the Civil War; this means before 1921. By social origin the basic mass of the delegates to the Congress were workers (60% of the voting members). For this reason, it was inconceivable that a Congress so composed would have elected a Central Committee a majority of whom would prove to be enemies of the party. The only reason why 70% of Central Committee members and candidates elected at the 17th Congress were branded as enemies of the party and of the people was because honest Communists were slandered, accusations against them were fabricated and revolutionary legality was gravely undermined.

The same fate met not only the Central Committee members but also the majority of the delegates to the 17th Party Congress. Of 1,966 delegates with either voting or advisory rights, 1,108 persons were arrested on charges of anti-revolutionary crimes, *i.e.,* decidedly more than a majority. This very fact shows how absurd, wild and contrary to common sense were the charges of counter-revolutionary crimes made out, as we now see, against a majority of participants at the 17th Party Congress. [Indignation in the hall.]

We should recall that the 17th Party Congress is historically known as the Congress of Victors. Delegates to the Congress were active participants in the building of our Socialist state; many of them suffered and fought for party interests during the pre-revolutionary years in the conspiracy and at the Civil War fronts; they fought their enemies valiantly and often nervelessly looked into the face of death. How then can we believe that such people could prove to be "2-faced" and had joined the camps of the enemies of socialism during the era after the political liquidation of Zinovievites, Trotskyites and rightists and after the great accomplishments of Socialist construction?

This was the result of the abuse of power by Stalin, who began to use mass terror against the party cadres.

What is the reason that mass repressions against activists increased more and more after the 17th Party Congress? It was because at that time Stalin had so elevated himself above the party and above the nation that he ceased to consider either the Central Committee or the party. While he still reckoned with the opinion of the collective before the 17th Congress, after the complete political liquidation of the Trotskyites, Zinovievites and Bukharinites, when as a result of that fight and Socialist victories the party achieved unity, Stalin ceased to an ever greater degree to consider the members of the Party's Central Committee and even the members of the Political Bureau. Stalin thought that now he could decide all things alone and all he needed were statisticians; he treated all others in such a way that they could only listen to and praise him.

After the criminal murder of S[ergei] M. Kirov, mass repressions and brutal acts of violation of Socialist legality began. On the evening of 1 Dec. 1934 on Stalin's initiative (without the approval of the Political Bureau—which was passed 2 days later, casually) the secretary of the Presidium of the Central Executive Committee, Yenukidze, signed the following directive:

"I. Investigative agencies are directed to speed up the cases of those accused of the preparation or execution of acts of terror.

"II. Judicial organs are directed not to hold up the execution of death sentences pertaining to crimes of this category in order to consider the possibility of pardon, because the Presidium of the Central Executive Committee USSR does not consider as possible the receiving of petitions of this sort.

"III. The organs of the Commissariat of Internal Affairs are directed to execute the death sentences against criminals of the above-mentioned category immediately after the passage of sentences."

This directive became the basis for mass acts of abuse against Socialist legality. During many of the fabricated court cases the accused were charged with "the preparation" of terroristic acts; this deprived them of any possibility that their cases might be re-examined, even when they stated before the court that their "confessions" were secured by force and when, in a convincing manner, they disproved the accusations against them.

It must be asserted that to this day the circumstances surrounding Kirov's murder hide many things which are inexplicable and mysterious and demand a most careful examination. There are reasons for the suspicion that the killer of Kirov, [Leonid V.] Nikolayev, was assisted by someone from among the people whose duty it was to protect the person of Kirov. A month and a half before the killing, Nikolayev was arrested on the grounds of suspicious behavior, but he was released and not even searched. It is an unusually suspicious circumstance that when the Chekist assigned to protect Kirov was being brought for an interrogation, on 2 Dec. 1934, he was killed in a car "accident" in which no other occupants of the car were harmed. After the murder of Kirov, top functionaries of the Leningrad NKVD were given very light sentences, but in 1937 they were shot. We can assume that they were shot in order to cover the traces of the organizers of Kirov's killing. [Movement in the hall.]

Mass repressions grew tremendously from the end of 1936 after a telegram from Stalin and [Andrei Aleksandrovich] Zhdanov, dated from Sochi on 25 Sept. 1936, was addressed to Kaganovich, Molotov and other members of the Political Bureau. The content of the telegram was as follows: "We deem it absolutely necessary and urgent that Comrade [Nikolai I.] Yezhov be nominated to the post of People's Commissar for Internal Affairs. [Henryk G.] Yagoda has definitely proved himself to be incapable of unmasking the Trotskyite-Zinovievite bloc. The OGPU is 4 years behind in this matter. This is noted by all party workers and by the majority of the representatives of the NKVD." Strictly speaking we should stress that Stalin did not meet with and therefore could not know the opinion of party workers.

This Stalinist formulation that the "NKVD (term used interchangeably with 'OGPU') [translator's note] is 4 years behind" in applying mass repression and that there is a necessity for "catching up" with the neglected work directly pushed the NKVD workers on the path of mass arrests and executions.

We should state that this formulation was also forced on the February-March plenary session of the Central Committee of the All-Union Communist Party (Bolsheviks) in 1937. The plenary resolution approved it on the basis of Yezhov's report "Lessons flowing from the harmful activity, diversion and espionage of the Japanese-German-Trotskyite agents," stating: "The plenum of the Central Committee of the All-Union Communist Party (Bolsheviks) considers that all facts revealed during the investigation into the matter of an anti-Soviet Trotskyite center and of its followers in the provinces show that the People's Commissariat of Internal Affairs has fallen behind at least 4 years in the attempt to unmask these most inexorable enemies of the people."

The mass repressions at this time were made under the slogan of a fight against the Trotskyites. Did the Trotskyites at this time actually constitute such a danger to our party and to the Soviet state? We should recall that in 1927, on the eve of the 15th Party Congress, only some 4,000 votes were cast for the Trotskyite-Zinovievite opposition, while there were 724,000 for the party line. During the 10 years that passed between the 15th Party Congress and the February-March Central Committee Plenum Trotskyism was completely disarmed; many former Trotskyites had changed their former views and worked in the various sectors building socialism. It is clear that in the situation of Socialist victory there was no basis for mass terror in the country.

Stalin's report at the February-March Central Committee Plenum in 1937, "Deficiencies of party work and methods for the liquidation of the Trotskyites and of other 2-facers," contained an attempt at theoretical justification of the mass terror policy under the pretext that as we march forward toward socialism class war must allegedly sharpen. Stalin asserted that both history and Lenin taught him this.

Actually Lenin taught that the application of revolutionary violence is necessitated by the resistance of the exploiting classes, and this referred to the era when the exploiting classes existed and were powerful. As soon as the nation's political situation had improved, when in Jan. 1920 the Red Army took Rostov and thus won a most important victory over Denikin, Lenin instructed Dzherzhinsky to stop mass terror and to abolish the death penalty. Lenin justified this important political move of the Soviet state in the following manner in his report at the session of the All-Union Central Executive Committee on 2 Feb. 1920:

"We were forced to use terror because of the terror practiced by the Entente, when strong world powers threw their hordes against us, not avoiding any type of conduct. We would not have lasted 2 days had we not answered these attempts of officers and White Guardists in a merciless fashion; this meant the use of terror, but this was forced upon us by the terrorist methods of the Entente. But as soon as we attained a decisive victory, even before the end of the war, immediately after taking Rostov, we gave up the use of the death penalty and thus proved that we intend to execute our own program in the manner that we promised. We say that the application of violence flows out of the decision to smother the exploiters, the big landowners and the capitalists; as soon as this was accomplished we gave up the use of all extraordinary methods. We have proved this in practice."

Stalin deviated from these clear and plain precepts of Lenin. Stalin put the party and the NKVD up to the use of mass terror when the exploiting classes had been liquidated in our country and when there were no serious reasons for the use of extraordinary mass terror.

This terror was actually directed not at the remnants of the defeated exploiting classes but against the honest workers of the party and of the Soviet state; against them were made lying, slanderous and absurd accusations concerning "2-facedness," "espionage," "sabotage," preparation of fictitious "plots," etc.

At the February-March Central Committee plenum in 1937, many members actually questioned the rightness of the established course regarding mass repressions under the pretext of combating "2-facedness."

Comrade [Pavel P.] Postyshev most ably expressed these doubts. He said: "I have philosophized that the severe years of fighting have passed, party members who have lost their backbones have broken down or have joined the camp of the enemy; healthy elements have fought for the party. These were the years of industrialization and collectivization. I never thought it possible that after this severe era had passed Karpov and people like him would find themselves in the camp of the enemy. (Karpov was a worker in the Ukrainian Central Committee whom Postyshev knew well.) And now, according to the testimony, it appears that Karpov was recruited in 1934 by the Trotskyites. I personally do not believe that in 1934 an honest party member, who had trod the long road of unrelenting fight against enemies for the party and for socialism, would now be in the camp of the enemies. I do not believe it.... I cannot imagine how it would be possible to travel with the party during the difficult years and then, in 1934, join the Trotskyites. It is an odd thing...." [Movement in the hall.]

Using Stalin's formulation, namely that the closer we are to socialism the more enemies we will have, and using the resolution of the February-March Central Committee Plenum passed on the basis of Yezhov's report—the provocateurs who had infiltrated the state security organs together with conscienceless careerists began to protect with the party name the mass terror against party cadres, cadres of the Soviet state and the ordinary Soviet citizens. It should suffice to say that the number of arrests based on charges of counter-revolutionary crimes had grown 10 times between 1936 and 1937.

It is known that brutal willfulness was practiced against leading party workers. The Party Statute, approved at the 17th Party Congress, was based on Leninist principles expressed at the 10th Party Congress. It stated that in order to apply an extreme method such as exclusion from the party against a Central Committee member, against a Central Committee candidate and against a member of the Party Control Commission, "it is necessary to call a Central Committee plenum and to invite to the plenum all Central Committee candidate members and all members of the Party Control Commission"; only if 2/3 of the members of such a general assembly of responsible party leaders find it necessary, only then can a Central Committee member or candidate be expelled.

The majority of the Central Committee members and candidates elected at the 17th Congress and arrested in 1937-1938 were expelled from the party illegally through the brutal abuse of the Party Statute, because the question of their expulsion was never studied at the Central Committee plenum.

Now when the cases of some of these so-called "spies" and "saboteurs" were examined it was found that all their cases were fabricated. Confessions of guilt of many arrested and charged with enemy activity were gained with the help of cruel and inhuman tortures.

At the same time Stalin, as we have been informed by members of the Political Bureau of that time, did not show them the statements of many accused political activists when they retracted their confessions before the military tribunal and asked for an objective examination of their cases. There were many such declarations, and Stalin doubtlessly knew of them.

The Central Committee considers it absolutely necessary to inform the Congress of many such fabricated "cases" against the members of the party's Central Committee elected at the 17th Party Congress.

An example of vile provocation, of odious falsification and of criminal violation of revolutionary legality is the case of the former candidate for the Central Committee Political Bureau, one of the most eminent workers of the party and of the Soviet government, Comrade [Robert I.] Eikhe, who was a party member since 1905. [Commotion in the hall.]

Comrade Eikhe was arrested on 29 Apr. 1938 on the basis of slanderous materials, without the sanction of the prosecutor of the USSR, which was finally received 15 months after the arrest.

Investigation of Eikhe's case was made in a manner which most brutally violated legality and was accompanied by willfulness and falsification.

Eikhe was forced under torture to sign ahead of time a protocol of his confession, prepared by the investigative judges, in which he and several other eminent party workers were accused of anti-Soviet activity.

On 1 Oct. 1939 Eikhe sent his declaration to Stalin in which he categorically denied his guilt and asked for an examination of his case. In the declaration he wrote: "There is no more bitter misery than to sit in the jail of a government for which I have always fought."

A 2d declaration of Eikhe has been preserved which he sent to Stalin on 27 Oct. 1939; in it he cited facts very convincingly and countered the slanderous accusations made against him, arguing that this provocatory accusation was on the one hand the work of real Trotskyites whose arrests he had sanctioned as first secretary of the West Siberian Krai Party Committee and who conspired in order to take revenge on him, and, on the other hand, the result of the base falsification of materials by the investigative judges.

Eikhe wrote in his declaration: "... On 25 Oct. of this year I was informed that the investigation in my case has been concluded and I was given access to the materials of this investigation. Had I been guilty of only 1/100 of the crimes with which I am charged, I would not have dared to send you this pre-execution declaration; however, I have not been guilty of even one of the things with which I am charged, and my heart is clean of even the shadow of baseness. I have never in my life told you a word of falsehood, and now, finding my 2 feet in the grave, I am also not lying. My whole case is a typical example of provocation, slander and violation of the elementary basis of revolutionary legality....

"... The confessions which were made part of my file are not only absurd but contain some slander toward the Central Committee of the All-Union Communist Party (Bolsheviks) and toward the Council of People's Commissars because correct resolutions of the Central Committee of the All-Union Communist Party (Bolsheviks) and of the Council of People's Commissars which were not made on my initiative and without my participation are presented as hostile acts of counter-revolutionary organizations made at my suggestion....

"I am now alluding to the most disgraceful part of my life and to my really grave guilt against the party and against you. This is my confession of counter-revolutionary activity.... The case is as follows: not being able to suffer the tortures to which I was submitted by Ushakov and Nikolayev—and especially by the first one—who utilized the knowledge that my broken ribs have not properly mended and have caused me great pain—I have been forced to accuse myself and others.

"The majority of my confession has been suggested or dictated by Ushakov, and the remainder is my reconstruction of NKVD materials from western Siberia for which I assumed all responsibility. If some part of the story which Ushakov fabricated and which I signed did not properly hang together, I was forced to sign another variation. The same thing was done to Rukhimovich, who was at first designated as a member of the reserve net and whose name later was removed without telling me anything about it; the same was also done with the leader of the reserve net, supposedly created by Bukharin in 1935. At first I wrote my name in, and then I was instructed to insert Mezhlauk. There were other similar incidents.

". . . I am asking and begging you that you again examine my case and this not for the purpose of sparing me but in order to unmask the vile provocation which like a snake wound itself around many persons in a great degree due to my meanness and criminal slander. I have never betrayed you or the party. I know that I perish because of vile and mean work of the enemies of the party and of the people, who fabricated the provocation against me."

It would appear that such an important declaration was worth an examination by the Central Committee. This, however, was not done, and the declaration was transmitted to Beria while the terrible maltreatment of the Political Bureau candidate, Comrade Eikhe, continued.

On 2 Feb. 1940 Eikhe was brought before the court. Here he did not confess any guilt and said as follows: "In all the so-called confessions of mine there is not one letter written by me with the exception of my signatures under the protocols which were forced from me. I have made my confession under pressure from the investigative judge who from the time of my arrest tormented me. After that I began to write all this nonsense. . . . The most important thing for me is to tell the court, the party and Stalin that I am not guilty. I have never been guilty of any conspiracy. I will die believing in the truth of party policy as I have believed in it during my whole life."

On 4 Feb. Eikhe was shot. [Indignation in the hall.] It has been definitely established now that Eikhe's case was fabricated; he has been posthumously rehabilitated.

Comrade [Yan E.] Rudzutak, candidate member of the Political Bureau, member of the party since 1905, who spent 10 years in a Czarist hard labor camp, completely retracted in court the confession which was forced from him. The protocol of the session of the Collegium of the Supreme Military Court contains the following statement by Rudzutak: ". . . The only plea which he places before the court is that the Central Committee of the All-Union Communist Party (Bolsheviks) be informed that there is in the NKVD an as yet not liquidated center which is craftily manufacturing cases, which forces innocent persons to confess; there is no opportunity to prove one's nonparticipation in crimes to which the confessions of various persons testify. The investigative methods are such that they force people to lie and to slander entirely innocent persons in addition to those who already stand accused. He asks the court that he be allowed to inform the Central Committee of the All-Union Communist Party (Bolsheviks) about all this in writing. He assures the court that he personally had never any evil designs in regard to the policy of our party because he had always agreed with the party policy pertaining to all spheres of economic and cultural activity."

This declaration of Rudzutak was ignored, despite the fact that Rudzutak was in his time the chief of the Central Control Commission, which was called into being in accordance with Lenin's concept for the purpose of fighting for party unity.... In this manner fell the chief of this highly authoritative party organ, a victim of brutal willfulness: he was not even called before the Central Committee's Political Bureau because Stalin did not want to talk to him. Sentence was pronounced on him in 20 minutes, and he was shot. [Indignation in the hall.] After careful examination of the case in 1955 it was established that the accusation against Rudzutak was false and that it was based on slanderous materials. Rudzutak has been rehabilitated posthumously.

The way in which the former NKVD workers manufactured various fictitious "anti-Soviet centers" and "blocs" with the help of provocatory methods is seen from the confession of Comrade Rozenblum, party member since 1906, who was arrested in 1937 by the Leningrad NKVD.

During the examination in 1955 of the Komarov case Rozenblum revealed the following fact: when Rozenblum was arrested in 1937 he was subjected to terrible torture during which he was ordered to confess false information concerning himself and other persons. He was then brought to the office of Zakovsky, who offered him freedom on condition that he make before the court a false confession fabricated in 1937 by the NKVD concerning "sabotage, espionage and diversion in a terroristic center in Leningrad." [Movement in the hall.] With unbelievable cynicism Zakovsky told about the vile "mechanism" for the crafty creation of fabricated "anti-Soviet plots."

"In order to illustrate it to me," stated Rozenblum, "Zakovsky gave me several possible variants of the organization of this center and of its branches. After he detailed the organization to me, Zakovsky told me that the NKVD would prepare the case of this center, remarking that the trial would be public. Before the court were to be brought 4 or 5 members of this center: Chudov, Ugarov, Smorodin, Pozern, Shaposhnikova (Chudov's wife) and others together with 2 or 3 members from the branches of this center.... The case of the Leningrad center has to be built solidly, and for this reason witnesses are needed. Social origin (of course, in the past) and the party standing of the witness will play than a small role. 'You, yourself,' said Zakovsky, 'will not need to invent anything. The NKVD will prepare for you a ready outline for every branch of the center; you will have to study it carefully and to remember well all questions and answers which the court might ask. This case will be ready in 4-5 months, or perhaps a half year. During all this time you will be preparing yourself so that you will not compromise the investigation and yourself. Your future will depend on how the trial goes and on its results. If you begin to lie and to testify falsely, blame yourself. If you manage to endure it, you will save your head and we will feed and clothe you at the government's cost until your death.' "

This is the kind of vile things which were then practiced. [Movement in the hall.]

Even more widely was the falsification of cases practiced in the provinces. The NKVD headquarters of the Sverdlov *oblast* "discovered" the so-called "Ural uprising staff"—an organ of the bloc of rightists, Trotskyites, Socialist Revolutionaries, church leaders—whose chief supposedly was the Secretary of the Sverdlov [Sverdlovsk] Oblast Party Committee and member of the Central Committee, All-Union Communist Party (Bolsheviks), Kabakov, who had been a party member since 1914. The investigative materials of that time show that in almost all *krais, oblasts* and republics there supposedly existed "rightist Trotskyite, espionage-terror and diversionary-sabotage organizations and centers" and that the heads of such organizations as a rule—for no known reason—were first secretaries of *oblast* or republic Communist Party committees or central committees. [Movement in the hall.]

Many thousands of honest and innocent Communists have died as a result of this monstrous falsification of such "cases," as a result of the fact that all kinds of slanderous "confessions" were accepted, and as a result of the practice of forcing accusations against oneself and others. In the same manner were fabricated the "cases" against eminent party and state workers—[Stanislav V.] Kossior, [Vlas B.] Chubar, [Ukrainian party leader Pavel] Postyshev, [Komsomol Secy. Gen. Aleksandr] Kosaryev and others. [Kossior and Chubar were party Politburo members.]

In those years repressions on a mass scale were applied which were based on nothing tangible and which resulted in heavy cadre losses to the party. The vicious practice was condoned of having the NKVD prepare lists of persons whose cases were under the jurisdiction of the Military Collegium and whose sentences were prepared in advance. Yezhov would send these lists to Stalin personally for his approval of the proposed punishment. In 1937-1938, 383 such lists containing the names of many thousands of party, Soviet, Komsomol, army and economic workers were sent to Stalin. He approved these lists.

A large part of these cases are being reviewed now, and a great part of them are being voided because they were baseless and falsified. Suffice it to say that from 1954 to the present time the Military Collegium of the Supreme Court has rehabilitated 7,679 persons, many of whom were rehabilitated posthumously.

Mass arrests of party, Soviet, economic and military workers caused tremendous harm to our country and to the cause of Socialist advancement. Mass repressions had a negative influence on the moral-political condition of the party, created a situation of uncertainty, contributed to the spreading of unhealthy suspicion, and sowed distrust among Communists. All sorts of slanderers and careerists were active.

Resolutions of the January plenum of the Central Committee, All-Union Communist Party (Bolsheviks), in 1938 had brought some measure of improvement to the party organizations. However, widespread repression also existed in 1938.

Only because our party has at its disposal such great moral-political strength was it possible for it to survive the difficult events in 1937-1938 and to educate new cadres. There is, however, no doubt that our march forward toward socialism and toward the preparation of the country's defense would have been much more successful were it not for the tremendous loss in the cadres suffered as a result of the baseless and false mass repressions in 1937-1938.

We are justly accusing Yezhov for the degenerate practices of 1937. But we have to answer these questions: Could Yezhov have arrested Kossior, for instance, without the knowledge of Stalin? Was there an exchange of opinions or a Political Bureau decision concerning this? No, there was not, as there was none regarding other cases of this type. Could Yezhov have decided such important matters as the fate of such eminent party figures? No, it would be a display of naivete to consider this the work of Yezhov alone. It is clear that these matters were decided by Stalin, and that without his orders and his sanction Yezhov could not have done this.

We have examined the cases and have rehabilitated Kossior, Rudzutak, Postyshev, Kosaryev and others. For what causes were they arrested and sentenced? The review of evidence shows that there was no reason for this. They, like many others, were arrested without the prosecutor's knowledge. In such a situation there is no need for any sanction, for what sort of a sanction could there be when Stalin decided everything[?]. He was the chief prosecutor in these cases. Stalin not only agreed to, but on his own initiative issued arrest orders. We must say this so that the delegates to the congress can clearly undertake [understand] and themselves assess this and draw the proper conclusions.

Facts prove that many abuses were made on Stalin's orders without reckoning with any norms of party and Soviet legality. Stalin was a very distrustful man, sickly suspicious; we knew this from our work with him. He could look at a man and say: "Why are your eyes so shifty today," or "Why are you turning so much today and avoiding to look me directly in the eyes?" The sickly suspicion created in him a general distrust even toward eminent party workers whom he had known for years. Everywhere and in everything he saw "enemies," "2-facers" and "spies."

Possessing unlimited power he indulged in great willfulness and choked a person morally and physically. A situation was created where one could not express one's own will.

When Stalin said that one or another should be arrested, it was necessary to accept on faith that he was an "enemy of the people." Meanwhile, Beria's gang, which ran the organs of state security, outdid itself in proving the guilt of the arrested and the truth of materials which it falsified. And what proofs were offered? The confessions of the arrested, and the investigative judges accepted these "confessions." And how is it possible that a person confesses to crimes which he has not committed? Only in one way—because of application of physical methods of pressuring him, tortures, bringing him to a state of unconsciousness, deprivation of his judgment, taking away of his human dignity. In this manner were "confessions" acquired.

When the wave of mass arrests began to recede in 1939, and the leaders of territorial party organizations began to accuse the NKVD workers of using methods of physical pressure on the arrested, Stalin dispatched a coded telegram on 20 Jan. 1939 to the committee secretaries of *oblasts* and *krais,* to the central committees of republic Communist parties, to the peoples commissars of internal affairs and to the heads of NKVD organizations. This telegram stated: "The Central Committee of the All-Union Communist Party (Bolsheviks) explains that the application of methods of physical pressure in NKVD practice is permissible from 1937 on in accordance with permission of the Central Committee of the All-Union Communist Party (Bolsheviks).... It is known that all bourgeois intelligence services use methods of physical influence against the representatives of the Socialist proletariat and that they use them in their most scandalous forms. The question arises as to why the Socialist intelligence service should be more humanitarian against the mad agents of the bourgeoisie, against the deadly enemies of the working class and of the *kolkhoz* workers. The Central Committee of the All-Union Communist Party (Bolsheviks) considers that physical pressure should still be used obligatorily, as an exception applicable to known and obstinate enemies of the people, as a method both justifiable and appropriate."

Thus, Stalin had sanctioned in the name of the Central Committee of the All-Union Communist Party (Bolsheviks) the most brutal violation of Socialist legality, torture and oppression, which led as we have seen to the slandering and self-accusation of innocent people.

Not long ago—only several days before the present congress—we called to the Central Committee Presidium session and interrogated the investigative judge Rodos, who in his time investigated and interrogated Kossior, Chubar and Kosaryev. He is a vile person, with the brain of a bird, and morally completely degenerate. And it was this man who was deciding the fate of prominent party workers; he was making judgments also concerning the politics in these matters, because having established their "crime," he provided therewith materials from which important political implications could be drawn.

The question arises whether a man with such an intellect could alone make the investigation in a manner to prove the guilt of people such as Kossior and others. No, he could not have done it without proper directives. At the Central Committee Presidium session he told us: "I was told that Kossior and Chubar were people's enemies, and for this reason, I, as an investigative judge, had to make them confess that they are enemies." [Indignation in the hall.]

He could do this only through long tortures, which he did, receiving detailed instructions from Beria. We must say that at the Central Committee Presidium session he cynically declared: "I thought that I was executing the orders of the party." In this manner Stalin's orders concerning the use of methods of physical pressure against the arrested were in practice executed.

These and many other facts show that all norms of correct party solution of problems were invalidated and everything was dependent upon the willfulness of one man.

The power accumulated in the hands of one person, Stalin, led to serious consequences during the Great Patriotic War.

When we look at many of our novels, films and historical "scientific studies," the role of Stalin in the Patriotic War appears to be entirely improbable. Stalin had foreseen everything. The Soviet Army, on the basis of a strategic plan prepared by Stalin long before, used the tactics of so-called "active defense," *i.e.,* tactics which, as we know, allowed the Germans to come up to Moscow and Stalingrad. Using such tactics, the Soviet Army, supposedly, thanks only to Stalin's genius, turned to the offensive and subdued the enemy. The epic victory gained through the armed might of the Land of the Soviets, through our heroic people, is ascribed in this type of novel, film and "scientific study" as being completely due to the strategic genius of Stalin.

We have to analyze this matter carefully because it has a tremendous significance not only from the historical, but especially from the political, educational and practical point of view.

What are the facts of this matter?

Before the war our press and all our political-educational work was characterized by its bragging tone: when an enemy violates the holy Soviet soil, then for every blow of the enemy we will answer with three blows, and we will battle the enemy on his soil and we will win without much harm to ourselves. But these positive statements were not based in all areas on concrete facts, which would actually guarantee the immunity of our borders.

During the war and after the war Stalin put forward the thesis that the tragedy which our nation experienced in the first part of the war was the result of the "unexpected" attack of the Germans against the Soviet Union. But, Comrades, this is completely untrue. As soon as Hitler came to power in Germany he assigned to himself the task of liquidating communism. The Fascists were saying this openly; they did not hide their plans. In order to attain this aggressive end all sorts of pacts and blocs were created, such as the famous Berlin-Rome-Tokyo axis. Many facts from the pre-war period clearly showed that Hitler was going all out to begin a war against the Soviet state and that he had concentrated large armed units, together with armored units, near the Soviet borders.

Documents which have now been published show that by 3 Apr. 1941, Churchill, through his ambassador to the USSR, Cripps, personally warned Stalin that the Germans had begun regrouping their armed units with the intent of attacking the Soviet Union. It is self-evident that Churchill did not do this at all because of his friendly feeling toward the Soviet nation. He had in this his own imperialistic goals—to bring Germany and the USSR into a bloody war and thereby to strengthen the position of the British Empire. Just the same, Churchill affirmed in his writings that he sought to "warn Stalin and call his attention to the danger which threatened him." Churchill stressed this repeatedly in his dispatches of 18 April and in the following days. However, Stalin took no heed of these warnings. What is more, Stalin ordered that no credence be given to information of this sort, in order not to provoke the initiation of military operations.

We must assert that information of this sort concerning the threat of German armed invasion of Soviet territory was coming in also from our own military and diplomatic sources; however, because the leadership was conditioned against such information, such data was dispatched with fear and assessed with reservation.

Thus, for instance, information sent from Berlin on 6 May 1941 by the Soviet military attache, Capt. Vorontsov, stated: "Soviet citizen Bozer... communicated to the deputy naval attache that according to a statement of a certain German officer from Hitler's headquarters, Germany is preparing to invade the USSR on 14 May through Finland, the Baltic countries and Latvia. At the same time Moscow and Leningrad will be heavily raided and paratroopers landed in border cities...."

In his report of 22 May 1941, the deputy military attache in Berlin, Khlopov, communicated that "...the attack of the German army is reportedly scheduled for 15 June, but it is possible that it may begin in the first days of June...."

A cable from our London embassy dated 18 June 1941 stated: "As of now Cripps is deeply convinced of the inevitability of armed conflict between Germany and the USSR which will begin not later than the middle of June. According to Cripps, the Germans have presently concentrated 147 divisions (including air force and service units) along the Soviet borders...."

Despite these particularly grave warnings, the necessary steps were not taken to prepare the country properly for defense and to prevent it from being caught unawares.

Did we have time and the capabilities for such preparations? Yes, we had the time and capabilities. Our industry was already so developed that it was capable of supplying fully the Soviet army with everything that it needed. This is proven by the fact that although during the war we lost almost half of our industry and important industrial and food production areas as the result of enemy occupation of the Ukraine, Northern Caucasus and other western parts of the country, the Soviet nation was still able to organize the production of military equipment in the eastern parts of the country, install there equipment taken from the western industrial areas, and to supply our armed forces with everything which was necessary to destroy the enemy.

Had our industry been mobilized properly and in time to supply the army with the necessary materiel, our wartime losses would have been decidedly smaller. Such mobilization had not been, however, started in time. And already in the first days of the war it became evident that our army was badly armed, that we did not have enough artillery, tanks and planes to throw the enemy back.

Soviet science and technology produced excellent models of tanks and artillery pieces before the war. But mass production of all this was not organized, and, as a matter of fact, we started to modernize our military equipment only on the eve of the war. As a result, at the time of the enemy's invasion of the Soviet land, we did not have sufficient quantities either of old machinery which was no longer used for armament production or of new machinery which we had planned to introduce into armament production. The situation with antiaircraft artillery was especially bad; we did not organize the production of anti-tank ammunition. Many fortified regions had proven to be indefensible as soon as they were attacked, because the old arms had been withdrawn and new ones were not yet available there.

This pertained, alas, not only to tanks, artillery and planes. At the outbreak of the war we did not even have sufficient numbers of rifles to arm the mobilized manpower. I recall that in those days I telephoned to Comrade Malenkov from Kiev and told him, "People have volunteered for the new army and demand arms. You must send us arms." Malenkov answered me, "We cannot send you arms. We are sending all our rifles to Leningrad, and you have to arm yourselves." [Movement in the hall.] Such was the armament situation.

In this connection we cannot forget, for instance, the following fact. Shortly before the invasion of the Soviet Union by the Hitlerite army, Korponos, who was chief of the Kiev Special Military District (he was later killed at the front), wrote to Stalin that the German armies were at the Bug River, were preparing for an attack and in the very near future would probably start their offensive. In this connection Korponos proposed that a strong defense be organized, that 300,000 people be evacuated from the border areas and that several strong points be organized there: anti-tank ditches, trenches for the soldiers, etc.

Moscow answered this proposition with the assertion that this would be a provocation, that no preparatory defensive work should be undertaken at the borders, that the Germans were not to be given any pretext for the initiation of military action against us. Thus, our borders were insufficiently prepared to repel the enemy.

When the Fascist armies had actually invaded Soviet territory and military operations began, Moscow issued the order that the German fire was not to be returned. Why? It was because Stalin, despite evident facts, thought that the war had not yet started, that this was only a provocative action on the part of several undisciplined sections of the German army and that our reaction might serve as a reason for the Germans to begin the war.

The following fact is also known. On the eve of the invasion of the territory of the Soviet Union by the Hitlerite army, a certain German citizen crossed our border and stated that the German armies had received orders to start the offensive against the Soviet Union on the night of 22 June at 3 o'clock. Stalin was informed about this immediately, but even this warning was ignored.

As you see, everything was ignored; warnings of certain army commanders, declarations of deserters from the enemy army and even the open hostility of the enemy. Is this an example of the alertness of the chief of the party and of the state at this particularly significant historical moment?

And what were the results of this carefree attitude, this disregard of clear facts? The result was that already in the first hours and days the enemy had destroyed in our border regions a large part of our air force, artillery and other military equipment; he annihilated large numbers of our military cadres and disorganized our military leadership; consequently we could not prevent the enemy from marching deep into the country.

Very grievous consequences, especially in reference to the beginning of the war, followed Stalin's annihilation of many military commanders and political workers during 1937-1941 because of his suspiciousness and through slanderous accusations. During these years repressions were instituted against certain parts of military cadres beginning literally at the company and battalion commander level and extending to the higher military centers; during this time the cadre of leaders who had gained military experience in Spain and in the Far East was almost completely liquidated.

The policy of large-scale repression against the military cadres led also to undermined military discipline, because for several years officers of all ranks and even soldiers in the party and Komsomol cells were taught to "unmask" their superiors as hidden enemies. [Movement in the hall.] It is natural that this caused a negative influence on the state of military discipline in the first war period.

And, as you know, we had before the war excellent military cadres which were unquestionably loyal to the party and to the fatherland. Suffice it to say that those of them who managed to survive despite severe tortures to which they were subjected in the prisons, have from the first war days shown themselves real patriots and heroically fought for the glory of the fatherland; I have here in mind such comrades as Rokossovsky (who, as you know, had been jailed), Gorbatov, Maretskov (who is a delegate at the present Congress), Podlas (he was an excellent commander who perished at the front) and many, many others. However, many such commanders perished in camps and jails, and the army saw them no more.

All this brought about the situation which existed at the beginning of the war and which was the great threat to our fatherland.

It would be incorrect to forget that after the first severe disaster and defeats at the front Stalin thought that this was the end. In one of his speeches in those days he said: "All that which Lenin created we have lost forever."

After this Stalin for a long time actually did not direct the military operations and ceased to do anything whatever. He returned to active leadership only when some members of the Political Bureau visited him and told him that it was necessary to take certain steps immediately in order to improve the situation at the front.

Therefore, the threatening danger which hung over our fatherland in the first period of the war was largely due to the faulty methods of directing the nation and the party by Stalin himself.

However, we speak not only about the moment when the war began, which led to serious disorganization of our army and brought us severe losses. Even after the war began, the nervousness and hysteria which Stalin demonstrated, interfering with actual military operations, caused our army serious damage.

Stalin was very far from an understanding of the real situation which was developing at the front. This was natural because during the whole Patriotic War he never visited any section of the front or any liberated city except for one short ride on the Mozhaisk Highway during a stabilized situation at the front. To this incident were dedicated many literary works full of fantasies of all sorts and so many paintings. Simultaneously, Stalin was interfering with operations and issuing orders which did not take into consideration the real situation at a given section of the front and which could not help but result in huge personnel losses.

I will allow myself in this connection to bring out one characteristic fact which illustrates how Stalin directed operations at the fronts. There is present at this Congress Marshal Bagramian who was once the chief of operations in the headquarters of the southwestern front and who can corroborate what I will tell you.

When there developed an exceptionally serious situation for our army in 1942 in the Kharkov region, we had correctly decided to drop an operation whose objective was to encircle Kharkov, because the real situation at that time would have threatened our army with fatal consequences if this operation were continued.

We communicated this to Stalin, stating that the situation demanded changes in operational plans so that the enemy would be prevented from liquidating a sizable concentration of our army.

Contrary to common sense, Stalin rejected our suggestion and issued the order to continue the operation aimed at the encirclement of Kharkov, despite the fact that at this time many army concentrations were themselves actually threatened with encirclement and liquidation.

I telephoned to [Marshal] Vasilevsky and begged him:

"Aleksandr Mikhailovich, take a map (Vasilevsky is present here) and show Comrade Stalin the situation which has developed." We should note that Stalin planned operations on a globe. [Animation in the hall.] Yes, Comrades, he used to take the globe and trace the frontline on it. I said to Comrade Vasilevsky: "Show him the situation on a map; in the present situation we cannot continue the operation which was planned. The old decision must be changed for the good of the cause."

Vasilevsky replied saying that Stalin had already studied this problem and that he, Vasilevsky, would not see Stalin further concerning this matter because the latter didn't want to hear any arguments on the subject of this operation.

After my talk with Vasilevsky I telephoned to Stalin at his villa. But Stalin did not answer the telephone, and Malenkov was at the receiver. I told Comrade Malenkov that I was calling from the front and that I wanted to speak personally to Stalin. Stalin informed me through Malenkov that I should speak with Malenkov. I stated for the 2d time that I wished to inform Stalin personally about the grave situation which had arisen for us at the front. But Stalin did not consider it convenient to raise the phone and again stated that I should speak to him through Malenkov, although he was only a few steps from the telephone.

After "listening" in this manner to our plea Stalin said: "Let everything remain as it is!"

And what was the result of this? The worst that we had expected. The Germans surrounded our army concentrations, and consequently we lost hundreds of thousands of our soldiers. This is Stalin's military "genius"; this is what it cost us. [Movement in the hall.]

On one occasion after the war, during a meeting of Stalin with members of the Political Bureau, Anastas Ivanovich Mikoyan mentioned that Khrushchev must have been right when he telephoned concerning the Kharkov operation and that it was unfortunate that his suggestion had not been accepted.

You should have seen Stalin's fury! How could it be admitted that he, Stalin, had not been right! He is after all a "genius," and a genius cannot help but be right! Everyone can err, but Stalin considered that he never erred, that he was always right. He never acknowledged to anyone that he made any mistake, large or small, despite the fact that he made not a few mistakes in the matter of theory and in his practical activity. After the Party Congress we shall probably have to re-evaluate many wartime military operations and to present them in their true light.

The tactics on which Stalin insisted without knowing the essence of the conduct of battle operations cost us much blood until we succeeded in stopping the opponent and going over to the offensive.

The military know that already by the end of 1941 instead of great operational maneuvers flanking the opponent and penetrating behind his back, Stalin demanded incessant frontal attacks and the capture of one village after another. Because of this we paid with great losses until our generals, on whose shoulders rested the whole weight of conducting the war, succeeded in changing the situation and shifting to flexible maneuver operations, which immediately brought serious changes at the front favorable to us.

All the more shameful was the fact that after our great victory over the enemy which cost us so much, Stalin began to downgrade many of the commanders who contributed so much to the victory over the enemy, because Stalin excluded every possibility that services rendered at the front should be credited to anyone but himself.

Stalin was very much interested in the assessment of Comrade Zhukov as a military leader. He asked me often for my opinion of Zhukov. I told him then, "I have known Zhukov for a long time; he is a good general and a good military leader."

After the war Stalin began to tell all kinds of nonsense about Zhukov, among others the following, "You praised Zhukov, but he does not deserve it. It is said that before each operation at the front Zhukov used to behave as follows: he used to take a handful of earth, smell it and say, 'We can begin the attack,' or the opposite, 'the planned operation cannot be carried out.'" I stated at that time, "Comrade Stalin, I do not know who invented this, but it is not true."

It is possible that Stalin himself invented these things for the purpose of minimizing the role and military talents of Marshal Zhukov.

In this connection Stalin very energetically popularized himself as a great leader; in various ways he tried to inculcate in the people the version that all victories gained by the Soviet nation during the Great Patriotic War were due to the courage, daring and genius of Stalin and of no one else. Exactly like Kuzma Kryuchkov [a famous Cossack who performed heroic feats against the Germans—translator's note], he put one dress on 7 people at the same time. [Animation in the hall.]

In the same vein, let us take, for instance, our historical and military films and some literary creations; they make us feel sick. Their true objective is the propagation of the theme of praising Stalin as a military genius. Let us recall the film *The Fall of Berlin*. Here only Stalin acts; he issues orders in the hall in which there are many empty chairs, and only one man approaches him and reports something to him—that is Poskrebyshev, his loyal shield-bearer. [Laughter in the hall.] And where is the military command? Where is the Political Bureau? Where is the government? What are they doing and with what are they engaged? There is nothing about them in the film. Stalin acts for everybody; he does not reckon with anyone; he asks no one for advice. Everything is shown to the nation in this false light. Why? In order to surround Stalin with glory, contrary to the facts and contrary to historical truth.

The question arises: And where are the military on whose shoulders rested the burden of the war? They are not in the film; with Stalin in, no room was left for them.

Not Stalin, but the party as a whole, the Soviet government, our heroic army, its talented leaders and brave soldiers, the whole Soviet nation—these are the ones who assured the victory in the Great Patriotic War. [Tempestuous and prolonged applause.]

The Central Committee members, ministers, our economic leaders, leaders of Soviet culture, directors of territorial party and Soviet organizations, engineers, and technicians—every one of them in his own place of work generously gave of his strength and knowledge toward ensuring victory over the enemy.

Exceptional heroism was shown by our hard core—surrounded by glory is our whole working class, our *kolkhoz* peasantry, the Soviet intelligentsia, who under the leadership of party organizations overcame untold hardships and, bearing the hardships of war, devoted all their strength to the cause of the defense of the fatherland.

Great and brave deeds during the war were accomplished by our Soviet women, who bore on their backs the heavy load of production work in the factories, on the kolkhozes and in various economic and cultural sectors; many women participated directly in the Great Patriotic War at the fronts; our brave youth contributed immeasurably at the front and at home to the defense of the Soviet fatherland and to the annihilation of the enemy.

Immortal are the services of the Soviet soldiers, of our commanders and political workers of all ranks; after the loss of a considerable part of the army in the first war months they did not lose their heads and were able to reorganize during the progress of combat; they created and toughened during the progress of the war a strong and heroic army and not only stood off pressure of the strong and cunning enemy but also smashed him.

The magnificent and heroic deeds of hundreds of millions of people of the East and of the West during the fight against the threat of Fascist subjugation which loomed before us will live centuries and millennia in the memory of thankful humanity. [Thunderous applause.]

The main role and the main credit for the victorious ending of the war belongs to our Communist Party, to the armed forces of the Soviet Union and to the tens of millions of Soviet people raised by the party. [Thunderous and prolonged applause.]

Comrades, let us reach for some other facts. The Soviet Union is justly considered as a model of a multi-national state because we have in practice assured the equality and friendship of all nations which live in our great fatherland.

All the more monstrous are the acts whose initiator was Stalin and which are rude violations of the basic Leninist principles of the nationality policy of the Soviet state. We refer to the mass deportations from their native places of whole nations, together with all Communists and Komsomols without any exception; this deportation action was not dictated by any military considerations.

Thus, already at the end of 1943, when there occurred a permanent breakthrough at the fronts of the Great Patriotic War benefiting the Soviet Union, a decision was taken and executed concerning the deportation of all the Karachai from the lands on which they lived. In the same period, at the end of Dec. 1943, the same lot befell the whole population of the Autonomous Kalmyk Republic. In Mar. 1944 all the Chechen and Ingush peoples were deported and the Chechen-Ingush Autonomous Republic was liquidated. In Apr. 1944 all Balkars were deported to faraway places from the territory of the Kabardyno-Balkar Autonomous Republic, and the republic itself was renamed the Autonomous Kabardynian [Kabardian] Republic. The Ukrainians avoided meeting this fate only because there were too many of them and there was no place to which to deport them. Otherwise, he would have deported them also. [Laughter and animation in the hall.]

Not only a Marxist-Leninist but also no man of common sense can grasp how it is possible to make whole nations responsible for inimical activity, including women, children, old people, Communists and Komsomols, to use mass repression against them and to expose them to misery and suffering for the hostile acts of individual persons or groups of persons.

After the conclusion of the Patriotic War the Soviet nation stressed with pride the magnificent victories gained through great sacrifices and tremendous efforts. The country experienced a period of political enthusiasm. The party came out of the war even more united; in the fire of the war party cadres were tempered and hardened. Under such conditions nobody could have even thought of the possibility of some plot in the party.

And it was precisely at this time that the so-called "Leningrad Affair" was born. As we have now proven, this case was fabricated. Those who innocently lost their lives included Comrades [Nikolai A.] Voznesensky, [A. A.] Kuznetsov, [Mikhail I.] Rodionov, [Petr S.] Popkov and others.

As is known, [Soviet Deputy Premier] Voznesensky and [Central Committee Secy.] Kuznetsov were talented and eminent leaders. Once they stood very close to Stalin. It is sufficient to mention that Stalin made Voznesensky first deputy to the chairman of the Council of Ministers, and Kuznetsov was elected secretary of the Central Committee. The very fact that Stalin entrusted Kuznetsov with the supervision of the state security organs shows the trust which he enjoyed.

How did it happen that these persons were branded as enemies of the people and liquidated?

Facts prove that the "Leningrad Affair" is also the result of willfulness which Stalin exercised against party cadres.

Had a normal situation existed in the party's Central Committee and in the Central Committee Political Bureau, affairs of this nature would have been examined there in accordance with party practice and all pertinent facts assessed; as a result, such an affair as well as others would not have happened.

We must state that after the war the situation became even more complicated. Stalin became even more capricious, irritable and brutal; in particular his suspicion grew. His persecution mania reached unbelievable dimensions. Many workers were becoming enemies before his very eyes. After the war Stalin separated himself from the collective even more. Everything was decided by him alone without any consideration for anyone or anything.

This unbelievable suspicion was cleverly taken advantage of by the abject provocateur and vile enemy Beria, who had murdered thousands of Communists and loyal Soviet people. The elevation of Voznesensky and Kuznetsov alarmed Beria. As we have now proven, it had been precisely Beria who had "suggested" to Stalin the fabrication by him and by his confidants of materials in the form of declarations and anonymous letters and in the form of various rumors and talks.

The party's Central Committee has examined this so-called "Leningrad Affair"; persons who innocently suffered are now rehabilitated, and honor has been restored to the glorious Leningrad party organization. [Ex-State Security Min. Viktor S.] Abakumov and others who had fabricated this affair were brought before a court, their trial took place in Leningrad and they received what they deserved.

The question arises: Why is it that we see the truth of this affair only now, and why did we not do something earlier, during Stalin's life, in order to prevent the loss of innocent lives? It was because Stalin personally supervised the "Leningrad Affair," and the majority of the Political Bureau members did not, at that time, know all of the circumstances in these matters, and could not therefore intervene.

When Stalin received certain materials from Beria and Abakumov, without examining these slanderous materials, he ordered an investigation of the "Affair" of Voznesensky and Kuznetsov. With this their fate was sealed. Instructive in the same way is the case of the Mingrelian nationalist organization which supposedly existed in Georgia. As is known, resolutions by the Central Committee, Communist Party of the Soviet Union, were made concerning this case in Nov. 1951 and in Mar. 1952. These resolutions were made without prior discussion with the Political Bureau. Stalin had personally dictated them. They made serious accusations against many loyal Communists. On the basis of falsified documents it was proven that there existed in Georgia a supposedly nationalistic organization whose objective was the liquidation of the Soviet power in that republic with the help of imperialist powers.

In this connection, a number of responsible party and Soviet workers were arrested in Georgia. As was later proven, this was a slander directed against the Georgian party organization. We know that there have been at times manifestations of local bourgeois nationalism in Georgia as in several other republics. The question arises: Could it be possible that in the period during which the resolutions referred to above were made, nationalist tendencies grew so much that there was a danger of Georgia's leaving the Soviet Union and joining Turkey? [Animation in the hall, laughter.] This is, of course, nonsense. It is impossible to imagine how such assumptions could enter anyone's mind. Everyone knows how Georgia has developed economically and culturally under Soviet rule.

Industrial production of the Georgian Republic is 27 times greater than it was before the revolution. Many new industries have arisen in Georgia which did not exist there before the revolution: iron smelting, an oil industry, a machine construction industry, etc. Illiteracy has long since been liquidated, which, in pre-revolutionary Georgia, included 78% of the population.

Could the Georgians, comparing the situation in their republic with the hard situation of the working masses in Turkey, be aspiring to join Turkey? In 1955 Georgia produced 18 times as much steel per person as Turkey. Georgia produces 9 times as much electrical energy per person as Turkey. According to the available 1950 census, 65% of Turkey's total population are illiterate, and of the women, 80% are illiterate. Georgia has 19 institutions of higher learning, which have about 39,000 students; this is 8 times more than in Turkey (for each 1,000 inhabitants). The prosperity of the working people has grown tremendously in Georgia under Soviet rule.

It is clear that as the economy and culture develop, and as the Socialist consciousness of the working masses in Georgia grows, the source from which bourgeois nationalism draws its strength evaporates.

As it developed, there was no nationalistic organization in Georgia. Thousands of innocent people fell victim of willfulness and lawlessness. All of this happened under the "genial" leadership of Stalin, "the great son of the Georgian nation," as Georgians liked to refer to Stalin. [Animation in the hall.]

The willfulness of Stalin showed itself not only in decisions concerning the internal life of the country but also in the international relations of the Soviet Union.

The July plenum of the Central Committee studied in detail the reasons for the development of conflict with Yugoslavia. It was a shameful role which Stalin played here. The "Yugoslav Affair" contained no problems which could not have been solved through party discussions among comrades. There was no significant basis for the development of this "Affair"; it was completely possible to have prevented the rupture of relations with that country. This does not mean, however, that the Yugoslav leaders did not make mistakes or did not have shortcomings. But these mistakes and shortcomings were magnified in a monstrous manner by Stalin, which resulted in a break of relations with a friendly country.

I recall the first days when the conflict between the Soviet Union and Yugoslavia began artificially to be blown up. Once, when I came from Kiev to Moscow, I was invited to visit Stalin who, pointing to the copy of a letter lately sent to Tito, asked me, "Have you read this?" Not waiting for my reply, he answered, "I will shake my little finger—and there will be no more Tito. He will fall."

We have dearly paid for this "shaking of the little finger." This statement reflected Stalin's mania for greatness, but he acted just that way: "I will shake my little finger—and there will be no Kossior"; "I will shake my little finger once more and Postyshev and Chubar will be no more"; "I will shake my little finger again—and Voznesensky, Kuznetsov and many others will disappear."

But this did not happen to Tito. No matter how much or how little Stalin shook, not only his little finger but everything else that he could shake, Tito did not fall. Why? The reason was that, in this case of disagreement with the Yugoslav comrades, Tito had behind him a state and a people who had gone through a severe school of fighting for liberty and independence, a people which gave support to its leaders.

You see to what Stalin's mania for greatness led. He had completely lost consciousness of reality; he demonstrated his suspicion and haughtiness not only in relation to individuals in the USSR, but in relation to whole parties and nations.

We have carefully examined the case of Yugoslavia and have found a proper solution which is approved by the peoples of the Soviet Union and of Yugoslavia as well as by the working masses of all the peoples' democracies and by all progressive humanity. The liquidation of the abnormal relationship with Yugoslavia was done in the interest of the whole camp of socialism, in the interest of strengthening peace in the whole world.

Let us also recall the "Affair of the Doctor-Plotters." [Animation in the hall.] Actually there was no "Affair" outside of the declaration of the woman doctor [Lydia F.] Timashuk, who was probably influenced or ordered by someone (after all, she was an unofficial collaborator of the organs of state security) to write Stalin a letter in which she declared that doctors were applying supposedly improper methods of medical treatment.

Such a letter was sufficient for Stalin to reach an immediate conclusion that there are doctor-plotters in the Soviet Union. He issued orders to arrest a group of eminent Soviet medical specialists. He personally issued advice on the conduct of the investigation and the method of interrogation of the arrested persons. He said that the academician [V. N.] Vinogradov should be put in chains, another one should be beaten. Present at this congress as a delegate is the former minister of state security, Comrade Ignatiev. Stalin told him curtly, "If you do not obtain confessions from the doctors we will shorten you by a head." [Tumult in the hall.] Stalin personally called the investigative judge, gave him instructions, advised him on which investigative methods should be used; these methods were simple—beat, beat and, once again, beat.

Shortly after the doctors were arrested we members of the Political Bureau received protocols with the doctors' confessions of guilt. After distributing these protocols Stalin told us, "You are blind like young kittens; what will happen without me? The country will perish because you do not know how to recognize enemies."

The case was so presented that no one could verify the facts on which the investigation was based. There was no possibility of trying to verify facts by contacting those who had made the confessions of guilt.

We felt, however, that the case of the arrested doctors was questionable. We knew some of these people personally because they had once treated us. When we examined this "case" after Stalin's death, we found it to be fabricated from beginning to end.

This ignominious "case" was set up by Stalin; he did not, however, have the time in which to bring it to an end (as he conceived that end), and for this reason the doctors are still alive. Now all have been rehabilitated; they are working in the same places they were working before; they treat top individuals, not excluding members of the government; they have our full confidence; and they execute their duties honestly, as they did before.

In organizing the various dirty and shameful cases, a very base role was played by the rabid enemy of our party, an agent of a foreign intelligence service—Beria, who had stolen into Stalin's confidence. In what way could this provocateur gain such a position in the party and in the state, so as to become the first deputy chairman of the Council of Ministers of the Soviet Union and a member of the Central Committee Political Bureau? It has now been established that this villain had climbed up the government ladder over an untold number of corpses.

Were there any signs that Beria was an enemy of the party? Yes, there were. Already in 1937, at a Central Committee plenum, former People's Commissar of Health Protection Kaminsky said that Beria worked for the Mussavat intelligence service. But the Central Committee plenum had barely concluded when Kaminsky was arrested and then shot. Had Stalin examined Kaminsky's statement? No, because Stalin believed in Beria, and that was enough for him. And when Stalin believed in anyone or anything, then no one could say anything which was contrary to his opinion; anyone who would dare to express opposition would have met the same fate as Kaminsky.

There were other signs also. The declaration which Comrade Snegov [the Trans-Caucasian party committee member] made at the party's Central Committee is interesting (parenthetically speaking, he was also rehabilitated not long ago, after 17 years in prison camps). In this declaration Snegov writes: "In connection with the proposed rehabilitation of the former Central Committee member Kartvelishvili-Lavryentiev, I have entrusted to the hands of the representative of the Committee of State Security a detailed deposition concerning Beria's role in the disposition of the Kartvelishvili case and concerning the criminal motives by which Beria was guided."

In my opinion it is indispensable to recall an important fact pertaining to this case and to communicate it to the Central Committee, because I did not consider it as proper to include in the investigation documents.

On 30 Oct. 1931, at the session of the Organizational Bureau of the Central Committee, All-Union Communist Party (Bolsheviks), Kartvelishvili, secretary of the Trans-Caucasian Krai Committee, made a report. All members of the Executive of the Krai Committee were present; of them I alone am alive. During this session J. V. Stalin made a motion at the end of his speech concerning the organization of the Secretariat of the Trans-Caucasian Krai Committee composed of the following: First Secretary, Kartvelishvili; Second Secretary, Beria (it was then for the first time in the party's history that Beria's name was mentioned as a candidate for a party position). Kartvelishvili answered that he knew Beria well and for that reason refused categorically to work together with him. Stalin proposed then that this matter be left open and that it be solved in the process of the work itself. 2 days later a decision was arrived at that Beria would receive the party post and that Kartvelishvili would be deported from the Trans-Caucasus.

This fact can be confirmed by Comrades Mikoyan and Kaganovich, who were present at that session.

The long unfriendly relations between Kartvelishvili and Beria were widely known; they date back to the time when Comrade Sergo [translator's note: "Sergo" was the popular nickname for Grigori K. Ordzhonikidze, a Politburo member who reportedly shot himself in 1937] was active in the Trans-Caucasus; Kartvelishvili was the closest assistant of Sergo. The unfriendly relationship impelled Beria to fabricate a "case" against Kartvelishvili. It is a characteristic thing that in this "case" Kartvelishvili was charged with a terroristic act against Beria.

The indictment in the Beria case contains a discussion of his crimes. Some things should, however, be recalled, especially since it is possible that not all delegates to the Congress have read this document. I wish to recall Beria's bestial disposition of the cases of [Lenin's friend Mikhail] Kedrov, Golubiev and Golubiev's adopted mother, Baturina—persons who wished to inform the Central Committee concerning Beria's treacherous activity. They were shot without any trial, and the sentence was passed *ex-post facto*, after the execution.

Here is what the old Communist Comrade Kedrov wrote to the Central Committee through Comrade Andreyev (Comrade Andreyev was then a Central Committee secretary):

"I am calling to you for help from a gloomy cell of the Lefortorsky prison. Let my cry of horror reach your ears; do not remain deaf; take me under your protection; please, help remove the nightmare of interrogations and show that this is all a mistake.

"I suffer innocently. Please believe me. Time will testify to the truth. I am not an agent-provocateur of the Tsarist Okhrana; I am not a spy; I am not a member of an anti-Soviet organization, of which I am being accused on the basis of denunciations. I am also not guilty of any other crimes against the party and the government. I am an old Bolshevik, free of any stain; I have honestly fought for almost 40 years in the ranks of the party for the good and the prosperity of the nation....

"...Today I, a 62-year-old man, am being threatened by the investigative judges with more severe, cruel and degrading methods of physical pressure. They (the judges) are no longer capable of becoming aware of their error and of recognizing that their handling of my case is illegal and impermissible. They try to justify their actions by picturing me as a hardened and raving enemy and are demanding increased repressions. But let the party know that I am innocent and that there is nothing which can turn a loyal son of the party into an enemy, even right up to his last dying breath.

"But I have no way out. I cannot divert from myself the hastily approaching new and powerful blows.

"Everything, however, has its limits. My torture has reached the extreme. My health is broken, my strength and my energy are waning, the end is drawing near. To die in a Soviet prison, branded as a vile traitor to the fatherland—what can be more monstrous for an honest man[?] And how monstrous all this is! Unsurpassed bitterness and pain grips my heart. No! No! This will not happen; this cannot be—I cry. Neither the party, nor the Soviet government, nor the People's Commissar, L. P. Beria, will permit this cruel irreparable injustice. I am firmly certain that given a quiet, objective examination, without any foul rantings, without any anger and without the fearful tortures, it would be easy to prove the baselessness of the charges. I believe deeply that truth and justice will triumph. I believe. I believe."

The old Bolshevik, Comrade Kedrov, was found innocent by the Military Collegium. But despite this he was shot at Beria's order. [Indignation in the hall.]

Beria also handled cruelly the family of Comrade Ordzhonikidze. Why? Because Ordzhonikidze had tried to prevent Beria from realizing his shameful plans. Beria had cleared from his way all persons who could possibly interfere with him. Ordzhonikidze was always an opponent of Beria, which he told to Stalin. Instead of examining this affair and taking appropriate steps, Stalin allowed the liquidation of Ordzhonikidze's brother and brought Ordzhonikidze himself to such a state that he was forced to shoot himself. [Indignation in the hall.] Such was Beria.

Beria was unmasked by the party's Central Committee shortly after Stalin's death. As a result of the particularly detailed legal proceedings it was established that Beria had committed monstrous crimes, and Beria was shot.

The question arises why Beria, who had liquidated 10s of thousands of party and Soviet workers, was not unmasked during Stalin's life? He was not unmasked earlier because he had utilized very skillfully Stalin's weaknesses; feeding him with suspicions, he assisted Stalin in everything and acted with his support.

Comrades: The cult of the individual acquired such monstrous size chiefly because Stalin himself, using all conceivable methods, supported the glorification of his own person. This is supported by numerous facts. One of the most characteristic examples of Stalin's self-glorification and of his lack of even elementary modesty is the edition of his *Short Biography*, which was published in 1948. This book is an expression of the most dissolute flattery, an example of making a man into a godhead, of transforming him into an infallible sage, "the greatest leader," "sublime strategist of all times and nations." Finally no other words could be found with which to lift Stalin up to the heavens.

We need not give here examples of the loathsome adulation filling this book. All we need to add is that they all were approved and edited by Stalin personally, and some of them were added in his own handwriting to the draft text of the book.

What did Stalin consider essential to write into this book? Did he want to cool the ardor of his flatterers who were composing his *Short Biography*. No! He marked the very places where he thought that the praise of his services was insufficient.

Here are some examples characterizing Stalin's activity, added in Stalin's own hand: "In this fight against the skeptics and capitulators, the Trotskyites, Zinovievites, Bukharinites and Kamenevites, there was definitely welded together, after Lenin's death, that leading core of the party ... that upheld the great banner of Lenin, rallied the party behind Lenin's behests and brought the Soviet people into the broad road of industrializing the country and collectivizing the rural economy. The leader of this core and the guiding force of the party and the state was Comrade Stalin."

Thus writes Stalin himself! Then he adds: "Although he performed his task of leader of the party and the people with consummate skill and enjoyed the unreserved support of the entire Soviet people, Stalin never allowed his work to be marred by the slightest hint of vanity, conceit or self-adulation."

Where and when could a leader so praise himself? Is this worthy of a leader of the Marxist-Leninist type? No. Precisely against this did Marx and Engels take such a strong position. This also was always sharply condemned by Vladimir Ilyich Lenin.

In the draft text of his book appeared the following sentence: "Stalin is the Lenin of today." This sentence appeared to Stalin to be too weak, so in his own handwriting he changed it to read: "Stalin is the worthy continuer of Lenin's work, or, as it is said in our party, Stalin is the Lenin of today." You see how well it is said, not by the nation but by Stalin himself.

It is possible to give many such self-praising appraisals written into the draft text of that book in Stalin's hand. Especially generously does he endow himself with praises pertaining to his military genius, to his talent for strategy.

I will cite one more insertion made by Stalin concerning the theme of the Stalinist military genius. "The advanced Soviet science of war received further development," he writes, "at Comrade Stalin's hands. Comrade Stalin elaborated the theory of the permanently operating factors that decide the issue of wars, of active defense and the laws of counter-offensive and offensive, of the co-operation of all services and arms in modern warfare, of the role of big tank masses and air forces in modern war, and of the artillery as the most formidable of the armed services. At the various stages of the war Stalin's genius found the correct solutions that took account of all the circumstances of the situation." [Movement in the hall.]

And further, writes Stalin: "Stalin's military mastership was displayed both in defense and offense. Comrade Stalin's genius enabled him to divine the enemy's plans and defeat them. The battles in which Comrade Stalin directed the Soviet armies are brilliant examples of operational military skill."

In this manner was Stalin praised as a strategist. Who did this? Stalin himself, not in his role as a strategist but in the role of an author-editor, one of the main creators of his self-adulatory biography.

Such, comrades, are the facts. We should rather say shameful facts.

And one additional fact from the same *Short Biography* of Stalin. As is known, *The Short Course of the History of the All-Union Communist Party (Bolsheviks)* was written by a commission of the Party Central Committee.

This book, parenthetically, was also permeated with the cult of the individual and was written by a designated group of authors. This fact was reflected in the following formulation on the proof copy of the *Short Biography* of Stalin: "A commission of the Central Committee, All-Union Communist Party (Bolsheviks), under the direction of Comrade Stalin and with his most active personal participation, has prepared a *Short Course of the History of the All-Union Communist Party (Bolsheviks)*."

But even this phrase did not satisfy Stalin: the following sentence replaced it in the final version of the *Short Biography*: "In 1938 appeared the book, *History of the All-Union Communist Party (Bolsheviks), Short Course*, written by Comrade Stalin and approved by a commission of the Central Committee, All-Union Communist Party (Bolsheviks)." Can one add anything more? [Animation in the hall.]

As you see, a surprising metamorphosis changed the work created by a group into a book written by Stalin. It is not necessary to state how and why this metamorphosis took place.

A pertinent question comes to our mind: If Stalin is the author of this book, why did he need to praise the person of Stalin so much and to transform the whole post-October historical period of our glorious Communist Party solely into an action of "the Stalin genius?"

Did this book properly reflect the efforts of the party in the Socialist transformation of the country, in the construction of Socialist society, in the industrialization and collectivization of the country and also other steps taken by the party which undeviatingly traveled the path outlined by Lenin? This book speaks principally about Stalin, about his speeches, about his reports. Everything without the smallest exception is tied to his name.

And when Stalin himself asserts that he himself wrote the *Short Course of the History of the All-Union Communist Party (Bolsheviks)*, this calls at least for amazement. Can a Marxist-Leninist thus write about himself, praising his own person to the heavens?

Or let us take the matter of the Stalin prizes. [Movement in the hall.] Not even the tsars created prizes which they named after themselves.

Stalin recognized as the best a text of the national anthem of the Soviet Union which contains not a word about the Communist Party; it contains, however, the following unprecedented praise of Stalin:

> "Stalin brought us up in loyalty to the people,
>   He inspired us to great toil and acts."

In these lines of the anthem is the whole educational, directional and inspirational activity of the great Leninist party ascribed to Stalin. This is, of course, a clear deviation from Marxism-Leninism, a clear debasing and belittling of the role of the party. We should add for your information that the Presidium of the Central Committee has already passed a resolution concerning the composition of a new text of the anthem, which will reflect the role of the people and the role of the party. [Loud, prolonged applause.]

And was it without Stalin's knowledge that many of the largest enterprises and towns were named after him? Was it without his knowledge that Stalin monuments were erected in the whole country—these "memorials to the living?" It is a fact that Stalin himself had signed on 2 July 1951 a resolution of the USSR Council of Ministers concerning the erection on the Volga-Don Canal of an impressive monument to Stalin; on 4 September of the same year he issued an order making 33 tons of copper available for the construction of this impressive monument. Anyone who has visited the Stalingrad area must have seen the huge statue which is being built there, and that on a site which hardly any people frequent. Huge sums were spent to build it at a time when people of this area had lived since the war in huts. Consider yourself, was Stalin right when he wrote in his biography that ". . . he did not allow in himself . . . even a shadow of conceit, pride, or self-adoration?"

At the same time Stalin gave proofs of his lack of respect for Lenin's memory. It is not a coincidence that, despite the decision taken over 30 years ago to build a Palace of Soviets as a monument to Vladimir Ilyich, this palace was not built, its construction was always postponed and the project allowed to lapse.

We cannot forget to recall the Soviet government resolution of 14 Aug. 1925 concerning "the founding of Lenin prizes for educational work." This resolution was published in the press, but until this day there are no Lenin prizes. This, too, should be corrected. [Tumultuous, prolonged applause.]

During Stalin's life, thanks to known methods which I have mentioned, and quoting facts, for instance, from the *Short Biography* of Stalin—all events were explained as if Lenin played only a secondary role, even during the October Socialist Revolution. In many films and in many literary works the figure of Lenin was incorrectly presented and inadmissibly depreciated.

Stalin loved to see the film *The Unforgettable Year of 1919,* in which he was shown on the steps of an armored train and where he was practically vanquishing the foe with his own saber. Let [Marshal] Kliment Yefremovich [Voroshilov], our dear friend, find the necessary courage and write the truth about Stalin; after all, he knows how Stalin had fought. It will be difficult for Comrade Voroshilov to undertake this, but it would be good if he did it. Everyone will approve of it, both the people and the party. Even his grandsons will thank him. [Prolonged applause.]

In speaking about the events of the October Revolution and about the Civil War, the impression was created that Stalin always played the main role, as if everywhere and always Stalin had suggested to Lenin what to do and how to do it. However, this is slander of Lenin. [Prolonged applause.] I will probably not sin against the truth when I say that 99% of the persons present here heard and knew very little about Stalin before the year 1924, while Lenin was known to all; he was known to the whole party, to the whole nation, from the children up to the graybeards. [Tumultuous, prolonged applause.]

All this has to be thoroughly revised, so that history, literature, and the fine arts properly reflect V. I. Lenin's role and the great deeds of our Communist Party and of the Soviet people—the creative people. [Applause.]

Comrades! The cult of the individual has caused the employment of faulty principles in party work and in economic activity; it brought about rude violation of internal party and Soviet democracy, sterile administration, deviations of all sorts, covering up of shortcomings and varnishing of reality. Our nation gave birth to many flatterers and specialists in false optimism and deceit.

We should also not forget that due to the numerous arrests of party, Soviet and economic leaders, many workers began to work uncertainly, showed over-cautiousness, feared all which was new, feared their own shadows and began to show less initiative in their work. Take, for instance, party and Soviet resolutions. They were prepared in a routine manner, often without considering the concrete situation. This went so far that party workers, even during the smallest sessions, read their speeches. All this produced the danger of formalizing the party and Soviet work and of bureaucratizing the whole apparatus.

Stalin's reluctance to consider life's realities and the fact that he was not aware of the real state of affairs in the provinces can be illustrated by his direction of agriculture.

All those who interested themselves even a little in the national situation saw the difficult situation in agriculture, but Stalin never even noted it. Did we tell Stalin about this? Yes, we told him, but he did not support us. Why? Because Stalin never traveled anywhere, did not meet city and *kolkhoz* workers; he did not know the actual situation in the provinces.

He knew the country and agriculture only from films. And these films had dressed up and beautified the existing situation in agriculture. Many films so pictured *kolkhoz* life that the tables were bending from the weight of turkeys and geese. Evidently Stalin thought that it was actually so.

Vladimir Ilyich Lenin looked at life differently; he was always close to the people; he used to receive peasant delegates, and often spoke at factory gatherings; he used to visit villages and talk with the peasants.

Stalin separated himself from the people and never went anywhere. This lasted 10s of years. The last time he visited a village was in Jan. 1928 when he visited Siberia in connection with grain deliveries. How then could he have known the situation in the provinces?

And when he was once told during a discussion that our situation on the land was a difficult one and that the situation of cattle breeding and meat production was especially bad, a commission was formed which was charged with the preparation of a resolution called "Means toward further development of animal breeding in kolkhozes and sovkhozes." We worked out this project.

Of course, our propositions of that time did not contain all possibilities, but we did charter ways in which animal breeding on the kolkhozes and sovkhozes would be raised. We had proposed then to raise the prices of such products in order to create material incentives for the *kolkhoz*, MTS [Machine & Tractor Stations] and *sovkhoz* workers in the development of cattle breeding. But our project was not accepted and in Feb. 1953 was laid aside entirely.

What is more, while reviewing this project Stalin proposed that the taxes paid by the kolkhozes and by the *kolkhoz* workers should be raised by 40 billion rubles; according to him the peasants are well-off and the *kolkhoz* worker would need to sell only one more chicken to pay his tax in full. Imagine what this meant! Certainly 40 billion rubles is a sum which the *kolkhoz* workers did not realize for all the products which they sold to the government. In 1952, for instance, the kolkhozes and the *kolkhoz* workers received 26,280 million rubles for all their products delivered and sold to the government.

Did Stalin's position then rest on data of any sort whatever? Of course not. In such cases facts and figures did not interest him. If Stalin said anything, it meant it was so—after all, he was a "genius," and a genius does not need to count, he only needs to look and can immediately tell how it should be. When he expresses his opinion, everyone has to repeat it and to admire his wisdom.

But how much wisdom was contained in the proposal to raise the agricultural tax by 40 billion rubles? None, absolutely none, because the proposal was not based on an actual assessment of the situation but on the fantastic ideas of a person divorced from reality. We are currently beginning slowly to work our way out of a difficult agricultural situation. The speeches of the delegates to the 20th Congress please us all; we are glad that many delegates deliver speeches, that there are conditions for the fulfillment of the 6th 5-Year Plan for animal husbandry, not during the period of 5 years, but within 2 to 3 years. We are certain that the commitments of the new 5-Year Plan will be accomplished successfully. [Prolonged applause.]

Comrades! If we sharply criticize today the cult of the individual which was so widespread during Stalin's life and if we speak about the many negative phenomena generated by this cult which is so alien to the spirit of Marxism-Leninism, various persons may ask: How could it be? Stalin headed the party and the country for 30 years, and many victories were gained during his lifetime. Can we deny this? In my opinion, the question can be asked in this manner only by those who are blinded and hopelessly hypnotized by the cult of the individual, only by those who do not understand the essence of the revolution and of the Soviet state, only by those who do not understand, in a Leninist manner, the role of the party and of the nation in the development of the Soviet society.

The Socialist revolution was attained by the working class and by the poor peasantry with the partial support of middle-class peasants. It was attained by the people under the leadership of the Bolshevik Party. Lenin's great service consisted of the fact that he created a militant party of the working class, but he was armed with Marxist understanding of the laws of social development and with the science of proletarian victory in the fight with capitalism, and he steeled this party in the crucible of revolutionary struggle of the masses of the people. During this fight the party consistently defended the interests of the people, became its experienced leader and led the working masses to power, to the creation of the first Socialist state.

You remember well the wise words of Lenin that the Soviet state is strong because of the awareness of the masses that history is created by the millions and 10s of millions of people.

Our historical victories were attained thanks to the organizational work of the party, to the many provincial organizations and to the self-sacrificing work of our great nation. These victories are the result of the great drive and activity of the nation and of the party as a whole; they are not at all the fruit of the leadership of Stalin, as the situation was pictured during the period of the cult of the individual.

If we are to consider this matter as Marxists and as Leninists, then we have to state unequivocally that the leadership practice which came into being during the last years of Stalin's life became a serious obstacle in the path of Soviet social development.

Stalin often failed for months to take up some unusually important problems concerning the life of the party and of the state whose solution could not be postponed. During Stalin's leadership our peaceful relations with other nations were often threatened, because one-man decisions could cause and often did cause great complications.

In the last years, when we managed to free ourselves of the harmful practice of the cult of the individual and took several proper steps in the sphere of internal and external policies, everyone saw how activity grew before their very eyes, how the creative activity of the broad working masses developed, how favorably all this acted upon the development of economy and of culture. [Applause.]

Some comrades may ask us: Where were the members of the Political Bureau of the Central Committee? Why did they not assert themselves against the cult of the individual in time? And why is this being done only now?

First of all we have to consider the fact that the members of the Political Bureau viewed these matters in a different way at different times. Initially, many of them backed Stalin actively because Stalin was one of the strongest Marxists and his logic, his strength and his will greatly influenced the cadres and party work.

It is known that Stalin, after Lenin's death, especially during the first years, actively fought for Leninism against the enemies of Leninist theory and against those who deviated. Beginning with Leninist theory, the party, with its Central Committee at the head, started on a great scale the work of Socialist industrialization of the country, agricultural collectivization and the cultural revolution. At that time Stalin gained great popularity, sympathy and support. The party had to fight those who attempted to lead the country away from the correct Leninist path; it had to fight Trotskyites, Zinovievites and rightists, and the bourgeois nationalists. This fight was indispensable. Later, however, Stalin, abusing his power more and more, began to fight eminent party and government leaders and to use terroristic methods against honest Soviet people. As we have already shown, Stalin thus handled such eminent party and government leaders as Kossior, Rudzutak, Eikhe, Postyshev and many others.

Attempts to oppose groundless suspicions and charges resulted in the opponent falling victim of the repression. This characterized the fall of Comrade Postyshev. In one of his speeches Stalin expressed his dissatisfaction with Postyshev and asked him, "What are you actually?" Postyshev answered clearly, "I am a Bolshevik, Comrade Stalin, a Bolshevik." This assertion was at first considered to show a lack of respect for Stalin; later it was considered a harmful act and consequently resulted in Postyshev's annihilation and branding without any reason as a "people's enemy."

In the situation which then prevailed I have talked often with Nikolai Aleksandrovich Bulganin; once when we 2 were traveling in a car, he said, "It has happened sometimes that a man goes to Stalin on his invitation as a friend. And when he sits with Stalin, he does not know where he will be sent next, home or to jail."

It is clear that such conditions put every member of the Political Bureau in a very difficult situation. And when we also consider the fact that in the last years the Central Committee plenary sessions were not convened and that the sessions of the Political Bureau occurred only occasionally, from time to time, then we will understand how difficult it was for any member of the Political Bureau to take a stand against one or another unjust or improper procedure, against serious errors and shortcomings in the practices of leadership.

As we have already shown, many decisions were taken either by one person or in a roundabout way, without collective discussions. The sad fate of Political Bureau member Comrade [Nikolai A.] Voznesensky, who fell victim to Stalin's repressions, is known to all. It is a characteristic thing that the decision to remove him from the Political Bureau was never discussed but was reached in a devious fashion. In the same way came the decision concerning the removal of [A. A.] Kuznetsov and [Mikhail I.] Rodionov from their posts.

The importance of the Central Committee's Political Bureau was reduced and its work was disorganized by the creation within the Political Bureau of various commissions—the so-called "quintets," "sextets," "septets" and "novenaries." Here is, for instance, a resolution of the Political Bureau of 3 Oct. 1946.

"Stalin's Proposal:

"1. The Political Bureau Commission for Foreign Affairs ('Sextet') is to concern itself in the future, in addition to foreign affairs, also with matters of internal construction and domestic policy.

"2. The Sextet is to add to its roster the Chairman of the State Commission of Economic Planning of the USSR, Comrade Voznesensky, and is to be known as a Septet.

"Signed: Secretary of the Central Committee J. Stalin."

What a terminology of a card player! [Laughter in the hall.] It is clear that the creation within the Political Bureau of this type of commissions—"quintets," "sextets," "septets" and "novenaries"—was against the principle of collective leadership. The result of this was that some members of the Political Bureau were in this way kept away from participation in reaching the most important state matters.

One of the oldest members of our party, Kliment Yefremovich Voroshilov, found himself in an almost impossible situation. For several years he was actually deprived of the right of participation in Political Bureau sessions. Stalin forbade him to attend the Political Bureau sessions and to receive documents. When the Political Bureau was in session and Comrade Voroshilov heard about it, he telephoned each time and asked whether he would be allowed to attend. Sometimes Stalin permitted it but always showed his dissatisfaction. Because of his extreme suspicion, Stalin toyed also with the absurd and ridiculous suspicion that Voroshilov was an English agent. [Laughter in the hall.] It's true—an English agent! A special tapping device was installed in his home to listen to what was said there. [Indignation in the hall.]

By unilateral decision Stalin had also separated one other man from the work of the Political Bureau—Andrey Andreyevich Andreyev. This was one of the most unbridled acts of willfulness.

Let us consider the first Central Committee plenum after the 19th Party Congress, when Stalin, in his talk at the plenum, characterized Vyacheslav Mikhailovich Molotov and Anastas Ivanovich Mikoyan and suggested that these old workers of our party were guilty of some baseless charges. It is not excluded that had Stalin remained at the helm for another several months, Comrades Molotov and Mikoyan would probably have not delivered any speeches at this congress.

Stalin evidently had plans to finish off the old members of the Political Bureau. He often stated that Political Bureau members should be replaced by new ones.

His proposal, after the 19th Congress, concerning the selection of 25 persons to the Central Committee Presidium, was aimed at the removal of the old Political Bureau members and the bringing in of less experienced persons so that these would extol him in all sorts of ways. We can assume that this was also a design for the future annihilation of the old Political Bureau members and in this way a cover for all shameful acts of Stalin, acts which we are now considering.

Comrades! In order not to repeat errors of the past, the Central Committee has declared itself resolutely against the cult of the individual. We consider that Stalin was excessively extolled. However, in the past Stalin doubtlessly performed great services to the party, to the working class and to the international workers' movement.

This question is complicated by the fact that all this which we have just discussed was done during Stalin's life under his leadership and with his concurrence; here Stalin was convinced that this was necessary for the defense of the interests of the working classes against the plotting of the enemies and against the attack of the imperialist camp. He saw this from the position of the interest of the working class, of the interest of the laboring people, of the interest of the victory of socialism and communism. We cannot say that these were the deeds of a giddy despot. He considered that this should be done in the interest of the party, of the working masses, in the name of the defense of the revolution's gains. In this lies the whole tragedy!

Comrades! Lenin had often stressed that modesty is an absolutely integral part of a real Bolshevik. Lenin himself was the living personification of the greatest modesty. We cannot say that we have been following this Leninist example in all respects. It is enough to point out that many towns, factories and industrial enterprises, kolkhozes and sovkhozes, Soviet institutions and cultural institutions have been referred to by us with a title—if I may express it so—of private property of the names of these or those government or party leaders who were still active and in good health. Many of us participated in the action of assigning our names to various towns, rayons, undertakings and kolkhozes. We must correct this. [Applause.]

But this should be done calmly and slowly. The Central Committee will discuss this matter and consider it carefully in order to prevent errors and excesses. I can remember how the Ukraine learned about Kossior's arrest. The Kiev radio used to start its programs thus: "This is radio (in the name of) Kossior." When one day the programs began without naming Kossior, everyone was quite certain that something had happened to Kossior, that he probably had been arrested.

Thus, if today we begin to remove the signs everywhere and to change names, people will think that these comrades in whose honor the given enterprises, kolkhozes or cities are named also met some bad fate and that they have also been arrested. [Animation in the hall.]

How is the authority and the importance of this or that leader judged? On the basis of how many towns, industrial enterprises and factories, kolkhozes and sovkhozes carry his name. Is it not about time that we eliminate this "private property" and "nationalize" the factories, the industrial enterprises, the kolkhozes and the sovkhozes? [Laughter, applause, voices: "That is right."] This will benefit our cause. After all the cult of the individual is manifested also in this way.

We should in all seriousness consider the question of the cult of the individual. We cannot let this matter get out of the party, especially not to the press. It is for this reason that we are considering it here at a closed congress session. We should know the limits; we should not give ammunition to the enemy; we should not wash our dirty linen before their eyes. I think that the delegates to the congress will understand and assess properly all these proposals. [Tumultuous applause.]

Comrades! We must abolish the cult of the individual decisively, once and for all; we must draw the proper conclusions concerning both ideological-theoretical and practical work.

It is necessary for this purpose:

First, in a Bolshevik manner to condemn and to eradicate the cult of the individual as alien to Marxism-Leninism and not consonant with the principles of party leadership and the norms of party life, and to fight inexorably all attempts at bringing back this practice in one form or another.

To return to and actually practice in all our ideological work the most important theses of Marxist-Leninist science about the people as the creator of history and as the creator of all material and spiritual good of humanity, about the decisive role of the Marxist Party in the revolutionary fight for the transformation of society, about the victory of communism.

In this connection we will be forced to do much work in order to examine critically, from the Marxist-Leninist viewpoint, and to correct the widely spread erroneous views connected with the cult of the individual in the sphere of history, philosophy, economy and of other sciences, as well as in literature and the fine arts. It is especially necessary that in the immediate future we compile a serious textbook of the history of our party which will be edited in accordance with scientific Marxist objectivism, a textbook of the history of Soviet society, a book pertaining to the events of the Civil War and the Great Patriotic War.

Secondly, to continue systematically and consistently the work done by the party's Central Committee during the last years, a work characterized by minute observation in all party organizations, from the bottom to the top, of the Leninist principles of party leadership, characterized, above all, by the main principle of collective leadership, characterized by the observation of the norms of party life described in the statutes of our party, and, finally, characterized by the wide practice of criticism and self-criticism.

Thirdly, to restore completely the Leninist principles of Soviet Socialist democracy, expressed in the Constitution of the Soviet Union, to fight willfulness of individuals abusing their power. The evil caused by acts violating revolutionary Socialist legality which have accumulated during a long time as a result of the negative influence of the cult of the individual has to be completely corrected.

Comrades! The 20th Congress of the Communist Party of the Soviet Union has manifested with a new strength the unshakable unity of our party, its cohesiveness around the Central Committee, its resolute will to accomplish the great task of building communism. [Tumultuous applause.] And the fact that we present in all their ramifications the basic problems of overcoming the cult of the individual which is alien to Marxism-Leninism, as well as the problem of liquidating its burdensome consequences, is an evidence of the great moral and political strength of our party. [Prolonged applause.]

We are absolutely certain that our party, armed with the historical resolutions of the 20th Congress, will lead the Soviet people along the Leninist path to new successes, to new victories. [Tumultuous, prolonged applause.]

Long live the victorious banner of our party—Leninism! [Tumultuous, prolonged applause ending in ovation. All rise.]

Foreign Communist Reaction

In Communist circles outside the USSR, few Communists expressed more than limited doubts as to the authenticity of the text. The British, French, Italian and U.S. Communist parties June 21-26 issued a series of declarations asserting their independence of Moscow's control and questioning the denunciation of Stalin. Actions by the parties of Communist East Europe and China continued to reflect policy changes announced by the Soviet party.

The British CP's Political Committee June 21 demanded an analysis "of the causes of degeneration in the functioning of Soviet democracy." It asked for "a more adequate estimate of the role of Stalin" and said British Communists had been forced to rely on "enemy sources" for the text of the Khrushchev speech. The London *Daily Worker* June 18 printed anti-Stalin extracts published by the N.Y. *Daily Worker* and Rome CP newspaper

L'Unita. The London *Worker* commented: "Only the leaders of the Soviet CP . . . can and ought to elucidate further."

The French CP Central Committee June 22 approved a June 18 French Politburo statement that it was "not just" to blame Stalin for "all that was negative in the activity of the CP in the Soviet Union." The French Politburo had called for a "profound Marxist analysis" of the growth of Stalinism. It said that "explanations given up to now . . . are not satisfactory," and it asked for copies of Khrushchev's speech. A 3-man delegation that included Waldeck Rochet, reported leader of opposition to French CP Secy. Maurice Thorez, left for Moscow June 25 for talks "concerning the 2 parties and the whole international workers' movement."

Italian CP Secy. Gen. Palmiro Togliatti said at a Rome meeting of the Italian Central Committee June 25 that the Khrushchev speech implied "co-responsibility on the part of those who today denounce the errors." He asked the USSR for "guarantees against the repetition of similar errors" and said the Italian CP must seek "an Italian way of development toward socialism." Togliatti urged "full autonomy for individual Communist movements and parties [and] bilateral relations between them." Leftwing Italian Socialist Pietro Nenni June 23 attacked the "Soviet system" for its lack of "political liberty." Rome reports June 23 said Nenni's Left Socialists were preparing to end their "unity of action" pact with the Italian CP.

The U.S. CP's National Committee said June 25 it had been "deeply shocked" by Khrushchev's revelations concerning Stalin and did not "share the view that the questions dealt with . . . are exclusively the affair of the CP of the Soviet Union." The statement refused to accept an "analysis" that attributed "such profound mistakes" to "a single individual." It asked for "a basic analysis of how such perversions of Socialist democracy . . . were permitted to develop and continue unchecked for 20 years." The American CP leaders said they had been "deeply disturbed by . . . information coming from Poland that organs and media of Jewish culture were summarily dissolved and their leaders executed." "Khrushchev's failure to deal with these outrages and the continuing silence of Soviet leaders requires an explanation." The statement noted the lack of "a whiff of self-criticism by the leadership of its own errors."

The Soviet CP newspaper *Pravda* for the first time referred indirectly to Khrushchev's denunciation of Stalin by reprinting without comment June 27 an article from the N.Y. *Daily Worker* criticizing Khrushchev's remarks. U.S. CP Secy. Gen. Eugene Dennis had said in the June 18 N.Y. *Worker* article that "the crimes that sullied the latter period of Stalin's leadership are unforgivable." He asked Soviet leaders: "Why did these things happen? Were they inevitable?" *Pravda,* the first Russian newspaper known to mention Khrushchev's speech, explained to its readers June 27 that the Dennis article referred to "materials published by the U.S. State Department and entitled 'Report by Khrushchev at the 20th Party Congress'." The Dennis article, as quoted by *Pravda* June 27, asked: "Did some of [the current Soviet leaders] try to bring about changes before the last 3 years? Could the past evils have been checked earlier? How big and serious are the changes now ... ?"

Dennis' criticism was also carried by the Polish CP newspaper *Trybuna Ludu* June 28.

N.Y. *Daily Worker* foreign editor Joseph Clark said July 3 that the June 27 *Pravda* reprint had deleted Dennis' references to Soviet liquidation of Jewish cultural leaders in East Europe and that, "if the charge was untrue, all *Pravda* had to do was deny it." Clark added July 3 that "an explanation is long overdue from the Soviet leaders about the physical annihilation of the top Soviet Jewish writers and poets" in the 1940s.

Russian Leaders Defend Their Past Behavior

A Soviet CP Central Committee resolution July 2 attempted to answer foreign Communist criticism of the role played by current Russian leaders under Stalin's regime. It said that the drive to uproot Stalinism had created "firm guarantees" of continued collective leadership and "that in the future phenomena similar to the personality cult can never appear in our party." The resolution said that "certain of our friends abroad have not got to the bottom of the personality cult and its consequences." Singling out Togliatti's criticism of the Russian interpretation of Stalin's rule, the Soviet CP statement said: "One cannot, in particular, agree with Comrade Togliatti when he asks whether Soviet society has not reached certain forms of degeneration." "Indisputably," the statement said, "the personality cult has inflicted serious harm on the cause of the CP and Soviet society," but in spite of this, "it could not change and has not changed the nature of the social order." "Even Stalin was not big enough to change the state."

The Central Committee repeated that Stalin's consolidation of power and popularity, backed by the "agent of international imperialism, Beria," had "made the struggle against the lawless deeds perpetrated at the time more difficult." The statement conceded that "it might be asked why" the core of leaders emerging during the war, often bypassing Stalin, "did not take an open stand [and] remove him from the leadership?" "This," it said, "could not be done." There was no "lack of personal courage" among party leaders, but "it is obvious that anyone who had acted in that situation against Stalin would not have received support from the people. Moreover, such a stand would in these conditions have been regarded as a ... blow against the unity of the party and the whole state, extremely dangerous in the presence of capitalist encirclement." "One should also bear in mind that many facts" on Stalin "became known only in recent times, after his death."

Togliatti, writing in the Rome newspaper *Paese Sera* July 3, voiced "unreserved approval" of the Soviet CP analysis of his "incorrect" criticisms. Togliatti said that the statement was a "clarification of questions that have been raised" in the international Communist movement, but he asked for further "frank discussion" of "differences [in] judgment." In an earlier July 3 edition of *Paese Sera,* Togliatti had refused to reconsider his past statements on the anti-Stalin campaign and western CP autonomy and said he had not seen the Soviet CP resolution text.

The N.Y. *Daily Worker* said July 3 that the Soviet party resolution would satisfy "many Marxists," but that "many will feel that the discussion must continue."

POST-STALIN ACTION

Friendship with West Urged

Khrushchev had said in his keynote address at the 20th Party Congress Feb. 14 that the current Soviet leaders "want to be friends with the U.S. and to cooperate with it in peace and international security and also in the economic and cultural fields." "We propose this with good intentions, without holding a knife behind our backs," he declared. He said the Communist world had become so strong that war with capitalist "imperialism" was no longer inevitable. He implied that recent world developments, including the advent of atomic weapons, had made obsolete the "Marxist-Leninist premise which says that while imperialism exists wars are inevitable."

Khrushchev said: "The reactionary forces...of the capitalist monopolies will continue to strive for war gambles and aggression" as long as they exist, but "now there are powerful social and political [Soviet-bloc] forces, commanding serious means capable of preventing the unleashing of war by the imperialists" or of "delivering a slashing rebuff" to "imperialists" who "try to start it." "It is ridiculous to think that revolutions are made to order. When we say that in the competition between...capitalism and socialism, socialism will triumph, this by no means implies" the use of armed force by Socialist countries. The world's working people will seek a Socialist society "after seeing for themselves the advantages that communism holds out." "We have always asserted . . . that the establishment of a new social order in any country is [an] internal affair." While "we recognize the necessity for the revolutionary transformation of capitalist society into Socialist society . . . . there are different forms of social revolution, and the allegation that we recognize force and civil war as the only way of transforming society does not correspond to reality." Acuteness of the struggle would depend "not so much on the proletariat as on the extent of the resistance put up by the exploiters." "Of course, in countries where capitalism . . . controls an enormous military and police machine, the serious resistance of the reactionary forces is inevitable," and "the transition to socialism [in such countries] will proceed and conditions of an acute class revolutionary struggle." But there had arisen "the possibility of employing the parliamentary form for the transition to socialism. For the Russian Bolsheviks..., this way was excluded." Since then, "radical changes have taken place," allowing "an approach to the question from another angle." "Socialism has become a great magnetizing force" and is "really conquering the minds of all toiling mankind." "Peaceful coexistence" is gaining "increasingly wider international recognition. Indeed, there are only 2 ways: either peaceful coexistence, or the most devastating war in history. There is no 3d alternative." But countries with "differing social systems cannot just simply exist side by side." "There must be progress to better relations, to stronger confidence among them, to cooperation."

(Khrushchev reported that Soviet CP membership had reached 7,215,505 as of Feb. 1, with 6,795,896 "regular members and 419,609 candidate members." That was "nearly treble the membership at the time of the 18th Congress and 330,000 more than" during the 19th Congress in 1952, he said. Khrushchev confirmed that a 7-hour work day would be introduced under the 6th Soviet 5-year plan, starting in 1956. Persons between 16 and 18 years old would have a 6-hour day, he said.)

Mikoyan, in his Feb. 16 speech at the congress, challenged "boastful Americans who swagger about their riches" to "enter into a competition with us" on economic lines "instead of the arms race." "Certain ossified forms" of Soviet diplomacy and foreign trade methods had been "discarded" by the post-Stalin regime, he said, and the "isolation of Soviet public and state organizations from the outer world has been liquidated." But in the event of "American aggression," he warned, hydrogen bombs might fall also on American towns, and "American imperialists" would find another war one of "destruction and annihilation," not "a source of enrichment."

Foreign Min. Vyacheslav M. Molotov, addressing the congress Feb. 18, urged vigilance and "a constant eye open for the aggressive plans of the imperialists," who were "hatching plans calculated to thwart" the USSR's development. He said this planning "has found expression in their 'containment' and especially their 'liberation' plans steeped in the spirit of aggression toward the countries of socialism." The Geneva summit meeting in 1955 showed "concrete possibilities for lessening international tension and for improving" East-West relations, he said, but "events showed that the road...is blocked by obstacles created by nobody else but the supporters of the policy 'from positions of strength,' which is doomed to suffer an inevitable fiasco."

Soviet Defense Min. Georgi K. Zhukov told the congress Feb. 18 that the USSR "does not threaten anybody and does not intend to attack anybody" but that it had a "first-class jet air force" that was "capable of solving any problems that will confront it in the event of an attack by an aggressor." He said the USSR was protected by "diverse atomic and thermonuclear weapons, powerful rocket-propelled and jet-propelled armaments of various types, including long-range missiles." Zhukov said the USSR would not accept restrictions on the use of thermonuclear weapons in the event of war. He added that nuclear weapons could not be limited to the battlefield, that Europe would be destroyed in an atomic war and that the USSR would carry the attack to the U.S. if attacked by the West.

Premier Bulganin told the congress Feb. 21 that the Soviet bloc's "consistent peace policy" had created "a realistic prospect for consolidating universal peace," although Soviet proposals have not always met "favorable response among those to whom they were addressed." "We deeply regret that but are nonetheless determined to explore new avenues to international cooperation," he said.

'Collective Leadership' Renewed

The 20th CP Congress ended Feb. 25 after the election of an enlarged Central Committee pledged to the renewed principle of collective leadership. Khrushchev's keynote report repudiating one-man rule was unanimously approved by the congress Feb. 24, as were Premier Bulganin's draft directives for the 6th 5-year plan. The congress Feb. 25 unanimously adopted a proposal by Khrushchev for the preparation of a new party program for submission to the next congress in 1960. This would replace the program, adopted by the 8th Congress in Dec. 1919, that called for worldwide proletarian revolution. The Soviet news agency Tass said Feb. 25 the new program would be based on "the historical experience of our party, the experience of fraternal parties of Socialist countries and the experience and achievements of the whole international Communist and workers' movement."

The Central Committee was expanded from 125 to 133 members, including 53 new ones. 46 members elected under Stalin in 1952 were dropped; most of them were victims of recent CP and government reshuffles in the provinces. Deaths accounted for other changes. Of 122 persons elected candidate (alternate) members of the Central Committee, 72 were chosen for the first time. Among new Central Committee members were: First Deputy Foreign Min. Andrei A. Gromyko; State Security Committee Chrmn. Ivan A. Serov; Internal Affairs Min. Nikolai P. Dudorov; Agriculture Min. Vladimir V. Matskevich.

The 11 members of the Central Committee's Presidium were reelected to the Central Committee, which reelected the same Presidium Feb. 27. Marshal Georgi K. Zhukov, Soviet defense minister, was one of 5 officials newly named as alternate Presidium members. He became the first professional soldier to reach that level, and Yekaterina A. Furtseva, first secretary of the Moscow CP, became the first woman. Other new alternates were *Pravda* editor Dmitri T. Shepilov, Kazakhstan CP chief Leonid I. Brezhnev, and Uzbek CP chief Nuritdin A. Mukhitdinov.

USSR Crushes Hungarian Revolt

The readiness of the new Soviet rulers to use military force was apparently proven by the USSR's bloody suppression of a major Hungarian uprising in 1956.

Student demonstrations in Hungary had escalated by Oct. 23 into armed revolt against the Soviet-backed Hungarian regime and the presence of Soviet troops in Hungary. After several days of fighting, the Soviet army units in Hungary suspended their resistance to the rebels, and they withdrew from Budapest Oct. 29-30. The Soviet government announced Oct. 30 that it was prepared to negotiate the withdrawal of Soviet forces it had stationed in Poland and Rumania as well as in Hungary under the Warsaw Treaty.

The Soviet withdrawal, however, proved to be only a tactical maneuver. Early Nov. 4 the Soviets mounted a powerful tank-led assault on the unsuspecting Hungarian rebels, and virtually all rebel resistance was subdued by Nov. 8. An estimated 200,000 Soviet troops and 5,500 tanks were used by the USSR to crush the revolt. 20,000-25,000 Hungarians and several thousand Russian troops were reported killed in the fighting in Budapest.

Cominform Abolished

The dissolution of the Cominform (Information Office of the Communist & Workers' Parties) was announced simultaneously Apr. 17 in the Russian and European Communist press in statements issued by the Central Committees of the Bulgarian, Hungarian, Italian, Polish, Rumanian, Russian, Czechoslovak and French Communist Parties. The statements said that in view of "the modifications that have taken place in the international situation in the past few years" member parties "recognized that the office as constituted in 1947 has exhausted its uses" and "should cease its activities, and the Information Office organ, *For a Lasting Peace, For a People's Democracy,* should cease publication."

The Italian CP newspaper *L'Unita* quoted the dissolution order as saying the move was undertaken to overcome "splits in the working class" and reinforce "working class unity." It said that the former Cominform member states would shape their policies "according to the particular national conditions of their own countries" and would "find new useful methods of establishing links with each other." Moscow dispatches said Apr. 16 that the Cominform's dissolution reportedly had been demanded by Marshal Tito of Yugoslavia in return for his country's reconciliation with the Soviet bloc. Tito had attacked Stalin's domination of Cominform policies and had been ousted from the group in 1948. Immediately after the break, Cominform headquarters had been shifted from Belgrade to Bucharest.

Molotov Loses Foreign Affairs Post

Vyacheslav Molotov's resignation as Soviet foreign minister was announced without explanation June 1 in Moscow. Dmitri Trofimovich Shepilov, 50, editor since 1952 of the Communist Party newspaper *Pravda,* was named Molotov's successor at the head of the Foreign Ministry. Molotov remained a first deputy premier.

The change in foreign ministers, which preceded a visit to Moscow begun June 2 by Yugoslav Pres. Tito, generally was interpreted in Yugoslavia and the West as a conciliatory Soviet gesture toward Tito as well as a symbol of change in Soviet diplomatic tactics. Tito frequently had implied during the past 8 years that he regarded Molotov as a major Soviet foe of the Yugoslav regime. The Soviet leadership's letters to Tito that led to the latter's break with the Cominform in 1948 had been signed by Stalin and Molotov. Contemporary observers had no verification of rumors that Molotov was a key member of the "hard" faction of the Soviet hierarchy opposed to Khrushchev's professed efforts to liquidate Stalinism and seek coexistence with the West.

Molotov was born Vyacheslav Skryabin, son of a dry goods clerk and cousin of composer Aleksandr N. Skryabin, in 1890 in Kazan, Russia. He gave up study of the violin to become a Bolshevik revolutionary in 1906 and adopted the name Molotov—derived from "molot," Russian for "hammer." He became a Politburo alternate and CP 2d secretary under Stalin in 1921, rose in power with Stalin after Lenin's death to become premier in 1930, switched to foreign minister in 1939 and performed unspecified work as deputy prime minister (with the late Andrei Y. Vishinsky serving as foreign minister) from 1949 until Stalin's death in 1953, when he was reassigned to the Foreign Ministry. He personified Stalin's anti-Western foreign policy and had been overshadowed by CP First Secy. Khrushchev and Premier Bulganin in Soviet "peace offensive" contacts with neutral and Western nations during the past year.

(Shepilov, a CP Central Committee Presidium alternate and career CP theoretician specializing in propaganda and foreign affairs, was born Nov. 5, 1905, in the Krasnodar area. He had directed the CP Central Committee Department of Agitation and Propaganda before becoming *Pravda* editor in 1952. He was rebuked in *Pravda* shortly before Stalin's death for having shown a favorable attitude toward theories of Nikolai A. Voznesensky, purged Soviet planning chief. Shepilov's prominence in Soviet affairs had increased since Stalin's death. He had accompanied Khrushchev and Bulganin to Communist China in 1953 and to Yugoslavia in 1955. He was believed by many Western observers to have put in motion Egypt's purchase of Czech arms during a visit to Cairo in July 1955.)

Molotov was named state control minister Nov. 21 to replace Vasily G. Zhavoronkov.

Other Jobs Change Hands

The Soviet government had announced Feb. 1 that Moscow Deputy Mayor N. P. Dudorov had been named to succeed Gen. Sergei N. Kruglov as interior minister. No explanation was given. Kruglov had succeeded Beria as interior minister in 1953, but Kruglov had lost control of the Soviet secret police to Gen. Ivan V. Serov in Apr. 1954. (The legal journal *Soviet State & Law* confirmed Feb. 9 that the secret MVD tribunal had been abolished in 1953. The tribunal handled mostly political cases and was able to condemn persons to labor camps without trial.)

Trofim D. Lysenko, who had made his genetic theories virtual dogma while serving as Stalinist ruler of biological science in the Soviet Union, was ousted as president of the All-Union Academy of Agricultural Sciences. The news agency Tass announced Apr. 9 that Deputy Premier Pavel P. Lobanov had succeeded him in the farm sciences post and that Agriculture Min. Vladimir V. Matskevich had been named a deputy premier. (It was reported in Moscow Apr. 2 that the Academy of Sciences had ordered the posthumous rehabilitation of purge victim Nikolai I. Vavilov and the publication of his Lysenko-opposed genetic studies.)

The cabinet announced Dec. 25 that First Deputy Premier Mikhail G. Pervukhin, an electrical engineer and expert on power and chemical industries, had replaced First Deputy Premier Maxim Z. Saburov as chairman of the State Commission for Electrical Current Planning.

Anti-Stalin Campaign

Following the initial denunciations of Stalin by his successors, reports from the USSR disclosed numerous instances of new names being bestowed on institutions previously named for Stalin, of efforts being made to right some of the wrongs that had been perpetrated while Stalin ruled and of the circulation of material documenting the charges of wholesale repression under Stalin.

Issues of *Pravda* arriving in New York Apr. 21 revealed that the Marx-Engels-Lenin-Stalin Institute in Moscow had been renamed the Institute of Marxism & Leninism. Moscow reported June 26 that the Stalin Auto Works (Zis cars and trucks) had been renamed Likhachev Auto Works in honor of Road Transport Min. Ivan Likachev, 60 (who had died June 25 and was buried June 26 in the Kremlin wall). The Soviet government June 14 renamed the Molotov Auto Works (Zim cars) Gorky Auto Works (to produce the Volga car).

The Soviet CP's theoretical magazine *Kommunist* June 30 published a group of notes and letters written by Lenin shortly before his death in Jan. 1924 and circulated to delegates at the Feb. 1956 CP congress in Moscow. Among them was the political "testament" intended for the May 1924 13th CP Congress, in which Lenin had praised Trotsky's abilities, termed Stalin "rude" and suggested Stalin's removal as Soviet CP Secretary General. The testament, which reportedly had not been referred to in the Soviet press since 1927, had appeared paraphrased and unidentified in the May 18 *Komsomolskaya Pravda.*

The Paris newspaper *France-Soir* had said June 11 that CP First Secy. Khrushchev, in a talk to a meeting of Soviet leaders in Moscow, had charged Stalin with "erotomania," with keeping a harem of young girls and with having killed his 2d wife (Nadezhda Alliluyeva, rumored a suicide Nov. 8, 1932).

The Frunze (USSR) newspaper *Sovetskaya Kirgizia* said May 19 that the deported Karachai and Balkar peoples had been settled in the Kirghiz SSR and were regaining minority rights and use of their languages. Settlement of the Chechen and Inguish peoples in the Kazakh SSR was said to have been reported in 1954.

Other Post-Stalin Changes

Soviet developments accompanying "de-Stalinization" included trial and prison reforms, the easing of press restrictions, the rehabilitation of many of Stalin's purge victims and an increase in efforts to produce more consumer items.

A decree signed by Presidium Chrmn. Kliment E. Voroshilov Apr. 19 and revealed May 4 ended special Internal Affairs Ministry (MVD) powers to try, convict and execute persons accused of political crimes under Dec. 1, 1934 and Sept. 9, 1937 decrees. Soviet Supreme Court Pres. Anatoli Volin said May 4 that the MVD's "Ossob" (extralegal tribunal) had been abolished by an unpublished 1953 decree and that review boards had been set up to check past MVD sentences.

MVD sources told a touring French Socialist delegation May 13 that the USSR had ended "deportation" to remote parts of the USSR except for serious political crimes and that the internment camp system would be replaced by ordinary prisons and "corrective labor colonies."

A Presidium decree signed by Voroshilov Apr. 25 and published May 8 revoked 5 decrees (3 dated 1940) freezing Soviet workers on their jobs and providing jail terms for unauthorized shifts or absenteeism. The decrees ordered labor law prisoners freed.

The Defense Ministry magazine *Voyenny Vestnik* (*Military Herald*) charged Apr. 24 that the Stalinist cult was responsible both for unpreparedness for World War II and for excessive war losses. The Defense Ministry newspaper *Krasnaya Zvezda* (*Red Star*) May 9, however, defended the principle of one-man military command and rejected *Voyenny Vestnik*'s charges.

The CP Central Committee organ *Partiinaya Zhizn* (*Party Life*) Apr. 28 called for "the widest freedom of discussion" in the USSR despite a current CP drive against "anti-party statements."

The Soviet government announced June 3 a transfer of its judicial and economic functions to republican governments in line with decentralization plans approved by the recent CP congress. The USSR Justice Ministry courts (but not secret police) under Konstantin P. Gorshenin were abolished and its legal functions were transferred to "legal institutions and judicial authorities in the union republics." A Legal Commission was established under the Soviet cabinet to codify Soviet laws and coordinate the republics' administration of justice. The Ministries of Foodstuffs, Meat & Dairy Industry, Fishing Industry, Procurement, Light Industry, Textile Industry, Building Materials Industry, Paper & Woodworking Industry, Automobile Transport & Highways and Health also were abolished. Their functions and the supervision of retail trade and catering were assigned to the republics in moves intended to achieve "more efficient industrial management, better use of available reserves for expanding production, and fuller satisfaction of the national economic requirements."

The Soviet CP newspaper *Pravda* July 6 editorially rejected any suggestion of forming opposition parties or political groups in the USSR as contrary to Leninist ideology. An editorial on the

CP and anti-Stalin campaign said "mass meeting democracy" of the workers must be subordinated with "iron discipline" to the will of one person, "the Soviet leader at work." *Pravda* said that "some people abroad are interested in having in the USSR artificially created non-Communist parties financed by foreign capital and serving its interests"; "as for our country the Communist Party has been and will be the only master of the minds and thoughts, the spokesman, leader and organizer of the people in their struggle for communism."

Khrushchev, attending a July 4 reception at the U.S. embassy in Moscow, had told Columbia University Prof. Philip E. Mosely that there was room in the Soviet hierarchy for differences between Russian leaders and that when "we disagree...we take a vote." In a June 28 article in *Pravda,* French Sen. Leo Hamon noted Soviet efforts at collective leadership and suggested that "an important part...could be played by a well-informed parliament where opinions were voiced publicly" and whose action would "exercise control" over the government "to prevent rash actions."

The English-language *Moscow News* had appeared Jan. 5, for the first time in 7 years. It made its reappearance as a semiweekly tabloid published by the Soviet Society for Cultural Relations with Foreign Countries. The paper had been suspended in Feb. 1949, when its founder, Anna Louise Strong, was expelled from the USSR.

The Apr. 13 issue of *Voprosi Istorii* (*Problems of History*) printed a rehabilitation of purged Red Army civil war leaders Aleksandr I. Yegorov, Vasili K. Bluecher, Yan B. Gamarnik, Andrei S. Bubnov (who had been reported alive in Moscow), Vladimir A. Antonov-Ovseyenko, Sergei S. Kamenev, Mikhail S. Kedrov, Mossei L. Rukhimovich and I. S. Unschlicht.

The Moscow magazine *Novy Mir* (*New World*), in what amounted to a rehabilitation of the writer Bruno Yasienski (who had been purged in 1937), began May 12 the publication of Yasienski's final novel, *The Plot of the Indifferent.*

The CP Central Committee Dec. 24 issued a report asserting that the USSR was "straining" to achieve its current 5-year-plan goals. The report said that the building of new factories would be decreased while efforts were made to improve housing and consumer goods production. Soviet economic planners were criticized for not adapting economic projects to limits imposed by the availability of materials. The report said that Soviet production of capital goods would be 11% higher and consumer goods 9% higher in 1956 than in 1955.

Diplomatic and press reports from Moscow during the 3 weeks preceding the CP Central Committee's pronouncement on economic plans had told of unrest among students and workers in the USSR. Among the reports were: Western diplomatic accounts, cited by the *N.Y. Times* Dec. 1, telling of a sitdown strike in the Kaganovich ball bearing plant in Moscow; Soviet press disclosures Dec. 4 that several prominent Kiev writers and Leningrad student leaders had been rebuked for deviations on ideology and art; a *France Soir* (Paris) dispatch from Stockholm Dec. 19 saying that the Putilov factory in Leningrad, as well as Moscow's Kaganovich plant, had been tied up by a strike for higher pay and better working conditions; reports from French and British diplomatic sources Dec. 20 that Moscow University students recently had refused to hear a speech by Khrushchev; reports from Washington diplomatic sources Dec. 20 that strikes had occurred in industries in the Ural Mountains and Don River valley; a denunciation by the Moscow newspaper *Sovetskaya Russiya* Dec. 22 of "demagogic" speeches made recently by students of the Urals Polytechnic Institute in Sverdlovsk, which the paper said was overcrowded.

1957

A Kremlin power struggle ended in 1957 with victory for Khrushchev, who ousted a faction headed by First Deputy Premier Vyacheslav M. Molotov. The purge took place after Andrei A. Gromyko replaced Dmitri T. Shepilov as foreign minister. The ouster of Marshal Georgi K. Zhukov as defense minister came later in the year. The machinery for planning and controlling the economy underwent major revision under the policy for decentralization. Further steps were taken in the rapprochement with Yugoslavia, and Soviet leaders continued their appeal for coexistence with the West. Khrushchev repeated his boast that the USSR would "catch up" with the U.S. in industrial and farm production, and Soviet citizens were promised further increases in consumer output.

LEADERSHIP UPHEAVAL

Gromyko Becomes Foreign Minister

Andrei A. Gromyko, 47, Soviet first deputy foreign minister and reputed protege of First Deputy Premier Vyacheslav M. Molotov, was appointed foreign minister Feb. 15 to replace Dmitri T. Shepilov. The announcement, made after a meeting of the Soviet CP Central Committee in Moscow Feb. 13-14, said that Shepilov would return to CP organizational and ideological work. Shepilov, a CP Presidium alternate and Central Committee secretary, had left party work and the editorship of *Pravda* to succeed Molotov as foreign minister. CP First Secy. Khrushchev told newsmen Feb. 18 that "Gromyko will carry out the policy set forth by Shepilov." Khrushchev, attending a Bulgarian embassy reception, said Soviet policy "does not depend on a man but [on] . . . the government." He asserted that Shepilov "has always defended the interests of the Soviet Union." Other appointments made by the Central Committee Feb. 15: Nikolai S. Patolichev, Byelo-Russian CP first secretary, as deputy foreign minister; Frol R. Koslov, Leningrad area CP first secretary, as candidate member of the CP Presidium.

(The Supreme Soviet Feb. 12 had named Aleksandr F. Gorkin chairman of a new 12-member Soviet Supreme Court to replace the old tribunal of 78 judges.)

Khrushchev Ousts Molotov Faction

The most sweeping revision of Soviet CP leadership since the Stalin purges of the 1930s was made public by the CP Central Committee July 3 when it announced that Molotov, Georgi M. Malenkov and Lazar M. Kaganovich had been dismissed from the Central Committee and its ruling Presidium for plotting against the leadership of Khrushchev. The 3, all formerly close associates of Stalin's, also were deprived of their government positions as deputy premiers.

A Central Committee communique July 3 accused the 3, particularly Molotov, of leading an "anti-party group" in the Presidium. Ex-Foreign Min. Dmitri T. Shepilov was charged with aiding the group and was ousted as a Presidium alternate (non-voting member), Central Committee member and CP secretary. Also dismissed as Presidium members were Mikhail G. Pervukhin and Maxim Z. Saburov. Pervukhin remained a Presidium alternate.

The Presidium was broadened to include 15 full members with the promotion, announced July 3, of alternate members Marshal Georgi K. Zhukov, Yekaterina A. Furtseva (first woman to attain full membership in the Presidium), Leonid I. Brezhnev, Frol R. Kozlov and Nikolai M. Shvernik, and the addition of new members Averky B. Aristov, Nikolai I. Belyayev, Otto V. Kuusinen and Nikolai G. Ignatov. Remaining as full Presidium members were Khrushchev and the 5 who apparently had backed him against the "anti-party group": Premier Bulganin, Soviet Pres. Kliment Voroshilov, Anastas I. Mikoyan, Mikhail A. Suslov and Aleksei I. Kirichenko. Retained or added as Presidium alternates were Pervukhin, Nuritdin A. Mukhitdinov, Petr N. Pospelov, Demyan S. Korotchenko, Andrei P. Kirilenko, Kirill T. Mazurov, Vasily P. Mzhavanadze and Janis E. Kalnberzins.

The Central Committee communique asserted that the Presidium shakeup had been approved by unanimous vote (Molotov abstaining) at a Central Committee plenary session held in Moscow June 22-29 to consider the "anti-party fractional methods" used by the the Molotov-Malenkov-Kaganovich group in an effort "to change the composition of the party's leading bodies." The communique charged that the 3 had offered "constant opposition, direct or indirect, to [the] course approved by the 20th Party Congress" and had opposed the elimination of "consequences of the personality cult." The Central Committee charged that the group had "resorted to methods of intrigue and formed a collusion against the Central Committee" in an attempt to hamper Soviet policies. It said that the faction specifically had (1) "opposed the Leninist policy of peaceful coexistence between states with different social systems," (2) "sought to frustrate...the reorganization of industrial management and the setting up of economic councils in the economic areas," and (3) fought the "introduction of a new system of [farm] planning, such as would release the initiative of the collective farms" and end "obligatory deliveries" from the peasants' "individual plot." (The Soviet government announced July 4 that requirements for compulsory deliveries of produce grown on individual plots would be abolished effective Jan. 1, 1958.)

Wide World

Nikita S. Khrushchev

The communique singled out Molotov for attack. It charged that he had "hampered in every way the implementation of the new pressing measures intended to ease international tensions and promote universal peace." It charged that Molotov had ignored decisions of the July 1955 Central Committee plenum and opposed an improvement of Soviet relations with Yugoslavia and Japan and the "conclusion of the [1955] Austrian state treaty." It said Molotov had fought the adoption and implementation of policies aimed at permitting "different ways of transition to socialism in different countries."

Reports reaching the U.S. July 5-8 from West European sources and Communist informants in Moscow, Prague and Warsaw gave this description of the power struggle in the Presidium between the Khrushchev and Molotov blocs:

●Led by Molotov and Malenkov, the opposition faction requested and obtained a special meeting of the CP Presidium June 17, ostensibly to discuss addresses to be given June 23 at a celebration of the 250th anniversary of the founding of Leningrad. The meeting was convened June 17 with only these 7 full (voting) Presidium members present: 4 opposition members (Molotov, Malenkov, Kaganovich and Pervukhin), Khrushchev and 2 pro-Khrushchev (Bulganin and Voroshilov). According to an account given by the Moscow correspondent of the Italian CP newspaper *L'Unita,* Khrushchev was confronted with demands that he relinquish control of the party to members of the Molotov faction. Despite the temporary defection of Bulganin and Voroshilov to the opposition, Khrushchev summoned absent Presidium members back to Moscow and by June 19 had presented a petition, signed by 70 of the Central Committee's 133 members, that the political split in the Presidium be discussed by the entire Central Committee.

●The Central Committee meeting opened in Moscow June 22, attended by 309 full and alternate members of the Central Committee and CP Central Control Commission. In the initial 35-hour discussion, Khrushchev demanded that debate be limited to party business while Molotov insisted on an examination of failures in Soviet foreign policy. Khrushchev reportedly addressed the Central Committee for 3 hours June 23, attacking the Molotov faction for anti-party conspiracy and sabotage of East-West disarmament talks and Soviet bloc unity. Molotov in turn charged Khrushchev with demogogic rule and with weakening Soviet heavy industry to match the U.S. in production of food and consumer goods. Marshal Zhukov speaking after it was evident that Khrushchev controlled a majority in the Central Committee, compared Molotov to the late secret police chief Lavrenti P. Beria and warned that the Red Army backed Khrushchev. In the self-criticism that followed, oppositionists confessed that they had plotted to unseat Khrushchev and all, except Molotov, were reported to have joined in approving their own dismissals.

The Presidium of the USSR Supreme Soviet, in an action paralleling that of the CP Central Committee, announced July 4 that leaders of the Molotov faction had been stripped of their government posts: Molotov as first deputy premier and state control minister, Malenkov as deputy premier and electric power stations minister and Kaganovich as first deputy premier. Aleksei S. Pavlenko was named to replace Malenkov as electric power stations minister, a post he had held before Malenkov assumed it in 1955. The Presidium disclosed July 5 that Pervukhin and Saburov, the USSR's top economic planners, had been ousted as first deputy premiers. Aleksei N. Kosygin, deputy chairman of the State Planning Commission, was made a deputy premier. Pervukhin was retained (temporarily) as head of the Ministry of Medium Machine Building Industry (reportedly atomic energy). The ouster of Pervukhin and Saburov from their ministerial posts reduced membership in the Soviet Council of Ministers' "inner cabinet" (premier and deputy premiers) to 4: Premier Bulganin, First Deputy Premiers Mikoyan and Joseph J. Kuzmin, and Deputy Premier Kosygin. (Mikoyan, attending the annual Independence Day reception at the U.S. embassy in Moscow, told Western newsmen July 4 that "everything will be the same, only better," as a result of the changes in the Soviet leadership. Mikoyan, accompanied at the reception by Foreign Min. Gromyko, said that the "opportunists" had "wanted to change our policies" of "peace, friendship and coexistence.")

(The Soviet CP journal *Partiinaya Zhizn* [*Party Life*] confirmed July 23 that the struggle for power had begun in the CP Presidium and had been resolved only at a full meeting of the party's Central Committee. The party organ said that Molotov, Malenkov and Kaganovich had plotted against the Central Committee by attempting to confine the rift to the Presidium. It said that the faction had hoped to present the Central Committee "with the accomplished fact of a changed leadership." *Partiinaya*

Zhizn asserted that the Molotov-Khrushchev struggle had shown the Central Committee "to be truly the highest organ of the party between [quadrennial CP] congresses." The magazine asserted that the Molotov faction had "miscalculated" in its effort to revive "a system that prevailed under Stalin, whom they served so long." "The anti-party group," it said, "did not realize the changes that had taken place in the course of 3 or 4 years" and were furthered by the 20th CP Congress in 1956.)

The ousters of Molotov, Malenkov and Kaganovich signaled the start July 4 of a massive campaign of public denunciation of the "oppositionists" and their policies. Party workers throughout the USSR, backed by the Soviet press and radio, were reported to have exceeded the Central Committee and government in their condemnation of the opposition. More than 8,000 denunciatory CP meetings were reported held in Moscow alone July 4-5. Workers in the Ural Mountains city of Molotov petitioned the Supreme Soviet July 5 to restore the city's original name of Perm. The Soviet liner *Molotov* officially was renamed the *Baltika* July 8.

Marshal Zhukov, in an address to CP members in the Defense Ministry reported July 5 by the ministry's newspaper, *Red Star,* said that the Red Army approved the ouster of the "anti-party group" and "will rally solidly around the party." Zhukov warned that the Red Army was "always prepared at the first call of our party and government to defend the interests of the state." Marshal Ivan Konev, Warsaw Pact commander, in a speech reported July 5 by *Red Star,* said that the armed forces were united in "condemning the splinter activities of Malenkov, Kaganovich and Molotov."

In the first criminal accusations to be made against one of the deposed leaders, Khrushchev July 6 called Malenkov "one of the most important organizers of the so-called Leningrad case," in which the late secret police chiefs Lavrenti Beria and Viktor S. Abakumov allegedly had liquidated leading Leningrad CP leaders under cover of a 1949 purge. Khrushchev told a Leningrad factory audience that the "anti-party group" had been forced to make public its plot when the CP Presidium began considering which of its members should take part in Leningrad's 250th anniversary celebration. Malenkov, he said, "was simply afraid to come to you here in Leningrad." Khrushchev charged that all 3 ousted Presidium members had been caught "hatching cunning schemes" to control key CP and government posts. Molotov had favored "tightening all [the] screws" in foreign policy to sabotage peaceful coexistence. Shepilov, "who had joined them..., showed himself to be most shamelessly 2-faced." But the CP and government, Khrushchev said, had taken "determined measures" to end their influence and reorganize the Soviet economy "to catch up with the [U.S.] in the production of meat, milk and butter" and "in industrial production per capita."

Nikolai Shvernik, one of the new appointees to the CP Presidium, broadened the accusations July 6 to include all opposition leaders, and linked them to Stalin's purges of the 1930s. Shvernik, in a Leningrad speech reported by *Pravda* July 7, said: "In correcting the violations of revolutionary legality permitted by Malenkov, Kaganovich and Molotov during the period of mass repressions [1936-38, according to language used by Khrushchev in his Feb. 1956 attack on Stalin], the party Control Commission has examined [and rehabilitated] in 1957 a great number of former party members." Shvernik repeated Khrushchev's charges that Malenkov had taken "an active part" in the "Leningrad affair." I. N. Turko, deputy chairman of the Leningrad Region Planning Committee, charged July 7 in *Leningradskaya Pravda* that Malenkov had tried to force him to sign "a notorious forgery" in Feb. 1949, at the high point of the Leningrad affair, when Turko was CP secretary for Yaroslavl and Malenkov a member of Stalin's Politburo. Turko, who failed to identify the "forgery" or say whether it was linked with the Leningrad affair, said that Malenkov had "accused [him] of all manner of things" and was "rude and ruthless, without honor or conscience."

The Soviet press and radio, in an apparent move to prepare for the ouster of Molotov, Malenkov and Kaganovich from the Communist Party, began reporting July 9 increasing numbers of protest meetings called to demand their expulsion. *Izvestia* warned July 9 that "the party cannot tolerate those who do not pursue the will of the majority... who try to bring dissension into its ranks."

Moscow radio reported July 10 that Malenkov had been appointed manager of a hydroelectric plant in Ust-Kameno-gorsk, 2,000 miles from Moscow in East Kazakhstan. The broadcast said that Molotov, Kaganovich and Shepilov also had been assigned to new but unspecified posts and that none of the ousted leaders would be prosecuted for their opposition tactics. It said that Malenkov's new post had been disclosed to expose "myths being spread by some of the Western journalists about the persecution of the members of the anti-party group."

In what observers termed a gesture of confidence in his victory over the Molotov group, Khrushchev, accompanied by Bulganin, left Moscow July 8 for a visit to Czechoslovakia. Addressing crowds July 9 in Zilina, en route to Prague, Khrushchev said: "We had some black sheep in a good flock." "They thought they would seize power, and you know how it ended. We took the black sheep by the tail and threw them out." Khrushchev, welcomed in Cerna by Antonin Novotny, Czechoslovak CP first secretary, hailed the Czechoslovak party for having "fully supported us—that is friendship." (Bulganin, whose position as premier reportedly was endangered by his initial support of the oppositionists, said at a Prague luncheon in his and Khrushchev's honor July 10 that "especially great merit" was due Khrushchev for his leading role in having "uncovered and destroyed the anti-party group.")

Leonid F. Ilyichev, Soviet Foreign Ministry spokesman, indicated July 11 that Molotov, Malenkov and Kaganovich would not be arrested or tried for their opposition tactics. Ilyichev characterized the ousted leaders as "anti-party, [but] not hostile..., something quite different from criminal."

Izvestia charged July 12 that Molotov had refused to abandon views that war was inevitable between the capitalist and Communist worlds. *Izvestia* said that Molotov, backed by Kaganovich and Malenkov, also had refused to accept revised Communist doctrine that held it possible for nations to become Communist without undergoing armed revolution and civil war. Marshal Zhukov, speaking at Navy Day ceremonies in Leningrad July 13, said that the 3 leaders of the "anti-party group" had been in disagreement with the Central Committee "on a number of important international and domestic policies" and had aimed at diverting the party into paths that "would not answer the interests of our homeland." Zhukov charged July 15 that the trio had resisted CP efforts "to expose and punish the culprits responsible for breaches of legality" during Stalin's regime.

Izvestia reported Aug. 31 that Molotov had been named ambassador to Outer Mongolia. He replaced Vasily I. Pisarev as Soviet ambassador in Ulan Bator (which was 3,000 miles from Moscow), and Pisarev became minister-counselor in Molotov's embassy. It was reported at about the same time that Kaganovich had been named manager of a cement plant east of the Ural Mountains and that Shepilov had been given a job as a teacher in the Soviet Far East.

International reaction to the sudden change in Soviet CP and government leadership varied. *Among views expressed:*

● U.S. State Secy. John Foster Dulles told newsmen in Washington July 8 that the change proved that "Communist-type despotisms are not as unchangeable as they sometimes appear." Dulles said that the shift had strengthened his conviction that communism in its present form was "a passing phase." "It appears," he said, "that time and circumstance have worked on some of the leaders in Moscow," showing that "power contests are not unusual" under communism. Dulles added July 16 that the Soviet shakeup confirmed "the existence in Russia" of an "irresistable" popular pressure "for more personal security, more personal freedom and more enjoyment of the fruits of their labor." He said that Soviet leaders had been "sharply divided" on current policies and that the Kremlin shift "was primarily a matter of internal politics," caused by "the question of how to cope with the internal pressures which were manifesting themselves." Dulles termed Khrushchev's ouster of the Molotov faction a victory of the "modernists" over the "fundamentalists." He asserted that the "modernists" seemed to favor policies that would "allow the people at least to hope for changes that would improve their lot." He said that Khrushchev, by "his promise to give more milk, butter and eggs than the [U.S.] produced," was "seeking to win a measure of popular favor."

● U.S. State Department spokesman Lincoln White July 5 indicated Eisenhower Administration skepticism that the change in leadership would affect Soviet policy toward the West. White suggested that "the proof of the pudding ... will be to see whether or not the [USSR] will now proceed with practical measures" to solve "such important international problems as disarmament and German unification."

● West German Chancellor Konrad Adenauer, in an interview published July 5, rejected theories that the Kremlin shakeup represented a victory for liberalism in the USSR. He likened the Khrushchev-Molotov battle to "the struggle of the tyrants after Lenin's death."

●Ex-British Prime Min. Sir Winston Churchill said July 6 that the USSR "was moving toward a different state of affairs and will aim at taking her part in this broad and easy composition of the human race."

● Indian Prime Min. Jawaharlal Nehru, in London for the British Commonwealth Prime Ministers Conference, said July 4 that the Soviet shift represented a return from "the high pitch of revolution" to "what might be called normality."

Zhukov Dismissed

The Soviet government announced Oct. 26 that Marshal Zhukov, 60, had been "released" as Soviet defense minister by the Presidium of the Supreme Soviet. It said that Marshal Rodion Y. Malinovsky, 59, had been named to succeed Zhukov in the post. (Malinovsky was replaced as commander of Soviet ground forces by Marshal Andrei A. Grechko, formerly Soviet commander in East Germany.) Zhukov, alleged to have supported Khrushchev against the "anti-party faction," had returned to Moscow earlier Oct. 16 from a tour of Yugoslavia and Albania. The announcement made no mention of an immediate change in Zhukov's position as sole military member of the Soviet CP Presidium. The Soviet army newspaper *Red Star*, however, implied that Zhukov's highly popular military leadership was at an end. It published a Defense Ministry statement declaring that the "Communist Party leadership is the source of strength of the Soviet army and navy." Khrushchev told newsmen at a Turkish embassy reception in Moscow Oct. 29 that Zhukov was in good health and soon would be given a post for which he was "experienced and qualified."

But the CP Central Committee announced Nov. 2 that Zhukov had been dismissed from the Central Committee and CP Presidium. His dismissal was presumed to have left Khrushchev in undisputed control of the Soviet hierarchy. Zhukov had been a member of the Presidium only since July 3.

The Central Committee communique, published Nov. 3 by the party newspaper, *Pravda*, was issued after several hundred senior Red Army officers had been summoned to a special meeting at the Kremlin Nov. 1. It charged that Zhukov had promoted his own "cult of personality" in the army and had tried to eliminate "the leadership and control of the party, its Central Committee and the government over the army and navy." It said that with "the help of sycophants," Zhukov "was praised to the sky . . . and his person and role in the Great Patriotic War [World War II] were overglorified." Zhukov was said to have belittled the "leading and inspired [war] role" of the CP and Russian people. The communique charged that, although "great political trust" had been placed in Zhukov, he had "proved to be a politically unsound person, inclining to adventurism" in his "understanding of . . . foreign policy [and] his conduct of the Defense Ministry." It asserted that party investigations prior to Zhukov's ouster had revealed "grave shortcomings in political work" within the Soviet army and navy.

The Central Committee said that Zhukov had conceded that the party's criticism was "in the main correct" and had voted for his own dismissal. Referring to his previous ouster from the Central Committee in 1946, Zhukov reminded the committee that he had not at that time acknowledged the correctness of the expulsion. The Central Committee condemnation of Zhukov was approved in speeches by 7 Red Army marshals, including Malinovsky, the new defense minister. The communique said the party secretariat had been ordered to find Zhukov a new post.

Marshal Ivan S. Konev, Warsaw Pact military forces commander, charged Nov. 3 in *Pravda* that Zhukov had been guilty of "errors in military science" and had shared with Stalin "serious responsibility" "for the fact that our border troops were caught unprepared by the sudden attack of the Fascist armies." Konev, World War II associate of Zhukov's (Zhukov's First White Russian Army and Konev's 2d Ukrainian Army had jointly captured Berlin), denounced Zhukov's alleged claims of credit for the Stalingrad and Berlin victories. He charged that Zhukov, "a person of unusual vanity," had seen himself as "a knight on a white horse."

The Soviet army and navy newspapers indicated Nov. 5 that Col. Gen. Aleksei S. Zheltov, Vice Adm. A. V. Komarov and Maj. Gen. A. G. Rytov, the chiefs of political work, respectively, in the army, navy and air force, would face censure for political failures under Zhukov's administration. The navy newspaper *Sovietskaya Flot* reported Nov. 5 that Averky B. Aristov, a CP Presidium member, had critized the Main Political Administration of the military forces for "shortcomings in leadership of political organs and party organizations of the fleet." *Red Star*, the Defense Ministry newspaper, said Nov. 5 that lack of awareness by party workers had bred "conceit, hauteur and contempt for subordinates" among Soviet army officers. (Zheltov's dismissal as head of the Main Political Administration was announced by the Defense Ministry Jan. 14, 1958. He was replaced by Col. Gen. Filipp I. Golikov.)

A U.S. State Department statement issued Nov. 2 termed Zhukov's downgrading evidence of the "strains and stresses" prevalent in the USSR and satellite nations. It noted that Zhukov's "disgrace" followed Soviet complaints that the U.S. had ignored requests for a Zhukov visit to the U.S. It termed Zhukov "a distinguished military leader" and expressed doubt that he had been responsible for "adventurism" in Soviet foreign policy. Pres. Eisenhower told newsmen Oct. 31 that Zhukov's ouster probably was linked to "some reason for the extraordinary frequency of changes in the Soviet ruling group since the death of Stalin." Mr. Eisenhower said that he hoped "Marshal Zhukov's resignation was completely voluntary and personal...." State Secy. Dulles said Oct. 29 that the U.S. was "on the alert" to the possibility of a new Soviet move abroad as a result of Zhukov's ouster but that he did not "think there is war around the corner." Dulles said that the Soviet leadership's attempt to destroy the "cult of personality" inevitably led "to pulling and hauling in different directions" within the Soviet hierarchy. He traced recent decisions to decentralize Soviet industry and scrap the 5-year plan to stresses within the system and said that "terrific convulsions" could be expected behind the USSR's "hard, calm exterior."

Party & Government Posts Change Hands

Uzbek CP First Secy. Nuritdin A. Mukhitdinov, a candidate member of the Soviet CP Presidium, was promoted to full Presidium membership Dec. 18 to fill the seat left by Zhukov. Mukhitdinov and Presidium members Aleksei I. Kirichenko and

Nikolai G. Ignatov were appointed to Central Committee secretaryships Dec. 18. Sabir K. Kamalov, Uzbek premier, was elected Dec. 28 to replace Mukhitdinov as Uzbek CP first secretary and in turn was succeeded as Uzbek premier Dec. 30 by Mansur Mirza-Akhmedov. Kirichenko was released Dec. 26 as Ukrainian CP first secretary to devote full time to Presidium and Central Committee tasks. Nikolai V. Podgorny became Ukrainian CP first secretary Dec. 26, and Leonti I. Naidek became Ukrainian CP 2d secretary. Ignatov was replaced as Gorki City CP chief Dec. 26 by N. N. Smelyakov, ex-machine building minister.

Yekaterina A. Furtseva, only woman in the CP Presidium, was replaced as Moscow City CP Committee first secretary Dec. 26 by Vladimir I. Ustinov to free her to assume new work in the Soviet CP secretariat. Nikolai P. Firyubin, Furtseva's husband, had been named a Soviet deputy foreign minister Sept. 30. (Ivan K. Zamchevsky replaced Firyubin as Soviet ambassador to Yugoslavia Sept. 30.) Frol R. Kozlov, CP Presidium member and Leningrad District CP chief, replaced Mikhail A. Yasnov as premier of the Russian Republic Dec. 19. Yasnov, Russian premier since 1956, was demoted to deputy premier. Kozlov was replaced as Leningrad District CP chief Dec. 26 by I. V. Spiridonov. Maxim V. Saburov, ex-deputy premier and planning chief ousted for complicity with the Molotov "anti-party" faction, was appointed Sept. 16 as deputy chief of the State Committee on Economic Relations with Foreign Countries, the USSR's foreign aid agency.

Control Machinery Revised

The Soviet Union's system for planning and controlling production was revised under a plan introduced in the Supreme Soviet May 7 by Khrushchev and approved by the Supreme Soviet May 10. Major details of the plan:

● 92 economic regions were designated (68 in the Russian Republic, 11 in the Ukraine, one in each of the 13 other Soviet republics). A council was set up in each region to direct production by all of the region's industries, including the construction of plant facilities, with emphasis on regional initiative but under direct control of the State Planning Commission. Joseph Josefovich Kuzmin, recently a member of the CP Central

Auditing Commission, was named State Planning Commission chairman and first deputy premier May 4; he replaced Nikolai M. Baibakov in the chairmanship.

• At least 24 Soviet government ministries were abolished and their work entrusted to republican governments and regional councils under Kremlin control. The industries for which ministries were abolished were: autos, machine building, instrument making and automation, machine tools and tools, building and road-making machinery, oil industry construction, tractors and agricultural machines, transport machinery, heavy machinery, electrical engineering, paper and wood processing, town and village construction, light industry, timber, oil, meat and dairy products, foodstuffs, building materials, fish, metallurgical and chemical works construction, coal-industry construction, coal, nonferrous metals, iron and steel.

• 14 ministries were shifted to the joint control of the republics and central Soviet government: Internal Affairs, Higher Education, Geology and Conservation of Mineral Resources, State Control, Public Health, Foreign Affairs, Culture, Defense, Communications, Agriculture, State Farms, Trade, Finance, Grain Products.

• 11 ministries concerned with defense production remained under central government control: Aircraft Industry, Foreign Trade, Merchant Marine, Defense Industry (absorbing General Machine Building), Railways, Radio Engineering, Medium Machine Building Industry (believed to be the atomic agency; First Deputy Premier Mikhail G. Pervukhin was appointed May 3 to succeed the late Avraamy P. Zavenyagin at the head of the ministry, but after his demotion in the Khrushchev crack-down on the "anti-party" faction, Pervukhin was replaced July 24 by Yefem Pavlovich Slavsky, ex-chief of the Main Administration for the Utilization of Atomic Energy and made chairman of a new State Committee for Foreign Economic Relations), Shipbuilding, Transport Construction, Chemical Industry, Electric Power Stations (absorbing Electric Power Station Construction).

Khrushchev said in his speech to the Supreme Soviet May 7 that the revised system would eliminate many production lags due to ministerial rivalries and red tape, but he denied that a "crisis in the Soviet economy" existed. The program as published May 11 after its ratification indicated that Kremlin control of industries probably would be tightened through the State Planning

Commission's enforcement of central policies, materials allotment, "state discipline" and its veto over decisions taken by regional economic councils.

The Soviet government Aug. 28 announced the abolition of the Ministry of State Control, which Molotov had headed at the time of his ouster from party and government posts. The Tass news agency reported that the Presidium of the Supreme Soviet had replaced the ministry with a Soviet Control Commission under the USSR's Council of Ministers (cabinet). Tass said that the new commission would "deal with new conditions" arising from the decentralization of industry and the increase in local government authority.

The Soviet government and CP Central Committee announced Sept. 25 that the current 5-year plan would be abandoned at the end of 1958 and replaced by a 7-year plan for industrial production from 1959 to 1965. The 7-year plan, to be developed by the State Planning Commission together with the governments of the Soviet republics, was said to have been made necessary by new scientific and raw materials discoveries and a "radical change in the system of current and future planning" under the USSR's industrial decentralization program.

The Ministries of Defense Industry, Aviation Industry, Shipbuilding Industry and Radio-Technical Industry were abolished Dec. 14 and replaced by State Committees for Defense, Aviation, Shipbuilding and Radio & Electronic Technology under the supervision of Dmitri F. Ustinov, ex-defense industries minister, who was named a deputy premier Dec. 14. Named to head the new State Committees were: Defense—A. V. Domrachev; Aviation—Petr V. Dementev; Shipbuilding—B. Y. Butom; Radio & Electronic—V. D. Kalmykov.

A decree approved by the Supreme Soviet Feb. 11 had given the 15 Soviet republics the authority to revise their legal codes with Soviet government guidance and to redesignate their internal regions and territories to improve efficiency. An economic commission on which each republic had 2 representatives was set up by the Soviet of Nationalities to advise the central government on economic measures.

Rapprochement with Yugoslavia

The USSR and Yugoslavia disclosed Aug. 3 that Khrushchev and Yugoslav Pres. Tito, meeting secretly in Rumania for 2 days, had reached agreement on "concrete forms of cooperation" between the Soviet and Yugoslav Communist parties. A statement broadcast on Moscow radio Aug. 3 said that delegations led by Khrushchev and Tito had agreed "to work for a further all-round development of relations." The statement "emphasized that particular importance is attached to the strengthening in every way of the unity and fraternal cooperation of the Communist and workers parties . . . of all the Socialist countries . . . and progressive forces throughout the world."

A similar Yugoslav government statement, issued Aug. 3 in Belgrade, stressed that the Yugoslav and Soviet leaders had agreed to develop relations "on the basis of equality, mutual assistance and cooperation, the respect of sovereignty and non-interference into internal affairs."

A compromise aid agreement, signed in Moscow July 29 and made public July 30, had renewed Soviet pledges of $250 million in economic and technical aid for construction of a hydroelectric and aluminum project in Montenegro and a 2d hydroelectric plant and fertilizer factory elsewhere in Yugoslavia. The accord provided for completion of the power stations in 1964, 3 years later than originally planned.

Khrushchev Presents Views to U.S.

A variety of subjects, including Soviet policy on war and disarmament, coexistence of and competition between communism and capitalism, and Soviet agricultural goals, were discussed by Khrushchev with 3 U.S. newsmen in a filmed, unrehearsed interview broadcast June 2 on CBS-TV's "Face the Nation." The interview, arranged by CBS public affairs director Irving S. Gitlin after 2 years of negotiations, was filmed May 28 in Khrushchev's Kremlin office. The interviewers were "Face the Nation" moderator Stuart Novins and Moscow correspondents Daniel Schorr of CBS and B. J. Cutler of the *N.Y. Herald*

Tribune. Khrushchev, who received an outline of subject matter but not questions in advance, made these major statements:

Disarmament—"The people of the world will not gain" if atomic tests are merely preannounced. "As long as there is an explosion, the air has been poisoned." "Our proposal is to put an end to all these tests." As a "useful first step" to "test the good-will of the 2 sides" and "prevent war," "why couldn't the U.S. and the other [Western] countries withdraw their troops from West Germany, from the other countries of the West... while we withdraw our troops from East Germany . . . Poland . . . Hungary . . . Rumania?"

War's effects—A nuclear war "would bring tremendous calamities to the whole of mankind" but "mankind would not be destroyed"; "ideas would continue to live, and the immortal idea... is communism."

Coexistence—"We will continue to compete, but we must live on this one planet. We think that is possible even though there would be ideological differences, because there are many questions which unite us."

U.S. 'war planning'—"God knows how many speeches are being made in your country saying in how many hours the Soviet Union can be destroyed by the power of the U.S. We don't indulge in any such things," but if "a madman should unleash a war, we would have to take our steps."

Socialism vs. capitalism—Russians wanted "competition" in which "the most healthy forces come into the forefront, and we believe that our Socialist system represents the most healthy elements because it is a younger system.... Your grandchildren in America will live under socialism, and please do not be afraid of that. Your grandchildren will not understand how their grandparents did not understand the progressive nature of a socialistic society."

Exchanges—"All restrictions on trade should be removed," and "there should be more exchanges of cultural delegations." About Soviet jamming of Voice of America broadcasts: "If it's a good voice, we do not jam it.... If it's a voice which cuts on the ear, then every person switches off one's radio or jams that radio because that voice gets on one's nerves."

Popular support of regime—"To divide us [the Soviet CP regime] from the people, that is an old tune, [and] no one is prepared to listen to that record any more." The CP "reflects the desires... of the people."

Soviet farm output—The USSR would equal the U.S.' per capita output of milk and butter in 1958, and "we hope to catch up" in livestock production "in 1960 or 1961."

East-West hostility—"Both sides might have had a more reasonable approach" after World War II, but "the deterioration . . . represented a desire on the part of the capitalistic countries to test us, because your political leaders say that they are prepared to deal with us only after the liberation of the so-called enslaved peoples, meaning the Socialist countries in Europe. . . . We look upon the capitalist society as slavery."

Soviet Views Amplified

During a visit to Czechoslovakia July 9-16, Khrushchev told crowds in Ostrava July 13 that "it is not bad if in improving the theory of Marx one throws in also a piece of bacon and a piece of butter." Khrushchev, defending his avowed aim of matching U.S. farm production, conceded that "when you have a hungry stomach it is sometimes very difficult to understand the theory of Marxism-Leninism." Khrushchev added, however, that Russia had become "the world's 2d industrial power, and we will catch up with" the U.S. "Nothing," he said, "can stop the birth of a new social order."

Referring to the 1956 Hungarian revolt as a "convincing example" of what happens when Communist regimes lose touch with their people, Khrushchev said July 13 that the "stupid mistakes" of ex-Hungarian CP leaders Matyas Rakosi and Erno Gero had permitted a "handful of counter-revolutionaries with help from abroad to make a bloodbath in Budapest." (A UN Special Committee on Hungary had charged the USSR June 20 with armed repression of the 1956 Hungarian uprising against Soviet occupation and Stalinist rule. The 5-member committee [Alsing Andersen of Denmark, chairman, Mongi Slim of Tunisia, Enrique Rodriguez Fabregat of Uruguay, R. S. S. Gunewardene of Ceylon and Keith C. O. Shann of Australia] asserted that Soviet armed forces had invaded Hungary to overthrow the legal revolutionary government of ex-Premier Imre Nagy and impose a puppet regime led by Premier Janos Kadar. The report was prepared under a Jan. 10 UN Gen. Assembly resolution. It was based on investigation of evidence provided by 111 witnesses, the majority of whom were Hungarian refugees. Moscow radio ridiculed the UN report June 20 as a U.S. "propaganda bomb," "fabricated by false testimonies" and created by "dark machinations under the [UN] flag." The broadcast charged the inquiry committee with violating provisions against UN "interference in the internal affairs of member states.")

A joint Soviet-Czechoslovak communique on talks held by Khrushchev, Soviet Premier Nikolai A. Bulganin, Czechoslovak Pres. Antonin Zapotocky, Czechoslovak Premier Viliam Siroky, Czechoslovak CP First Secy. Antonin Novotny and Czechoslovak National Assembly Speaker Zdenek Fierlinger, issued July 16 on the departure of Khrushchev and Bulganin from Prague, called on all Communists to perform their "sacred duty" in "unflagging struggle" against "all expression of factionalism" within their parties. The statement urged a "determined fight against revisionism" and "any signs of detachment from the masses or conservatism." The Czechoslovaks stated their condemnation of "the anti-party views and factional activities of the Malenkov-Kaganovich-Molotov group."

In the first public Soviet CP comment on Communist Chinese Pres. Mao Tse-tung's thesis that contradictions were possible in a Soviet-style society, *Pravda* said July 16 that Chinese experimentation with Communist ideology was of "great importance for the Marxist-Leninist theory in general." Terming Mao's speech "an outstanding event in China's political life," the Soviet CP newspaper said it "furnishes the Chinese people with a new clear-cut orientation in the new situation" of socialism. Mao's speech, it said, "has multiplied the strength of the millions of supporters of socialism in China who have turned to a decisive offensive against . . . rightwing bourgeois elements."

Writing in the Soviet CP journal *Kommunist,* Khrushchev appealed Aug. 27 to the "inexhaustible forces" of the Soviet people to aid in an "unremitting struggle" against hostile ideologies propounded by dogmatists and liberals. He denounced the party's "hardheads," "parrots" and "Talmudists" for opposing his schemes for reorganizing Soviet agriculture and industry. The article, written on the subject of literature, warned Soviet writers to learn from the events that preceded the Hungarian revolt. It criticized those who demanded total "freedom of creative work." Referring to the Stalin "tragedy," Khrushchev charged that Malenkov, despite "his high position," not only had not restrained Stalin but had "very deftly used

weaknesses and habits of Stalin in the last years of his life."
Khrushchev said Malenkov had fallen "under the complete influence" of Beria, "a sworn enemy of the people," and had
become Beria's "shadow and tool," aiding him in his anti-Soviet
activities.

Coexistence Call Renewed

Answering an appeal by British philosopher Earl Russell for
East-West summit talks, Khrushchev wrote Dec. 7 that "we
favor a meeting between the leaders of the [U.S.] and the [USSR].
It depends, therefore, on the leaders of the [U.S.] whether or not
such a meeting will take place." Khrushchev's reply to Russell's
Nov. 23 appeal (published Dec. 19 by the *New Statesmen,* a
British weekly) asserted that "in the present situation, war is not
fatally inevitable."

In messages to 82 UN-member states and Switzerland,
Soviet Premier Bulganin Dec. 12 renewed his call for a non-
aggression pact between NATO and Warsaw Pact nations and
appealed for worldwide support for the USSR's policies of
"peaceful coexistence." Bulganin's message, similar in content to
letters received from him by Pres. Eisenhower Dec. 10 and by
West German Chancellor Konrad Adenauer, British Prime Min.
Harold Macmillan and French Premier Felix Gaillard Dec. 11,
warned that "the danger of a nuclear war has greatly increased."
It derided the "dangerous illusion" that NATO nations permitting use of their territory for nuclear missile bases still would
be able to fight "local or small wars" with "so-called tactical
nuclear weapons." Bulganin made these proposals for ending the
East-West deadlock in Europe:

● An East-West summit meeting to seek a general European
political settlement and a disarmament accord.

● An immediate ban on nuclear weapons tests by the U.S.,
Britain and USSR for at least 2 to 3 years.

● Agreement on a system for establishing a demilitarized zone
through central Europe.

In his note to Adenauer, Bulganin proposed the creation of
an "atom free zone" across Europe to include East and West
Germany, Poland and Czechoslovakia. He reiterated earlier
offers by Khrushchev to withdraw Soviet forces from East
Germany and other East European nations in return for a with-

drawal of U.S. forces from West Europe. He repeated warnings that West German acceptance of U.S. nuclear missile bases could bring annihilation of German cities. Additional Bulganin letters, repeating Soviet terms for an East-West settlement and appealing to sectional interests of each country, were received by the Netherlands and Belgium Dec. 12, by Italy, Turkey, Norway and Canada Dec. 13 and by Greece and Denmark Dec. 14.

DOMESTIC AFFAIRS

The Budget

The 1957 Soviet budget, calling for expenditures of 604,580,653,000 rubles ($151,145,163,250 at the official 4-to-1 rate of exchange) and revenues of 617,155,967,000 rubles ($154,288,991,750) was approved Feb. 9 by the USSR Supreme Soviet. 96.7 billion rubles ($24,175,000,000) were allocated to the armed forces, compared with 97.8 billion rubles ($24.45 billion) in 1956. During the discussion of the budget in the Supreme Soviet Feb. 9, Finance Min. Arseny G. Zverev and First Deputy Premier Mikhail G. Pervukhin (State Planning Commission chairman) agreed to a 737 million-ruble increase in scheduled expenditures, including 68 million rubles more for anti-TB medicines (raised from 379 million rubles to 447 million after Health Min. Maria D. Kovrygina warned of a high rate of TB in the USSR). Pervukhin also promised efforts to increase the outlay for consumer goods by 1.086 billion rubles.

The Supreme Soviet Dec. 20 unanimously approved a 627,742,125,000-ruble state budget and economic plan for 1958. Presented Dec. 19 by Zverev, the budget (increased Dec. 20 from the 626.7 billion rubles requested by the government) called for the following 1958 expenditures: military—96.3 billion rubles (96.7 billion in 1957); economic development—257.1 billion rubles (376 billion in 1957); education, health, science, social insurance—212.2 billion rubles; scientific research—18.2 billion rubles; construction and housing—36.8 billion rubles (29.9 billion in 1957); administration—11.96 billion rubles. The 1958 budget estimated total state income at 641.9 billion rubles (614.5 billion in 1957) despite the exemption from income taxes, effective Jan. 1, of married couples with children and unmarried working women. Zverev listed total state expenditures for 1957 as 598.2 billion rubles or 99.9% of the amount budgeted. The *N.Y. Times* reported Dec. 20 that, reflecting the USSR's industrial decentralization campaign and concomitant reductions in the 1958 economic development budget, the 1958 budgets of the Soviet republics had been set at 319.1 billion rubles, an increase of 125 billion over 1957.

Other Developments

A decree approved by the Supreme Soviet Feb. 11 provided for the creation of labor disputes commissions, with equal worker and management representation, to replace union rates-and-disputes committees in all working organizations. Workers were given the right to appeal commission decisions against them to their local unions. The labor newspaper *Trud* said Feb. 14 that machinery for handling worker grievances had been overhauled because union officials had been inclined to side with management, to the disadvantage of workers with just complaints, in order to meet production quotas.

The Supreme Soviet Feb. 11 voted the "rehabilitation" of the Balkar, Chechen & Inguish, Kalmyk, Karachai and Kabardian national minority groups, all banished to Central Asia and Kazakhistan during World War II for disloyalty to Stalin's regime. The decree called for their reestablishment in the Kalmyk, Chechen-Inguish and Kabardino-Balkar autonomous republics and a Karachai-Cherkess autonomous region in the Caucasus.

The government reported that 99% of eligible voters went to the polls and indorsed Communist-slate candidates by votes of 98.9% to 99.9% in elections of regional, city and rural soviets Mar. 3 in the Russian, Ukrainian, White (Byelo-) Russian, Lithuanian, Moldavian, Tadzhik, Turkmen & Uzbek republics. Similar results were reported in elections Mar. 10 in Armenia, Azerbaidzhan, Estonia, Kirghizia, Kazakhstan and Latvia.

Prof. M. S. Vovsi, one of the Jewish physicians accused of planning the murders of Soviet officials in the 1953 "doctors plot" but later cleared, was awarded the Order of Lenin July 11 for 35 years' service to Soviet medicine, science and education.

The Young Communist League (Komsomol) revealed July 26 that it had expelled an undisclosed number of members for "religious worship," "immoral behavior" and "breaking away from the organization." The youth organization, reporting on its "great check-up" in *Komsomolskaya Pravda,* listed its membership as 18.5 million.

The government Aug. 25 ordered price reductions of 10% to 32% on 7 categories of consumer items.

The USSR ushered in the "space age" Oct. 4 when *Sputnik 1,* the earth's first man-made satellite, was launched into orbit around the earth by Soviet scientists. Western sources determined later that the launching rocket was fired at 7:21 p.m. Greenwich Mean Time from an initially undisclosed site later identified as the Baikonur "cosmodrome" at Tyuratam in Kazakhstan. The achievement was announced by the Soviet government Oct. 5. Prof. (Lt. Gen.) Anatoli A. Blagonravov, a leading Soviet missile and space expert, said in a U.S. TV interview Oct. 6 that *Sputnik 1* had not been launched as part of the USSR's International Geophysical Year contribution. Khrushchev, interviewed in Moscow Oct. 7, offered to subject future launchings to international control. The world's 2d artificial satellite, *Sputnik 2,* was launched successfully into orbit by Soviet scientists Nov. 3 with a dog named Laika as passenger. Western sources determined later that the launching took place at 2:32 a.m. Greenwich Mean Time from the Kazakhstan site used for *Sputnik 1.*

Khrushchev, addressing the Ukrainian Supreme Soviet in Kiev, confirmed Dec. 24 that the USSR's 1957 grain harvest had fallen short of the record 1956 levels (124 million tons) but had equalled the 1955 crop (103 million tons). Nikolai I. Belyayev, key Khrushchev agriculture aide and a Soviet CP Presidium member, was named Dec. 26 to replace Ivan D. Yakovlev as Kazakh CP first secretary, presumably to speed production of grain in newly opened farm areas of Kazakhstan. Fazyl K. Karibzhanov replaced Nikolai I. Zhurin as Kazakh CP 2d secretary.

1958

Khrushchev consolidated his control of the Soviet Communist Party and government in 1958 by ousting Premier Nikolai Bulganin and becoming premier himself. By the end of the year, Bulganin was ready to confess that he had been a leader of the Molotov-led "anti-party" faction purged by Khrushchev in 1957. Aleksandr N. Shelepin, long associated with Khrushchev, replaced Gen. Ivan A. Serov as chief of the KGB, the USSR's security organization. Khrushchev repeated his desire to coexist peacefully with the West and to negotiate agreements to ban nuclear tests, control arms and prevent surprise attack by either East or West. The USSR joined Britain and the U.S. in suspending nuclear tests. Khrushchev indicated to East European Communist countries that the USSR would use force to put down anti-Soviet revolts. Farm reforms and other domestic programs were pressed to make Soviet life more agreeable.

KHRUSHCHEV IN COMMAND

Khrushchev Succeeds Bulganin as Premier

CP First Secy. Nikita S. Khrushchev replaced Nikolai A. Bulganin Mar. 27 as chairman of the USSR Council of Ministers, or premier. Khrushchev, 63, long believed to control both party and government, thus abandoned the public image of collective Soviet leadership and concentrated in one person the party and state powers separated since Stalin's death.

Khrushchev's elevation to premier came at a joint session of the newly elected Supreme Soviet following the routine resignation of Bulganin and his cabinet. Nominated by Soviet Pres. Kliment E. Voroshilov in the name of the CP Central Committee, Khrushchev was approved by unanimous voice vote of the 1,378 Supreme Soviet deputies present at the session. His election followed the reelection of Voroshilov as chairman of the Supreme Soviet Presidium—equivalent to president—and the approval of 32 others (Bulganin included, Khrushchev omitted) as members of the Presidium. Khrushchev's accession to the premiership had been believed probable since 1957, when Bulganin reportedly had backed the anti-Khrushchev faction led by Molotov. Khrushchev, addressing the Supreme Soviet following his installation as premier, declared: "I shall do everything to justify your confidence and shall not spare strength, health or life to serve you." "We shall conquer capitalism with a high level of work and a higher standard of living."

Bulganin was named board chairman of the USSR State Bank Mar. 31 as part of a general cabinet revision presented by Khrushchev and approved the same day by the Supreme Soviet. The bank chairmanship, which Bulganin had held in 1938-41, entitled him to cabinet membership despite his loss of ministerial rank. Bulganin also apparently retained his position in the Supreme Soviet Presidium.

Khrushchev's cabinet revision reestablished the rank of first deputy premier, abolished after the Molotov dispute. Deputy Premier Anastas I. Mikoyan and Frol R. Kozlov, a member of the CP Presidium and premier of the Russian Republic were promoted to the rank of first deputy premier. Other changes: Krasnodar CP chief Dmitri S. Polyansky replaced Kozlov as

Russian premier; Aleksandr F. Zasyadko of the State Planning Commission became a deputy premier and was replaced on the Planning Commission by Aleksandr A. Ishkov; Georgi V. Perov was named first deputy chairman of the State Planning Commission to replace Deputy Premier Aleksei N. Kosygin. Khrushchev retained the heads of all 19 government ministries and of all state committees with cabinet status except Aleksandr V. Domrachev, replaced as chairman of the Defense Technology Committee by Konstantin N. Rudnev. Col. Gen. Ivan A. Serov remained chairman of the State Security Committee (KGB).

The new Soviet cabinet, announced Mar. 31: Premier—Khrushchev; First Deputy Premiers—Miyokan and Kozlov; Deputy Premiers—Kosygin, Zasyadko, Dmitri F. Ustinov, Joseph J. Kuzmin; Foreign Affairs—Andrei A. Gromyko; Defense—Marshal Rodion Y. Malinovsky; Finance—Arseny V. Zverev; Interior—Nikolai P. Dudorov; Foreign Trade—Ivan G. Kabanov; Culture—Nikolai A. Mikhailov; Health—Maria D. Kovrygina; Agriculture—Vladimir V. Matskevich; Higher Education—Vyacheslav P. Yelyutin; Geology & Resources—Piotr Y. Antropov; Merchant Marine—Viktor G. Bakayev; Railways—Boris P. Beshchev; Communications—Nikolai D. Psurtsev; Medium Machine Building Industry—Yefim P. Slavsky; Trade—Dmitri V. Pavlov; Transport Construction—Yevgeny F. Kozhevnikov; Chemical Industry—Sergei M. Tikhomirov; Grain Products—Leonid R. Korniyets; Electric Power Stations—Aleksei S. Pavlenko.

A statement issued Mar. 27 by U.S. State Department press officer Lincoln White noted that Khrushchev had been the "real spokesman for the foreign and domestic policies of the Soviet Union." It said that his elevation to premier "clarifies a situation in which Mr. Khrushchev has been participating at meetings of heads of government, even though he occupied no official position."

Mikhail G. Pervukhin, Soviet foreign aid chief (chairman of the State Commission for Economic Relations with Foreign Countries), had been appointed Feb. 20 as Soviet ambassador to East Germany. Pervukhin, downgraded in the CP Presidium during the removal of ex-Foreign Min. Molotov in 1957, replaced ex-Amb.-to-East Germany Georgi M. Pushkin. Semyon A. Skachkov, Kharkov region economic council chairman and ex-first deputy transportation and machine building minister, succeeded Pervukhin Feb. 20 as foreign aid head.

The reorganization of the Chemical Industry Ministry as a non-cabinet governmental committee for the chemical industry was announced June 9 by Tass.

A Soviet CP Central Committee communique disclosed June 19 that Dmitri S. Polyansky, premier of the Russian Republic, and Nikolai V. Podgorny, first secretary of the Ukrainian CP, had been promoted to alternate membership in the CP Presidium. Leonid F. Ilyichev, Soviet Foreign Ministry press chief, had been named June 13 to replace Fyodr V. Konstantinov as head of the Soviet CP agitation and propaganda (Agitprop) section. Mikhail A. Kharlamov was named Foreign Ministry press chief. Konstantinov retained his post as editor of the CP ideological journal *Kommunist*.

First Deputy Foreign Min. Nikolai S. Patolichev, 50, formerly a Ukrainian CP secretary under Khrushchev, was named Aug. 26 to succeed Ivan G. Kabanov as foreign trade minister.

Bulganin Admits 'Anti-Party' Role

Ex-Premier Bulganin confessed before the Central Committee in Moscow Dec. 18 that he had joined and assumed "nominal" leadership of the "anti-party" group ousted by Khrushchev. Admitting that Khruschev's charges against him were "correct," Bulganin said: "When in 1957 the anti-party activities of Malenkov, Kaganovich, Molotov and Shepilov actively developed I joined them. I supported them and became their partisan..., nominally their leader. The anti-party group met in my office and there concerted their anti-party reactionary work." Bulganin said that the faction "always took a special stand which did not correspond to the general [party] line" in "domestic and foreign policy which the Central Committee had to rule on."

Bulganin denounced ex-Foreign Min. Molotov as a "man estranged from life and the people, who knew nothing of industry and agriculture." He described Malenkov as "an intriguer capable of any dirty trick and any abomination." Bulganin said that the party's "stern" action against the faction "helped me to realize all the harm of the group and to see the rottenness of the anti-party swamp in which I found myself."

A Central Committee communique issued at the end of the Moscow meeting Dec. 19 assailed the "anti-party" faction as a "despised group of reactionaries" who had attempted to prevent the attainment of goals set by the 20th CP Congress in 1956. It gave no indication, however, that Bulganin would be ousted as a Central Committee member or as chairman of the Stavropol Economic Council.

Khrushchev, in a CP Central Committee address reported Nov. 13 by *Izvestia,* had confirmed that Bulganin had been deposed for membership in the "anti-party group." Khrushchev charged that Bulganin had worked at organizing the group's "factional-splitting" activities.

(Stenographic records of the Dec. 15-19 Central Committee meeting were made public Jan. 6, 1959. They revealed that Soviet leaders in effect had denounced Bulganin as a liar for minimizing his role in the "anti-party group." Agriculture Min. Vladimir V. Matskevich declared that it was "untrue" that Bulganin "only joined the group at the last moment." Tatar CP First Secy. Semyon D. Ignatyev asserted that Bulganin's confession "sounded ... feeble and unconvincing.")

Bulganin had been removed Aug. 15 as chairman of the USSR State Bank and was appointed chairman of the Economic Council for the Stavropol region of the northern Caucasus. Bulganin was replaced as State Bank chairman by ex-Deputy Finance Min. A. K. Korovushkin. Bulganin's dismissal as a member of the CP Presidium was disclosed in Moscow Sept. 6.

Serov Loses KGB Command

Red Army Gen. Ivan A. Serov, 53, was transferred Dec. 9 from his post as chairman of the USSR's State Security Committee (KGB), responsible for Soviet internal security, espionage and counter-espionage. *Izvestia* announced that Serov, first chief of the security system revised after the execution of Lavrenti P. Beria in 1953, had been given other, unspecified duties. Serov, regarded as a Stalinist, had been elevated to security chief by the USSR's "collective leadership" of 1953-54. A former Ukrainian security chief and Red Army political commissar believed to have directed the deportation of Baltic peoples in the 1940s, Serov was the sole remaining Soviet cabinet member not intimately connected with Khrushchev.

Aleksandr N. Shelepin, 40, former Communist youth leader, succeeded Serov Dec. 25 as KGB chairman. Shelepin, who rose to prominence under Khrushchev as first secretary of the All-Union Komsomol (Communist youth league) Central Committee, had served since April as head of the CP Central Committee's section for mass organizations.

•

FOREIGN POLICY

East-West Relations

Many Soviet initiatives and statements during 1958 indicated a desire on the part of the USSR's leaders to promote amity with the West.

Khrushchev urged Jan. 27 that Eastern and Western heads of government meet and "attempt to agree on simple things first" before moving on to more complex and serious East-West disputes. Khrushchev, attending an Indian embassy reception in Moscow, listed an East-West non-aggression pact as one of the "simple things" that could be resolved easily. Khrushchev said: "You say you do not want to attack us. We do not want to attack you. Why don't we then get together and put that on paper?" Reminded that Western defense pacts had evolved from doubts of Soviet peaceful intentions, Khrushchev said: "We have everything we want. We do not have to take anything. All we want is peace."

U.S. Pres. Eisenhower disclosed Mar. 5 that Soviet leaders had been "kind enough" to send him a personal message offering to hold proposed East-West summit talks in the U.S. Mr. Eisenhower said at his news conference in Washington that he would favor a U.S. summit meeting, if the discussions proved to be lengthy, because a meeting in the U.S. would interfere less with the performance of his Presidential duties. Khrushchev personally offered Mar. 12 to attend summit talks in the U.S. Interviewed in Moscow by correspondents of the Warsaw *Trybuna Ludu,* Khrushchev said he realized "that because of a number of circumstances it is hard for the President...to leave his country." But Khrushchev, who conceded that a foreign ministers' conference to prepare summit talks was "probably inevitable," added that if "all substantive issues are discussed at a foreign ministers' meeting, why should we organize a summit conference?"

The USSR Mar. 31 announced an indefinite suspension of its nuclear tests and called on the U.S. and Britain to do the same.

Khrushchev formally appealed to Pres. Eisenhower and British Prime Min. Macmillan Apr. 4 for the U.S. and Britain to halt nuclear weapons tests, as the Soviet Union had done. The similar notes to the U.S. and British leaders were Khrushchev's first as Soviet premier. He renewed Soviet offers to establish an unspecified system of "appropriate international control" over nuclear test detonations. He stressed, however, that if the U.S. and Britain failed to halt atomic tests effective Mar. 31 (date of the Soviet ban), the USSR would be "free of the assumed commitment to end nuclear tests." Khrushchev asserted that continued nuclear tests had served to "whip up the arms race...thereby increasing greatly the danger of atomic war which looms over mankind." He declared that "the termination of experiments with atomic and hydrogen weapons will greatly improve the international political atmosphere [and] create more favorable conditions for the solution of other unresolved international problems." (Speaking at a rally in Budapest Apr. 4, Khrushchev challenged the U.S. and Britain to "prove their good intentions" by halting further atomic tests. He said: "If Eisenhower really thinks that we have stopped...tests for propaganda reasons, then why don't he and other Western statesmen conduct the same propaganda and stop the tests?")

Khrushchev informed the U.S. May 31 that the USSR was ready to begin East-West technical talks on enforcing an agreement to suspend nuclear tests. Khrushchev, replying to a May 9 proposal by Pres. Eisenhower for early talks on test-detection problems, announced Soviet willingness to begin such talks "within the next 3 weeks." Khrushchev, who accepted Mr. Eisenhower's suggestion for the inclusion of British and French nuclear experts, proposed that Polish, Czechoslovak and perhaps other scientists participate in the conference. He suggested that the conference be held in Moscow and aim at ending its work "within 3 or 4 weeks." (The talks were held in Geneva July 1-Aug. 22.) Khrushchev chided Mr. Eisenhower for his failure to reply to "the question of immediately discontinuing the tests." He expressed "anxiety" lest the technical talks "lead to a delay in settling the main issue, namely the suspension of tests."

The detonation of 2 Soviet nuclear devices in the USSR's atomic test area north of the Arctic Circle was reported Sept. 30 by the U.S. Atomic Energy Commission (AEC). The tests were the first reported held by the USSR since the Soviet announcement Mar. 31 of its unilateral suspension of nuclear tests. 2 more Soviet nuclear tests were reported by the AEC Oct. 2 and another Oct. 6. A Soviet government statement issued Oct. 3 by Tass confirmed that the USSR had resumed nuclear weapons tests. It said that the resumption had been "forced" by U.S. and British nuclear tests, which were "unprecedented in scope" and designed to gain "maximum unilateral military advantages" from the Soviet test cessation. The statement renewed Soviet offers to join the U.S. and Britain in an "immediate" and "universal" cessation of nuclear tests.

U.S. proposals for the convening Oct. 31 in Geneva of U.S.-British-Soviet talks on an international nuclear test ban had been accepted by Khrushchev in an interview published by *Pravda* Aug. 29 and in a Soviet note delivered to the U.S. and Britain Aug. 30. The U.S. and Britain announced Oct. 31 that they were suspending nuclear tests for a year on condition that the USSR did likewise. The Soviets then suspended tests Nov. 3.

Proposals for East-West technical talks on measures to prevent surprise attack by either East or West, raised by Pres. Eisenhower in a Jan. 12 note to then-Soviet Premier Bulganin, had been renewed July 2 by Premier Khrushchev. In a letter to Mr. Eisenhower, Khrushchev urged a meeting of experts from the U.S., USSR and possibly other nations to examine "recommendations on measures to prevent the possibility of surprise attack." Khrushchev, who ignored Mr. Eisenhower's prior suggestion of similar talks, proposed that the experts attempt to draft specific recommendations "within a definite time limit." He suggested that their recommendations be submitted at an eventual East-West summit meeting. The Soviet note, which dismissed Western views on preventing surprise attacks (said to have been transmitted to the USSR May 28), restated these Soviet suggestions for a guarantee against such attacks: (1) establishment of "control posts at railway junctions, big ports and motor highways"; (2) "definite disarmament steps...[and]

aerial surveys in areas that are of major importance from the viewpoint of preventing a surprise attack"; (3) removal "of the bulk of the armed forces of the 2 groups of powers in Europe to a depth of 800 kilometers east and west of the demarcation line between these forces"; (4) creation of "an aerial inspection zone which would include a part of Soviet territory in the Far East and a corresponding part of the [U.S.'] territory." (Preliminary talks were held in Geneva Nov. 10-Dec. 18 but ended in failure to agree even on an agenda.)

Khrushchev said July 12 that the USSR was prepared to negotiate a limited arms-control agreement with the West but could not accept complete disarmament with inspection until the development of mutual trust between East and West. Speaking at a Czechoslovak-Soviet rally in Moscow, Khrushchev said that Western demands for comprehensive disarmament inspection were designed to "deal out the enemy's vulnerable spots and to prepare aggression." "Is it possible," he asked, "when there is not even a minimum of trust, to start . . . multilateral control and inspection?" "Those who put the question" do not "speak seriously either about disarmament, control or trust," he declared. Khrushchev pledged, however, that "when there is full trust, when we see that nothing is being lined up against us . . . then we will be ready to open up all our borders and to show all we have." (In notes to the U.S. and West European governments July 15 the USSR inclosed a draft treaty of friendship providing for limited controlled disarmament, reduction of foreign forces in Germany and the establishment of an atom-free zone in mid-Europe.)

N.Y. Herald Tribune columnist Walter Lippmann, reporting Nov. 10-11 on a Kremlin interview granted by Khrushchev Oct. 24, said that Khrushchev had urged Western acceptance of the Socialist revolution in China, the USSR and Eastern Europe and of the nationalist revolution in Africa, the Middle East and Asia. Khrushchev, Lippmann reported, showed respect for the U.S.' military might but dismissed the U.S.' NATO policies on the ground that NATO Europe could be easily dominated by a rearmed Germany or by Soviet IRBMs (intermediate-range ballistic missiles) based in Eastern Europe. (Lippmann traced this attitude to Soviet mastery of the IRBM and short-range missile types and the presumed lack of an effective Soviet ICBM [intercontinental ballistic missile] that could break the U.S.-Soviet military balance.) Khrushchev predicted that the danger of Western-inspired nuclear warfare would increase as the West sought to block Soviet world leadership. He said the USSR's eventual predominance was guaranteed by the Soviet system's "multiplication of benefits" stemming from efforts, under the new 7-year plan, to surpass the U.S. in production and living standards.

Sen. Hubert H. Humphrey (D., Minn.) interviewed Khrushchev in the Kremlin Dec. 1. On his return to the U.S. Dec. 8, Humphrey told newsmen that the interview had convinced him that there would be no settlement of U.S.-Soviet political differences "for a long time." Humphrey predicted, however, that current Soviet economic plans "would depend on peace" "at least for 7 years."

Soviet Amb.-to-U.S. Georgi N. Zarubin and William S. B. Lacey, U.S. State Secy. John Foster Dulles' special assistant on East-West exchanges, had signed in Washington Jan. 27 a compromise agreement to establish a program of increased cultural, educational, technical and sports exchanges between the U.S. and USSR. The accord, under negotiation in Washington since Oct. 28, 1957, provided for official exchange visits by about 500 U.S. and 500 Soviet citizens during 1958. It also pledged each country to encourage private U.S.-Soviet tourism. The accord's specific provisions: (1) agreement "in principle" on a direct New York-to-Moscow air route with details subject to further negotiation; (2) "regular" radio and TV exchanges of cultural and educational broadcasts, special exchanges of news and political programs and radio, TV and record experts; (3) exchanges of specific numbers of delegations in industry, agriculture and medicine; (4) visits by writers, composers, performing artists, women's and youth organization representatives and talks on exchanges by U.S. and Soviet parliamentarians; (5) exchanges of feature and documentary films and film personalities, simultaneous premieres, talks on joint documentary film productions; (6) scientific exchanges, particularly in medicine and agriculture; (7) exchanges of staff and students between Moscow and Columbia, Leningrad and Harvard universities; (8) exchanges of athletes and publications. Zarubin, who left the U.S. Jan. 29 to become deputy to Soviet Foreign Min. Andrei A. Gromyko, told newsmen Jan. 27 that he regarded the exchange accord as his most important achievement in 5 years as Soviet ambassador in Washington.

A Soviet-U.S. film sale agreement, signed in Moscow Oct. 9 by Pres. Eric Johnston of the U.S.' Motion Picture Export Association and Vladimir Surin of the Soviet Culture Ministry, provided for the sale at $60,000-$67,000 each of 10 U.S. and 7 Soviet feature films for exhibition in the U.S. and USSR. The accord also provided for exchange visits by film personalities, and this section of the agreement was put into effect Nov. 18 when 18 Soviet motion picture personalities, including producer Yuri Raizman and actress Tamara Markova, arrived in New York for a 12-day U.S. visit. (An educational delegation led by First Deputy Education Min. A. I. Markushevich had arrived in Washington Nov. 16 for a 5-week tour of U.S. schools.)

A Soviet-U.S. cultural agreement signed in Washington Dec. 29 by Vladimir S. Alkhimov of the Soviet embassy and Frederick T. Merrill, director of the State Department's East-West Contacts Staff, provided for construction of a U.S. science-cultural exhibit in Moscow and a similar Soviet exhibit in New York in 1959. The U.S. exhibit, to be built in Moscow's Sokolniki Park, was to be managed by ex-Asst. Commerce Secy. Harold C. McClellan.

(The U.S. State Department's East-West Contacts Office reported Jan. 17, 1959 that 38 U.S. delegations and 33 Soviet groups had made reciprocal visits to the U.S. and USSR during 1958 under exchange accords. 5,000 U.S. tourists were reported to have visited the USSR, and 4 groups of 20 Soviet tourists traveled in the U.S.)

Satellites Warned Vs. Revolt

Visiting Hungary, Khrushchev Apr. 5 and 8 warned Hungarians in apparently contradictory statements against a repetition of their 1956 anti-Red uprising. Speaking in Sztalinvaros (later renamed Dunaujvaros), Khrushchev told steelworkers and Communist officials Apr. 5 that they "must not again depend on the Russians coming to your assistance in the event of another counter-revolution." "You must help your-selves" and be "so tough that the enemy will always be aware that the Hungarian working class will not waiver for a single instant," he said. Apologizing for his implied criticism, Khrushchev told workers that they must "distinguish clearly between friends and foes," be "more disciplined" and "raise your productivity."

Khrushchev modified his stand and assured a crowd in Tatabanya Apr. 8 that if anti-Communists attempted a *"putsch or a counter-revolution in any Socialist country,"* the other "Socialist countries and the armed forces of the Soviet Union are always prepared to unite, to provide help and to answer the provocation." Khrushchev said that his Sztalinvaros remarks, which had been deleted from the text broadcast by Budapest radio, had been intended to explain "that you must arrange matters so that there will be no new counter-revolution and we Russians will not be obliged to come to your assistance." Khrushchev, reportedly angered by the Tatabanya audience's cool response to his speech, said: "If you don't like my criticism, swallow it anyway and see that it does not leave a bitter taste in your mouth."

Ending his visit to Hungary, Khrushchev Apr. 9 defended Soviet intervention in the Hungarian revolt and denied "the lies and slanders of the imperialists who said in 1956 that it was the Hungarian workers who rebelled." Khrushchev conceded, however, that "the counter-revolutionaries ... were able to mobilize on their side a part of the people." He told Csepel Island industrial workers: "There was bloodshed in Budapest. We knew that part of the workers were fighting and that the West would accuse us of intervention. But it is the duty of a Socialist country to come to the aid of another Socialist country."

Yugoslavia Rejects Soviet Discipline

A Soviet CP Central Committee ultimatum demanding Yugoslav resumption of Soviet-bloc discipline was rejected in a Yugoslav CP message drafted May 19-20 and delivered in Moscow a few days later. The Yugoslav reply was said to have reaffirmed Yugoslavia's intention to remain independent and to have warned against any repetition of the 1948 Soviet-Yugoslav break.

A renewal of the Soviet rift with Yugoslavia was apparently confirmed May 27 when the Soviet government informed Yugoslavia that the USSR had postponed for 5 years the implementation of $285 million in Soviet credits pledged to Yugoslavia. The Yugoslav Tanjug news agency said May 28 that the aid delay had been "unilaterally proposed" in a note handed Yugoslav Amb.-to-USSR Veljko Mikunovic by Soviet

Foreign Min. Gromyko. The Soviet note reportedly suggested that Yugoslavia could be compensated partially for the postponement by an expansion of normal Soviet-Yugoslav trade. The postponed Soviet credits comprised $110 million pledged in Jan. 1956 for mine, fertilizer plant and power-station development and $175 million promised in Aug. 1956 for construction, with East German equipment, of a Montenegrin hydroelectric-and-aluminum project. The 2 loans had been postponed shortly after the Oct. 1956 Hungarian revolt but had been restored in July 1957 as part of Soviet efforts to restore normal relations with Yugoslavia.

In notes to the USSR and East Germany June 3, the Yugoslav government denounced the postponement and said Yugoslavia would refuse to negotiate any delay in pledged Soviet-bloc credits. The Yugoslav government warned that it would be forced to seek compensation unless the Soviet pledges were fulfilled. Yugoslav Foreign Ministry spokesmen May 31 had rejected, as "completely arbitrary," Soviet contentions that the delay was necessitated by recent decisions to expand the USSR's chemical industries.

In a message to Yugoslav Pres. Tito on Tito's 66th birthday, Khrushchev May 25 had expressed hope that "existing misunderstandings" between Yugoslavia and the Soviet bloc "will be overcome." But in his first public statement on the renewed Yugoslav-Soviet rift, Khrushchev June 3 condemned Yugoslav Communist leaders as "revisionists" and defended the 1948 Cominform denunciation of Yugoslavia as "basically correct." Khrushchev told the Bulgarian CP Congress in Sofia that Yugoslav leaders had acted as "spies of the imperialist camp" against the Soviet bloc. Khrushchev described modern revisionism as a Trojan Horse designed "to corrupt workers and Socialist parties from the inside, to split the unity of the Socialist camp and bring disorder and confusion to Marxist-Leninist ideology." Khrushchev derided Yugoslav and Western efforts to "find any shades of difference" in Soviet, East European or Communist Chinese attitudes toward revisionism. He indorsed recent Chinese statements that the 1948 offensive against Yugoslavia was correct and in "the interests of the revolutionary movement." He charged Yugoslavia with sheltering "predatory" leaders of the 1956 Hungarian revolt and said the USSR had made it clear that it would counter any future Yugoslav action "against any Socialist country."

Support of Arabs Increased

In a step underlining Soviet efforts to consolidate good relations with Arab nations, Egyptian Industry Min. Aziz Sidky and Mikhail G. Pervukhin, then chairman of the USSR's State Commission for Economic Relations with Foreign Countries, signed in Moscow Jan. 29 agreements providing for a reported 700 million-ruble 12-year loan at 2.5% and for increased technical assistance to Egypt. The loan was to be repaid in cotton and other farm products and "freely convertible currencies." The accord reportedly provided for many Soviet technicians to go to Egypt to work on projects planned under a 5-year, $750 million Egyptian development program.

Khrushchev May 15 pledged his support for an eventual union of "the Arab people" under Pres. Gamal Abdel Nasser of the United Arab Republic (Egypt). Khrushchev said at a Kremlin reception for Nasser, who was ending a state visit to the USSR, that Nasser had the USSR's "sympathy" and "will have the necessary help" for an Arab union "under your [Nasser's] leadership." Khrushchev assured Nasser of Soviet wishes that "no boot of a colonizer ever tread again on the soil of Egypt." Nasser reiterated his thanks to the USSR for breaking a Western "arms monopoly in our region" by shipping military equipment to Egypt. He said that his travels through the USSR had convinced him that only "imperialist, hostile, false propaganda says you are arming and preparing for war."

A joint Khrushchev-Nasser statement signed and issued in Moscow May 15 pledged UAR support for Soviet policies aimed at an East-West summit meeting, cessation of nuclear tests and Communist Chinese admission to the UN. It promised Soviet backing for "the legitimate rights of the Arabs of Palestine" and the "liberation" of African and Asian peoples. It condemned France's "barbarous war" in Algeria and other alleged aggressions against Yemen and Indonesia.

Cairo informants said May 17 that Nasser had won Khrushchev's agreement to a reduction of 20%-30% in the price of arms purchased from the Soviet bloc by Egypt and Syria and a 15% cut in the price of industrial goods ordered by the UAR.

An agreement signed in Cairo Dec. 22 by UAR Industry Min. Aziz Sidky and Chrmn. Pavel Nikitin of the Soviet cabinet's Foreign Relations Committee provided for Soviet construction of 5 airfields in Egypt and factories in the Suez Canal Zone.

DOMESTIC PROGRAMS

Better Life for All Sought

Programs for increasing the supply of consumer goods and reducing working hours were introduced in 1958 in an avowed effort to make life more pleasant for most Soviet citizens.

Prices were increased by the government by as much as 50% Jan. 2 for autos, motorcycles, vodka, wines, and carpets but were reduced for bread, some cameras and TV sets in an effort to offset an estimated 6 billion-ruble state revenue loss resulting from the abolition Jan. 1 of income taxes on small families, childless women and widows.

Plans to reduce by one hour the 8-hour work day of Soviet industrial workers and 7-hour day of Soviet miners were announced Apr. 21 by the CP Central Committee and Central Trades Union Council. The new measure, to be introduced by Sept. 1959, would cut the 6-day work week to 40 hours for workers in heavy industry and to 35 hours for miners. The USSR's State Committee on Wages & Labor was ordered to revise production and wage schedules, apparently by increased use of piecework rates, to narrow the gap between upper and lower Soviet wage levels.

The CP Central Committee, in special session May 6-7, approved Khrushchev's plans for a Soviet "offensive" on consumer goods production. The Central Committee said May 9 that the production drive would bring "considerable" increases in available clothing, shoes and household goods. "Offensive" goals set for achievement by 1965: artificial and synthetic fiber output to be increased by 460%, plastics and synthetic resins 800%, synthetic rubber 340%, artificial leather footwear 230%, woolen fabric 230%, cotton textiles 600%, artificial knitwear 900%. (Khrushchev said at a Czechoslovak embassy reception in

Moscow May 9 that the USSR would need "help" from East European states to meet its chemical and synthetics goal. He recommended that "sizeable orders" be placed with the U.S., British and West German chemical industries. He said that "when we make war, we make it on this basis—an offensive for more consumer goods.")

Soviet industrial officials were warned May 19 that nonfulfillment of production and delivery schedules had been made criminal offenses, punishable by "strict disciplinary measures" or fines of up to 3 months' salary. *Pravda* disclosed that industrial decentralization decrees adopted Apr. 24 by the Supreme Soviet Presidium also would impose penalties for "local tendencies" developing at the expense of the national economy. *Pravda* said the decrees gave governments and planning commissions of the USSR's 15 republics "full responsibility" for achieving economic goals.

The Soviet government and CP Oct. 4 announced orders of an immediate halt in the construction of all but apartment, hospital and school building projects. They ordered the scrapping of all recreational and administrative construction that could not be altered for housing or hospital use. The statements charged that unnecessary construction work was hampering fulfillment of pledges to end housing shortages.

In a televised speech Nov. 6 on the eve of the 41st anniversary of the Bolshevik revolution, Deputy Premier Mikoyan pledged continued efforts to raise the Soviet standard of living. Mikoyan appealed for expanded foreign trade. He assured the West that "war is not inevitable" despite current Soviet-U.S. differences.

The new 7-year plan—designed to increase Soviet industrial production by 80% during 1959-65—was presented to the CP Central Committee by Khrushchev Nov. 12 and made public in Moscow Nov. 14. The plan, providing for production increases of 85%-88% in heavy industry, 62%-65% in consumer goods and 70% in agriculture, was approved by the Central Committee Nov. 13. In a statement published Nov. 14 by Moscow newspapers, Khrushchev claimed that the new 7-year plan would give the USSR the highest per capita production rate in Europe by 1965 and in the world by 1970. Challenging the capitalist West to an all-out production race, Khrushchev predicted that the plan eventually would "insure" the USSR "the world's highest standard of living." He pledged that the USSR would continue efforts to introduce the 7-hour day in offices and factories and the 6-hour day in mines. The new 7-year plan was presented to the Soviet people as "an integral element" of a 14-year program to double or triple industrial production in 15 years. It promised them an increase of 62%-65% in national income and an average 40% increase in real wages. It pledged construction of 15 million city apartments and 7 million rural homes to alleviate the USSR's housing shortage.

The Supreme Soviet Dec. 23 approved a 1959 national budget providing for income of 723,369,159,000 rubles ($180,842,289,750 at official exchange rates) and expenditures of 707,637,887,000 rubles ($176,909,471,750). Introduced by Finance Min. Arseny Zverev, the budget programmed these major expenditures for 1959: industrial and other investments—484.3 billion rubles ($121.1 billion); defense—96.1 billion rubles ($24 billion); government administration—11.5 billion rubles ($2.9 billion); agriculture—30.3 billion rubles ($7.57 billion); education, health, social insurance and maternity benefits—232 billion rubles ($58 billion). The 1959 budget provided for increases of 12.69% in income and 12.74% in expenditures over the 1958 budget. Publicly acknowledged defense expenditures were reduced by 200 million rubles from 1958 levels (but many military appropriations were normally concealed in the investment, research and educational budgets).

Farm Reforms Started

Agriculture Min. Vladimir V. Matskevich disclosed Jan. 8 that 39 agricultural zones had been established in a move to decentralize farm planning and to spur output. Matskevich said that Soviet milk output had increased by 11% in 1957 (to 57.6 million metric tons), meat output by 14% (71.2 pounds per capita in 1956).

Gradual abolition of the machine and tractor-station system for supplying equipment to Soviet collective farms was proposed by Khrushchev in a speech in Minsk Jan. 22 (made public Jan. 25). He said that "the bureaucratic distribution of machinery" from the estimated 8,500 stations had caused "huge losses to the state" and should be replaced by collective farm ownership of equipment. He also urged consideration of proposals for collectivizing livestock that currently was owned privately. The CP Central Committee reported Feb. 27 that it had approved Khrushchev's plans to break up the state-owned farm machine-station system. It announced that, at a meeting Feb. 25-26, it had ratified the proposed sale of state farm equipment to collective farms. It urged the convening of a nationwide meeting of collective farmers in 1959 to discuss "further development of the collective farm system." The abolition of the machine-station system was approved by the Supreme Soviet at a joint session Mar. 31. Khrushchev, in his report to the Supreme Soviet, had conceded Feb. 28 that "some comrades" in the CP leadership had opposed ending the machine-station network on the ground that this would weaken state ownership of the means of production. He defended the move as necessary to increase food production. He proposed transformation of the machine stations into repair and sales centers, with the network's 1.5 1/2 million mechanics and 186,000 engineers absorbed into the collective farm system.

Khrushchev, speaking Apr. 26 in Kiev, blamed ex-Premier Georgi M. Malenkov for many Soviet agricultural failures during the Stalin regime. Khrushchev charged that Malenkov had opposed CP Central Committee decisions to cut farm taxes and to eliminate compulsory deliveries of collective farm products to the state. The compulsory deliveries, instituted early in the Soviet regime, were made at token prices. They served the dual purpose of levying direct taxes on the collective farm system and insuring a minimal supply of food for state disposal. A 2d quota of food was subject to "state purchase" at higher prices, while most remaining products were free for direct consumer sales at retail prices.

The CP Central Committee June 19 abolished the compulsory deliveries and replaced the system with government procurement of foodstuffs as ordinary "purchases" at higher, but undisclosed, price levels. The decision, intended to spur efficient collective farm production by restoring limited agricultural competition in the USSR, was considered to be part of Khrushchev's campaign for increased farm output at lower cost.

A CP communique said June 19 that the Central Committee, meeting in Moscow June 17-18, had also ordered an end to collective farm "payment in kind" for services of the recently abolished machine-station system. Collective farms were ordered placed on a cash basis and were freed of all debts-in-kind incurred for machine-station services or for nonfulfillment of compulsory delivery quotas. The announcement made clear that the government would continue to set collective farm production quotas and prices. It said, however, that prices would be revised to reflect actual production costs and stimulate cost-cutting and competition among collectives. It informed party workers that lowering farm production costs would be their "most important task" under the new system. It indicated that prices and procurement purchases would be rigged to force collectives into increased specialization.

Khrushchev asserted Oct. 14 that "the whole world will be amazed at the prospects of the development of Socialist economy" when goals of the USSR's new 7-year plan (1959-65) were made public. Speaking at a meeting in Stavropol, Khrushchev said that conditions were good for "gaining new victories" in the USSR's "movement forward to raise the living standards of the people." Ignoring reports that rain and cold had reduced current Soviet grain harvests, he claimed that state grain purchases Jan. 1-Oct. 10 were 14 million metric tons greater than in 1953 and meat purchases 62% greater for the same period. (The Soviet government disclosed Nov. 5 that 1958 grain deliveries to the state had reached a record 57 million metric tons after a harvest nearly equal to that of 1955. It reported that grain deliveries to the state had totalled 35 million tons in 1957.)

Speaking at the CP Central Committee's opening session, Premier Khrushchev charged Dec. 15 that the Malenkov-Molotov anti-party group had been responsible for Soviet agricultural failures while boasting of their achievements. Khrushchev's speech, reportedly the first to be made public while a Central Committee meeting still was in progress, claimed that recent Soviet agricultural progress began with his assumption of party leadership in Sept. 1953. It charged Malenkov with lying when he announced a 1952 grain harvest of 131 million metric tons when, in fact, the harvest had totalled 91 million tons. Khrushchev said that the faction had opposed (1) the drive "for catching up with the United States in per capita production of livestock" and (2) the development of virgin lands in Siberia and the eastern USSR.

A CP Central Committee communique Dec. 19 indorsed Khrushchev's agricultural policies, particularly the virgin-land development program, as "of decisive significance in increasing the output of grain and the improvement of the entire farming system."

Other Developments

The Soviet government had announced Jan. 6 that it would reduce its armed forces by 300,000 men during 1958. First Deputy Foreign Min. Vasily V. Kuznetsov and Gen. Mikhail S. Malinin, deputy army chief of staff, told newsmen that 41,000 men would be released from Soviet forces in East Germany, 17,000 from units in Hungary, the remainder from units in the USSR. Reductions would be made in army, navy and air force rosters. Western observers estimated that the new cuts, added to announced reductions of 640,000 in 1955-6 and 1,200,000 in 1956-7, would bring Soviet armed manpower down to 2,500,000 men. Kuznetsov termed the planned cuts a "new, serious contribution to the cause of easing tensions and creating confidence in the relations between states." He called on the NATO powers to follow the USSR's "act of goodwill" as an example and to act similarly to end the arms race. (The completion of the 300,000-man troop reduction by Jan. 1, 1959 was reported by Tass Jan. 30, 1959.)

The Defense Ministry confirmed Jan. 14 that Col. Gen. Aleksei S. Zheltov had been dismissed as chief of the armed forces' Main Political Administration. Zheltov, criticized for laxness in army, navy and air force political indoctrination following Marshal Georgi K. Zhukov's ouster as defense minister, was replaced by Col. Gen. Filip I. Golikov. It was disclosed Feb. 11 that Zheltov had been reassigned to work with the CP Central Committee and civil defense organizations.

Khrushchev, addressing the 13th Komsomol (Young Communist League) Congress in Moscow, called Apr. 19 for revision of the Soviet school system to prepare "every boy and girl, regardless of the position of his parents... for labor on a basis common for all." Khrushchev charged that many students had been helped into Soviet higher schools by "influential" parents guilty of a "snobbish mistaken attitude toward manual labor." He noted that of 1.15 million secondary school graduates in 1957, only 450,000 had gained entrance to higher schools (1/2 on part-time basis). He also urged expansion of the USSR's trade and technical school systems. (Secy. Aleksandr N. Shelepin of the

Komsomol Central Committee said at the Congress' opening session Apr. 15 that insufficient Komsomol indoctrination had permitted many Soviet youths to "fall prey" to Western propaganda and become idlers. V. E. Semichastny was named Apr. 19 to succeed Shelepin as Komsomol first secretary.)

A Khrushchev plan for revising the Soviet school system to provide increased vocational training and to encourage youth to begin full or part-time work at ages 14-15 was published throughout the USSR Sept. 21. The proposal, approved by the CP Central Committee Nov. 13, called for: (1) linking more education to "useful work" rather than to higher education available only to 1/3 or 1/4 of lower school graduates; (2) "all pupils without exception" to be "involved in socially useful labor in industry" or agriculture by age 15; (3) entry to universities to be made conditional on trade union and CP recommendation, with undergraduates required to continue part-time work. The new system would give all students obligatory schooling for 7 or 8 years, with major stress on science, technical training, labor education and "Communist morals." Students who wished to continue their studies would be compelled to prove themselves through work and further tests.

1,378 Communist Party candidates were elected to the Supreme Soviet in uncontested single-list elections Mar. 16. Returns reported Mar. 18 showed that 99.97% of the USSR's 133,836,325 registered voters had cast ballots. 580,641 negative or write-in ballots were cast against Soviet of the Union candidates, 363,736 negative ballots against Soviet of Nationalities candidates. 3 members of an official U.S. election delegation—Prof. Cyril E. Black of Princeton University, Richard Scammon of the Governmental Affairs Institute and managing editor Hedley W. Donovan of *Fortune* magazine— had arrived in the USSR Mar. 4 and observed ballot counting Mar. 17 in Moscow's Moskvoretski election district. They met Mar. 17 with Khrushchev and told newsmen Mar. 18 that Khrushchev had defended the Soviet election system but had conceded that nominations and voting were at all times controlled fully by the CP. Khrushchev also told the delegation: "We are all convinced we will overtake you. Our rate and tempo of growth is 3 or 4 times yours. I don't know when the lines will cross, but they are bound to do so. It's not a question of theory, but of facts." He warned that the U.S. "will always lag behind the Soviet Union from now on, not because Americans are less intelligent than the Soviet people," but because all Soviet youths had educational opportunities to "develop their talents."

The Soviet Defense Ministry newspaper *Krasnaya Zvezda (Red Star)*, lauding party leadership of the armed forces, reversed its past criticism of Stalin's World War II role and said Jan. 4 that he had been a "faithful Marxist-Leninist" who had ably analyzed the conduct of the war and had maintained the morale of Soviet forces.

Writing in the Jan. 30 issue of *Kommunist*, Marshal Aleksandr I. Yeremenko, World War II Stalingrad commander, lauded Khrushchev's contribution to the victory and dismissed past versions of Stalin's vital role in the battle as "not . . . historical reality."

Stalin's revised official biography, delayed for 2 years following Khrushchev's Feb. 1956 destalinization speech, appeared Feb. 14 with the publication of Vol. 40 of the *Great Soviet Encyclopedia*. The biography credited Stalin with the USSR's successful transformation into an industrial power and with preserving the early Bolshevik regime, but it condemned him for the purges of the 1930s, the unpreparedness for the attack by Nazi Germany and the failure to prevent the postwar break with Tito. It asserted that Stalin's serious errors began in 1934, when he "began to believe in his own infallibility and to act alone without taking account of the [CP] Central Committee's advice."

In an interview granted French newsman Serge Groussard Mar. 19 and published Apr. 9 by *Le Figaro* of Paris, Khrushchev expressed these views on Soviet Jews: "A true Jewish cultural community is no more realizable than a political community." The Jewish autonomous region of Birobidzhan failed due to "historical conditions" that made Jews individualistic and left Khrushchev "skeptical about the permanence of Jewish collectivities," including those of Israel. (The Anti-Defamation League of B'nai B'rith, in a report Aug. 17 entitled "Anti-Semitism in the Soviet Union Today," accused the Soviet government of "cultural genocide" against the USSR's Jewish population. The report asserted that Jews had been systematically removed from Soviet public life and that of 450 Jewish intellectuals arrested in 1948, 24 had been executed in 1952 "while the others have disappeared.")

The CP Central Committee June 8 dismissed 10-year-old charges of "formalistic perversion" against Dmitri D. Shostakovich, Aram Khatchaturian, the late Sergei Prokofieff and other leading Soviet composers and writers. A CP decree blamed the 1948 charges on the "cult of personality" under Stalin and ordered *Pravda* and all CP units to make amends for their "one-sided" criticism of Soviet artists. The decree made clear, however, that the party would continue to control music to guard against "unhealthy alien phenomena" and "modernistic tendencies." The decree also rehabilitated works by Soviet composers Vissarion Y. Shebalin, Gabriel Popov, Nikolai Y. Myaskovsky, Konstantin Dankevich and German Zhukovsky and writers Wanda Wasilewska and Aleksandr Y. Korneychuk.

A campaign for the expulsion from the USSR of author Boris Pasternak, winner of the 1958 Nobel Prize for Literature for his novel *Doctor Zhivago,* was begun Oct. 29 by Soviet officials and propaganda agencies. Speaking at a Moscow rally attended by Khrushchev, Secy. Vladimir Y. Semichastny of the Young Communist League called Oct. 29 for Pasternak to resettle in "his capitalist paradise" outside the USSR, and Semichastny pledged that the Soviet government would not hinder Pasternak's departure. 800 members of the Moscow branch of the Soviet Writers Union unanimously petitioned the government Oct. 31 to strip Pasternak of his Soviet citizenship and banish him if he refused to leave the USSR voluntarily. Pasternak, whose renunciation of the Nobel Prize was not reported in the USSR until Nov. 1, appealed to Khrushchev and the CP Central Committee Nov. 1 for permission to remain in the USSR. In a letter made public by Tass, Pasternak pleaded: "I am tied to Russia by birth, by life and by work. I cannot imagine my fate separated from and outside of Russia." "Leaving my homeland would equal death for me." Tass repeated Nov. 1 that Pasternak was free to go to Stockholm to accept the Nobel Prize and that the Soviet government would "not raise any obstacles" to his remaining abroad "permanently."

A new Soviet legal code approved by the Supreme Soviet Dec. 25 and published Dec. 27 incorporated some Western legal provisions for protection of accused persons. The new code (1) omitted punishment for relatives who failed to denounce traitors, (2) forbade prosecutors "to shift the burden of proof on the accused," (3) forbade evidence obtained "by force, threats and other unlawful means," (4) omitted past acceptance of confessions as final proof of guilt, and (5) permitted defense counsel for a defendant as soon as his preliminary investigation was completed. (The code provided up to 10 years of imprisonment for violations of Soviet airspace or flight regulations.)

1959

Khrushchev paid an unprecedented 2-week visit to the U.S., where he conferred with American leaders and outlined before the UN a plan for complete disarmament. At the 21st Soviet Communist Party Congress, Khrushchev predicted worldwide military and economic dominance for communism. The USSR renewed its assurances of support to the Arab nations. Action was taken to speed the expansion and integration of the economies of the East European Communist nations. Soviet leaders pressed efforts to improve and modernize Soviet agriculture and industry and to increase the output of consumer goods. There appeared to be increasing signs of a "thaw" in Soviet life and foreign relations, and the rehabilitations of previously denounced party and other figures continued.

Khrushchev Foresees Red Dominance of World

Premier Nikita S. Khrushchev told world Communist leaders Jan. 27 that the USSR had built an intercontinental missile arsenal that assured the Soviets of military dominance over the West. Addressing 1,375 Soviet delegates and heads of 70 foreign Communist parties, who had gathered in Moscow for the 21st Soviet Communist Party Congress, Khrushchev predicted that Soviet economic successes eventually would give communism "a complete and final victory" throughout the world.

Despite the Soviet ICBM lead, Khrushchev declared in this keynote address, the USSR was prepared to end the production and testing of missiles and nuclear weapons and to destroy its stockpile of these weapons as part of an East-West disarmament pact.

Khrushchev told his audience that Communist nations would continue to fight Yugoslav-inspired revisionism and that Western hopes for a split between the USSR and Communist China were "doomed to failure." He reported that there already were 33 million Communist party members in 83 countries (8,239,000 of them being members or candidate members of the Soviet CP), and he predicted that Soviet successes would attract to communism "new countries that had recently thrown off the yoke of imperialism."

(Despite the Soviet attack on Yugoslavia's Communist revisionism, Soviet and Yugoslav representatives in Moscow Jan. 28 signed a trade agreement providing for the exchange of $108 million worth of goods in 1959. The 1958 Soviet-Yugoslav trade pact had provided for the exchange of goods worth $124 million.)

More 'Anti-Party' Members Unmasked

Mikhail G. Pervukhin, Soviet ambassador to East Germany, and Maxim Z. Saburov, former deputy chairman of the State Committee for Foreign Economic Relations, were identified publicly Jan. 29 as members of the Molotov-Malenkov-Kaganovich "anti-party" group. Both men, leading economic planners and still members of the CP Central Committee, appeared before the 21st CP Congress in Moscow Feb. 3-4, 1959 to confess their errors as anti-party plotters.

Pervukhin and Saburov, demoted without explanation from their party and government posts in 1957, initially were linked with the anti-party group in a speech to the Congress Jan. 29 by Secy. Ivan V. Spiridonov of the Leningrad CP Committee. Spiridonov rejected ex-Premier Bulganin's confession of participation in the anti-party group and called on the plotters, including Pervukhin and Saburov, to make "an accounting to the congress... for your mistakes." The alleged anti-party group plot to depose Premier Khrushchev and take control of the Soviet government June 18, 1957 was described to the congress Jan. 30 by Aleksei I. Kirichenko, a CP Presidium member. Kirichenko said that only Khrushchev's June 14, 1957 summoning of the CP Central Committee had balked a party coup by Molotov, Malenkov, Bulganin, Kaganovich, Saburov and Pervukhin.

Pervukhin went before the CP Congress Feb. 3 and confessed his "mistake" in siding with the anti-party group against Khrushchev. Pervukhin insisted, however, that he had backed the plotters only in their economic policies and not in their attempt to replace Khrushchev as party leader. Pervukhin, first anti-party group member to admit that Khrushchev's ouster had been sought, confessed that he had been "incorrect" to doubt "the expediency" of Khrushchev's plan for reorganizing the USSR's industrial management system.

Saburov told the Congress Feb. 4 that his support of the anti-party group had been a result of his "political instability." He disclosed that currently he was employed as a factory manager in Syzran, a Volga River city near Kiubyshev. He admitted that he had supported attacks on Khrushchev and other Presidium members although he did not agree with the aims of the anti-party group. He asserted that he was trying "to atone" for his "mistake" by serving well in his current factory post.

Chrmn. Aleksandr N. Shelepin of the USSR's State Security Committee reported to the CP Congress Feb. 4 that police excesses committed by the late Lavrenti Beria had been eliminated and that the USSR's security system was continuing its battle against "agents smuggled into our country by the imperialist states." Shelepin pledged that his organization would do everything possible to "guarantee the security of the Soviet state and its citizens." Shelepin asserted that "the consequences of the hostile activity of Beria . . . have been eradicated. . . . Every Soviet citizen can rest assured that nothing like that shameful business will ever repeat itself."

(The congress adjourned Feb. 5 after adopting the new 7-year economic plan proposed by Khrushchev. The congress approved labor reforms incorporated in the new plan for establishing the 40-hour work week and 7-hour day by 1962 and for the introduction, beginning in 1964, of a 30-hour week for mine workers and 35-hour week for all others. The congress which took no action against alleged anti-party plotters, empowered the CP Central Committee to review "appeals about decisions on expulsions from the party [and] on party punishment." It unanimously adopted Khrushchev's suggestion that the 22d CP Congress be postponed from 1960 to 1961.)

A new official history of the Soviet Communist Party, published June 3, listed Marshal Kliment Y. Voroshilov, Soviet chief of state, among those CP Presidium members who had refused to "come out strongly" for Khrushchev during his "stubborn and bitter fight" in 1957 against the anti-party group. The book identified Mikhail A. Suslov, Yekaterina A. Furtseva, Nikolai M. Shvernik and Anastas Mikoyan as the Presidium members who had backed Khrushchev in his political battle with the Molotov-Malenkov-Kaganovich bloc. Prepared by a group headed by Boris N. Ponomarev of the CP Central Committee, the history denounced Stalin for "the evils of his cult of personality" and gave Khrushchev major credit for ending Stalin-era excesses. (East European political informants cited Feb. 21 by the *N.Y. Times* reported that Voroshilov had been an active member of the anti-party faction in its attempt to oust Khrushchev. Voroshilov, 78, was said to be the only member of the faction who had not confessed his role against Khrushchev and who had never joined the public denunciation of Stalin-era excesses.)

Khrushchev in the U.S., Urges Disarming

During an unprecedented visit to the U.S. Sept. 15-27, Khrushchev conferred at length with Pres. Eisenhower and other U.S. leaders and presented to the UN General Assembly a Soviet plan for "general and complete disarmament" within 4 years. At a White House dinner tendered by Mr. Eisenhower Sept. 15, Khrushchev said he had come to the U.S. to seek peace because "if we quarrel, then not only our countries can suffer colossal damage but the other countries of the world will also be involved in a world shambles." "Our countries have different social systems," he said. "We believe our system is better—and you believe yours to be better. But... we should not bring quarrels out onto the arena of open struggle. Let history judge which of us is right."

In his speech before the UN General Assembly in New York Sept. 18, Khrushchev presented a plan for all the nations of the world to disband their armed forces: "Military bases in foreign territories shall be abolished" during the 4-year disarmament period. "All atomic and hydrogen bombs at the disposal of states shall be destroyed and their further production terminated. The energy of fissionable materials shall be used exclusively for peaceful . . . purposes." The individual states would retain "only strictly limited contingents of police, of militia, agreed upon for each country, armed with small arms, . . . to maintain internal order and protect the personal security of the citizens." Khrushchev suggested that an "international control body comprising all states" be established to initiate a "system of control over all disarmament measures."

"If at present... the Western powers do not manifest their readiness to embark on general and complete disarmament," Khrushchev added, "then the Soviet government is ready [to agree on]... partial steps of disarmament and the strengthening of security."

W. Averell Harriman, former New York governor and wartime ambassador to the USSR, had been told by Khrushchev in 3 lengthly Kremlin interviews June 23-24 that the USSR would not retreat from its stated intentions to oust the Western Allies from Berlin and to surpass the U.S. in industrial production.

161

Harriman's account of the interviews, published in North American Newspaper Alliance articles and in the July 13 issue of *Life* magazine, portrayed Khrushchev as "blunt and threatening" in his assessment of the Berlin situation. Harriman quoted Khrushchev as warning the West that "if you send in tanks [to Berlin], they will burn, and make no mistake about it." "If you want war, you can have it," he warned, "but remember, it will be your war. Our rockets will fly automatically."

Harriman quoted Khrushchev as saying he was convinced that communism would triumph over capitalism and that this victory would be foreshadowed, in 1970, by the USSR's achievement of 70% of the U.S.' 1957 production levels. Khrushchev held that the U.S.' system of democratic capitalism was doomed by its reliance on war for profits whereas the USSR was recovering from its backwardness and the excesses of Stalin's rule. He noted that the 21st Soviet CP Congress had declared that war was not inevitably caused by degenerating capitalism and imperialism and that Soviet-U.S. accords could prevent war.

Harriman said that Khrushchev was accompanied by Soviet Foreign Min. Gromyko at the interviews but that Khrushchev asserted that Gromyko could say nothing except "what we tell him to" and had been instructed to tell the West that "these days of the [Berlin] occupation are gone forever."

Soviet terms for establishing "peaceful coexistence" between East and West were explained by Khrushchev in an article in the October edition of the U.S. quarterly *Foreign Affairs*. Khrushchev's article contained a warning that the world faced "2 ways out: either war . . . or peaceful coexistence." He listed these 3 basic Soviet conditions for coexistence: (1) the abandonment of Western efforts to "roll back" communism from Eastern Europe, China and other areas it had taken over since World War II; (2) the acceptance of Soviet proposals for settling the disputes over Germany and Berlin and for suppressing "West German militarists and revanchists," and (3) the removal of U.S. restrictions on trade with the USSR to provide a "good basis for improvement of relations between our countries."

In his *Foreign Affairs* article, Khrushchev denied U.S. Vice Pres. Richard M. Nixon's contention that coexistence was a negative concept based on perpetual division of the world into opposing camps. Khrushchev said that "the coexistence of states with different social systems does not mean that they will only fence themselves off from one another by a high wall and undertake...not to throw stones." Coexistence, Khrushchev held, was the first step toward "peaceful competition for the purpose of satisfying man's needs in the best...way." He asserted that the 20th CP Congress had "made it perfectly clear...that the allegations that the Soviet Union intends to overthrow capitalism in other countries by 'exporting' revolution are absolutely unfounded." The USSR, he said, aimed at maintaining "the positions of ideological struggle without resorting to arms in order to prove that one is right." Khrushchev challenged the leaders of the capitalist countries to "try out in practice whose system is better...,[to] compete without war." He assured Western leaders that if "the Soviet Union and the countries friendly to it are not attacked, we shall never use any weapons either against the United States or...any other countries." "Peaceful coexistence is the only way which is in keeping with the interests of all nations," Khrushchev said. "To reject it would mean under existing conditions to doom the whole world to a terrible and destructive war at a time when it is fully possible to avoid it."

First Deputy Premier Anastas I. Mikoyan had visited the U.S. Jan. 4-20 for a tour during which he met Pres. Eisenhower and other U.S. leaders. He asserted that the USSR was eager to settle East-West differences but was not willing to alter its policies on major issues.

At a dinner in Washington Jan. 5, Mikoyan had hinted that a meeting between Mr. Eisenhower and Khrushchev might deal successfully with many East-West problems. According to Mikoyan: (a) Soviet leaders had no aggressive intentions against the U.S. but were hoping for peaceful East-West competition; (b) the Stalin regime's excesses were being corrected by measures to reduce police powers and decentralize industrial and agricultural management; (c) the USSR seriously regarded itself as threatened by U.S. overseas military bases and the proposed nuclear armament of West Germany; (d) the USSR intended to withdraw its occupation forces from Berlin within 6 months and was willing to discuss proposals for UN supervision of a "free Berlin."

Addressing the Chicago Law Club as a guest of Adlai E. Stevenson's, Mikoyan conceded Jan. 9 that the USSR had suffered from police abuses, but he insisted that these had been eliminated by the reduction of police powers and the strengthening of the court system. He asserted that there had been no death sentences for "political matters" since the ouster of Soviet security chief Lavrenti P. Beria (who was executed in Dec. 1953, some 5 months after his removal from office).*

At a press conference at UN Headquarters in New York Jan. 15, Mikoyan held that "capitalism will continue so long as the people...involved will support" it and that when they end this support, "they will overthrow it." Therefore, he said, "our people do not need or want to interfere in the internal affairs of other countries" but would prefer to "compete with and emulate each other" in raising living standards.

First Deputy Premier Frol R. Kozlov also toured the U.S. during 1959. He told reporters aboard his California-bound plane July 3 that: He favored the doctrine of "separate roads to socialism" as advanced by Khrushchev in 1955. National Communist parties were linked only by their common belief in Marxism; none, including the U.S. CP, were dominated by the USSR, which "has never interfered in the internal affairs of even the smallest country, let alone of such a mighty country as the United States."

At a farewell press conference in New York July 12, Kozlov said he fully agreed with Khrushchev's 1957 prediction that "your grandchildren in America will live under socialism," but he rejected, as a "profound delusion," U.S. "apprehensions that ideological differences between us are the major obstacles to peaceful coexistence between our countries." He asserted that the ideological dispute between capitalism and communism "will be settled by history...through peaceful competition" and "the struggle for securing higher living standards." "We are convinced," he added, "that victory in this competition will be with us."

---

*Among those officially reported executed after Dec. 1953 but before Mikoyan's visit were: ex-Soviet State Security Min. Viktor Abakumov and 3 ministerial assistants, deaths announced Dec. 23, 1954; ex-Georgian Internal Security Min. N. M. Rukhadze, ex-Georgian State Control Min. A. N. Rapava and 4 other Georgian Soviet government and police officials, deaths announced Nov. 22, 1955; ex-Azerbaidzhan Premier Jafar Bagirov, ex-Azerbaidzhan Vice Commissar for Security R. A. Makarian, K. I. Grigorian and T. M. Bortschev, deaths announced May 28, 1956.

Support of Arabs Renewed

United Arab Republic Pres. Gamal Abdel Nasser announced at a Cairo rally Feb. 21 that he and Khrushchev had exchanged pledges of renewed Soviet-UAR goodwill and cooperation. Nasser said he had written to ask Khrushchev about "the future intentions of the Soviet Union" toward the UAR after Khrushchev had rebuked the UAR for suppressing domestic Communists. Nasser said Khrushchev had replied Feb. 20 that the UAR's handling of Egyptian and Syrian Communists (Egypt and Syria were then federated) was "a matter of internal policy which concerned the [UAR] alone."

Reports that the USSR might let some of its 3 million Jews emigrate to Israel were rejected by *Izvestia* Feb. 21 as "provocative fabrications." The government newspaper said that mass emigration of Soviet Jews to Israel would increase Israel's military potential against the Arab states and would not be tolerated by the USSR. *Izvestia* charged that the reports had been spread by the West "to sow seeds of mistrust" between the USSR and the Arab states.

East European Economic Integration

The Council of Mutual Economic Aid, representing the USSR, Poland, Czechoslovakia, Hungary, Rumania, Bulgaria and Albania, met in Tirana May 13-16 and agreed on plans for faster expansion and integration of the economies of the member states. A final communique disclosed council decisions: (a) to build a new East European electricity grid that would link the East German, Polish, Czechoslovak, Hungarian and Rumanian power networks with the USSR's Ukrainian and Kaliningrad (East Prussia) grids; (b) to increase Soviet-bloc production in 1959-65 by 53.5% for coking coal, by 180% for pig iron and by 170% for steel and rolled steel; (c) to increase machine construction specialization, with East Germany and Poland to produce special steel rolling mills, the USSR and Czechoslovakia ordinary mills, Hungary and East Germany wire machinery, Rumania and the USSR oil refining and drilling equipment; (d) to increase Soviet-bloc internal trade by 170% in 1959-65.

DOMESTIC AFFAIRS

Khrushchev Seeks Farm Improvements

Touring Ukrainian and Moldavian farm areas, Khrushchev called on Soviet collective farmers May 10-12 to improve food production and to increase efficiency in an effort to meet 7-year-plan farm goals and overtake the U.S. in food output. Addressing farmers in Krasnaya Slobodka in the province of Kiev, Khrushchev said May 10 that the USSR's economic goal was "more products with a minimum expenditure of means and labor." He urged the production of quality crops suitable to the land being farmed and lauded the Ukraine's introduction of Iowa corn-growing techniques. He urged Ukrainians to reconsider the suggestion of forming large farm cities along the lines of the *agrogorod* ("agro-city") system proposed in 1951 but never adopted. Speaking in Kiev May 11, Khrushchev urged that collectives keep members' wages at reasonable minimum levels to increase surpluses for investment in communal production and services. He expressed fear of a return of the *kulak* (wealthy farmer) mentality among members of successful collectives. Khrushchev told a Kishinev audience that the USSR could surpass the "developed capitalist countries in [farm] production . . . only under conditions of sharp improvements of the productivity of labor" through mechanization and organization.

The CP Central Committee, meeting in the Kremlin Dec. 22-25, approved plans to tighten regional party control over Soviet agriculture. It asked the CP Presidium to study proposals to create regional agricultural associations or trusts to control the collective farm system. The party-controlled associations would be similar to commissions recently established to direct Soviet industrial enterprises.

A communique issued by the Central Committee indicted Kazakhstan's leadership for "serious shortcomings" that were found responsible for a 26% decline in Kazakhstan grain output in 1959 (but it predicted that the USSR would produce 62 million tons of milk and 845,000 tons of butter in 1959 and surpass U.S. output of both products). At the Central Committee meeting, Khrushchev attacked Kazakhstan CP Secy. Nikolai I. Belyayev

Dec. 25 for trying to conceal his "bad, very bad," administration of Kazakhstan agriculture. Khrushchev warned Belyayev, despite their "friendship," that "when an executive fails to cope with an assignment he is replaced." Khrushchev included in his criticism Kazakhstan Premier Dinmukhamed A. Kunayev and Soviet Agriculture Min. Vladimir V. Matskevich.

Industrial Modernization Pressed

At an extraordinary plenary session held in Moscow June 24-29, the CP Central Committee ordered Soviet economic planners to submit detailed programs by Sept. 1 for the modernization of Soviet industry required to meet 7-year-plan goals.

Resolutions approved at the plenum and made public in a June 30 communique proclaimed this program for eliminating waste and inefficiency and for building a modern Soviet industrial system: (a) technical progress and "material stimulus" for higher production; (b) "the reconstruction and development of existing enterprises" and "more effective use of capital investment" (investments for modernization were said to renew themselves 2-1/2 times faster than investments in new plant); (c) "integrated mechanization and automation of production" as the key to increased output (50% of the USSR's labor force was said to be engaged in "ancillary work," 65% of construction workers in "manual work" and 25% of all Soviet workers in "poorly mechanized loading and unloading"); (d) specialization and cooperation to create "new economic links" among the USSR's industrial regions and to suppress regional "parochialism"; (e) an increased "role for science in technical progress" and the elimination of duplication and waste in research; (f) improved CP control of the Soviet economy and executive decisions and the replacement by "younger experts" of "leaders who have stopped growing."

The Central Committee warned that officials who failed to carry out the new industrial program would be "severely punished." It ordered the State Planning Commission and other industrial agencies to submit within 3 to 6 months "new proposals for improving financial controls in industry and construction" and "designs of new machinery and of new equipment for mass production."

Khrushchev said at the plenum June 29 that Soviet industrial production had increased by 11% during 1959's first 5 months. But he warned that the USSR's industrial successes were endangered by waste, low productivity, "arbitrary use of capital investment and material resources for local needs" and "shortcomings in the engineering industry" and bureaucracy. Khrushchev charged that Soviet industrial managers (*nachalstvo*) had protected themselves from criticism and change. He warned that party organizations would be ordered to check on the performance of leading personnel.

The government and CP Central Committee Oct. 16 ordered immediate steps to increase consumer goods production by 42% over 1958 output within 2 years. Announcements published in the press pledged a redesigning of all Soviet consumer goods to "match the best foreign samples" and substantial increases in output to meet the USSR's "ceaselessly growing" demand. The statements conceded that the Soviet Union had "a shortage of TV sets, pianos, children's bicycles, washing and sewing machines, refrigerators" and other household appliances. Party and industrial planners were ordered "to take measures for a considerable increase in the production and expansion of the variety, in improvement of quality of these goods." (The Soviet book *The Economy of the USSR in 1958* reported that 1958 Soviet production was devoted 28.4% to consumer goods and 71.6% to industrial goods.)

Toward the year's end the State Committee on Labor & Wages issued regulations limiting Soviet workers' productivity bonuses to 50% of their basic pay and linking bonuses to production costs rather than to quantity.

Signs of 'Thaw' Continue

Among other apparent signs of a "thaw" in Soviet life and foreign relations was the announcement in *Izvestia* Mar. 29 that Sebastopol and other Crimean areas would be opened to foreign tourists in the summer.

Additional political rehabilitations of purged former Communist leaders were disclosed in a new edition of the 10-volume *Soviet Small Encyclopedia*. Among those rehabilitated (dates of their death in parenthesis) were: A. Y. Arosev (1938), writer and diplomat; Yan A. Berzin (1941), Latvian Communist International leader; P. P. Blonsky (1941), psychologist; Gleb I. Bokii (1941), secret police official; Mikhail I. Vasiliev-Uzhin (1937), Soviet Supreme Court deputy chairman 1934-7; I. I. Vatzetis (1938), Frunze Military Academy director; Aleksandr K. Voronsky (1943), writer and Trotskyite; Aleksei K. Gastev (1941), poet and former director of the Central Institute of Labor; Mikhail P. Gerasimov (1939), poet, and Artem Vesyoly (1939), writer.

Khrushchev, addressing the 3d Soviet Writers Congress in the Kremlin May 23, ordered an end to the campaign against "revisionism" in Soviet literature. He told the 2,000 delegates of the Soviet Writers Union that the "revisionists have suffered full defeat" and must be aided "in their transition from mistaken views to the correct principled positions." Khrushchev specifically cleared Vladimir Dudintsev, author of the novel *Not by Bread Alone,* who, Khrushchev said, had "noted certain negative features" of Soviet life "in an exaggerated... form" but "was not against the Soviet system." Khrushchev told the writers that First Deputy Premier Mikoyan had urged him to read *Not by Bread Alone* because it contained "some observations that sound as if he [Dudintsev] had been eavesdropping on you [Khrushchev]."

At its opening session May 18, the Writers Congress had approved the rehabilitation of Konstantin M. Simonov, condemned for his role in the publishing of *Not by Bread Alone,* Ilya Ehrenburg, criticized for his novel *The Thaw,* and Margarita Aliger, nonconformist poet denounced by Khrushchev in 1957 for deviationism.

Major Posts Change Hands

Health Min. Maria D. Kovrygina was released from her post Jan. 1 and was replaced by Health Min. Sergei V. Kurashov of the Russian republic.

Deputy Premier Joseph J. Kuzmin was dismissed Mar. 20 as chairman of the USSR's State Planning Commission and deprived of his deputy premiership. He was replaced as chief Soviet planner by Deputy Premier Aleksei N. Kosygin, 55, deputy chairman of the State Planning Commission and chief aide to First Deputy Premier Mikoyan on consumer goods production. Kuzmin, 55, credited with carrying out Khrushchev's plans for decentralization of Soviet industry, was named chairman of a new State Scientific-Economic Council established Feb. 28 to coordinate all Soviet scientific research with development planning. He retained cabinet minister's rank. (Deputy Premier Aleksandr F. Zasyadko was appointed Apr. 22, 1960 to replace Kuzmin as chairman of the State Scientific-Economic Council.)

First Secy. Vladimir Y. Semichastny of the Communist Youth League (Komsomol) was replaced Mar. 25 by Sergei Pavlovich Pavlov, former secretary of the Moscow Komsomol.

Aleksei I. Adzhubei, 34, editor of *Komsomolskaya Pravda* and a son-in-law of Khrushchev's, was appointed May 26 to succeed Konstantin A. Gubin as editor of *Izvestia,* the Soviet government newspaper.

Ex-Heavy Machine Building Min. Konstantin Petukhov replaced Yuri Maksarev Dec. 25 as chairman of the State Science & Technology Committee.

Other Developments

The Supreme Soviet Presidium Apr. 7 issued decrees abolishing the Agricultural, Communal and Communal & Housing Construction banks and centralizing all Soviet banking functions in the Soviet State Bank and Capital Investment Bank.

Chairman A. Stepanov of the State Committee on Labor & Wages disclosed Apr. 14 that the salaries and privileges of Soviet scientists would be made dependent on the quality of their work rather than on their titles and academic rank. A new constitution for the Soviet Academy of Sciences, approved by the Soviet government, apparently gave scientists more control over research. The new constitution increased the powers of the academy's General Assembly, emphasized that the academy Presidium was subordinate to the assembly and put the academy directly under the control of the Soviet cabinet.

Under decrees issued June 27, all universities and specialized high schools were removed from the control of the Ministry of Higher & Special High School Education and placed under the direct supervision of the 15 Soviet republics. The changes, made as part of Khrushchev's program for decentralizing most Soviet institutions, gave the republics control of school financing and curriculum.

The 1960 Soviet budget, providing for revenues of 772.1 billion rubles and expenditures of 744.8 billion rubles, was presented to the Supreme Soviet Oct. 27 and approved Oct. 30. As presented, the budget, whose size set a peacetime record, earmarked major expenditures for science and heavy industry but maintained defense spending at the 1959 levels of 96.1 billion rubles, or 12.9% of the total budget. The Supreme Soviet, however, raised the expenditures figure to 745,808,593,000 rubles and the revenues total to 772,990,487,000 rubles.

1960

A carefully planned East-West summit conference in Paris collapsed on its opening day after the shooting down of a U.S. reconnaissance plane over the USSR some 2 weeks before the conference was to start. Khrushchev, who blocked the conference by insisting that it could not start unless Pres. Eisenhower apologized for the spy-plane incident, went to New York 4 months later to appear at a UN meeting, where efforts to reschedule the summit conference proved futile. World Communist leaders met during 1960 and supported the Khrushchev view—against the Communist Chinese stand—in favor of peaceful Communist coexistence with the West. The Soviet government decided to make an additional 1,200,000-man cut in its armed forces. Increases in industrial production were reported, but there appeared to be trouble in the farm program.

Khrushchev in France, Warns Vs. Germany

Premier Khrushchev, visiting France Mar. 23-Apr. 3, warned repeatedly that a rebirth of German militarism threatened France and Europe and could be stopped most effectively by a French-Soviet alliance based on principles of peaceful coexistence. Answering French Pres. Charles de Gaulle's greeting at Orly Airport Mar. 23, Khrushchev said: "It is not rare to find still in the Soviet Union, as in France, unexploded bombs and shells.... In these cases our engineers take them in hand carefully ... and they eliminate these dangerous vestiges of the war. We others, government leaders, we must do the same in cleaning from our old and beautiful earth the remains of these somber years of war. It is a difficult ... task, but the people will say 'thank you' to us."

Khrushchev said at a Paris rally of the France-USSR Society Mar. 23 that Soviet foreign policy was based on "Leninist" principles that implied "complete renunciation of war," but he added that the USSR could not give "guarantees that communism will not advance ... and will not spread to the non-Communist world." Quoting the late Frederic Joliot-Curie's "remarkable words that ideas travel without visas," Khrushchev declared: "We are no hypocrites.... We do believe in the ideas of communism, we do believe that they will win out. But ... we have always been opposed to the spreading of any social system by violence."

In a toast to de Gaulle and France at an Elysee Palace state dinner later Mar. 23, Khrushchev said: "We know that in France you are aware ... of the threat of a [German] revenge ... and want to prevent the growth of this threat by different methods from ours." "We are of the opinion that, so that militarism and aggression should no longer threaten the peace of Europe, it is necessary to finish with the last traces of the 2d World War and to conclude a peace treaty with Germany.... All the former partners of the anti-Hitler coalition would gain from it, as well as the German people."

Meeting Mar. 25 with French National Assembly deputies who were members of various French-Soviet friendship groups, Khrushchev declared that "the possibility of a [territorial] change in favor of Germany from the East is excluded completely and forever. Germany will seek, therefore, finally an opening to the West. You will recall my words." Khrushchev admitted that he had come to France with the hope that he could prevent the total rearmament of West Germany. He asserted that if he succeeded in preventing the repetition of pre-World War II history, "I will have fulfilled my duty toward the Soviet people." "Now Hitler is no more," he declared, "but German militarism and the spirit of revenge are always alive." Defending the 1939 German-Soviet pact, which preceded the invasion and partition of Poland, Khrushchev said it had been made necessary by British and French efforts to turn Nazi aggression from themselves against the USSR.

Khrushchev's talks with de Gaulle ended without agreement on any major East-West dispute. They agreed, however, to have their representatives negotiate a "long-term commercial agreement" providing for "a substantial increase in trade between the 2 countries." They signed protocols (a) for "exchanges of information...[and] personnel and the carrying out of programs...in the fields of oceanography,...biological reactions, neurophysiology, the fight against cancer and leukemia,...chemistry and physics" and (b) for specific exchanges of personnel, information and equipment "to promote reciprocal scientific and technical collaboration in...peaceful use of atomic energy."

(Khrushchev confirmed Oct. 7 that the USSR had given "*de facto* recognition" to the rebel Algerian Provisional Government and would grant "the utmost aid possible to help them obtain their freedom" from France. Khrushchev, addressing the UN Correspondents Association in New York, said that the USSR was sympathetic to the Algerian rebels and to all "colonial peoples fighting for their independence." Rebel Premier Ferhat Abbas visited the USSR Oct. 6-10 and then said he had been promised Soviet aid.)

Spy Plane Affair Wrecks Summit Parley

2 weeks before a carefully planned East-West summit conference was scheduled to open in Paris, a U.S. U-2 high-altitude reconnaissance plane was shot down May 1 near Sverdlovsk in the central USSR while on a military intelligence mission. The incident effectively wrecked the East-West meeting, and it caused a heightening of U.S.-Soviet animosity that persisted for months.

The U-2 mission, initially denied by the U.S., was admitted after the USSR announced the capture of the pilot, ex-USAF First Lt. Francis Gary Powers, 30. Powers was described as a civilian pilot employed by the Lockheed Aircraft Corp. for the U.S.' National Aeronautics & Space Administration, ostensibly to fly the U-2 for a weather research project. Powers, stationed at a U.S. air base at Incirlik, near Adana, Turkey, actually was flying intelligence missions for the Central Intelligence Agency.

The disclosure of the U.S. reconnaissance flight and of its interception in "the interior of the Soviet land" was made by Khrushchev May 5 in an address to the Supreme Soviet. Khrushchev said an unmarked U.S. plane had been sent across the USSR's frontier on May Day "from Turkey, Iran or Pakistan" and had been "shot down" on orders from Moscow. He said that a similar flight had taken place Apr. 9 but that the plane had been permitted to leave the USSR unmolested and no diplomatic protest made. He declared angrily that the 2d flight was "an aggressive provocation aimed at wrecking the summit conference" and had been stopped.

Khrushchev warned May 8 that nations that permitted their airfields to be used for US air intelligence missions against the USSR risked destruction from Soviet missiles. Speaking at a Czechoslovak embassy reception in Moscow, Khrushchev addressed his warning to "those countries that ... allow others to fly from their bases to our territory." "If you leased your territory to others and are not the masters of your land, ... we shall find the range," he declared. Khrushchev reportedly singled out Norwegian Amb.-to-USSR Oscar Gundersen and Pakistani Amb.-to-USSR Salman Ali to make clear his intent.

The East-West summit conference collapsed at its opening session in Paris May 16 when Khrushchev refused to begin talks unless Pres. Eisenhower formally apologized for sending U.S. aircraft across the USSR. Efforts of French Pres. Charles de

Gaulle and British Prime Min. Harold Macmillan to persuade Khrushchev to continue the conference failed May 17 despite Mr. Eisenhower's assurances that U.S. espionage flights over the USSR had been suspended after the May 1 incident and would not be resumed. Khrushchev's use of the plane incident to break up the summit meeting apparently violated his pledge, issued May 14 on his arrival in Paris, to "make the conference a success" for "the consolidation of the peace and security of nations."

Making clear that he considered Mr. Eisenhower personally responsible for the U.S.' military reconnaissance of the USSR and the deterioration of U.S.-Soviet relations, Khrushchev May 16 withdrew his invitation for a scheduled June visit of the President to the USSR. He said the "provocative flights of American military planes" had deprived the USSR of the "possibility to receive the President with the proper cordiality with which the Soviet people receive welcome guests."

Khrushchev stated these 3 conditions—to be met by the U.S.—for possible continuance of the Paris meetings: (1) condemnation of "the inadmissible provocative actions of the United States Air Force with regard to the Soviet Union"; (2) assurances that the U.S. would "refrain from continuing such actions," and (3) punishment of "those who are directly guilty" of the flights.

Without waiting for Mr. Eisenhower's reply, Khrushchev said that the U.S.' policy, justifiable "only when states are in a state of war," had doomed "the summit conference to failure in advance." Khrushchev declared that he could not "be among the participants in negotiations where one of them has made treachery the basis of his policy with regard to the Soviet Union." For a summit meeting to have a chance of success, the U.S. would have to confess "that it has committed aggression and admit that it regrets it," he declared.

Pres. Eisenhower replied that the U.S. had ended the spy flights and would not resume them. But he said the U.S. would "never" accept Khrushchev's "ultimatum" for summit talks.

Khrushchev Backs Cuba Vs. U.S.

Khrushchev warned July 9-11 that the USSR would support the Castro regime with rockets if the U.S. intervened in Cuba. He said that the USSR no longer considered the Monroe Doctrine a valid basis for U.S. domination of Latin America.

In a televised Kremlin speech to a Soviet teachers' convention, Khrushchev asserted July 9 that the USSR would back Cuba's Fidel Castro against "the intrigue of the American imperialists" and that "figuratively speaking, in case of necessity, Soviet artillerymen can support the Cuban people with their rocket fire." Khrushchev held that the U.S.' reduction of Cuban sugar imports was intended "to strangle the economy of Cuba" and could be a prelude to military intervention against Castro. He said the USSR had "rockets which can land precisely in a ... target 13,000 kilometers away," and "this ... is a warning to those who would like to solve international problems by force and not by reason."

Khrushchev said at a Kremlin news conference July 12 that "the Monroe Doctrine has outlived its time" and "has died ... a natural death." It was the Monroe Doctrine, Khrushchev charged, that had permitted the U.S. to perpetuate the reign of colonialism and monopolies in Latin America. Khrushchev said that "should the United States imperialists undertake aggressive action against the Cuban people upholding their national independence, we would support the Cuban people." Khrushchev indicated that this support would extend to Cuban efforts to evict the U.S. from its naval base at Guantanamo Bay, but he denied as "silly fabrication" the idea that the USSR itself wanted military bases in Cuba. The USSR's "best base is the Soviet Union, from where Soviet rockets can hit unerringly any sector in any part of the globe," he declared.

Tass Oct. 28-29 published 2 versions of Khrushchev's clarification of his July 9 statement promising to aid Cuba with rockets if the U.S. attacked Cuba. Khrushchev's clarification was made in Moscow Oct. 22 in an interview with Carlos Franqui, director of the Cuban newspaper *Revolucion*. In a summary of the interview released by Tass Oct. 28, Khrushchev was quoted as saying that he would like his promise to defend Cuba to be regarded as a "symbolic" offer. Tass added: "For this purpose, Khrushchev said, it is essential that the imperialists' threats of [military] intervention against Cuba should not materialize,

. . . and then there will be no need to confirm the reality of our statement about armed assistance to . . . Cuba." In the full text of the interview, released by Tass Oct. 29, Khrushchev was quoted as agreeing with Franqui that "if this [military] threat is carried out [against Cuba], [Soviet] rockets are adequately prepared" to come to Cuba's defense.

The U.S. State Department charged in a note to the Organization of American States (OAS) Oct. 28 that Soviet-bloc nations had shipped "thousands of tons" of weapons to Cuba "to give armed support to the spread of its [Cuban] revolution to other parts of the Americas." The State Department charged Nov. 18 that Soviet-bloc arms shipments to Cuba since Jan. 1, 1959 had totaled "at least 28,000 tons."

In a commercial-aid pact signed by Castro and Soviet First Deputy Premier Anastas I. Mikoyan in Havana Feb. 13, the USSR had agreed to buy 1,000,000 tons of Cuban sugar annually in 1960-4 at world market prices (currently 3¢ a pound), to give Cuba a $100 million credit repayable in 12 years at 2.5% interest and to furnish technical assistance to Cuba during 1961-4. The credit was to be used to buy equipment, machinery and materials.

Khrushchev in U.S. for UN Meeting

The 15th regular annual session of the UN General Assembly was convened Sept. 20 at UN headquarters in New York. The opening session was attended by many governmental heads and chiefs of state, mainly from Soviet bloc, Asian and African nations, some of whom had come to New York in response to Khrushchev's demand for a UN summit meeting on disarmament and other major world problems. Khrushchev, in a major address to the Assembly Sept. 24, attacked UN Secy. Gen. Dag Hammarskjold by proposing the abolition of his office.

Khrushchev, defending the USSR's foreign policies on issues ranging from the problems of the Congo and Cuba to disarmament, charged that Hammarskjold and the UN Secretariat had fallen under the domination of the Western powers. Khrushchev suggested that the post of secretary general be replaced by a 3-man board composed of one representative each of the Soviet, Western and neutralist blocs. *Among remarks Khrushchev made in his address:*

Divided world—Despite the social and scientific gains of the 20th Century, millions of humans continued to live in bondage and starvation, and the world remained divided between conflicting military camps. "2 points of view regarding world developments plainly opposed one another already in the first postwar years. One line aimed at an international *detente,* at ending the arms race, ... and the exclusion of war from the life of society." "There is, however, a 2d line ... aimed at fanning the 'cold war' ... [and] the destruction of all the foundations of international cooperation." Peace can be assured only if "the nations wage an active struggle ... to tie the hands of the militarist monopolist quarters."

Spy flights—The collapse of the Paris East-West summit talks and the disarmament negotiations was due to the "aggressive incursion" into Soviet airspace of the U.S.' reconnaissance plane. The incident showed the world that it was the U.S.' policy "to supplant international law with piracy and honest negotiations ... with perfidy." It was carried out by "provocation-mongers ... seeking to create an atmosphere in which the nations would live in constant fear." The incident "demonstrated ... graphically the danger for peace that is constituted by the web of American military bases which has enmeshed dozens of states in Europe, Asia, Africa and Latin America."

Cuba—"Courageous Cuba has become the object of all kinds of attacks, intrigues and subversion, economic aggression and ... threats of aggression." These attacks were due to the fact that "having expelled dictator Batista, the Cuban people have freed themselves from foreign exploitation, and have taken their fate into their own hands, firmly declaring to the United States monopolists: 'No more plundering of our country.'" "The United Nations must do all it can to remove from Cuba the ... threat of [outside] interference."

Congo—The Congo Republic, "on the 3d day after the proclamation of her independence, fell victim to aggression." Belgian military intervention to regain monopolist control of the country's mineral wealth was part of a "conspiracy against the Congo, the strings of which extend from Brussels to the capitals of other major NATO powers." The "colonialists" were aided in their "crude methods and direct interference" by "Mr. Hammarskjold and his staff," whose use of the UN Force "disorganized the life of the state and paralyzed ... the legitimate government." "The Assembly should give a rebuff to the colonialists and their stooges and call Mr. Hammarskjold to order so that he should not abuse his position."

Abolition of colonialism—"Is it not time to mount the final offensive against colonialism... [just as] a century or more ago civilized mankind launched an offensive against the slave trade... The Soviet government believes that the time has come to raise the question of the complete and final elimination of the colonial regime... in all its forms." The USSR "submits for consideration... a draft declaration in which the following demands are solemnly proclaimed":

1. "To grant immediately to all colonial countries, trusteeship territories and other non-self-governing territories complete independence and freedom. ... The colonial regime... should be abolished completely...."

2. "To eliminate... all strongholds of colonialism in the shape of possessions and leasehold areas on the territories of other states."

3. To require "equality and respect for sovereign rights and territorial integrity of all states, ... allowing no manifestations of colonialism."

Aid—"A positive role in overcoming... backwardness of countries that are being liberated would be played by [UN and bilateral] economic and technical assistance." "The allocation of only 1/10 of the funds that the great powers are spending for military purposes would increase the amount of assistance to underdeveloped countries by $10 billion a year. ... It is the moral duty of states that possessed colonies... to return to the liberated peoples... at least a part of the values taken by them through cruel exploitation of the population and through pillage of the natural resources."

Disarmament—The USSR was submitting to the Assembly a revised draft plan for general and complete disarmament which "in many respects... meets halfway the position of the Western powers." "The Soviet government is deeply convinced that only a radical solution of the disarmament problem which would provide for the complete prohibition of nuclear weapons... [would deliver] mankind from the threat of nuclear war."

New UN executive—"The time has come to create conditions for a more effective work both of the United Nations as a whole and of this organization's executive working body." Hammarskjold, who had been nominated for his post by the Western powers, showed himself responsive to their needs in his use of UN forces for "colonialist" purposes in the Congo. The "post of the secretary general... should be abolished." The UN included "the military blocs of the Western powers, socialist states and neutralist countries." "We consider it reasonable... for the [UN] executive body... to be constituted not as one person—the secretary general—but as 3 representatives" of the 3 groups.

During the Assembly session, 5 neutralist nations failed in an effort to bring Khrushchev and Pres. Eisenhower together for a new summit conference on current international tensions. The summit proposal, sponsored by the leaders of India, Indonesia, Yugoslavia, Ghana and the United Arab Republic, was introduced Sept. 30 but rejected by Mr. Eisenhower Oct. 2 and Khrushchev Oct. 3.

Mr. Eisenhower suggested that if the USSR were ready to begin serious negotiations on disarmament or any other important issue, it could do so through the UN or normal diplomatic channels. He said he would not "participate in a mere gesture which... might convey a thoroughly misleading and unfortunate impression to the peoples of the world." Khrushchev said Oct. 3 that he was prepared to meet with Pres. Eisenhower only if Mr. Eisenhower apologized in advance for the U.S.' spy-plane flights.

Simultaneously with the neutralist efforts to arrange an Eisenhower-Khrushchev meeting, British Prime Min. Harold Macmillan met separately twice with Pres. Eisenhower and with Khrushchev Sept. 27-Oct. 4 to discuss conflicting Western and Soviet views.

Khrushchev said Oct. 7 that he had been assured by Macmillan that a Big 4 summit conference would be held soon after Pres. Eisenhower's successor took office. Khrushchev, interviewed by the UN Correspondents Association, declared that Soviet leaders would "keep our word" to maintain the *status quo* in Berlin and Germany if the promised summit meeting were held. He made clear, however, that if there were "no desire" to hold a conference or to reach an agreement on Germany, "a peace treaty will be signed [with East Germany], and that will mean the end of the occupation regime in West Berlin." He told newsmen that he had suggested to Macmillan that, rather than hold a summit meeting on the German problem, "it might be better to convene a conference of all the competent countries... to sign a [German] peace treaty. But... Macmillan assured me that a summit conference would take place."

A demand by Khrushchev that Hammarskjold resign was rejected by Hammarskjold Oct. 3 on the ground that it was his responsibility to protect the UN and its smaller member states from great-power domination. Hammarskjold's refusal to "throw the [UN] organization to the winds" and permit his replacement by a 3-man executive board was greeted by a standing ovation of all Assembly delegates except those of India, Ghana, Guinea, the Soviet bloc and Khrushchev, who pounded his desk in displeasure. The demand for Hammarskjold's resignation had been voiced by Khrushchev earlier that day in an Assembly address replying to U.S. charges that his executive board proposal would wreck the UN. Denouncing Hammarskjold as "biased with regard to the Socialist countries," Khrushchev repeated Soviet charges that he had abused his post and had put UN troops at the service of "colonialist forces" seeking "to impose a new yoke on the Congo."

The Assembly Oct. 11 rejected by a 54-13 vote a Soviet demand that the disarmament question be debated immediately by the full Assembly rather than be sent to the Political Committee. The Assembly upheld the Western-supported recommendations of the Steering Committee that the disarmament question be dealt with according to normal Assembly procedure, by reference to the Political Committee. Khrushchev led the Soviet attack on U.S. Amb. James Wadsworth's contentions that a debate on disarmament by the full Assembly would turn "a serious discussion into a table-thumping propaganda spectacle." Declaring that "the last shreds of our patience and of our hope are at stake now," Khrushchev warned that "if war were to break out, it will break out throughout the globe.... If war is to be foisted on us, we shall fight for our country, and we shall gain the victory,... but the losses will be uncountable and appalling, and you shall be answerable, gentlemen." Khrushchev warned that the "production of [Soviet] rockets now is a matter of mass delivery, like sausages that come out from the automatic machines." Khrushchev told newsmen after the session that the rejection of his demand for debate had brought the world "closer to war."

In his farewell appearance at the Assembly, Khrushchev threatened Oct. 13 to order a Soviet boycott of disarmament talks unless they were limited to his proposals for total world disarmament. Reading to the Assembly a Soviet draft resolution that reiterated his 1959 plan for "general and complete disarmament," Khrushchev warned that the USSR would withdraw from the Assembly's Political Committee, the UN Disarmament Commission and the 10-nation (Geneva) Committee on Disarmament unless the Political Committee "works out specific directives, at least on the basic principles of disarmament" as outlined in the Soviet paper. He warned that Britain, "the well-known ... unsinkable aircraft carrier, would cease to exist on the very first day of ... war." Referring to the U.S., he said: "If you want war, keep provoking it and you'll get it."

A boisterous Assembly session in which Soviet delegates insulted Western speakers and Assembly Pres. Frederick H. Boland of Ireland, and in which Khrushchev banged his desk with his shoe, had been suspended angrily by Boland Oct. 12 after he had broken his gavel trying to restore order. The uproar occurred during debate on demands by Khrushchev for rapid Assembly consideration of the Soviet draft declaration against colonialism. Khrushchev, who had warned Asian and African delegates that "it is with your hands that the colonialists want to do this dirty deed—to prevent the adoption of the declaration," interrupted a later speech by Philippine delegate Lorenzo Sumulong to charge that Sumulong was a "jerk" and "lackey" of imperialism. Khrushchev then returned to his desk, removed his shoe, waved it at Sumulong and pounded his desk with it as Sumulong resumed an attack on Soviet colonialism in East Europe.

Khrushchev's final UN appearance was marked by (a) USSR failure to win immediate Assembly debate of Soviet charges of U.S. aerial aggression and (b) Soviet success in forcing Assembly consideration of the Soviet draft declaration on the abolition of colonialism.

Khrushchev, reporting on his visit to the UN Assembly, told an audience in Moscow's Luzhniki Sports Palace Oct. 20 that U.S. press reports said "the Pentagon had decided to send submarines armed with rockets with nuclear warheads which would cruise in the Baltic Sea close to the shores of the Soviet Union." The U.S., he said, "cannot but know that our country also has submarines with atomic engines armed with rockets." Khrushchev said, however, that the Soviet A-subs would not cruise near the U.S. because that would be "a criminal policy of the brink of war that was proclaimed by [the late U.S. State

Secy. John Foster] Dulles." Khrushchev said he had achieved "considerable results" by attending the UN session and attracting other world leaders to its important debates. He labeled the Soviet draft on the abolition of colonialism a "great success" and said that only the opposition of Western leaders had prevented rapid UN action on Soviet disarmament proposals.

COMMUNIST WORLD

Red Allies Back 'Peaceful Coexistence'

The leaders of 12 ruling Communist parties met in Bucharest, Rumania June 22 and reaffirmed their unified support of Khrushchev's thesis of "peaceful coexistence." Their accord, made public in a communique issued June 27 by Tass, followed reports of Communist Chinese opposition to Khrushchev's avowed efforts to negotiate settlements of some East-West disputes. The Bucharest meeting, called during a gathering of Communist leaders for the 3d congress of the Rumanian CP, was attended by party representatives from Albania, Bulgaria, Czechoslovakia, East Germany, Hungary, North Korea, North Viet Nam, Outer Mongolia, Poland, Red China, Rumania and the USSR.

The 12 parties declared their unanimous belief that "all the conclusions of the [Nov. 1957 Moscow] declaration...and manifesto of peace—on peaceful coexistence between countries with differing social systems, on the possibility of preventing wars in the present era, on the necessity of peoples' vigilance with regard to the danger of war since the existence of imperialism retains the ground for aggressive wars—can be fully applied in the present situation too."

In a series of speeches following his arrival in Bucharest June 18, Khrushchev reaffirmed his belief that war was not inevitable and called for flexibility in interpreting Marx and Lenin. In a 2-hour speech to the Rumanian congress June 21, Khrushchev declared "with certainty that under present conditions war is not inevitable" and that "he who does not understand this does not believe in the...great attractive force of socialism, which has manifestly demonstrated its superiority over capitalism." Khrushchev said: Communist leaders must be prepared to "creatively develop Marxist-Leninist theory" in order to meet modern needs; "we cannot repeat ... what Lenin said many decades ago about imperialism and always repeat that imperialist wars are inevitable as long as socialism has not triumphed all over the world"; these views were "based on what the great Lenin said in completely different historical conditions" and disregarded the fact that the "forces of socialism grow and strengthen more and more"; "in our day only madmen and maniacs" call for a new war.

Speaking at a rally marking the end of the Bucharest congress, Khrushchev repeated his thesis but warned that "imperialists" still were "wild animals that will attack when one is not looking." He said at a Rumanian CP Central Committee reception later that day that imperialist nations were tempted to make war because they were uncertain of the future but that "we Communists do not want war because we believe our cause will bring final victory." "We are going to make the imperialists dance like fishes in a saucepan—and that without a war," Khrushchev declared.

Communist China's interpretation of the Bucharest actions, published June 29 in *Jenmin Jih Pao (People's Daily)*, the Chinese CP organ, and issued though the Hsinhua news agency, rejected Khrushchev's emphasis on the noninevitability of war. The Chinese statement paid lip service to Khrushchev's thesis, but it declared that "imperialism is imperialism after all," and "imperialists will under no circumstances give up of their own accord their policies of aggression and war and withdraw ... from the stage of history just because of the[ir] sad plight.... The nearer they approach their doom the more they will put up a frantic fight." "Only when the imperialist ... and the capitalist system ... are really abolished can there really be lasting world peace," it asserted.

The Chinese-Soviet ideological rift had become evident in April with the publication of conflicting theses in connection with observances of Lenin's 90th birthday. A summation of Chinese views on the inevitability of imperialist war was contained in the Apr. 26 issue of *Peking Review*. Attacking "attempts of the modern revisionists to distort and carve up the teachings of Lenin," it charged that by acting as if "the peace movement is everything, the final aim is nothing," these persons were seeking a peace that "may be acceptable to the imperialists" but would "destroy" the "revolutionary will" to socialism. In a direct challenge to Khrushchev's view that nuclear war would mean destruction for both camps, the Chinese article said: "The result [of atomic war] will certainly not be the anihilation of mankind"; "on the debris of a dead imperialism, the victorious people would create very swiftly a civilization thousands of times higher than the capitalist system."

Khrushchev's doctrine of peaceful coexistence and the non-inevitability of war had been defended in a major ideological statement published June 12 by the Soviet CP newspaper *Pravda*. In an attack on "left sectarians" and "leftist doctrinaires," *Pravda* rejected the attempts of "some persons" to stigmatize the "peaceful coexistence of countries with different political systems, the struggle to halt the arms race ... and the talks between leaders of the Socialist and capitalist countries as ... deviation from the positions of Marxism-Leninism." It said that "the complex struggle for communism ... could not be waged while renouncing in advance agreements on compromises on specific questions." In a presumed reference to Chinese efforts to proceed directly from revolution to the creation of pure communism by the establishment of the commune system, it said: "We consider erroneous and incorrect the statement of leftists in the international Communist movement ... that since we have taken power ... we can at once introduce communism by passing certain historical stages in its development." "Lenin demonstrated the unsoundness and harm of ... the leftists who rejected the idea of Communist compromises with other parties and groups" during the struggle to build socialism. *Pravda* added June 13 that the thesis "that today war is not inevitable and can be avoided" had been "scientifically substantiated" according to the tenets of Marxism-Leninism.

World Red Leaders Unite on Manifesto

A manifesto issued from Moscow Dec. 6 by the leaders of 81 national and regional Communist parties proclaimed the unity of all Communists in a continuing struggle against capitalism. The manifesto was then generally believed to represent an ideological truce between Soviet insistence on the possibility of peaceful coexistence and Chinese demands for more aggressive policies, not excluding war. Published simultaneously in Communist newspapers throughout the world as a new guide for Communist policy, the manifesto superseded the 1957 Moscow declaration on the need for peaceful coexistence.

The manifesto was based on agreements reached at a world congress of Communist leaders begun in Moscow Nov. 10 and generally believed to have ended Nov. 30. Participants, among them Khrushchev and Chinese Pres. Liu Shao-chi, were said to have debated their ideological differences for 10 days before turning their conclusions over to a committee that wrote the final manifesto. A preliminary communique issued Dec. 1 had foreshadowed issuance of the manifesto. The document was taken as proof that neither the USSR nor Communist China had been able to impose its views on the direction of future Communist policy. The manifesto's citation of Marxist theory in support of a more aggressive Communist strategy, however, was believed to have given ideological vindication to the Chinese position.

Liu was reported to have presented Chinese views in a 4-1/2-hour address at the meeting Nov. 22, Liu was said to have been supported by Communist party leaders from Latin America, some Asian countries and Albania. Khrushchev, however, reportedly retained the backing of a majority of delegates, including the leaders of the Eastern European parties, for his continued emphasis on coexistence.

Khrushchev's coexistence thesis was defended in a series of *Pravda* articles, viewed as attacks on the Chinese position, published during the meeting. A front-page editorial called Nov. 23 for a struggle against "revisionism, dogmatism and sectarianism" and all opponents of coexistence, "the only correct principle for international relations." A 2d editorial Nov. 28 demanded an end to "dogmatism, sectarianism and all attempts to convert living, creative Marxism-Leninism into a set of dessicated, petrified formulas detached from life."

The Chinese position was outlined in articles appearing Oct. 31 in *Red Flag,* the CP theoretical journal, and *Jenmin Jih Pao (People's Daily).* Conceding that revolutions could not be exported, the Chinese said: "Development of the revolutionary forces of the...various countries and their successes in revolution" were fundamental to the success of communism; "the modern revisionists and certain muddleheaded people [allege]...that revolution cannot be carried out if world peace is to be preserved; this is preposterous."

Khrushchev, speaking at a Kremlin reception attended by Liu Nov. 7, asserted that peace, not war, was necessary and "inevitable." He said: "We are working toward communism, but war will not help us reach our goal—it will spoil it. We shall win only through the minds of men. We must rest on the position of peaceful coexistence and non-intervention. It is not necessary to whip people along this road."

Partial text of the Moscow manifesto (English translation distributed by Tass):

Introduction—Representatives of the Communist and workers parties have discussed at this meeting urgent problems of the present international situation and of the further struggle for peace, national independence, democracy and socialism.

The meeting has shown unity of views among the participants on the issues discussed. The Communist and workers' parties have unanimously reaffirmed their allegiance to the Declaration & Peace Manifesto adopted in 1957. These program documents of creative Marxism-Leninism determined the fundamental positions of the international Communist movement on the more important issues of our time....They remain the banner and guide to action for...the international Communist movement.

The course of events in the past 3 years has demonstrated the correctness of the analysis of the international situation and the outlook for world development as given in the Declaration & Peace Manifesto....

The chief result of these years is the rapid growth of the might and international influence of the world Socialist system, the vigorous process of disintegration of the colonial system under the impact of the national liberation movement, the intensification of class struggles in the capitalist world, and the continued decline and decay of the world capitalist system; the superiority of the forces of socialism over those of imperialism, of the forces of peace over those of war, is becoming ever more marked in the world arena....

Socialism winning struggle—Our time, whose main content is the normalization from capitalism to socialism initiated by the great October Revolution, is a time of struggle between the 2 social systems, a time of socialistic revolutions and nationalistic liberalistic revolutions, a time of the breakdown of imperialism, of the abolition of the colonial system, a time of transition of more peoples to the socialistic position, of the triumph of socialism and communism on a world-wide scale....

The strength and invincibility of socialism have been demonstrated in recent decades in titanic battles between the new and old worlds. Attempts by the imperialists and their shock force—fascism—to check the course of historical development by force of arms ended in failure. Imperialism proved powerless to stop the Socialist revolutions in Europe and Asia. Socialism became a world system....

Today it is the world Socialist system and the forces fighting against imperialism, for a Socialist transformation of society, that determine the main content, main trend and main features of the historical development of society. Whatever efforts imperialism makes, it cannot stop the advance of history. The complete triumph of socialism is inevitable....

The time is not far off when socialism's share of world production will be greater than that of capitalism. Capitalism will be defeated in the decisive sphere of human endeavor, the sphere of material production. . . .

Capitalist decay, U. S. decline—The world capitalist system is going through an intense process of disintegration and decay. Its contradictions have accelerated the development of monopoly capitalism into state monopoly capitalism.

By tightening the monopolies' grip on the life of the nation, state-monopoly capitalism closely combines the power of the monopolies with that of the state with the aim of saving the capitalist system and increasing the profits of the imperialist bourgeoisie to the utmost by exploiting the working class and plundering large sections of the population.

But no matter what methods it resorts to the monopoly bourgeoisie cannot rescue capitalism. . . .

The instability of capitalist economy is growing. Although production in some capitalist countries is increasing to some degree or other, the contraditions of capitalism are becoming the more acute on a national as well as international scale. . . .

These facts once again refute the lies which bourgeois ideologists and revisionists spread to the effect that modern capitalism has become 'peoples capitalism,' that it has established a so-called 'welfare state' capable of overcoming the anarchy of production and economic crises and assuring well-being for all working people. . . .

The decay of capitalism is particularly marked in the United States of America, the chief imperialist country of today. U.S. monopoly capital is clearly unable to use all the productive forces at its command. The [U.S.] . . . has become a land of especially big chronic unemployment. Increasing undercapacity operation in industry has become permanent in that country. Despite the enormous increase in military appropriations, which is achieved at the expense of the standard of living of the working people, the rate of growth of production has been declining in the post-war years. . . .

The most developed capitalist country has become a country of the most distorted, militarized economy. More than any other capitalist country, the United States drains Asia, and especially Latin America, of their riches, holding up their progress. U.S. capitalist penetration into Africa is increasing. U.S. imperialism has become the biggest international exploiter. . . .

The pillars of the capitalist system have become so decayed that the ruling imperialist bourgeoisie in many countries . . . form military-political alliances under United States leadership to fight in common against the Socialist camp and to strangle the national-liberation, working-class and Socialist movements. . . .

Peoples against imperialism—The peoples are rising with growing determination to fight imperialism. A great struggle is getting under way between the forces of labor and capital, democracy and reaction, of freedom and colonialism. . . .

The actions of the Negro people in the United States for their fundamental rights are assuming a mass character. . . .

All this is graphic evidence that the tide of anti-imperialist, national-liberation, anti-war and class struggles is rising ever higher.

A new stage has begun in the development of the general crisis of capitalism.

This is shown by the triumph of socialism in a large group of European and Asian countries embracing 1/3 of mankind, the powerful growth of the forces fighting for socialism throughout the world and the steady weakening of the imperialists' positions in the economic competition with socialism, the tremendous new upsurge of the national-liberation struggle and the mounting disintegration of the colonial system, the growing instability of the entire world economic system of capitalism. . . .

This stage is distinguished by the fact that it has set in, not as a result of the world war, but in the conditions of competition and struggle between the 2 systems. . . . It has taken place at a time when a successful struggle by the peace-loving forces to bring about and promote peaceful coexistence has prevented the imperialists from undermining world peace by their aggressive actions. . . .

Socialism enters new era—A new stage has begun in the development of the world Socialist system. The Soviet Union is successfully carrying on the full-scale construction of a Communist society. Other countries of the Socialist camp are successfully laying the foundations of socialism, and some of them have already entered the period of construction of a developed Socialist society. . . .

The Soviet people, successfully carrying out the 7-year economic development plan, are rapidly building up a material and technical basis for communism. Soviet science has ushered in what is virtually a new era in the development of world civilization. . . . The Soviet Union is the first country in history to be blazing a trail to communism for all mankind. It is the most striking example and most powerful bulwark for the peoples of the world in their struggle for peace, democratic freedoms, national independence and social progress.

The people's revolution in China dealt a crushing blow at the positions of imperialism in Asia and contributed in great measure to the balance of the world forces changing in favor of socialism. By giving a further powerful impetus to the national-liberation movement, it exerted tremendous influence on the peoples, especially those of Asia, Africa and Latin America. . . .

. . . The success of the policy of Socialist industrialization has led to a great economic upsurge in the Socialist countries, which are developing their economy much faster than the capitalist countries. . . .

In recent years all the people's democracies have solved, or have been successfully solving, the most difficult problem of Socialist construction, that of transferring the peasantry, on a voluntary basis, . . . to the road of large-scale cooperative farming on socialist lines. . . .

. . . The Communist and workers parties of the Socialist countries consider it their internationalist duty . . . to carry out, by joint effort and as speedily as possible, the historic task of surpassing the world capitalist system in over-all industrial and agricultural production and then outstrip the economically most developed capitalist countries in per capita output and in the standard of living. . . .

National paths to socialism—One of the greatest achievements of the world Socialist system is the practical confirmation of the Marxist-Leninist thesis that national antagonisms diminish with the decline of class antagonisms. . . .

The common interest of the peoples of the Socialist countries and the interests of peace and socialism demand the proper combination of the principles of Socialist internationalism and socialist patriotism in politics. . . .

The declaration of 1957 points out quite correctly that undue emphasis on the role of national peculiarities and departure from the universal truth of Marxism-Leninism regarding the Socialist revolution and Socialist construction prejudice the common cause of socialism.

The declaration also states quite correctly that Marxism-Leninism demands creative application of the general principles of Socialist revolution and Socialist construction, depending on the specific historical conditions in the country concerned, and does not permit of a mechanical copying of the policies and tactics of the Communist parties of other countries. Disregard of national peculiarities may lead to the part of the proletariat being isolated from reality, from the masses, and may injure the Socialist cause.

Manifestations of nationalism and national narrow-mindedness do not disappear automatically with the establishment of the Socialist system. If fraternal relations and friendship between the Socialist countries are to be strengthened, it is necessary that the Communist and workers' parties pursue a Marxist-Leninist internationalist policy . . . and that a resolute struggle be waged to eliminate the survivals of bourgeois nationalism and chauvinism. . . .

Imperialism breeds war—War is a constant companion of capitalism. The system of exploitation of man by man and the system of extermination of man by man are 2 aspects of the capitalist system. Imperialism has already inflicted 2 devastating world wars on mankind and now threatens to plunge it into an even more terrible catastrophe. . . .

. . . U.S. imperialism is the main force of aggression and war. . . .

The U.S. imperialists, together with the imperialists of Britain, France and West Germany, have drawn many countries into NATO, CENTO, SEATO and other military blocs. Under the guise of combatting the 'Communist menace,' it ['U.S. imperialism'] has enmeshed the so-called 'free world' . . . in a network of military bases spearheaded first and foremost against the Socialist countries. . . .

The imperialist forces of the U.S., . . . Britain and France have made a criminal deal with West German imperialism. In West Germany militarism has been revived and the restoration is being pushed ahead of a vast regular army under the command of Hitler generals, which the U.S. imperialists are equipping with nuclear and rocket weapons and other modern means of mass annihilation. . . .

War not inevitable—The aggressive nature of imperialism has not changed. But real forces have appeared that are capable of foiling its plans of aggression. War is not fatally inevitable. Had the imperialists been able to do what they wanted, they would already have plunged mankind into the abyss of the calamities and horrors of a new world war.

But the time is past when the imperialists could decide at will whether there should or should not be war. More than once in the past years the imperialists have brought mankind to the brink of world catastrophe by starting local wars. The resolute stand of the Soviet Union, of the other Socialist states and of all the peaceful forces put an end to the Anglo-Franco-Israeli intervention in Egypt, and averted a military invasion of Syria, Iraq and [other countries] . . .

. . . Experience shows that it is possible to combat effectively the local wars started by the imperialists and to stamp out successfully the hotbeds of such wars.

The time has come when the attempts of the imperialist aggressors to start a world war can be curbed. World war can be prevented by the joint efforts of the world Socialist camp, the international working class, the national-liberation movement . . . and all peace-loving forces.

In the opinion of Communists the tasks which must be accomplished first of all if peace is to be safeguarded are to stop the arms race, ban nuclear weapons, their tests and production, dismantle foreign war bases and withdraw foreign troops from other countries, disband military blocs, conclude a peace treaty with

Germany, turn West Berlin into a demilitarized free city, thwart the aggressive designs of the West German revanchists and prevent the revival of Japanese militarism....

But should the imperialist maniacs start war, the peoples will sweep capitalism out of existence and bury it.

Peaceful coexistence—The foreign policy of the Socialist countries rests on the firm foundation of the Leninist principle of peaceful coexistence and economic competition between the Socialist and capitalist countries.

The near future will bring the forces of peace and socialism new successes. The USSR will become the leading industrial power of the world. China will become a mighty industrial state. The Socialist system will be turning out more than half the world's industrial product.... The superiority of the forces of socialism and peace will be absolute.

In these conditions a real possibility will have arisen to exclude world war from the life of society even before socialism achieves complete victory on earth, with capitalism still existing in a part of the world....

In a world divided into 2 systems, the only correct and reasonable principle of international relations is the principle of peaceful coexistence of states with different social systems advanced by Lenin and further elaborated in the Moscow Declaration & the Peace Manifesto of 1957, in the decisions of the 20th and 21st Congresses of the CPSU....

Peaceful coexistence of countries with different systems or destructive war— this is the alternative today. There is no other choice. Communists emphatically reject the U.S. doctrine of cold war and brinkmanship, for it is a policy leading to thermonuclear catastrophe....

... Peaceful coexistence of states does not imply renunciation of the class struggle, as the revisionists claim. The coexistence of states with different social systems is a form of class struggle between socialism and capitalism....

Peaceful coexistence of countries with different social systems does not mean conciliation of the Socialist and bourgeois ideologies. On the contrary, it implies intensification of the struggle of the working class, of all the Communist parties, for the triumph of Socialist ideas. But ideological and political disputes between states must not be settled through war....

Disarmament—The meeting considers that the implementation of the program for general and complete disarmament put forward by the Soviet Union would be of historic importance....

To realize this program means to eliminate the very possibility of waging wars between countries. It is not easy to realize, owing to the stubborn resistance of the imperialists....

Through an active, determined struggle by the Socialist and other peace-loving countries, by the international working class and the broad masses in all countries, it is possible to ... force the imperialists into an agreement on general disarmament....

Anti-colonialist wars—National-liberation revolutions have triumphed in vast areas of the world. About 40 new sovereign states have arisen in Asia and Africa in the 15 postwar years. ... A new historical period has set in in the life of mankind: the peoples of Asia, Africa and Latin America that have won their freedom have begun to take an active part in world politics.

The complete collapse of colonialism is imminent. The breakdown of the system of colonial slavery under the impact of the national-liberation movement is a development ranking 2d in historic importance only to the formation of the world Socialist system....

Communists have always recognized the progressive, revolutionary significance of national-liberation wars; they are the most active champions of national independence. . . .

The peoples of the colonial countries win their independence both through armed struggle and by nonmilitary methods. . . .

Anti-colonialist bourgeoisie—In present conditions the national bourgeoisie of the colonial and dependent countries unconnected with imperialist circles is objectively interested in the accomplishment of the principal tasks of anti-imperialist, anti-feudal revolution and, therefore, retains the capacity of participating in the revolutionary struggle against imperialism and feudalism. In that sense it is progressive. But it is unstable; though progressive, it is inclined to compromise with imperialism and feudalism. . . .

As social contradictions grow, the national bourgeoisie inclines more and more to compromising with domestic reaction and imperialism. The people, however, begin to see that the best way to abolish age-long backwardness and improve their living standard is that of non-capitalistic development. Only thus can the peoples free themselves from exploitation, poverty and hunger. . . .

'National democracies' backed—In the present historical situation, favorable domestic and international conditions arise in many countries for the establishment of an independent national democracy; that is, a state which consistently upholds its political and economic independence, fights against imperialism and its military blocs, against military bases on its territory, a state which fights against the new forms of colonialism and the penetration of imperialist capital, a state which rejects dictatorial and despotic methods of government, a state in which the people are insured broad democratic rights and freedoms (freedom of speech, press, assembly, demonstrations, establishment of political parties and social organizations), the opportunity to work for the enactment of an agrarian reform and other democratic and social changes, and for participation in shaping government policy.

The formation and consolidation of national democracies enables the countries concerned to make rapid social progress and play an active part in the peoples' struggle for peace, against the aggressive policies of the imperialist camp, for the complete abolition of colonial yoke.

The Communist parties are working actively for a consistent completion of the anti-imperialist, anti-feudal, democratic revolution, for the establishment of national democracies. . . .

Abolition of colonialism—The entire course of the world history of recent decades prompts the complete and final abolition of the colonial system in all its forms and manifestations. All the peoples still languishing in colonial bondage must be given every support in winning their national independence. All forms of colonial oppression must be abolished. . . .

This meeting expresses solidarity with all the peoples of Asia, Africa, Latin America and Oceania who are carrying on a heroic struggle against imperialism. . . .

The meeting extends heartfelt regards and support to the heroic Algerian people fighting for freedom. . . . It wrathfully condemns the inhuman system of racial persecution and tyranny in the Union of South Africa (*apartheid*). . . .

All the Socialist countries . . . see it as their duty to render the fullest moral and material assistance to the peoples fighting to free themselves from imperialist and colonial tyranny. . . .

New revolutionary opportunities—The new balance of world forces offers the Communist and workers parties new opportunities of carrying out the historic tasks they face in the struggle for peace, national independence, democracy and socialism....

The main blow in present conditions is directed with growing force at the capitalist monopolies,... at the whole system of state monopoly capitalism, which defends their interests....

The monopolies seek to abolish, or cut down to a bare minimum, the democratic rights of the masses. The reign of open fascist terror continues in some countries. In a number of countries, fascism is expanding in new forms: dictatorial methods of government are combined with fictitious parliamentary practices that have been stripped of democratic content and reduced to pure form....

The working class, peasantry, intellectuals and the petty and middle urban bourgeoisie are vitally interested in the abolition of monopoly domination. Hence there are favorable conditions for rallying these forces....

Communists vs. reformists—Communists regard the struggle for democracy as a component of the struggle for socialism....

This sets the Marxist-Leninist parties completely apart from the reformists, who consider reforms within the framework of the capitalist system as the ultimate goal and deny the necessity of Socialist revolution....

Now that more sections of the population are joining in an active class struggle, it is of the utmost importance that Communists should extend their work in trade unions and cooperatives, among the peasantry, the youth, the women, in sports organizations and the unorganized sections of the population. There are new opportunities now to draw the younger generation into the struggle for peace and democracy, and for the great ideals of communism. Lenin's great behest—to go deeper into the masses, to work wherever there are masses, to strengthen the ties with the masses in order to lead them—must become a major task for every Communist party....

'Popular front' sought—The split in the ranks of the working class, which the ruling classes, the rightwing Social-Democratic leadership and reactionary trade union leaders are interested to maintain on a national and international scale, remains the principal obstacle to the accomplishment of the goals of the working class....

The Communists are firmly convinced that the ideological differences obtaining between themselves and the Social Democrats must not hinder exchanges of opinion on the pressing problems of the working-class movement and the joint struggle, especially against the war danger....

...It is safe to say that on overcoming the split in its ranks, on achieving unity of action of all its contingents, the working class of many capitalist countries could deliver a staggering blow to the policy of the ruling circles in the capitalist countries and make them stop preparing a new war, repel the offensive of monopoly capital....

...The Communists...are prepared to hold discussions with Social-Democrats...to compare views, ideas and experience with the aim of removing deeprooted prejudices and the split among the working people and of establishing cooperation.

Peaceful revolution possible—The imperialist reactionaries, who seek to arouse distrust for the Communist movement and its ideology, continue to intimidate the masses by alleging that the Communists need wars between states to overthrow the capitalist system and establish a Socialist system.

The Communist parties emphatically reject this slander. The fact that both world wars, which were started by the imperialists, ended in Socialist revolutions by no means implies that the way to social revolution goes necessarily through world war, especially now that there exists a powerful world system of socialism. Marxists-Leninists have never considered that the way to social revolution lies through wars between states.

The choice of social system is the inalienable right of the people of each country. Socialist revolution is not an item of import and cannot be imposed from without. It is a result of the internal development of the country concerned. . . .

The Communist parties, which guide themselves by the Marxist-Leninist doctrine, have always been against the export of revolution. . . .

. . . The forms and course of development of the Socialist revolution will depend on the specific balance of the class forces in the country concerned, on the organization and maturity of the working class and its vanguard, and on the extent of the resistance put up by the ruling classes. . . .

The Communist parties reaffirm the propositions put forward by the declaration of 1957 with regard to the forms of transition of different countries from capitalism to socialism. The declaration points out that the working class and its vanguard—the Marxist-Leninist party—seek to achieve the Socialist revolution by peaceful means. . . .

Today in a number of capitalist countries the working class, headed by its vanguard, has the opportunity . . . to unite a majority of the people, win state power without civil war and insure the transfer of the basic means of production to . . . the people. . . .

In the event of the exploiting classes' resorting to violence . . . the possibility of nonpeaceful transition to socialism should be borne in mind. Leninism teaches, and experience confirms, that the ruling classes never relinquish power voluntarily. In this case the degree of bitterness and the forms of the class struggle will depend not so much on the proletariat as on the resistance put up by the reactionary circles to the will of the overwhelming majority of the people, on these circles' using force. . . .

The actual possibility of the one or the other way of transition to socialism in each individual country depends on the concrete historical conditions. . . .

Yugoslav 'revisionism' condemned—The Communist parties have ideologically defeated the revisionists in their ranks who sought to divert them from the Marxist-Leninist path. . . .

The Communist parties have unanimously condemned the Yugoslav variety of international opportunism, a variety of modern revisionist theories in concentrated form. After betraying Marxism-Leninism, which they termed obsolete, the leaders of the League of Communists of Yugoslavia opposed their anti-Leninist revisionist program to the declaration of 1957; they set . . . Yugoslavia against the international Communist movement as a whole, severed their country from the Socialist camp [and] made it dependent on so-called aid from United States and other imperialists. . . .

The Yugoslav revisionists carry on subversive work against the Socialist camp and the world Communist movement. Under the pretext of an extra-bloc policy, they engage in activities which prejudice the unity of all the peace-loving forces and countries. Further exposure of the leaders of the Yugoslav revisionists, and active struggle to safeguard the Communist movement and the working-class movement from the anti-Leninist ideas of the Yugoslav revisionists, remains an essential task of the Marxist-Leninist parties. . . .

Marxist 'dogmatism' denounced—The further development of the Communist and working class movement calls, as stated in the Moscow declaration of 1957, for continuing a determined struggle on 2 fronts—against revisionism, which remains the main danger, and against dogmatism and sectarianism. . . .

Dogmatism and sectarianism in theory and practice can also become the main danger at some stage of development of individual parties, unless combated unrelentingly.

They rob revolutionary parties of the ability to develop Marxism-Leninism through scientific analysis and apply it creatively according to the specific conditions, they isolate Communists from the broad masses of the working people, doom them to passive expectation or leftist, adventurist actions in the revolutionary struggle, prevent them from making a timely and correct estimate of the changing situation and of new experience, using all opportunities to bring about the victory of the working class and all democratic forces in the struggle against imperialism, reaction and war danger, and thereby prevent the peoples from achieving victory in their just struggle. . . .

At a time when imperialist reaction is joining forces to fight communism, it is particularly imperative vigorously to consolidate the world Communist movement. . . .

. . . The interests of the Communist movement require solidarity in adherence by every Communist party to the estimates and conclusions concerning the common tasks in the struggle against imperialism, for peace, democracy and socialism, jointly reached by the fraternal parties at their meetings. . . .

Communists independent & united—All the Marxist-Leninist parties are independent and have equal rights, they shape their policies according to the specific conditions in their respective countries and in keeping with Marxist-Leninist principles, and support each other. The success of the working-class cause in any country is unthinkable without the internationalist solidarity of all Marxist-Leninist parties. . . .

The Communist and workers parties hold meetings whenever necessary to discuss urgent problems, to exchange experience, acquaint themselves with each other's views and positions, work out common views through consultations and coordinate joint actions in the struggle for common goals. . . .

USSR leads Marxist offensive—The Communist and workers' parties unanimously declare that the Communist Party of the Soviet Union has been, and remains, the universally recognized vanguard of the world Communist movement, being the most experienced and steeled contingent of the international Communist movement. The experience which the Communist Party of the Soviet Union has gained in the struggle for the victory of the working class, in Socialist construction and in the full-scale construction of communism, is of fundamental significance for the whole of the world Communist movement.

The example of the Soviet Communist Party and its fraternal solidarity inspire all the Communist parties in their struggle for peace and socialism, and represent the revolutionary principles of proletarian internationalism applied in practice. . . .

The meeting sees the further consolidation of the Communist parties on the basis of Marxism-Leninism, of proletarian internationalism, as a primary condition for the unification of all working-class, democratic and progressive forces, as a guarantee of new victories in the great struggle waged by the world Communist and working-class movement for a happy future for the whole of mankind, for the triumph of the cause of peace and socialism.

DOMESTIC AFFAIRS

Khrushchev Strengthened in Shakeup

A major shakeup in the leadership of the Soviet government and CP was approved at a plenary meeting of the CP Central Committee in Moscow May 4 and made public May 5. The shifts generally were considered to have strengthened Khrushchev in his unchanged positions of chairman (premier) of the USSR Council of Ministers (cabinet) and as first secretary of the CP Central Committee.

In the most significant of the announced changes, First Deputy Premier Frol R. Kozlov became a CP Central Committee secretary and presumably Khrushchev's chief aide on the committee. Aleksei N. Kosygin resigned as chairman of the State Planning Commission to replace Kozlov as first deputy premier, and Vladimir N. Novikov assumed Kosygin's former post.

The other reassignments: CP Central Committee—Yekaterina A. Furtseva, Aleksei I. Kirichenko, Averky B. Aristov, Petr N. Pospelov and Nikolai G. Ignatov resigned as committee secretaries. Pospelov and Aristov were released to "devote their energies" to the Russian SFSR CP Central Committee. Secretaries retained were Khrushchev (first), Mikhail A. Suslov, Otto V. Kuusinen, Nuritdin A. Mukhitdinov and Leonid I. Brezhnev. CP Central Committee Presidium—Aleksei I. Kirichenko and Nikolai I. Belyayev, recently demoted from other posts in the Ukraine and Kazakhstan, were dropped from Presidium membership. Kosygin, Nikolai V. Podgorny and Dmitri S. Polyansky were promoted from alternates to full membership. Full members retained were Pres. Kliment Voroshilov, First Deputy Premier Mikoyan, Aristov, Brezhnev, Khrushchev, Furtseva, Ignatov, Kozlov, Kuusinen, Mukhitdinov, Mikhail A. Suslov and Nikolai A. Shvernik. Council of Ministers—Vladimir N. Novikov and Ignatov became deputy premiers. Kozlov joined Mikoyan as a first deputy premier. Mrs. Furtseva replaced Nikolai A. Mikhailov as culture minister.

The retirement of Marshal Voroshilov, 79, Soviet chief of state, was announced May 7. Brezhnev was elected the same day to replace him. Voroshilov who had held the post of chairman of the Presidium of the USSR's Supreme Soviet, a post equivalent to president of the USSR, resigned for health reasons.

Aleksei Kirichenko, then CP Presidium member believed responsible for party recruitment and personnel, had been named Jan. 13 to replace Nikolai V. Kiselev as first secretary of the Rostov regional CP. Kirichenko, 51, a Ukrainian and major general during World War II, had been considered a close friend of Khrushchev's. His transfer from Moscow was a demotion. Kirichenko was dismissed from his Rostov post June 15.

Nikolai Belyayev's dismissal as first secretary of the Kazakhstan CP had been disclosed Jan. 15 by Tass dispatch, which reported his receipt of a labor medal but omitted mention of his rank. Soviet censors released foreign dispatches reporting his dismissal Jan. 16. Belyayev, who had been a friend of Khrushchev's, had been rebuked by Khrushchev for failures in Kazakh grain production. *Pravda* reported Jan. 29 that Belyayev had been demoted to first secretary of the Stavropol (Caucasus) region CP Central Committee, but he was ousted from this post also June 25.

(Deputy Premier Aleksandr F. Zasyadko was appointed Apr. 22 to replace ex-Deputy Premier Joseph J. Kuzmin as chairman of the USSR's State Scientific-Economic Council, established in 1959 to coordinate Soviet scientific research with economic planning.

(Finance Min. Arseny G. Zverev, 60, resigned May 16 for health reasons and was replaced by Deputy Finance Min. Vasily F. Garbuzov.)

Propaganda Intensification Ordered

The CP Central Committee Jan. 10 had ordered Soviet propagandists to improve and intensify their explanation of Communist policies and goals to create an "unshakeable belief in the cause of the party and people" and to provide "moral stimuli for work" according to the principle that "he who does not work, neither shall he eat." The Central Committee expressed its concern that current propaganda efforts were "divorced from life," did "not embrace the masses" and had only a "narrow sphere of influence." It emphasized that propaganda must be given renewed vigor and must be directed toward ordinary people in their "practical tasks." It said that the "ideological struggle" remained despite the coexistence movement and that Soviet peoples had to be educated in a "spirit of patriotism and national pride." It asserted that the effectiveness of the new propaganda campaign, to be directed at all groups by all media, would be "manifested first of all in concrete production results."

MVD Abolished

The USSR's central Ministry of Internal Affairs—the MVD—was abolished Jan. 13 by order of the Supreme Soviet Presidium on recommendation of the Soviet Council of Ministers. MVD functions, which included control of police, border forces, special military units, penal colonies, labor camps, frontier forces and state archives, were transferred to the internal affairs ministries of the 15 Soviet republics. Interior Min. Nikolai P. Dudorov, MVD chief since 1956, apparently retained his post as interior minister of the Russian republic.

Many MVD functions had been transferred to the State Security Committee (KGB) under the administrative decentralization program begun since Stalin's death and the ouster and execution of Interior Min. Lavrenti P. Beria in 1953. The KGB, headed by Aleksandr Shelepin, retained its status as a special body directly responsible to the Soviet cabinet.

Armed Forces Cut by 1,200,000 Men

A 1,200,000-man reduction of Soviet armed forces—from 3,623,000 men to 2,423,000—was proposed by Khrushchev Jan. 14 and was approved unanimously by the Supreme Soviet the next day. The proposal for a massive unilateral reduction of Soviet military manpower was made by Khrushchev in the course of a 3-hour state-of-the-nation speech to the Supreme Soviet.

Khrushchev said the Soviet troop reduction was made possible by the USSR's increasing nuclear missile forces. "In our country," he asserted, "the armed forces have been to a considerable extent transferred to rocket and nuclear arms. These arms are being perfected and will continue to be perfected until the day they are banned." "The proposed reduction will in no way reduce the firepower of our armed forces, and this is the main point," he declared. "The air force and the navy have lost their previous importance," and their conventional arms are "not being reduced but replaced," Khrushchev said. "Almost the whole of the air force is being replaced by rocket equipment. We have by now cut down sharply and... will continue to cut down and even discontinue the manufacture of bombers and other obsolete machinery." "In the navy," he continued, "the submarine fleet assumes great importance, whilst above-water ships can no longer play" their former role.

Khrushchev emphasized that "we already possess so many nuclear weapons, both atomic and hydrogen, and the necessary rockets for sending these weapons to the territory of a potential aggressor, that should any madman launch an attack on our state or on other Socialist states, we would be able literally to wipe the... countries which attack us off the face of the earth." Alluding to Soviet discovery of a new superweapon, he boasted that, "though the weapons we have now are formidable,... the weapon we have today in the hatching stage is even more perfect and even more formidable." This new Soviet arm, "in the portfolio of our scientists and designers, is a fantastic weapon," he declared.

Khrushchev gave the Supreme Soviet the following review of Soviet troop strength since 1927: 1927—"After the civil war...the number of service personnel was cut to 586,000." 1937—"As the result of... aggression in the Far East and the growth of fascism in Germany..., [Soviet forces] amounted to 1,433,000." 1941—"The outbreak of World War II and the growing danger of a... German invasion compelled...[an increase] to 4,207,000." 1945—Soviet forces totalled 11,365,000 by the end of World War II. 1948—Postwar demobilization cut manpower to 2,874,000. 1955—"NATO threat and atomic blackmail" compelled a buildup to 5,763,000 men. 1959—Soviet forces totalled 3,623,000 men.

Khrushchev's proposal for reducing Soviet troop strength was embodied in a law passed unanimously by the Supreme Soviet Jan. 15. A formal appeal to "the parliaments and governments of all the nations of the world" to emulate the Soviet action was approved unanimously by the Supreme Soviet the same day. The text of the appeal was delivered to U.S. State Secy. Christian A. Herter Jan. 18 by Soviet Amb.-to-U.S. Mikhail A. Menshikov.

Marshal Vasily D. Sokolovsky, 63, armed forces chief of staff, was reported May 2 to have retired for health reasons. Marshal Matvei V. Zakharov, 62, former Soviet commander in East Germany, was named his successor. Col. Gen. Ivan I. Yakubovsky recently had replaced Zakharov in the East German post.

The Warsaw Pact nations announced July 24 that Marshal Andrei A. Grechko, 57, Soviet first deputy defense minister, had been named to succeed Marshal Ivan S. Konev as supreme commander of Warsaw Pact forces. Konev, 63, was said to have requested retirement for health reasons. Grechko had commanded the First Guards Army on the Ukrainian front during World War II, the Kiev Military District after the war, and Soviet occupation troops in East Germany in 1953-57. Grechko had returned to the USSR in 1957 to become commander of all Soviet land forces.

Grechko reported in the Defense Ministry newspaper *Krasnaya Zvezda (Red Star)* Sept. 7 that the Soviet government and CP had approved a new code of military discipline. The new code implemented an Oct. 1957 decision of the CP Central Committee to reassert party control over the USSR's armed forces. Grechko said that "the new regulations emphasize that firm military discipline is achieved by the education of high moral, political and militant qualities of personnel," induced by "persuasion" rather than force. The code abolished solitary confinement, reduced terms of arrest and replaced arrest with reprimands for many types of violations. It replaced the Soviet military code in use since 1946.

Economic Programs

Khrushchev told the Supreme Soviet Jan. 14 that "the year 1959 ... will go down in history as the opening year of full-scale construction of a Communist society in our country. ... During the year industrial production rose by more than 11% instead of the 7.7[%] provided for by the [7-year] plan. The industrial output of consumer goods ... actually rose by 10.3%. The gross grain harvest in 1959 was lower than it was in ... 1958 because of the drought," but needed grains were purchased. "The national income rose in 1959 by 8%, or by about 100 billion rubles. More than 13 million factory workers and salaried staffs had been put on 7-1/2- and 6-hour working days by the end of the year ... [and this program] will have been completed before this year is out."

The USSR's final economic report for 1959, issued Jan. 21 by the Central Statistical Board, declared that Soviet production had increased by 11% during 1959 but conceded that estimated grain output had fallen by 13% from 141 million metric tons in 1958 to 124,800,000 metric tons in 1959. Production of most heavy industrial items and consumer goods generally exceeded 1959 goals. But many industrial categories (natural gas, turbines and generators, electric motors, metallurgical, oil and chemical equipment, locomotives and railway cars, prefabricated housing, radios and refrigerators) failed to meet planned targets. Farm machinery output dropped 30% below 1958 levels because of "reorganization" of the industry. Foreign trade, however, increased from 1958's 34.6 billion rubles ($8.65 billion) to 41 billion rubles ($10.25 billion). The report cited these production figures for major industrial and consumer items: steel—59,900,000 metric tons; pig iron—43 million metric tons; oil—129-1/2 million metric tons; coal—506-1/2 million metric tons; cement—38,800,000 metric tons; electricity—264 billion kilowatt hours; mineral fertilizers—12,900,000 metric tons; gas—37.2 billion cubic meters; shoes—389 million pairs; cotton cloth—4.6 billion square meters; wool cloth—416 million square meters; apartment units—2,200,000; TV sets—1,300,000; radios—4 million; sewing machines—2,900,000; washing machines—724,000; refrigerators—426,000; autos—124,500.

A new Soviet production index, prepared by Rand Corp. economists and reported in the *American Economic Review*, supported recent Soviet progress claims. Using 1950 production as a base (equal to 100), the Rand index rated Soviet production at 202.3 in 1958. It estimated these annual Soviet production increases in 1953-58 (official claims in parentheses): 1953—9.6% (11.8%); 1954—10.2% (13.3%); 1955—10.1% (12.4%); 1956—8.6% (10.6%); 1957—9.7% (10%); 1958—7.4% (9.7%).

The Soviet government announced Dec. 26 that 7-year-plan production targets had been increased for certain sectors of the USSR's economy due to unexpected gains in industrial output. The announcement said the decision had been made at a cabinet meeting convened Dec. 23 by Khrushchev to study evidence that the USSR's gross production had increased by 23% (planned increase: 17%) in 1958-9, the first 2 years of the plan. The cabinet was said to have approved Khrushchev's suggestion that the production surplus, valued at 120 billion (old) rubles, be reinvested to speed "development of industry and agriculture and for meeting the growing demands of the population."

(*Pravda* charged Mar. 29, however, that productivity in Donets [Donbas] Basin coal mines was lower in 1960 than before World War II despite intensive mechanization. *Pravda* blamed mismanagement, bungling, poor planning and indifference for the failure of the 15-year modernization program in the Donets mines, producers of 1/3 of the USSR's 500 million tons of coal per year.)

Soviet foreign trade increased by 7.4 billion rubles to a total value of 42 billion rubles during 1959 (imports 20.3 billion rubles, exports 21.7 billion rubles), Foreign Trade Min. Nikolai S. Patolichev reported Mar. 9 in *Pravda*. Patolichev said the USSR's foreign trade had increased by 62% over 1955, compared with increases of 53% for West German trade and 22% for the U.S.' He reported that the USSR had imported 5.4 billion rubles worth of machinery and equipment and had exported 4.5 billion rubles worth, primarily to Asia and Africa. Soviet trade with Communist China totaled 8.2 billion rubles in 1959, most of it in Soviet shipments of industrial, electrical and transportation equipment. The USSR's trade with the Communist bloc totaled 31.6 billion rubles, its trade with non-Communist nations 10.4 billion.

(Polish Deputy Premier Piotr Jaroszewicz disclosed July 20, on his return from a 4-day Budapest meeting of the Soviet-bloc Council on Mutual Economic Assistance, that CEMA [COMECON] nations had agreed to plan coordination of their economies for 20 years. The 8 CEMA countries planned to mesh their raw material, capital investment and industrial production planning and lessen East European trade ties with the West, Jaroszewicz said. But agreements for the expansion of British-Soviet trade from $7,980,000 to $11,200,000 worth of goods in each direction in the year ending June 30, 1961 were announced by Britain's Board of Trade in London Oct. 7. And a $200 million Soviet-Italian trade pact was announced Oct. 11 in Moscow. It provided for the delivery to Italy of 12 million tons of Soviet crude oil.)

Price cuts ranging up to 30% were announced Feb. 29 for consumer goods items including furs, sewing machines, guns and some food items.

Khrushchev May 5 described to the Supreme Soviet a program of fiscal reforms intended to revalue the ruble approximately to equal the U.S. dollar and to eliminate income taxes in the USSR. All salaries, prices and monetary accounts would be reduced to 1/10 of the former amounts in old rubles. Unlike the 1947 revaluation, Soviet citizens would be permitted to convert unrestricted amounts of currency. The abolition of personal income taxes was to begin in October and be completed by 1965. All income taxes on persons earning less than 1,000 rubles monthly were to be ended with no reduction in pay. Taxes on persons earning more than 1,000 rubles monthly also would be abolished, but all salaries of 1,000 to 2,000 rubles monthly would be reduced by 1/2 the tax saving, and those over 2,000 rubles monthly would be reduced by amounts equal to the tax saving. Khrushchev pledged that the extra money made available to workers in the lower wage brackets would be matched by increased supplies of consumer goods. Exhorting Soviet workers to achieve 7-year-plan goals by 1963, 2 years ahead of schedule, he promised that all savings realized would be applied to consumer goods production. A Soviet cabinet decree Nov. 15 revalued the ruble from 4 rubles to the U.S. dollar to 90 kopecks to the dollar (one ruble to equal $1.11), effective Jan. 1, 1961. The new ruble's gold content was fixed at .987412 gram and the Soviet State Bank's gold purchasing price at one ruble per gram. Soviet citizens were to receive one new ruble for 10 old rubles.

The CP Central Committee Aug. 8 approved a 5-year 17 billion-ruble program for building warehouses and retail stores. The objective was to improve the distribution of consumer goods. The construction of 105,000 new stores and retail outlets throughout the USSR in 1961 was ordered in Soviet government decrees reported in August. The decree provided for an investment of 17.345 billion rubles for store construction and authorized the Foreign Trade Ministry to buy "high quality goods abroad" to "satisfy the taste of the population."

A fiscal 1961 budget proposing expenditures of 78.5 billion new rubles—a peacetime record—was presented to the Supreme Soviet Dec. 20 by Finance Min. Vasily F. Garbuzov. The new budget estimated state revenues at 78.9 billion new rubles and expenditures at 9.255 billion new rubles for defense, 4 billion new rubles for science and 29 billion new rubles for capital investments, a 50% increase over the 1960 capital investment budget.

Chrmn. Vladimir N. Novikov of the State Planning Commission told the Supreme Soviet Dec. 20 that the heavy investment program would give the USSR the capacity to meet 1961 production goals fixed at 71,300,000 tons of steel, 164 million tons of crude oil and 327 billion kilowatt hours of electricity. The revised 1961 budget and national economic plan were approved Dec. 25 by unanimous vote of the Supreme Soviet, meeting in Moscow. The revised budget provided for expenditures of 77.589 billion new rubles and income of 78.993 billion. The national economic plan called for production increases of 9.5% for heavy industry and 6.9% for consumer goods.

Decrees establishing an All-Russian Economic Council to supervise and coordinate the 70 regional economic councils of the Russian SFSR had been published June 19. The new council, headed by Deputy Premier Vasily M. Ryabikov of the Russian republic, was given authority and responsibility for efficient direction of the regional councils to insure fulfillment of the republic's economic plan. The council apparently was designed to eliminate inefficiency, "localism," and other abuses reported since the creation of regional economic councils in 1957 to implement Khrushchev's plans for decentralization of the Soviet economy.

Pravda charged Dec. 19 that leaders of the Tatar and Bashkir autonomous republics of the Russian SFSR had cost the USSR's economy millions of rubles through lack of cooperation, economic rivalry and other "local tendencies." *Izvestia* articles reported that thousands of workers had left construction sites of the Bratsk, Siberia hydroelectric project due to poor living conditions.

Farm Problems Disclosed

Agriculture Min. Vladimir V. Matskevich was dismissed Dec. 29 and named chairman of a newly-formed economic district in Kazakhstan's "virgin-lands" development area. Matskevich, recently criticized for Soviet farm production failures, was replaced by Mikhail A. Olshansky. The CP Central Committee agricultural journal *Selskaya Zhizn (Rural Life)* had reported Oct. 1 that 3/4 of Kazakhstan's virgin-land grain crop had been harvested but that 1,000,000 hectares of grain remained uncut despite the onset of winter frosts. The trade union newspaper *Trud* had reported Sept. 29 that numbers of tractorists and mechanics had left their jobs in Kazakhstan as a result of rulings refusing them payment in grain for their work.

Pravda reported Oct. 10 that "rates of increase of head of cattle and output of livestock lag behind the average annual rates envisaged in the 7-year plan."

First Secy. Aleksandr U. Petukhov of the Bryansk Oblast CP was dismissed Dec. 14 and replaced by Mikhail K. Krakhmalev for his "failure" to solve agricultural problems of the area, in the Russian SFSR.

A Soviet agricultural statistics handbook disclosed that more than 1/2 the USSR's production of key farm items came from the small private plots allowed collective farmers and city dwellers. In 1959, these plots were said to have produced 82% of the USSR's eggs, 70% of its potatoes, 50% of its meat and milk and 45% of its vegetables. Soviet collective farms had declined in number from 200,000 at the end of World War II to 54,600 in 1959 because of the consolidation of smaller farms and the conversion of inefficient collectives into state farms. The collective farm labor force was said to vary from 18,003,700 in January to 30,703,700 in June, averaging 24,100,000. Soviet collectives were said to average 13,000 acres with a membership of 343 families.

Other Developments

The Central Statistical Board Jan. 21 reported a substantial increase in the number of Soviet graduates. In 1959 colleges and universities produced 106,000 engineers, 200,000 teachers, more than 100,000 physicians, nurses and medical aides, 260,000 technicians and 125,000 agricultural specialists.

Soviet jamming of BBC Russian-language transmissions to the USSR was halted Feb. 3. Cessation of jamming had been pledged in a Dec. 1959 Anglo-Soviet cultural pact. (Some BBC broadcasts to other East European countries still were blocked.)

Plans for the creation of a University of Friendship of Peoples, eventually to enroll 3,000 to 4,000 foreign students, were announced by Krushchev Feb. 20 during a trip to Indonesia. Students, to be brought mainly from Asia, Africa and Latin America, would be given free tuition, housing and care at the school's Moscow campus and free transportation to and from the USSR. The school was opened by Khrushchev Nov. 17 with an entering class of 500.

The Soviet Communist Party had 8,017,000 full members and 691,000 candidate members at the beginning of 1960, the CP magazine *Partiinaya Zhizn (Party Life)* reported Mar. 12.

Soviet agreement to permit U.S. tourists to visit Voronezh in the Don Valley and Tarnopol in the Western Ukraine and to extend to 30 days the limit on visits to Riga, in the Latvian SSR, was reported in Moscow Apr. 18 by Cosmos Travel Bureau, a U.S. firm.

Decrees published in the Soviet press Aug. 10 ordered republican and local economic councils to give priority to a 3-year program of school construction. Local authorities were ordered to divert materials and funds from housing to the school program. The decree disclosed that the USSR's school building program for 1959 had been only 89% fulfilled and that many Soviet students were attending classes on a 2- and 3-shift basis.

Memoirs published Feb. 29 by Marshal Vasily Chuikov credited Khrushchev with a major role in liaison and planning for the World War II defense of Stalingrad but made no mention of Marshal Georgi Zhukov, formerly considered the Stalingrad victor.

4 U.S. helicopters were ordered by the Soviet embassy in Washington Mar. 13, at a cost of $2 million, for the personal use of Khrushchev and other Soviet leaders.

Several former high officials in the Soviet hierarchy who had been given minor positions after they were forced out of the party leadership by Khrushchev and his allies were reported to have retired during March and April. Ex-Premier Bulganin's retirement as chairman of the Stavropol Region Economic Council was reported by Moscow sources Mar. 23. Bulganin, 65, reportedly had been permitted to return to the Moscow area on a 3,000-ruble monthly pension after complaining to Khrushchev about harassment by Stavropol officials.

Ex-Foreign Min. Molotov, ex-Heavy Industry Min. Kaganovich and ex-Premier Malenkov, ousted for allegedly leading an "anti-party" plot against Khrushchev, were absent or dismissed from the posts given them after their defeat by Khrushchev, according to reports from Moscow. UPI reported Apr. 15 that Molotov, 70, Soviet ambassador to Outer Monoglia was ill in a Moscow hospital. UPI reported Apr. 16 that Kaganovich, 66, manager of a cement factory in the Urals, had retired to Moscow. AP reported May 3 that Malenkov had been dismissed as manager of a hydroelectric station in Ust-Kamenogorsk, Kazakhstan.

1961

The Sino-Soviet ideological rift, long an open secret, was brought out into the open in 1961 at the 22d Soviet Communist Party Congress. The congress approved a party program to serve as a guide for Soviet-bloc actions, policies and goals for 20 years. It also adopted revised rules designed to promote democracy within the party. Khrushchev emphasized repeatedly that Soviet foreign policy was based on co-existence with the West, but he said the USSR would continue to support wars of national liberation against colonial/imperialist regimes. Khrushchev met with the new U.S. President, John F. Kennedy, but their discussions evidently produced no agreements. The Soviet military demobilization was reversed in 1961, and the Warsaw Pact powers decided on a general build-up of their forces. The USSR ended the nuclear-test moratorium and detonated the 2 most powerful bombs ever exploded. Khrushchev asserted that the expanding Soviet economy would soon overtake the U.S. economy. But farm problems persisted, and Khrushchev won approval of a drastic overhaul of agricultural administration.

The ideological rift between the Soviet leaders and the Chinese and Albanian Communist leaders was brought into the open by Soviet Premier Nikita Khrushchev at the 22d Congress of the Soviet Communist Party, held Oct. 17-31. Khrushchev denounced Albania as the stronghold of Stalinism and of opposition to the liberalization and de-Stalinization campaigns he (Khrushchev) had initiated. Khrushchev's charges were opposed by Communist Chinese Premier Chou En-lai, who, in effect, confirmed Communist China's support of the Albanian deviation. Condemnations of Stalin were repeated by many speakers at the congress, and the congress ordered Stalin's body removed from the Lenin mausoleum and reburied near the Kremlin wall.

The congress, the party's supreme policy-ratifying body, was attended by 4,008 voting delegates and 405 advisory delegates of the Soviet CP and by delegations of observers from 83 foreign countries. The foreign delegates included groups from Communist China, the U.S. and Cuba, but not from Albania or Yugoslavia.* The meeting took place in the newly built Palace of the Congresses on the Kremlin grounds. The meeting's aims had been widely publicized by the Soviet press and radio: the examination and approval of a new Communist program, the 3d in the party's history, which would serve as a guide for the construction of "Communist society" in the USSR in 20 years. The new program was introduced Oct. 18 together with a new Communist Party statute whose avowed purpose was to democratize the party's membership, organization and procedures. But the congress' direction changed abruptly when Khrushchev began a new attack on Stalinist tendencies in the USSR and other Soviet-bloc nations.

---

* A communique pledging to continue efforts toward the improvement of Soviet-Yugoslav relations had been signed in Moscow July 13 by Soviet Foreign Min. Andrei A. Gromyko and Yugoslav Foreign Min. Koca Popovic. The communique, issued at the end of a 7-day Soviet visit by Popovic, declared that the 2 countries' policies "are similar or coincide on the major international questions." It expressed hope that "cooperation between the 2 countries in the questions of the struggle for peace and the reduction of international tension will go on developing successfully."

Russia's Rift with Albania & China

The CP congress' denunciation of the Albanian Communist regime of Gen. Enver Hoxha was begun by Khrushchev Oct. 17 in his speech at the first session. It was evident to informed observers, however, that Communist China was the true target of the Soviet attack on Albania. According to the official paraphrased text of the speech (the paraphrase in single quotes, Khrushchev's quoted words in double quotes): 'The CPSU policy aimed at eliminating the harmful consequences of the cult the individual did not meet with due understanding on the part of the leaders of the Albanian Party of Labor. Indeed they began to oppose that policy.... [The CPSU] will continue to do all in its power to ensure that Albania marches shoulder to shoulder with all the socialist countries.' "This stand of the Albanian leaders is due to the fact that ... they are using the same methods as were current in our country at the time of the personality cult."

Western newsmen attending the congress reported Oct. 17 that Communist Chinese Premier Chou ostentatiously refrained from joining in the general applause for Khrushchev's remarks about Albania. Western reporters were barred from the congress after the first session.

(Khrushchev coupled his attack on Albania with a reiteration of the Soviet bloc's condemnation of Yugoslavia. He said: "Revisionist ideas pervade ... the leadership of the League of Communists of Yugoslavia. The line they had adopted—that of development in isolation from the world Socialist community—is harmful and perilous. It plays into the hands of imperialist action....")

Khrushchev's attack on Albania was renewed Oct. 18. Khrushchev charged that Albania's leaders "adopted a course of sharp deterioration of relations with our party and with the Soviet Union.... This became especially evident" in 1960.

Communist China's refusal to join in the attack on Albania was made clear Oct. 19 in a speech by Chou, the first foreign delegate to address the congress. Although he reiterated assurances of Chinese friendship for the USSR, Chou reportedly said: "If there are quarrels in the Socialist camp we consider that they should be settled through bilateral contacts and that a public denunciation does not contribute to the cohesion of the Socialist camp." (A text of the Chou address published Oct. 20 by *Pravda* contained the similar warning that "open one-sided condemnation of a fraternal party can only grieve our friends and gladden our enemies.") It was reported that Khrushchev, by refraining from applauding Chou's speech, caused other delegates to stop.

Led by Soviet First Deputy Premier Anastas I. Mikoyan, Soviet and foreign Communist leaders backed the attack on Albania in speeches at the congress Oct. 20. Mikoyan's address contained specific charges against Albanian CP First Secy. Hoxha and Premier Mehmet Shehu. Mikoyan said Hoxha had warned that "whoever goes against my policy will be shot." Others supporting Khrushchev included Walter Ulbricht of East Germany, Palmiro Togliatti of Italy, Janos Kadar of Hungary, Antonin Novotny of Czechoslovakia and Gheorghe Gheorghiu-Dej of Rumania.

The Chinese position was given implicit support Oct. 21 in speeches in which Pres. Ho Chi Minh of North Viet Nam and Premier Kim Il Sung of North Korea made no reference to the Albanian heresy. Similar support was indicated Oct. 24 by Japanese CP First Secy. Sanzo Nosaka.

Communist China's support of Albania was alluded to openly by Khrushchev in an address at the congress Oct. 26. He said: "If the Chinese comrades wish to make efforts toward normalizing the relations between the Albanian party . . . and the fraternal parties, there is hardly anyone who can contribute to the solution of this problem more than the Communist Party of China." "To end the cult of the personality," he declared, "Shehu, Hoxha and others have to give up their leading positions."

The congress approved and made public Oct. 31 a resolution calling on Albanian leaders to "renounce their erroneous views and to return to the road of unity" with the international Communist movement.

Stalinism & 'Anti-Party' Group Attacked

The first indication of the renewed campaign against Stalinism came Oct. 17 in an inaugural congress address in which Khrushchev said that the USSR would test a 50-megaton nuclear bomb and might withdraw its year-end deadline for a separate peace treaty with East Germany. Khrushchev, submitting the CP Central Committee's report on its activities since the 21st CP Congress (1959), spoke for 6-1/2 hours. He described the period as one of Communist successes in every field of endeavor. But he made it clear that he considered continuation of his policies necessary for a peaceful Communist victory over capitalism.

According to the official paraphrase of Khrushchev's speech (paraphrase in single quotes, Khrushchev's words in double quotes): '...The policy adopted by the 20th Congress has fully triumphed.... Had the cult of the individual not been condemned..., it would have threatened a cleavage between party and people.... The results would have been a weakening of Soviet positions on the world scene.... The party realized...that the errors and distortions and abuses of power it had laid bare might arouse a certain bitterness and even discontent within the party and among the people.... But the party boldly faced the difficulties; honestly and frankly it told the people the truth, being deeply convinced that the people would rightly understand....' 'The Leninist policy line...was opposed by a factional anti-party group consisting of [Vyacheslav M.] Molotov, [Lazar M.] Kaganovich, [Georgi M.] Malenkov, [Kliment E.] Voroshilov, [Nikolai] Bulganin, [Mikhail G.] Pervukhin, [Maxim Z.] Saburov and [Dmitri T.] Shepilov.... Somewhat later, in Oct. 1957, the plenary meeting of the Central Committee of the CPSU firmly repelled attempts by the former defense minister, [Georgi K.] Zhukov, to take an adventurous course intended to dissociate the armed forces from the party and oppose the Soviet army to the party leadership.' "The party cast aside the bankrupt factionalists...and closed its ranks."

A fuller text of Khrushchev's address, published in Moscow newspapers Oct. 18, contained this description of these events: The original opposition to the de-Stalinization campaign was led within the CP Presidium by 4 of its 11 members—Molotov, Kaganovich, Malenkov and Voroshilov; "their position was no accident; they bear personal responsibility for mass repressions" during the Stalin era; these 4 then gained the support of 4 more Presidium members: Bulganin, Pervukhin, Saburov and Shepilov; "having plotted in secret meeting, the factionalists demanded an extraordinary session of the Presidium. They counted on...seizing the leadership of the party and the country"; they were "exposed and ideologically routed" when other Presidium members learned of their plot and confronted them at a specially summoned Central Committee plenum in June 1957.

Khrushchev's address was the first confirmation of rumors that Marshal Voroshilov had been implicated. Voroshilov, 80, was present when Khrushchev made his denunciation; he had been elected earlier Oct. 17 to membership in the congress' 41-member Presidium.

The attack on the anti-party group was continued in most speeches at the congress. First Secy. Kirill T. Mazurov of the Byelorussian CP charged Oct. 19 that Malenkov had helped organize a purge of "1/2 the members of the party" in 1935-6. First Secy. Ivan V. Spiridonov of the Leningrad Region CP charged the same day that Malenkov, together with the late Lavrenti Beria, had been responsible for the "Leningrad affair," in which thousands of "innocent people" had been purged and many executed in 1934. (The "Leningrad affair" involved the assassination of local party leader Sergei Kirov. His murder, which some observers thought had been committed by an *agent provocateur,* had been cited by Stalin as a major reason for the purges of the 1930s.) First Secy. Nikolai V. Podgorny of the Ukrainian CP accused Kaganovich of purging innocent Ukrainian writers in 1947.

First Deputy Premier Anastas Mikoyan charged Oct. 20 that if the anti-party faction had not been defeated in 1957, Molotov's policies might have led to a new world war. He said: "Molotov rejected the line of peaceful coexistence, reducing this concept to the absence of war . . . and to a denial of the possibility of avoiding world war"; "to the present day Molotov adheres . . . to his conservative-dogmatic views."

Voroshilov was silenced by the congress' chairman Oct. 23 when he attempted to reply from the floor to Russian Republican Premier Dmitri S. Polyansky's charges of his complicity in the pre-war purges of the Soviet army.

Molotov was represented Oct. 25 as having continued his opposition to Khrushchev's policies. Pavel A. Satyukov, editor of *Pravda,* told the congress that Molotov had written the Central Committee to denounce the new 20-year party program as "anti-revolutionary" and "pacifist." He was said to have written that, "without serious conflict, without war, advance toward communism is impossible." Otto V. Kuusinen, a CP Presidium member, charged Molotov Oct. 26 with the authorship of a program for "further intrigues" against the party.

Voroshilov, in a personal confession read to the congress for him Oct. 27, admitted that he had unknowingly taken part in the anti-party group's plotting, but he said he rejected their aims. He asked to be forgiven. Khrushchev accepted his apology and urged party leaders be "considerate" in their assessment of him.

Khrushchev, in his final address to the full congress, said Oct. 27 that "a memorial should be erected in Moscow to commemorate the comrades who became victims of arbitrary rule" under Stalin. Khrushchev told the congress that evidence existed that Kirov had been murdered by Stalin's secret police. Khrushchev declared that Stalin's close associates Sergei Ordzhonikidze and Alesha Svanidse (brother of Stalin's first wife) had committed suicide rather than share his guilt. Khrushchev said: "Thousands of absolutely innocent people perished [in the purges]."

The resolution ordering the removal of Stalin's body from the Red Square mausoleum, where it lay in public view beside Lenin, was approved unanimously by the congress Oct. 30. Submitted by Podgorny, the resolution said that "the abuses of power, the mass reprisals against honest Soviet people and other actions during the period of the personality cult make it impossible to leave the coffin with his body in the V. I. Lenin mausoleum." Stalin's name was effaced from the Red Square tomb Oct. 31, and his body was removed Nov. 1 and reinterred at the foot of the Kremlin wall.

Khrushchev Restates Foreign Policies

The USSR's foreign policies were given a major restatement by Khrushchev Oct. 17 in a 6-1/2 hour address at the opening session of the 22d CP Congress. In his address, Khrushchev said:

Germany—As a result of talks held by Soviet Foreign Min. Andrei A. Gromyko with U.S. Pres. Kennedy and State Secy. Dean Rusk, "we have the impression that the Western powers were displaying a certain understanding of the situation and that they were inclined to seek a solution for the German problem and for the West Berlin issue on a mutually acceptable basis." "If the Western powers show readiness to settle the German problem, the question of a deadline for the signing of a German peace treaty will not be of such importance. Then we shall not insist on the signing of the peace treaty before Dec. 31, 1961." The

USSR's aims, however, remained the transformation of West Berlin into a "demilitarized free city" and the signing of a German peace treaty which would "do away with the vestiges" of World War II.

A-tests—"The tests of new nuclear weapons are proceeding successfully.... We have a 100-megaton bomb, but it will not be exploded because if we did we might break our own windows.... We shall explode a 50-megaton bomb and thus test the instruments for the 100-megaton bomb."

War danger—"We believe that now the forces of socialism ... are mightier than the aggressive imperialist forces. But even if we should agree with the United States President, who quite recently stated that our forces were equal, even then it is plainly unreasonable to use the threat of war." "The chief aggressive force is the United States, center of world reaction," and its NATO allies, particularly the "West German militarists and revenge-seekers." The world could be destroyed if "some Western officer" made a mistake and unleashed nuclear forces. "We now have at our disposal intercontinental ballistic missiles, anti-aircraft rocket equipment and rockets for the land, naval and air forces. A nuclear-powered submarine fleet is being built up and equipped with ballistic and targetseeking rockets." If the Western powers "dare attack the Socialist countries and hurl mankind into the abyss of a war of annihilation, that mad act will be their last."

Peaceful coexistence—Despite the current crisis, war was not inevitable. "There now is a prospect of achieving peaceful coexistence for the entire period in which the social and political problems now dividing the world will have to be solved." The indications are that it may actually be feasible "to banish world war from the life of society even before the complete triumph of socialism on earth, with capitalism surviving in part of the world."

Export of revolution—"We are convinced that in the end the Socialist system will triumph everywhere. But this in no way implies that we will seek to achieve its triumph by interfering in the internal affairs of other countries. You cannot bring in ideas on bayonets ... or on rockets." But "imperialist attempts to interfere in the affairs of insurrectionary people would constitute acts of aggression endangering world peace," and "in the event of imperialist export of counter-revolution, the Communists will call on the peoples of all countries to ... mobilize."

Disarmament & disengagement—The Soviet Union was prepared to "seek jointly with the Western powers a mutually acceptable and agreed [disarmament] settlement through talks." It also was ready to negotiate (a) a zone of disengagement between Soviet and Western troops, (b) the reduction of foreign-based armed forces, (c) atom-free zones in Europe and Asia, (d) a NATO-Warsaw Treaty nonaggression pact.

UN leadership—The UN's executive "machinery has grown rusty in the cold war years and has been operating fitfully.... It is the time to grant genuinely equal rights in all UN agencies to the 3 groups of states that have come into being in the world—socialist, neutralist and imperialist." Action must be taken to "restore the legitimate rights of...[Communist] China in the United Nations."

CP Program Sets 20-Year Policies

The initial draft of the new program for the Communist Party of the Soviet Union, written to Khrushchev's order, had been approved unanimously by the CP Central Committee June 19. The draft program, designed as a guide for actions, policies and goals of the Soviet bloc for at least 20 years, was widely regarded as virtually a Khrushchev revision of Marxist-Leninist doctrine. It was generally considered a move by Khrushchev to make himself the undisputed ideological leader of the Communist world. The program was approved in revised form by the 22d Congress of the Soviet Communist Party Oct. 31 although the original draft continued to be regarded generally as Khrushchev's true plan.

The lengthy draft, filling 9 pages of *Pravda* (the June 30 edition), was described by the CP as its "3d program, a program for the building of Communist society." The first program, adopted by the Bolshevik Party's 2d Congress in 1903, had called for the overthrow of the Czarist-bourgeois regime in Russia and the establishment of the dictatorship of the proletariat. The 2d program, adopted by the 8th Congress in 1919, was the Leninist plan for creating a Socialist society. Both programs were carried out, and "socialism triumphed in the Soviet Union completely and finally," the CP draft asserted.

The draft 3d program asserted that "peaceful coexistence of the Socialist and capitalist countries" was "necessary for the development of human society." Such coexistence was a "Leninist principle" and "a mighty obstacle in the path of the imperialist aggression," it declared. It held that communism could triumph without world war.

The draft proclaimed that "the present generation of Soviet people shall live under communism."

The draft predicted that during 1961-70 the USSR "will surpass the strongest and richest capitalist country, the U.S.A., in production per head of population; the people's standard of living and their cultural and technical standards will improve substantially; everyone will live in easy circumstances"; "the demand of the Soviet people for well-appointed housing will, in the main, be satisfied; hard physical work will disappear; the USSR will become the country with the shortest working day."

During 1971-80, the draft predicted, "the material and technical basis of communism will be created and there will be an abundance of material and cultural benefits for the whole population; Soviet society will come close to a state where it can introduce the principle of distribution according to needs, and there will be a gradual transition to one form of ownership—public ownership. Thus, a Communist society will, on the whole, be built in the USSR. The construction of Communist society will be fully completed in the subsequent period."

"The program can be fulfilled successfully under conditions of peace," the draft said. But "aggravation of the international situation, and the resulting necessary increase of expenditure on defense, may prevent realization of the plan for an upsurge of the well-being of the Soviet people."

Partial text of the Soviet CP draft program (English translation distributed by Tass):

INTRODUCTION—The great October Socialist Revolution ushered in a new era in the history of mankind, the era of the downfall of capitalism and the establishment of communism. Socialism has triumphed in the Soviet Union and has achieved decisive victories in the people's democracies. . . .

More than 100 years ago Karl Marx and Friedrich Engels . . . wrote in the *Communist Manifesto:* "A specter is haunting Europe, the specter of communism." . . . A tremendously long road . . . had to be traversed before communism . . . became the great force of modern times. . . .

In the early 20th century the center of the international revolutionary movement shifted to Russia. Russia's heroic working class, led by the Bolshevik party headed by Vladimir Ilyich Lenin, became its vanguard. The Communist Party inspired and led the Socialist revolution; it was the organizer and leader of the first workers' and peasants' state in history....

In adopting its first program at its 2d Congress in 1903 the Bolshevik party called on the working class and all working people of Russia to fight for the overthrow of the Czarist autocracy and then of the bourgeois-landlord system and for the establishment of the dictatorship of the proletariat. In Feb. 1917, the Czarist regime was swept away. In Oct. 1917, the proletarian revolution abolished the capitalist system.... A Socialist country came into being for the first time in history. The creation of a new world began.

The first program of the party had been carried out.

Adopting its 2d program at the 8th Congress in 1919, the party promulgated the task of building a Socialist society.... The Soviet people under the leadership of the Communist Party put into practice the plan for Socialist construction drawn up by Lenin. Socialism triumphed in the Soviet Union completely and finally.

The 2d program of the party has likewise been carried out.

The gigantic revolutionary exploits accomplished by the Soviet people roused and inspired the masses in all countries and continents.... The Socialist revolution in European and Asian countries has resulted in the establishment of the world Socialist system....

1/3 of mankind is building a new life under the banner of scientific communism.... The Socialist world is expanding; the capitalist world is shrinking. Socialism will inevitably succeed capitalism everywhere. Such is the objective law of social development....

Our effort, whose main content is the transition from capitalism to socialism, is an effort and struggle between the 2 opposing social systems, an effort of Socialist and national liberation revolutions, of the breakdown of imperialism and the abolition of the colonial system, an effort of the transition of more and more people to the Socialist path, of the triumph of socialism and communism on a world-wide scale....

Today the Communist Party of the Soviet Union (CPSU) is adopting its 3d program, a program for the building of Communist society. The new program is a constructive generalization of the experience of Socialist constructions; it takes account of the revolutionary movement throughout the world and ... defines the main tasks and principal stages of Communist construction.

The supreme goal of the party is to build a Communist society on whose banner will be inscribed: "From each according to his ability, to each according to his needs." The party's motto, "Everything in the name of man, for the benefit of man," will be put into effect in full....

PART ONE—THE TRANSITION FROM CAPITALISM TO COMMUNISM IS THE ROAD OF HUMAN PROGRESS.

1. The Historical Necessity of the Transition from Capitalism to Socialism

The epoch-making turn of mankind from capitalism to socialism, initiated by the October Revolution, is a natural result of the development of society. Marxism-Leninism discovered the objective laws of social development and revealed the contradictions inherent in capitalism, the inevitability of their bringing about a revolutionary explosion and of the transition of society to communism.

Capitalism is the last exploiting system. Having developed its productive forces to an enormous extent, it became a tremendous obstacle to social progress. Capitalism alone is responsible for the fact that the 20th century, a century of colossal growth of the productive forces and of great scientific progress, has not yet put an end to the poverty of hundreds of millions of people, has not provided an abundance of material and spiritual values for all men on earth....

Under capitalism, the basic and decisive means of production belong to the numerically small capitalist class, while the vast majority of the population consists of proletarians and semi-proletarians, who own no means of production and are therefore compelled to sell their labor-power and by their labor create profits and riches for the ruling classes of society....

The development of large-scale capitalist production—production for profit, for the appropriation of surplus value—leads to the elimination of small independent producers.... The economic laws of its [capitalism's] development necessarily give rise to a huge reserve army of unemployed, which is constantly replenished by ruined peasants and urban petty bourgeoisie. The exploitation of the working people is continuously increasing, social inequality is becoming more and more marked ... and the sufferings and privations of the millions are growing worse.

Capitalism, by concentrating millions of workers in its factories, socializing the process of labor, imparts a social character to production; nevertheless it is the capitalists who appropriate the fruits of labor. This fundamental contradiction of capitalism ... manifests itself in production anarchy and in the fact that the purchasing power of society falls short of the expansion of production and leads periodically to destructive economic crises....

The working class, which is the most consistent revolutionary class, is the chief motive force of the revolutionary transformation of the world.... In fulfilling its historic mission as the revolutionary remaker of the old society and creator of a new system, the working class has become the exponent, not only of its own class interests, but of the interests of all working people. It is the natural leader of all forces fighting against capitalism.

The dictatorship of the proletariat and the leadership of the Marxist-Leninist party are indispensable conditions for the triumph of the Socialist revolution and the building of socialism....

Capitalism has entered its final stage, the stage of monopoly capitalism, of imperialism....

Imperialism is decaying and moribund capitalism; it is the eve of the Socialist revolution. The world capitalist system as a whole is ripe for the social revolution of the proletariat....

The revolutionary defeat of imperialism does not take place all over the world simultaneously....

V. I. Lenin developed the theory of the Socialist revolution in new historical conditions, elaborated the theory of the possibility of socialism triumphing first in one capitalist country taken singly.

Russia was the weakest link in the imperialist system and the focal point of all its contradictions. On the other hand, she had all the conditions necessary for the victory of socialism. Her working class was the most revolutionary and best organized in the world and had considerable experience of class struggle. It was led by a Marxist-Leninist party armed with an advanced, revolutionary theory and steeled in class battles....

2. Historic Significance of the October Revolution & of the Victory of Socialism in the USSR

The great October Revolution breached the imperialist front in Russia,... firmly established the dictatorship of the proletariat and created a new type of state—the Soviet state—and a new type of democracy—democracy for the working people....

...Soviet power nationalized industry, the railways, banks and the land. It abolished landed proprietorship and fulfilled the peasants' age-long dream of land....

The Socialist revolution in Russia shook the entire structure of world capitalism to its very foundations; the world split into 2 opposing systems.

For the first time there emerged in the international arena a state which put forward the great slogan of peace and began carrying through new principles in relations between peoples and countries....

The enemies of Leninism maintained that Russia was not mature enough for a Socialist revolution, that it was impossible to build socialism in one country. But the enemies of Leninism were put to shame....

The party proved equal to that historic task.... On the basis of a thorough scientific analysis, Lenin elaborated the policy of the proletarian state for the entire period of transition from capitalism to socialism. He evolved the New Economic Policy (NEP), designed to bring about the victory of socialism....

The party upheld that plan in an acute struggle against skeptics and capitulators, against the Trotskyists, Right opportunists, nationalist-deviators and other hostile groups....

The point at issue at the time was: either perish or forge full steam ahead and overtake the capitalist countries economically.

The Soviet state had first of all to solve the problem of industrialization. In a historically brief period, without outside help, the Soviet Union built up a large-scale modern industry. By the time it had fulfilled 3 5-year plans (1928-1941) the Soviet Union had become a mighty industrial power that had achieved complete economic independence from the capitalist countries....

Led by the party, aided and fully supported by the working class, the peasantry took the road to socialism. Millions of small individual farms went into voluntary association to form collective farms. A large number of Soviet state farms and machine and tractor stations were established....

To build socialism it was necessary to raise the cultural level of the people; that task too was accomplished. A cultural revolution was carried out in the country. It freed the working people from spiritual slavery and ignorance and gave them access to the cultural values accumulated by mankind....

Socialism, which Marx and Engels scientifically predicted as inevitable and the plan for the construction of which was mapped out by Lenin, has become a reality in the Soviet Union....

The Socialist principle "From each according to his abilities, to each according to his work" has been put into effect in the Soviet Union....

The entire life of Socialist society is based on the principle of broad democracy. Working people take an active part, through the Soviets, trade unions and other mass organizations, in managing the affairs of the state and in solving problems of economic and cultural advancement. Socialist democracy includes both political freedoms—freedom of speech, of the press and of assembly, the right to elect and to be elected and also social rights—the right to work, to rest and leisure, to education, to material security in old age and in case of illness or disability; equality of citizens of all races and nationalities; equal rights for women and men in all spheres of political, economic and cultural activity. Socialist democracy, unlike bourgeois democracy, does not merely proclaim the rights of the people, but makes it really possible for the people to exercise them. Soviet society insures the real liberty of the individual. The highest manifestation of this liberty is man's emancipation from exploitation, which is what primarily constitutes genuine social justice.

Socialism has created conditions for the rapid progress of science.... The man-made satellites of the earth and the sun, powerful space rockets and interplanetary space ships, atomic power stations and the first triumphal orbiting of the globe, accomplished by a Soviet citizen,... have become symbols of the creative energy of ascendant communism.

The solution of the national question is one of the greatest achievements of socialism.... Socialist society has not only guaranteed the political equality of nations, but has also abolished the economic and cultural backwardness inherited from the old system....

... For nearly 2 out of little more than 4 decades, the Soviet people were compelled to devote their energies to the repulsion of invasions by the imperialist powers and to post-war economic rehabilitation. The Soviet system was put to a particularly severe test during the Great Patriotic War, the most trying war in history. By winning that war, the Soviet people proved that there are no forces in the world capable of stopping the progress of Socialist society....

Soviet experience has shown that the peoples are able to achieve socialism only as a result of the Socialist revolution and the dictatorship of the proletariat....

Soviet experience has shown that socialism alone can put an end to the exploitation of man by man, production anarchy, economic crises, unemployment and the poverty of the people, and insure planned, continuous and rapid development of the economy and steady improvement of the people's standard of living.

Soviet experience has shown that the working class can fulfill its historical mission as the builder of a new society only in a sound alliance with the non-proletarian working masses, primarily the peasantry.

Soviet experience has shown that the victory of the Socialist revolution alone provides all possibilities and conditions for the abolition of all national oppression, for the voluntary union of free and equal nations and nationalities in a single state.

Soviet experience has shown that the Socialist state is the main instrument for the Socialist transformation of society....

Soviet experience has shown that socialism and peace are inseparable. The might of socialism serves peace....

Soviet experience has fully borne out the Marxist-Leninist theory that the Communist Party plays a decisive role in the formation and development of Socialist society....

Soviet experience has shown that fidelity to the principles of Marxism-Leninism, of proletarian internationalism,... are imperative conditions for the victory of socialism....

3. The World Socialist System

The Soviet Union is not pursuing the tasks of Communist construction alone but in fraternal community with the other Socialist countries.

The defeat of German fascism and Japanese militarism in World War II... created favorable conditions for the overthrow of capitalist and landlord rule by the peoples in a number of European and Asian countries.... Yugoslavia likewise took the Socialist path. But the Yugoslav leaders by revisionist policy contraposed Yugoslavia to the Socialist camp and the international Communist movement, thus threatening the loss of the revolutionary gains of the Yugoslav people.

The Socialist revolutions in Europe and Asia dealt imperialism a further powerful blow.... The revolutions in European and Asian countries are the biggest event in world history since Oct. 1917.

A new form of political organization of society, people's democracy, a variety of the dictatorship of the proletariat, emerged....

There emerged a world Socialist system, a social, economic and political community of free sovereign peoples pursuing the Socialist and Communist path, united by common interests and goals and the close bonds of international Socialist solidarity....

The combined forces of the Socialist camp guarantee each Socialist country against encroachments of imperialist reaction. The consolidation of the Socialist countries in a single camp, its increasing unity and steadily growing strength, ensure the complete victory of socialism within the framework of the system as a whole....

It has been borne out in practice and recognized by all Marxist-Leninist parties that the processes of Socialist revolution and construction are founded on a number of basic objective laws applicable to all countries entering upon the Socialist path....

... The distinctive features of the relations existing between the countries of the Socialist community are complete equality, respect for independence and sovereignty and fraternal mutual assistance.... In the world community of Socialist countries, none have, nor can have, any special rights or privileges.

The experience of the world Socialist system has confirmed the need for the closest unity of countries that fall away from capitalism, for their united effort in the building of socialism and communism. The line of Socialist construction in isolation, detached from the world community of Socialist countries, is theoretically untenable because it conflicts with the objective laws governing the development of Socialist society....

All the Socialist countries make their contribution to the building and development of the world Socialist system and the consolidation of its might....

The cooperation of the Socialist countries enables each country to use its resources and develop its productive forces to the full and in the most rational manner. A new type of international division of labor is taking shape in the process of the economic, scientific and technical cooperation of the Socialist countries, the coordination of their economic plan, the specialization and combination of production....

Nationalism is the chief political and ideological weapon used by international reaction and the remnants of the domestic reactionary forces against the unity of the Socialist countries....

... Yet while they oppose nationalism and national egoism, Communists always show utmost consideration for the national feelings of the masses.

The world Socialist system is advancing steadfastly toward decisive victory in its economic competition with capitalism. It will shortly surpass the world capitalist system in aggregate industrial and agricultural production....

4. Crisis of World Capitalism

Imperialism has entered the period of decline and collapse. The inexorable process of decay has seized capitalism from top to bottom—its economic and political system, its politics and ideology. Imperialism has forever lost its power over the bulk of mankind. The main content, main trend and main features of the historical development of mankind are being determined by the world Socialist system....

World War I and the October Revolution ushered in the general crisis of capitalism. The 2d stage of this crisis developed at the time of World War II and the Socialist revolutions in a number of European and Asian countries. World capitalism has now entered a new, 3d stage of that crisis, the principal feature of which is that its development was not due to a world war....

In the imperialist stage state-monopoly capitalism comes to the fore. The emergence and growth of monopolies leads to the direct intervention of the state, in the interests of the financial oligarchy, in the process of capitalist reproduction. It is in the interests of the financial oligarchy that the bourgeois state institutes various types of regulation and resorts to the nationalization of some branches of the economy....

The oppression of finance capital keeps growing. Giant monopolies controlling the bulk of social production dominate the life of the nation. A handful of millionaires and multimillionaires wield arbitrary power over the entire wealth of the capitalist world and make the life of entire nations mere small change in their selfish deals....

The state is becoming a committee for the management of the affairs of the monopoly bourgeoisie....

The proponents of social-democratism and revisionism are making out state-monopoly capitalism to be socialism. The facts give the lie to this contention. State-monopoly capitalism does not change the nature of imperialism.... It widens the rift between labor and capital....

Attempts at state regulation of the capitalist economy cannot eliminate competition and anarchy of production, cannot insure the planned development of the economy on a nationwide scale because capitalist ownership and exploitation of wage-labor remain the basis of production....

The new phenomena in imperialist development corroborate the accuracy of Lenin's conclusions on the principal objective laws of capitalism in its final stage and on its increasing decay. Yet this decay does not signify complete stagnation ... and does not rule out growth of capitalist economy at particular times and in particular countries.

All in all, capitalism is increasingly impeding the development of the contemporary productive forces. Mankind is entering the period of a great scientific and technical revolution....

Socialism alone is capable of effecting it and of applying its fruits in the interests of society.

Technical progress under the rule of monopoly capital is turning against the working class.... Capitalist automation is robbing the worker of his daily bread. Unemployment is rising, the living standard is dropping....

Modern capitalism has made the market problem extremely acute. Imperialism is incapable of solving it, because lag of effective demand behind growth of production is one of its objective laws. Moreover, it retards the industrial development of the underdeveloped countries. The world capitalist market is shrinking relative to the more rapidly expanding production capacity....

Monopoly capital has, in the final analysis, doomed bourgeois society to a low rate of production growth.... A considerable part of the production plant stands idle, while millions of unemployed wait at the factory gates. Farm production is artificially restricted although millions are underfed in the world. People suffer want in material goods, but imperialism is squandering them on war preparations....

State-monopoly capitalism stimulates militarism to an unheard-of degree....

While enriching some groups of the monopoly bourgeoisie, militarism leads to the exhaustion of nations, to the ruin of the peoples languishing under an excessive tax burden, mounting inflation and a high cost of living. Within the lifetime of one generation imperialism plunged mankind into the abyss of 2 destructive world wars.... The new war being hatched by the imperialists threatens mankind with unprecedented human losses and destruction....

Fear of revolution, the successes of the Socialist countries and the pressure of the working-class movement compel the bourgeoisie to make partial concessions with respect to wages, labor conditions and social security....

Even the relatively high standard of living in the small group of capitalistically developed countries rests upon the poverty of the Asian, African and Latin-American peoples, upon non-equivalent exchange, discrimination of female labor, brutal oppression of Negroes and immigrant workers, and also upon the intensified exploitation of the working people in those countries.

The bourgeois myth of "full employment" has proved to be sheer mockery, for the working class is suffering continuously from mass unemployment and insecurity....

The development of capitalism has dissipated the legend of the stability of small peasant farming.... The monopolies have seized dominant positions in agriculture as well. Millions of farmers and peasants are being driven off the land....

The uneven development of capitalism alters the balance of forces between countries and makes the contradictions between them more acute. The economic and with it the political and military center of imperialism has shifted from Europe to the United States. United States monopoly capital...has seized the main sources of raw materials, the markets and the spheres of investment, has built up a covert colonial empire and become the biggest international exploiter.... United States imperialism is in effect performing the function of a world gendarme, supporting reactionary dictatorial regimes and decayed monarchies, opposing democratic, revolutionary changes and launching aggressions against peoples fighting for independence....

The contradictions between the principal imperialist powers are growing deeper.... The Anglo-American, Franco-American, Franco-German, American-German, Anglo-German, Japanese-American and other contradictions are becoming especially acute....

The American monopolies and their British and French allies are openly assisting the resurgence of West German imperialism, which is cynically advocating aggressive aims of revenge and preparing a war against the Socialist countries and other European states....

The bourgeois system came into being with the alluring slogans of liberty, equality, fraternity. But the bourgeoisie made use of these slogans merely to elbow out the feudal gentry and to assume power. Instead of equality a new gaping abyss of social and economic inequality appeared. Not fraternity but ferocious class struggle reigns in bourgeois society....

The ideologists of imperialism hide the dictatorship of monopoly capital behind specious slogans of freedom and democracy. They declare the imperialist powers to be countries of the "free world" and [yet] represent the ruling bourgeois circles....

The bourgeoisie gives extensive publicity to the allegedly democratic nature of its election laws, singing special praise to its multi-party system and the possibility of nominating many candidates. In reality, however, the monopolists deprive the masses of the opportunity to express their will and elect genuine champions of their interests.... They mislead the masses, imposing their own candidates upon the electorate. The different bourgeois parties are usually not more than different factions of the ruling bourgeoisie....

The financial oligarchy resorts to the establishment of Fascist regimes... particularly when the masses try to make use even of their democratic rights....

Thus, the world imperialist system is rent by deep-rooted and acute contradictions....

5. International Revolutionary Movement of the Working Class

...The example of victorious socialism has a revolutionizing effect on the minds of the working people of the capitalist world; it inspires them to fight against imperialism and greatly facilitates the struggle.

...A new contingent of the world proletariat—the young working-class movement of the newly-free, dependent and colonial countries of Asia, Africa and Latin America—has entered the world arena. Marxist-Leninist parties have arisen and matured. They are becoming a universally recognized national force enjoying ever greater prestige and followed by large sections of the working people....

The capitalist countries are continuously shaken by class battles. Militant actions of the working class in defense of its economic and political interests are growing in number....

The reactionary forces in individual capitalist countries can no longer cope with the growing forces of democracy and socialism. Struggle and competition between the capitalist states do not preclude, however, a certain unity among them in the face of the increasing strength of socialism and the working-class movement. The imperialists form reactionary alliances; they enter into mutual agreements and set up military blocs and bases spearheaded not only against the Socialist countries, but also against the revolutionary liberation movement....

The world situation today is more favorable to the working-class movement....

In the new historical situation, the working class of many countries can, even before capitalism is overthrown, compel the bourgeoisie to carry out measures that transcend ordinary reforms.... By uniting large sections of the working people, the working-class can make ruling circles cease preparations for a new world war, renounce the idea of starting local wars and use the economy for peaceful purposes....

The working class directs its main blow against the capitalist monopolies. All the main sections of a nation have a vital interest in abolishing the unlimited power of the monopolies. This makes it possible to unite all the democratic movements opposing the oppression of the finance oligarchy....

The proletariat advances a political program for combating the power of the monopolies with due regard to the present as well as the future interests of its allies. It advocates broad nationalization on terms most favorable to the people, control by parliament, the trade unions and other democratic representative bodies over the nationalized industries and over the entire economic activity of the state. It backs the peasants' demands for radical land reforms and works for the realization of the slogan "The land to those who till it."...

It is in this struggle that the alliance of the working class and all working people is shaped. . . .

General democratic struggles against the monopolies do not delay the Socialist revolution but bring it nearer. The struggle for democracy is a component of the struggle for socialism. The broader the democratic movement, the higher becomes the level of the political consciousness of the masses and the more clearly they see that only socialism clears for them the way to genuine freedom and well-being. . . .

The proletarian revolution in a country, being part of the world Socialist revolution, is accomplished by the working class of that country and the masses of its people. The revolution is not made to order. It cannot be imposed on the people from without. . . .

Together with the other Marxist-Leninist parties, the Communist Party of the Soviet Union regards it as its internationalist duty to call on the peoples of all countries to . . . firmly repel imperialist interference in the affairs of the people of any country risen to revolt and thereby prevent imperialist export of counter-revolution. . . .

Communists have never held that the road to revolution lies necessarily through wars between countries. Socialist revolution is not necessarily connected with war. . . . Revolutions are quite feasible without war. The great objectives of the working class can be realized without world war. Today the conditions for this are more favorable than ever.

The working class and its vanguard—the Marxist-Leninist parties—prefer to achieve the transfer of power from the bourgeoisie to the proletariat by peaceful means, without civil war. . . .

The working class, supported by the majority of the people, . . . can defeat the reactionary, anti-popular forces, win a solid majority in parliament, transform it from a tool serving the class interests of the bourgeoisie into an instrument serving the working people, launch a broad mass struggle outside parliament, smash the resistance of the reactionary forces and provide the necessary conditions for a peaceful Socialist revolution. . . .

Where the exploiting classes resort to violence against the people, the possibility of a non-peaceful transition to socialism should be borne in mind. Leninism maintains, and historical experience confirms, that the ruling classes do not yield power of their own free will. Hence, the degree of bitterness of the class struggle and the forms it takes will depend not so much on the proletariat as on the strength of the reactionary groups' resistance to the will of the overwhelming majority of the people, and on the use of force by these groups at a particular stage of the struggle for socialism. In each particular country the actual applicability of one method of transition to socialism or the other depends on concrete historical conditions.

It may well be that as the forces of socialism grow, the working-class movement gains strength and the positions of capitalism are weakened, there will arise in certain countries a situation in which it will be preferable for the bourgeoisie, as Marx and Lenin foresaw it, to agree to the means of production being purchased from it and for the proletariat to "pay off" the bourgeoisie. . . .

. . . However varied the forms of a new, people's state power in the period of Socialist construction, their essence will be the same—dictatorship of the proletariat, which represents genuine democracy, democracy for the working people. . . .

The dictatorship of the proletariat is a dictatorship of the overwhelming majority over the minority; it is directed against the exploiters, against the oppression of peoples and nations, and is aimed at abolishing all exploitation of man by man.... Its chief content is not violence but creation, the building of a new, classless society, and the defense of its gains against the enemies of socialism.

Overcoming the split in its ranks is an important condition for the working class to fulfill its historic mission.... The Communist parties favor cooperation with the Social-Democratic parties....

At the same time Communists criticize the ideological positions and Right-opportunist practice of social-democracy and expose the Right Social-Democratic leaders, who have sided openly with the bourgeoisie and renounced the traditional Socialist demands of the working class....

...Revisionism, Right opportunism, which is a reflection of bourgeois influence, is the chief danger within the Communist movement today.... The ideology of revisionism is most fully embodied in the program of the League of Communists of Yugoslavia.

Another danger is dogmatism and sectarianism, which cannot be reconciled with a creative development of revolutionary theory [but would] lead to the dissociation and isolation of Communists from the masses of the working people, doom them to passive expectation or incite them to Leftist adventurist actions in the revolutionary struggle....

The Communist parties are independent, and they shape their policies with due regard to the specific conditions prevailing in their own countries. They base relations between themselves on equality and the principles of proletarian internationalism.... The Communist Party of the Soviet Union, like the other Communist parties, regards it as its internationalist duty to abide by the appraisals and conclusion which the fraternal parties have reached jointly concerning their common tasks in the struggle against imperialism, for peace, democracy and socialism, and by the declaration and the statement adopted by the Communist parties at their international meetings....

6. The National-Liberation Movement

...Imperialism suppressed the national independence and freedom of the majority of the peoples and put the fetters of brutal colonial slavery on them, but the rise of socialism marks the advent of the era of emancipation of the oppressed peoples. A powerful wave of national-liberation revolutions is sweeping away the colonial system and undermining the foundations of imperialism. Young sovereign states have arisen, or are arising, in one-time colonies or semi-colonies....

...The peoples who are throwing off the shackles of colonialism have attained different levels of freedom....

The young sovereign states do not belong either to the system of imperialist states or to the system of Socialist states. But the overwhelming majority of them have not yet broken free from world capitalist economy even though they occupy a special place in it....

The existence of the world Socialist system and the weakening of imperialism offer the peoples of the newly free countries the prospect of a national renascence, of ending age-long backwardness and poverty, and achieving economic independence....

Foreign capital will retreat only before a broad union of patriotic democratic forces pursuing an anti-imperialist policy. The pillars of feudalism will crumble only under the impact of a general democratic movement. None but far-reaching agrarian reforms and a broad peasant movement can sweep away those remnants of medievalism that fetter the development of the productive forces and solve the food problem ... of Asia, Africa and Latin America....

A national-liberation revolution does not end with the winning of political independence. Independence will be unstable and will become fictitious unless the revolution brings about radical changes in the social and economic spheres and solves the pressing problems of national rebirth.

... The alliance of the working class and the peasantry is the fundamental condition for the success of the struggle to carry out far-reaching democratic changes and achieve economic and social progress. This alliance must form the core of a broad national front....

In many countries, the liberation movement of the peoples that have awakened proceeds under the flag of nationalism. Marxists-Leninists draw a distinction between the nationalism of the oppressed nations and that of the oppressor nations. The nationalism of an oppressed nation contains a general democratic element directed against oppression, and Communists support it because they consider it historically justified at a given stage....

The national bourgeoisie is dual in character. In modern conditions the national bourgeoisie in those colonial, one-time colonial and dependent countries where it is not connected with the imperialist circles is objectively interested in accomplishing the basic tasks of an anti-imperialist and antifeudal revolution....

But as the contradictions between the working people and the propertied classes grow and the class struggle inside the country becomes more aggravated, the national bourgeoisie shows an increasing inclination to compromise with imperialism and domestic reaction....

One of the basic issues confronting these peoples is, which road of development ... to take, whether the capitalist road or the noncapitalist....

Capitalism is the road of suffering for the people. It will not insure rapid economic progress nor eliminate poverty; social inequality will increase. The capitalist development of the countryside will ruin the peasantry still more....

Socialism is the road to freedom and happiness for the peoples. It insures rapid economic and cultural progress. It transforms a backward country within the lifetime of one generation.... Planned Socialist economy is an economy of progress and prosperity by its very nature....

It is for the peoples themselves to decide which road they are to choose. In view of the present balance of the world forces and the actual feasibility of powerful support on the part of the world Socialist system, the peoples of the former colonies can decide this question in their own interest....

The CPSU considers fraternal alliance with the peoples who have thrown off colonial or semi-colonial tyranny to be a cornerstone of its international policy.... The CPSU regards it as its internationalist duty to assist the peoples who have set out to win and strengthen their national independence, all peoples who are fighting for the complete abolition of the colonial system.

7. The Struggle Against Bourgeois & Reformist Ideology

A grim struggle is going on between 2 ideologies—Communist and bourgeois—in the world today....

The new historic epoch has brought the revolutionary world outlook of the proletariat a genuine triumph. Marxism-Leninism has gripped the minds of progressive mankind.

Bourgeois doctrines and schools have failed in the test of history. They have been and still are unable to furnish scientific answers to the questions posed by life....

A revolutionary change in the minds of vast human masses is a long and complex process. The more victories the world Socialist system achieves, the deeper the crisis of world capitalism and the sharper the class struggle, the more important becomes the role of Marxist-Leninist ideas in unifying and mobilizing the masses to fight for communism. The ideological struggle is a most important element of the class struggle of the proletariat....

The defenders of the bourgeois system, seeking to keep the masses in spiritual bondage, invent new "theories" designed to mask the exploiting character of the bourgeois system and to embellish capitalism....

The advocates of the bourgeois state call it a "welfare state."... But the masses see from their own experience that the bourgeois state is an obedient tool of the monopolies and that the vaunted "welfare" is welfare for the magnates of finance capital, but suffering and torture for hundreds of millions of working men....

The monopolies are reviving Fascist ideology—the ideology of extreme chauvinism and racism....

Imperialist reaction makes extensive use of chauvinism to incite nationalist conflicts, persecute entire nationalities and national groups (anti-Semitism, racial discrimination against Negroes and the peoples of the underdeveloped countries)....

Clericalism is acquiring ever greater importance in the political and ideological arsenal of imperialism. The clericals do not confine themselves to using the Church and its ramified machinery. They now have their own big political parties which in many capitalist countries are in power....

Anti-communism is becoming the main instrument of reaction in its struggle against the democratic forces of Asia, Africa and Latin America. It is the meeting ground of imperialist ideology and the ideology of the feudal, pro-imperialist elements and the reactionary groups of the bourgeoisie of the countries which have gained their freedom from colonial tyranny....

The ideological struggle of the imperialist bourgeoisie is spearheaded primarily against the working class and its Marxist-Leninist parties. Social-democratism in the working-class movement and revisionism in the Communist movement reflect the bourgeois influence on the working class.

The contemporary Right-Wing Social-Democrats are the most important ideological and political prop of the bourgeoisie within the working-class movement.... The Right wing of social-democracy has completely broken with Marxism and contraposed so-called democratic socialism to scientific socialism. Its adherents deny the existence of antagonistic classes and the class struggle in bourgeois society; they forcefully deny the necessity of the proletarian revolution and oppose the abolition of the private ownership of the means of production. They assert that capitalism is being "transformed" into socialism.

The Right-wing Socialists began by advocating social reforms in place of the Socialist revolution and went as far as to defend state-monopoly capitalism....

Now they openly renounce socialism. Formerly the Right-wing Socialists refused to recognize the class struggle to the point of recognizing the dictatorship of the proletariat. Today they deny...the very existence of antagonistic classes....

8. Peaceful Coexistence & the Struggle for World Peace

The CPSU considers that the chief aim of its foreign-policy activity is to provide peaceful conditions for the building of a Communist society in the USSR and developing the world Socialist system and together with the other peace-loving peoples to deliver mankind from a world war of extermination.

The CPSU maintains that forces capable of preserving and promoting world peace have arisen and are growing in the world. It is becoming possible to establish essentially new relations between states....

... Imperialism is the only source of the war danger. The imperialist camp is making preparations for the worst crime against mankind—a world thermonuclear war that can bring unprecedented destruction to entire countries and wipe out entire nations....

The peoples must concentrate their efforts on curbing the imperialists in good time and preventing them from making use of lethal weapons. The important thing is to ward off a thermonuclear war, not to let it break out. This can be done by the present generation....

Capitalism established its rule with fire and sword, but socialism does not require war to spread its ideals. Its weapon is its superiority over the old system in social organization, political system, economy, the improvement of the standard of living and spiritual culture.

The Socialist system is a natural center of attraction for the peace-loving forces of the globe....

It is possible to avert a world war by the combined efforts of the mighty Socialist camp, the peace-loving non-Socialist countries, the international working class and all the forces championing peace. The growing superiority of the Socialist forces over the forces of imperialism ... will make it actually possible to banish world war from the life of society even before the complete victory of socialism on earth, with capitalism surviving in part of the world. The victory of socialism throughout the world will do away completely with the social and national causes of all wars....

Socialism has offered mankind the only reasonable principle of maintaining relations between states at a time when the world is divided into 2 systems—the principle of the peaceful coexistence of states with different social systems, put forward by Lenin.

Peaceful coexistence of the Socialist and capitalist countries is an objective necessity for the development of human society....

Peaceful coexistence serves as a basis for the peaceful competition between socialism and capitalism on an international scale and constitutes a specific form of class struggle between them ...

The Communist Party of the Soviet Union advances the following tasks in the field of international relations:

●To use, together with the other Socialist countries, peaceful states and peoples, every means of preventing war and providing conditions for the complete elimination of war from the life of society;

●To pursue a policy of establishing sound international relations, and work for the disbandment of all military blocs ... the discontinuance of the "cold war" ... and the abolition of all air, naval, rocket and other military bases on foreign territory;

●To work for general and complete disarmament under strict international control;

●To strengthen relations of fraternal friendship and close cooperation with the countries of Asia, Africa and Latin America which are fighting to attain or consolidate national independence, with all peoples and states that advocate the preservation of peace;

●To pursue an active and consistent policy of improving and developing relations with all capitalist countries ... and other countries, with a view to safeguarding peace;

•To contribute in every way to the militant solidarity of all contingents and organizations of the international working class, which oppose the imperialist policy of war....

The CPSU and the Soviet people as a whole will continue to oppose all wars of conquest, including wars between capitalist countries, and local wars aimed at strangling people's emancipation movements, and consider it their duty to support the sacred struggle of the oppressed peoples and their just anti-imperialist wars of liberation....

PART 2—THE TASKS OF THE COMMUNIST PARTY OF THE SOVIET UNION IN BUILDING A COMMUNIST SOCIETY

Communism—The Bright Future of All Mankind

The building of a Communist society has become an immediate practical task for the Soviet people. The gradual dvelopment of socialism into communism is an objective law; it has been prepared by the development of Soviet Socialist society throughout the preceding period....

Communism is a classless social system with one form of public ownership of the means of production and full social equality of all members of society; under it, the all-around development of people will be accompanied by the growth of the productive forces through continuous progress in science and technology, all sources of public wealth will gush forth abundantly, and the great principle, "From each according to his ability, to each according to his needs," will be implemented. Communism is a highly organized society of free, socially conscious working people in which public self-government will be established, in which labor for the good of society will become the prime and vital requirement of everyone, a necessity recognized by one and all, and the ability of each person will be employed to the greatest benefit of the people....

Under communism, the classes, and the socio-economic and cultural distinctions, and differences in living conditions, between town and countryside disappear completely....

Under communism, all people will have equal status in society, will stand in the same relation to the means of production, will enjoy equal conditions of work and distribution, and will actively participate in the management of public affairs....

People's requirements will be satisfied from public sources. Articles of personal use will come into the full ownership of each member of society and will be at his disposal.

Communist society, which is based on highly organized production and advanced technology, alters the character of work, but it does not release the members of society from work....

... Labor and discipline will not be a burden to people, labor will no longer be a mere source of livelihood—it will be a genuinely creative process and a source of happiness.

Communism represents the highest form of organization of public life. All production units and self-governing associations will be harmoniously interlinked by a common planned economy and a uniform rhythm of social labor.

Under communism the nations will draw closer and closer together in all spheres on the basis of a complete identity of economic, political and spiritual interests, of fraternal friendship and cooperation....

In defining the basic tasks to be accomplished in building a Communist society, the party is guided by Lenin's great formula: "Communism is Soviet power plus the electrification of the whole country."...

In the current decade (1961-1970), the Soviet Union, in creating the material and technical basis of communism, will surpass the strongest and richest capitalist country, the USA, in production per head of population, the people's standard of living, and their cultural and technical standards will improve substantially, everyone will live in easy circumstances, all collective and state farms will become highly productive and profitable enterprises, the demand of the Soviet people for well-appointed housing will, in the main, be satisfied, hard physical work will disappear, the USSR will become the country with the shortest working day.

In the next decade (1971-1980) the material and technical basis of communism will be created and there will be an abundance of material and cultural benefits for the whole population, Soviet society will come close to a stage where it can introduce the principle of distribution according to needs, and there will be a gradual transition to one form of ownership—public ownership. Thus, a Communist society will, on the whole, be built in the USSR. The construction of Communist society will be fully completed in the subsequent period....

1. The Tasks of the Party in the Field of Economic Development & in the Creation and Promotion of the Material & Technical Basis of Communism

The main economic task of the party and the Soviet people is to create the material and technical basis of communism within 2 decades. This means the complete electrification of the country and the perfection on this basis of the techniques, technologies and organization of social production in industry and agriculture....

As a result, the USSR will possess productive forces of unparalleled might, it will surpass the technical level of the most developed countries and occupy first place in the world in per capita production. This will serve as a basis for the gradual transformation of Socialist social relations into Communist social relations and for a development of industry and agriculture that will make it possible to meet in abundance the requirements of society and all its members....

(1) *The development of industry; its role in creating the productive forces of communism.*

The creation of the material and technical basis of communism, the task of making Soviet industry technologically the best and strongest in the world, calls for the further development of heavy industry....

A first-class heavy industry, the basis for the country's technical progress and economic might, has been built up in the Soviet Union. The CPSU will continue to devote unflagging attention to the growth of heavy industry.... In the new period of the Soviet Union's development, the growth and technological progress of heavy industry must insure the expansion of those branches of the economy producing consumer goods to meet ever more fully the requirements of the people....

With these aims in view, the CPSU plans the following increases in total industrial output:

● Within the current 10 years, by approximately 150%, exceeding the contemporary level of U.S. industrial output.

● Within 20 years, by not less than 500%, leaving the present over-all volume of U.S. industrial output far behind.

To achieve this, it is necessary to raise productivity of labor in industry by more than 100% within 10 years, and by 300% to 350% within 20 years. In 20 years' time labor productivity in Soviet industry will exceed the present level of labor productivity in the U.S.A. by roughly 100% and considerably more in terms of per-hour output due to the reduction of the working day of the USSR....

... The electrification of the whole country will on the whole be completed in the course of the 2d decade.

The annual output of electricity must be brought up to 900,000-1,000,000 million kilowatt hours by the end of the first decade, and to 2,700,000-3,000,000 million kilowatt hours by the end of the 2d decade....

As atomic energy becomes cheaper, the construction of atomic power stations will be expanded....

The further rapid expansion of the output of metals and fuels, the basis of modern industry, remains one of the major economic tasks. Within 20 years metallurgy will develop sufficiently to produce about 250 million tons of steel a year....

Within the 20-year period the comprehensive automation of production will be effected on a large scale, with more and more shops and plants being fully automated....

The CPSU will concentrate its efforts on insuring a rapid increase in the output of consumer goods....

A ramified network of modern roads will be built throughout the country. The automobile fleet will increase sufficiently to fully meet freight and passenger traffic requirements; car hire centers will be organized on a large scale. Air transport will become a means of mass passenger traffic extending to all parts of the country....

...All regions of the country will have reliable telephone and radio communications and a link-up system of television stations.

Full-scale Communist construction calls for a more rational geographic distribution of the industries, to save social labor and insure the comprehensive development of areas and the specialization of their industries, do away with the overpopulation of big cities, facilitate the elimination of substantial distinctions between town and countryside, and further even out the economic levels of different parts of the country....

The party will do everything to enhance the role of science in the building of the Communist society. It will encourage research to discover new possibilities for the development of the productive forces and the rapid and extensive application of the latest scientific and technical achievements, a decisive advancement in experimental work, including research directly at enterprises, and the efficient organization of scientific and technical information and of the whole system of studying and disseminating progressive Soviet and foreign methods...

New techniques and the reduction of the working day call for better organization of work. Technical progress and better production organization must be fully utilized to increase labor productivity and reduce production costs at every enterprise. This implies a higher rate of increase in labor productivity as compared with remuneration, better rate-fixing, prevention of loss of working time, and operation on a profitable basis at all stages of production.

Most important will be the task of systematically improving the qualifications of those working in industry and other branches of the economy in connection with technical progress. The planned training, instruction and rational employment of those released from various jobs due to mechanization and automation are essential....

(2) *Development of agriculture and social relations in the countryside.*

... The party organizes a great development of productive forces in agriculture, which will enable it to accomplish 2 basic, closely related tasks: (a) To build up an abundance of high-quality food products for the population and of raw materials for industry, and (b) to effect the gradual transition of social relations in the Soviet countryside to Communist relations and eliminate, in the main, the distinctions between town and country.

The chief means of achieving progress in agriculture and satisfying the growing needs of the country in farm produce are comprehensive mechanization and consistent intensification: high efficiency of crop farming and stock-breeding based on science and progressive experience in all *kolkhozes* and state farms, a steep rise in the yielding capacity of all crops and greater output per hectare with the utmost economy of labor and funds.... Agriculture will approach the level of industry in technical equipment and the organization of production, farm labor will turn into a variety of industrial labor, and the dependence of agriculture upon the elements will decrease considerably and ultimately drop to a minimum.

The development of virgin and disused land and establishment of new large-scale state farms, the reorganization of the machine-and-tractor stations, the sale of implements of production to the collective farms, and the enhancement of material incentives for agricultural workers—all constitute an important stage in the development of agriculture.

The further advance of the countryside to communism will proceed through the development and improvement of the 2 forms of Socialist farming—the *kolkhozes* and state farms.

The *kolkhoz* system is an integral part of Soviet Socialist society. It is a way charted by V. I. Lenin for the gradual transition of the peasantry to communism....

... The *kolkhoz* blends the personal interests of the peasants with common, nationwide interests, blends individual with collective interest in the results of production, and offers extensive opportunities for raising the incomes and the well-being of peasants on the basis of growing labor productivity....

Economic advancement of the *kolkhoz* system creates conditions for the gradual rapprochement and, in the long run, also for the merging of *kolkhoz* property and the property of the whole people into one Communist property.

The state farms, which are the leading Socialist agricultural enterprises, play an ever-increasing role in the development of agriculture. The state farms must serve the *kolkhozes* as a model of progressive, scientifically managed, economically profitable social production, of high efficiency and labor productivity....

A. BUILDING UP AN ABUNDANCE OF AGRICULTURAL PRODUCE

In order fully to satisfy the requirements of the entire population and of the national economy in agricultural produce, the task is to increase the aggregate volume of agricultural production in 10 years by about 150%, and in 20 years 250%.... In the first decade the Soviet Union will outstrip the United States in output of the key agricultural products per head of population.

Accelerated growth of grain production is the chief link in the further development of all agriculture and a basis for the rapid growth of stock-breeding. The aggregate grain crops will more than double in 20 years, and their yielding capacity will double.

... The output of animal products will rise: meat about 3-fold in the first 10 years and nearly 4-fold in 20 years, and milk more than double in the first decade and nearly 3-fold in 20 years....

Productivity of labor in agriculture will rise not less than 150% in 10 years, and 5-to-6-fold in 20 years. The rapid rise of the productivity of farm labor—at a higher rate than in industry—will serve to eliminate the lag of agriculture behind industry....

...All state farms and *kolkhozes* will be supplied electric power for production and domestic purposes from the state power grid, and also from power stations built in the countryside....

...Qualified workers with special agricultural training and proficient in the use of new machinery will increasingly predominate in the *kolkhozes* and state farms.

To insure high, stable, steadily increasing harvests, to deliver agriculture from the baneful effects of the elements, especially droughts, to steeply raise land fertility, and to rapidly advance livestock breeding, it is necessary:

● To introduce in all parts of the country scientific systems of land cultivation and animal husbandry in keeping with local conditions and the specialization of each farm, insuring the most effective use of the land and the most economically expedient combination of branches,... to insure that every *kolkhoz* and state farm masters the most advanced methods of crop farming with the application of efficient crop rotation and the sowing of highgrade seeds only, to build up reliable fodder resources in all districts and to introduce the foremost stock-breeding techniques....

● To effect a scientifically expedient disposition of agriculture by natural economic zones and districts, and a more thorough and stable specialization of agriculture....

● To effect a consistent introduction of chemicals in all branches of agriculture, to meet all its needs in mineral fertilizers and chemical means of combating weeds, blights, diseases and plant and animal pests, and to insure the best use of local fertilizers....

● To apply broadly biological achievements and microbiology... to improve soil fertility,... to irrigate and water millions of hectares of land in the arid areas,... to expand field-protective afforestation, building of water reservoirs, irrigation of pastures and melioration of overmoist land, and to combat, systematically, the water and wind erosion of soil....

...Research institutions and experimental stations must become important links in agricultural management, and scientists and specialists must become the direct organizers of farm production. Each region or group of regions of the same zonal type should have agricultural research centers, with their own large-scale farms and up-to-date material, and technical resources, to work out recommendations... applicable to the given district. Agricultural research and educational establishments must be chiefly located in rural areas and be directly associated with farm production, so that students may learn while working and work while learning.

B. THE KOLKHOZES & STATE FARMS ON THE ROAD TO COMMUNISM; REMOLDING SOCIAL RELATIONS IN THE COUNTRYSIDE

The economic basis for the development of *kolkhozes* and state farms lies in the continuous growth and best use of their productive forces, improvement of the organization of production and methods of management, steady rise of labor productivity and strict observance of the principle: higher payment for good work, for better results....

...The state will promote the growth of the productive forces of the *kolkhoz* system and the economic advancement of all *kolkhozes*. Concurrently, the *kolkhoz* peasantry must also contribute more widely to the building of Communist society.

The state will insure the full satisfaction of the needs of the *kolkhozes* in modern machinery, chemicals and other means of production, will train new hundreds of thousands of skilled farm workers, and will considerably increase capital investments in the countryside, in addition to the greater investments by the *kolkhozes* themselves. . . .

Strict observance of their contracted commitments to the state by the *kolkhozes* and their members is an irrevocable principle of their participation in the development of the national economy.

. . . It is essential to coordinate the planning of state purchases and the productions plans of the *kolkhozes,* with utmost consideration for the interests of agricultural production, its correct disposition and specialization.

. . . It is essential that the level of state purchasing prices encourage the *kolkhozes* to raise labor productivity and reduce production expenses, since greater farm output and lower production costs are the basis of greater incomes for the *kolkhozes*. . . .

. . . The *kolkhozes* cannot develop without continuously extending their commonly owned assets for production, insurance, cultural and community needs. At the same time, it must be a standing rule for every *kolkhoz* to raise its members' incomes from collective farming and to enhance their living standard as labor productivity rises.

. . . Increasingly equal economic conditions must be provided that will improve the incomes of *kolkhozes* existing under unequal natural-economic conditions in different zones, and also within the zones, in order to put into effect more consistently the principle of equal pay for equal work. . . . Farming on all *kolkhozes* must be conducted in accordance with a strict principle of profitability.

In its organizational work and economic policy, the party will strive to overcome the lag of the economically weak *kolkhozes* and to turn all *kolkhozes* into economically strong, high-income farms in the course of the next few years. . . .

The economic advancement of the *kolkhozes* will make it possible to perfect *kolkhoz* internal relations; to raise the degree to which production is socialized, to bring the rate setting, organization and payment of labor closer to the level and the forms employed at state enterprises and effect a transition to a guaranteed monthly wage, to develop community services more broadly. . . .

. . . When collective production at the *kolkhozes* is able to replace in full that of the supplementary individual plot of the *kolkhoz* members, when the collective farmers see for themselves that their supplementary individual farming is unprofitable, they will give it up of their own accord.

As the productive forces increase, inter-*kolkhoz* production ties will develop and the socialization of production will transcend the limits of individual *kolkhozes.* The building, jointly by several *kolkhozes,* of enterprises and cultural and other welfare institutions . . . should be encouraged. As the commonly-owned assets increase, the *kolkhozes* will participate more and more in establishing enterprises and cultural and other welfare institutions for general public use, boarding schools, clubs, hospitals and holiday homes. All these developments, which must proceed on a voluntary basis and when the necessary economic conditions are available, will gradually impart to *kolkhoz*-cooperative property the nature of public property.

The state farms have a long way to travel in their development—to attain high rates of growth of labor productivity, to steadily reduce production costs and raise farm efficiency. This calls for the economically expedient specialization of state farms. . . . They must become mechanized and well-organized first-class factories of grain, cotton, meat, milk, wool, vegetables, fruit and other products. . . .

The material and technical basis of the state farms will be extended and improved, and the living and cultural conditions at the state farms will approach those in towns. State farm management should follow a more and more democratic pattern which will allot a greater role to the personnel and to general meetings and production conferences in deciding production, cultural and other community issues.

As the *kolkhozes* and state farms develop, their production ties with each other and with local industrial enterprises will grow stronger.... Agrarian-industrial associations will gradually emerge wherever economically expedient....

As production in *kolkhozes* and state farms develops and social relations within them advance, agriculture rises to a higher level, affording the possibility of transition to Communist forms of production and distribution.... By virtue of high labor productivity all *kolkhozes* will become economically powerful. *Kolkhoz* members will be adequately provided and their requirements fully satisfied out of collective-farm production.... The payment of labor will be the same as at nationally-owned enterprises and they will be provided all forms of social security (pensions, holidays, etc.) out of *kolkhoz* and state funds.

Gradually, the *kolkhoz* villages will grow into amalgamated urban communities with modern housing facilities.... The rural population will ultimately draw level with the urban population in cultural and living conditions....

(3) *Management of the national economy and planning.*

The building of the material and technical basis of communism calls for a continuous improvement in economic management. Chief emphasis at all levels of planning and economic management must be laid on the most rational and effective use of the material, labor and financial resources and natural wealth and on the elimination of excessive expenditures. The immutable law of economic development is to achieve in the interests of society the highest results at the lowest cost.

Planning must at all levels concentrate on the rapid development and introduction of new techniques....

... The quality of goods produced by Soviet enterprises must be considerably higher than that of the best capitalist enterprises. For this purpose, it is necessary to apply a broad set of measures, including public control, and to enhance the role of quality indexes....

Communist construction presupposes the maximum development of democratic principles of management coupled with a strengthening and improvement of centralized economic management by the state. The economic independence and the rights of local organs and enterprises will continue to expand within the framework of the single national economic plan....

Centralized planning should chiefly concentrate on working out and ensuring the fulfillment of the key targets of the economic plans with the greatest consideration paid to recommendations made at lower levels, on coordinating and dove-tailing plans drawn up locally; on spreading scientific and technical achievements and advanced production experience; on enforcing a single state policy in the spheres of technical progress, capital investment, distribution of production, payment of labor, prices, and finance, and a unified system of accounting and statistics....

Firm and consistent discipline, day-to-day control, and determined elimination of elements of parochialism and of a narrow departmental approach in economic affairs are necessary conditions for successful Communist construction.

There must be a further expansion of the role and responsibility of local bodies in economic management. The transfer of a number of functions of economic management by the all-union bodies to those of the republics, by republican bodies to those of the regions and by regional bodies to those of the districts should be continued.... The improvement of the work of economic councils within the economic administration areas will also be accompanied by greater coordination of the work of other economic bodies, in order better to organize the planned comprehensive economic development of such major economic areas as the Urals, the Volga area, Siberia, Transcaucasia, the Baltic area, Central Asia, etc.

Extension of operative independence and of the initiative of enterprises on the basis of the state-plan targets is essential....

The direct and most active participation of trade unions in elaborating and realizing economic plans, in matters concerning the labor of factory and office workers, in setting up organs of economic administration and of management of enterprises, must be extended more and more at top level and locally. The role of the collectives of factory and office workers in ... the work of enterprises must be enhanced.

In the process of Communist construction economic management will make use of material and moral incentives for high production figures.... In the course of the advance to communism the importance of moral labor incentives, public recognition of achieved results and the sense of responsibility of each for the common cause will become continuously greater....

There must be a continuous improvement in rate setting, the system of labor payments and bonuses, in the financial control over the quantity and quality of work, in the elimination of leveling and the stimulation of collective forms of incentives raising the interest of each employe in the high efficiency of the enterprise as a whole.

It is necessary in Communist construction to make full use of commodity-money relations in keeping with their new substance in the Socialist period.... When the transition to a Communist form of people's property and the Communist system of distribution is completed, commodity-money relations will become economically outdated and will wither away.

The important role of the budget in distributing the social product and national income will prevail throughout the period of full-scale Communist construction. There will be a further strengthening of the monetary and credit system, a consolidation of Soviet currency, a steady rise of the rate of exchange of the ruble by virtue of its growing purchasing power, and a strengthening of the role of the ruble in the international arena.

It is necessary to promote profitable operation of enterprises.... Prices must, to a growing extent, reflect the socially necessary outlays of labor, insure return of production and circulation expenditures and a certain profit for each normally operating enterprise. Systematic, economically justified price reductions based on growth of labor productivity and reduction of production costs are the main trend of the price policy in the period of Communist construction....

2. *The Tasks of the Party in Improving the Living Standards of the People*

... The CPSU sets the historically important task of achieving in the Soviet Union a living standard higher than that of any of the capitalist countries.

This task will be effected by: (A) Raising the individual payment of employes according to the quantity and quality of work, coupled with reduction of retail prices and abolition of taxes paid by the population, (B) Increase of the public funds distributed among members of society irrespective of the quantity and quality of their labor, that is, free of charge (education, medical treatment, pensions, maintenance of children at children's institutions, transition to cost-free use of public amenities, etc.).

The rise of the real incomes of the population will be outstripped by rapid increase in the amount of commodities and services and by far-flung construction of dwellings and cultural and service buildings.

Soviet people will be more prosperous than people in the developed capitalist countries even if average incomes will be equal, because in the Soviet Union the national income is distributed fairly among the members of society....

The party acts upon Lenin's thesis that Communist construction must be based upon the principle of material incentive. In the coming 20 years payment according to one's work will remain the principal source for satisfying the material and cultural needs of the working people.

The disparity between high and comparatively low incomes must gradually shrink.... As the living standard of the entire population rises, low income levels will approach the higher, and the disparity between the incomes of peasants and workers, low-paid and high-paid personnel and the populations of different parts of the country, will gradually shrink.

...As the country advances towards communism, personal needs will be increasingly met out of public consumption funds.... The transition to Communist distribution will be completed after the principle of distribution according to one's work will exhaust itself, that is, when there will be an abundance of material and cultural wealth and labor will become life's prime necessity for all members of society.

A. PROVISION OF A HIGH LEVEL OF INCOME & CONSUMPTION FOR THE WHOLE POPULATION

The national income of the USSR in the next 10 years will increase nearly 150%, and about 400% in 20 years. The real income per head of population will increase by more than 250% in 20 years.

In the course of the coming 10 years the real incomes of factory and office workers (including public funds) per employed person will, on the average, be almost doubled, and in 20 years will increase by approximately 200% to 250%. The increase in the real incomes of factory, office and professional workers paid relatively lower wages will be brought to a level at which low-paid brackets throughout the country will be eliminated within 10 years. The real incomes of factory and office workers receiving the minimum wages will be approximately trebled....

By virtue of higher rates of growth of the labor productivity of collective farmers their real incomes will grow more rapidly than the incomes of factory workers and will, on an average per employed person, more than double in the next 10 years and increase more than 4-fold in 20 years....

...The general level of popular consumption will rise rapidly. The entire population will be able to satisfy to the full its need in high quality and varied foodstuffs.... The demand of all sections of the population for high-quality consumer goods: attractive clothes, footwear and goods improving and adorning the daily life of Soviet people, such as comfortable modern furniture, up-to-date domestic goods, a wide range of goods for cultural purposes, etc., will be amply satisfied....

...Good shopping facilities will be arranged throughout the country....

The 2d decade will see an abundance of material and cultural benefits for the whole population, and material prerequisites will be created to complete the transition to the Communist principle of distribution according to need in the period to follow.

B. SOLUTION OF THE HOUSING PROBLEM & IMPROVEMENT OF LIVING CONDITIONS

... As a result of the 2d decade, every family, including newlyweds, will have a comfortable flat conforming to the requirements of hygiene and cultured living. Peasant houses of the old type will, in the main, give place to new modern dwellings, or—whereever possible—they will be rebuilt and appropriately improved. In the course of the 2d decade housing will be gradually provided to all citizens rent free.

An extensive program of public-services construction and of improvements in all towns and workers' estates will be carried out.... Well-appointed small and middle-size towns will be increasingly developed....

Public-transport facilities (tramways, buses, trolley buses and subways) will become free in the course of the 2d decade, and at the end of it such public amenities as water, gas and heating will also be free.

C. REDUCTION OF WORKING HOURS & THE FURTHER IMPROVEMENT OF WORKING CONDITIONS

In the coming 10 years the country will go over to a 6-hour working day with one day off a week, or 34-to-36-hour working week with 2 days off, and in underground and harmful jobs to a 5-hour working day or a 30-hour, 5-day working week.

By virtue of a corresponding rise in labor productivity, transition to a still shorter working week will be begun in the 2d decade.

The Soviet Union will thus have the world's shortest and, concurrently, the most productive and highest-paid working day....

The length of the annual paid holidays of working people will be increased.... Gradually the minimum length of leave for all industrial, professional and office workers will increase to 3 weeks and subsequently to one month....

D. HEALTH SERVICES & MEASURES FOR INCREASED LONGEVITY

The Socialist state is the only state which undertakes to protect and continuously improve the health of the whole population.... There will be an extensive program designed to prevent and sharply reduce diseases, wipe out mass infectious diseases and further increase longevity. The needs of the urban and rural population in all forms of highly-qualified medical services will be met in full....

In addition to the existing free medical services, accommodation of sick persons at sanatoria and the dispensing of medicines will become gratuitous. In order to afford the population an opportunity to rest in an out-of-town environment, holiday homes, boarding houses, country hotels and tourist camps will be built, where working people will be accommodated at a reasonable charge or by way of a bonus, as well as at a discount or gratis.

The party considers it a most important task to ensure the education ... of a sound young generation harmoniously developed physically and spiritually. This calls for utmost encouragement of all forms of mass sport and physical training....

E. IMPROVEMENT OF FAMILY CONDITIONS & OF THE POSITION OF WOMEN. MAINTENANCE OF CHILDREN & INCAPACITATED PEOPLE AT PUBLIC EXPENSE

The remnants of the unequal position of women in domestic life must be totally eliminated. Social and living conditions must be provided to enable women to combine happy motherhood with increasingly active and creative participation in social labor and social activities, and in scientific and artistic pursuits. Women must be given relatively lighter and yet sufficiently well-paid jobs....

It is essential to provide conditions to reduce and lighten the domestic work of women, and later to make possible the replacement of domestic work by public forms of satisfying the daily needs of the family....

... The service at catering establishments and the quality of catering must be radically improved, so that meals at public catering establishments should be tasty and nourishing and should cost the family less than meals cooked at home. Price reductions in public catering will keep ahead of price reductions for foodstuffs in the shops. By virtue of this, public catering will be able to take precedence over home cooking within 10 to 15 years.

The transition to free public catering (mid-day meals) at enterprises and institutions and for collective farmers at work will begin in the 2d decade.

... The development of a ramified network of children's institutions will make it possible ... in the 2d decade for every family to keep children and adolescents free of charge at children's establishments if they so desire....

... The state, the trade unions and the *kolkhozes* will in the course of the 20 years gradually undertake maintenance of all citizens incapacitated through old age or some disability....

By fulfilling the tasks set by the party for the improvement of the well-being of the people, the Soviet Union will make considerable headway towards the practical realization of the Communist principle of distribution according to need.

At the end of the 20 years public consumption funds will total about half of the aggregate real income of the population....

The set program can be fulfilled with success under conditions of peace. Complications in the international situation and the resultant necessity of increasing defense expenditures may hold up the fulfillment of the plans for raising the living standard of the people....

3. The Tasks of the Party in the Spheres of State Development & the Further Promotion of Socialist Democracy

The dictatorship of the proletariat ... has played an epoch-making role by insuring the victory of socialism in the USSR. In the course of Socialist construction, however, it underwent changes. After the exploiting classes had been abolished, the state function of suppressing their resistance ceased to exist. The chief functions of the Socialist state—economic and organizational, cultural and educational—have developed in full measure. The Socialist state has entered a new phase.

The state has begun to grow over into a nationwide organization of the working people of Socialist society. Proletarian democracy is becoming more and more a Socialist democracy of the people as a whole. The working class is the only class in history that does not aim to perpetuate its power. Having brought about a complete and final victory of socialism—the first phase of communism—and the transition of society to the fullscale construction of communism, the dictatorship of the proletariat has fulfilled its historic mission and has ceased to be indispensable in the USSR from the point of view of the tasks of internal development.

The state, which arose as a state of the dictatorship of the proletariat, has become a state of the entire people.... Since the working class is the foremost and best organized force of Soviet society, it plays a leading role also in the period of the full-scale construction of communism. The working class will have completed its function of leader of society after communism is built and classes disappear.

The party holds that the dictatorship of the working class will cease to be necessary before the state withers away. The state as an organization embracing the entire people will survive until the complete victory of communism.

... It must organize the building up of the material and technical basis of communism, and the transformation of Socialist relations into Communist relations, must exercise control over the measure of work and rate of consumption, promote welfare, protect the rights and freedoms of Soviet citizens, Socialist law and order and Socialist property, instill in the people conscious discipline and a Communist attitude to labor, guarantee the defense and security of the country, promote fraternal cooperation with the Socialist countries, uphold world peace and maintain normal relations with all countries.

Vigorous extension and perfection of Socialist democracy, active participation of all citizens in the administration of the state, in the management of economic and cultural development, improvement of the government apparatus, and increased control over its activity by the people constitute the main direction in which Socialist statehood develops in the period of the building of communism.

As Socialist democracy develops, the organs of state power will gradually be transformed into organs of public self-government. The Leninist principle of democratic centralism, which insures the proper combination of centralized leadership with the maximum encouragement of local initiative, the extension of the rights of the union republics and greater creative activity of the masses, will be promoted.

(1) *The soviets and promotion of the democratic principles of government.*

The role of the soviets, which have become an all-inclusive organization of the people embodying their unity, will grow as Communist construction progresses. The soviets, which combine the features of a government body and a social organization, operate more and more like social organizations, with the masses participating in their work extensively and directly....

... It is desirable that at least 1/3 of the total number of deputies to a soviet should be elected anew each time so that more ... working people may learn to govern the state.

The party considers systematic renewal of the leading bodies necessary.... It is advisable to introduce the principle that the leading officials of the union, republican and local bodies should be elected to their offices, as a rule, for not more than 3 consecutive terms. In those cases when the personal gifts of the official in question are generally believed to make his further activity ... useful and necessary, his reelection may be allowed. His election shall be considered valid ... if not less than 3/4 of the votes are cast in his favor.

... It is necessary to develop more and more fully regular accountability of soviets and deputies to their constituents and the right of the electorate to recall ahead of term deputies who have not justified confidence placed in them, publicity and the free and full discussion of all the important questions of government and of economic and cultural developments at the meetings of soviets, regular accountability of executive government bodies to meetings of soviets, ... criticism of shortcomings in the work of government, economic and other organizations....

The rights of the local Soviets of Working People's Deputies (local self-government) will be extended. Local soviets will make final decisions on all questions of local significance.

... As *kolkhoz*-cooperative and public property draws closer together, a single democratic body administering all enterprises, organizations and institutions at district level will gradually take shape....

Discussion by the people of draft laws and other decisions of both national and local significance must become the rule. The most important draft laws should be put to a nationwide referendum....

... The party regards inspection by people's control bodies as an effective means of drawing large sections of the people into the management of state affairs, and control over the strict observance of legality as a means of perfecting the government apparatus, eradicating bureaucracy and promptly realizing proposals made by the people....

... The principle of electivity and accountability to representative bodies and to the electorate will be gradually extended to all the leading officials of government bodies.

An effort should be made to insure that the salaried government staffs are reduced, that ever larger sections of the people learn to take part in administration and that work on government staffs eventually ceases to constitute a profession.

... It is necessary consistently to exercise the principle of collective leadership at all levels of the government and economic apparatus....

The transition to communism means the fullest extension of personal freedom and the rights of Soviet citizens....

Justice in the USSR ... is based on truly democratic lines: Election and accountability of the judges and people's assessors, the right to recall them before expiration of their term, the publicity of court proceedings, and the participation of prosecutors and lawyers appointed by social organizations in the work of courts with strict observance of legality and all the rules of judicial procedure....

... As long as there are criminal offenses, it is necessary severely to punish those who commit crimes dangerous to society, violate the rules of the Socialist community and refuse to live by honest labor....

Higher standards of living and culture and greater social consciousness of the people will pave the way to the ultimate replacement of judicial punishment by measures of public influence and education. Under socialism, anyone who has strayed from the path of a working man can return to useful activity....

(2) *The further heightening of the role of social organizations. The state and communism.*

The role of social organizations increases in the period of the fullscale construction of communism. The trade unions acquire particular importance as schools of administration and economic management, as schools of communism.... The trade unions shall:

● Work constantly to increase the Communist consciousness of the masses, organize an emulation movement for Communist labor and help the people in learning to manage state and social affairs, take an active part in controlling the measure of labor and rate of consumption.

● Encourage the activity of factory and office workers, enlisting their aid in the work for continuous technical progress, for higher productivity of labor, for the fulfillment and over-fulfillment of state plans and assignments.

● Work steadfastly for the improvement of the skill of factory and office workers and their working and living conditions, protect the material interests and rights of the working people.

● Insure that housing and cultural development plans are fulfilled and that public catering, trade, social insurance and health resort services are improved.

● Insure control over the spending of public consumption funds....

● Improve cultural services and recreation facilities ..., encourage physical training and sports....

... The YCL [Young Communist League] organizations must concentrate on educating the youth in a spirit of utmost devotion to their people, the Communist Party and country, the Communist cause, constant preparedness for labor for the good of the country and for overcoming all difficulties and improving the general education and technical knowledge of all young men and women....

The party regards it as a major task of the social organizations to promote labor emulation and Communist forms of labor in every possible way, to encourage the activity of working people in building a Communist society, to work for the improvement of the living conditions of the people. Social organizations... should be encouraged to play a greater part in promoting public order, particularly through the people's volunteer squads and comradely courts....

As Socialist statehood develops, it will gradually become public Communist self-government, which will embrace the soviets, trade unions, cooperatives and other mass organizations of the people....

Public functions similar to those performed by the state today in the sphere of economic and cultural management will be preserved under communism and will be modified and perfected as society develops.... The bodies in charge of planning, accounting, economic management and cultural advancement, now government bodies, will lose their political character and will become organs of public self-government. Communist society will be a highly organized community of working men. Universally recognized rules of Communist conduct will be established whose observance will become an organic need and habit with everyone.

Historical development is bound to lead to the withering away of the state. To insure that the state withers away completely, it is necessary to provide both internal conditions—the building of a developed Communist society—and external conditions—the [resolution of] contradictions between capitalism and communism in the world arena in favor of communism.

(3) *The strengthening of the armed forces and the defense potential of the Soviet Union.*

... The Leninist principle of peaceful coexistence has been, and remains, the general principle of the foreign policy of the Soviet state.

The Soviet Union perseveringly seeks to bring about the realization of the proposals for general and complete disarmament under strict international control. But the imperialist countries stubbornly refuse to accept these proposals, and feverishly build up their armed forces. They refuse to reconcile themselves to the existence of the world Socialist system, and openly proclaim their insane plans for the liquidation of the Soviet Union and the other Socialist states through war. This obliges the Communist Party... and all the peoples of the USSR... to be constantly prepared to take up arms in defense of their country.

The party maintains that as long as imperialism survives, the threat of aggressive wars will remain.... The Soviet Union sees it as its internationalist duty to guarantee, together with the other Socialist countries, the reliable defense and security of the entire Socialist camp.

... The Soviet state will see to it that its armed forces are powerful; that they have the most up-to-date means of defending the country—atomic and thermonuclear weapons, rockets of every range, and they keep all types of military equipment and all weapons up to standard....

The CPSU is doing everything to insure that the Soviet armed forces... are prepared at any moment to administer a crushing rebuff to imperialist aggressors. One-man leadership is a major principle of the organization of the Soviet armed forces....

Party leadership of the armed forces, and the increased role and influence of the party organizations in the army and navy are the bedrock of military development....

4. ... The Party in the Field of National Relations

Under socialism the nations flourish, and their sovereignty grows stronger. The development of nations does not proceed along lines of strengthening national barriers, national narrowmindedness and egoism, as it does under capitalism, but along lines of their association, fraternal mutual assistance and friendship....

People of many nationalities live together and work in harmony in the Soviet republics. The boundaries between the constituent republics of the USSR are increasingly losing their former significance....

Fullscale Communist construction constitutes a new stage in the development of national relations in the USSR in which the nations will draw still closer together until complete unity is achieved....

The party approaches all questions of national relationships arising in the course of Communist construction from the standpoint of proletarian internationalism and firm pursuance of the Leninist national policy....

The party sets the following tasks in the sphere of national relations:

A. To continue the all-around economic and cultural development of all the Soviet nations, insuring their increasingly close fraternal cooperation, mutual aid, unity and affinity in all spheres of life...; to make full use of, and advance the forms of, national statehood of the peoples of the USSR.

B. In the economic sphere, it is necessary to pursue the line of comprehensive development of the economies of the Soviet republics, effect a rational geographic location of production and a planned working of natural wealth, and promote Socialist division of labor among the republics, unifying and combining their economic efforts, and properly balancing the interests of the state as a whole and those of each Soviet republic....

... Benefits growing in the course of Communist construction must be fairly distributed among all nations and nationalities;

C. To work for the further all-around development of the Socialist cultures of the peoples of the USSR the big scale of Communist construction and the new victories of Communist ideology are enriching the cultures of the peoples of the USSR which are Socialist in content and national in form. The ideological unity of the nations and nationalities is growing.... An international culture common to all the Soviet nations is developing....

Attaching decisive importance to the development of the Socialist content of the cultures of the peoples of the USSR the party will promote their further mutual enrichment and rapprochement to the consolidation of their international basis, and thereby the formation of the future single worldwide culture of Communist society....

D. To continue promoting the free development of the languages of the USSR and the complete freedom of every citizen of the USSR to speak, and to bring up and educate his children in any language....

The voluntary study of Russian in addition to the native language is of positive significance, since it facilitates reciprocal exchanges of experience and access of every nation and nationality to the cultural gains of all the other peoples of the USSR and to world culture.

E. To pursue consistently as heretofore the principles of internationalism in the field of national relations, ...to conduct a relentless struggle against manifestations and survivals of nationalism and chauvinism of all types, against trends of national narrow-mindedness and exclusiveness, idealization of the past and the veiling of social contradictions and habits....

5. ... *The Party in the Spheres of Ideology, Education, Instruction, Science & Culture*

...Even after the Socialist system has triumphed, there persist in the minds and behavior of people survivals of capitalism, which hamper the progress of society....

The party considers that the paramount task in the ideological field in the present period is to educate all working people in a spirit of ideological integrity and devotion to communism and cultivate in them a Communist attitude to labor and the social economy, to eliminate completely the survivals of bourgeois views and morals, to insure the all-round, harmonious development of the individual, to create a truly rich spiritual culture....

Increased Communist consciousness of the people furthers the ideological and political unity of the workers, collective farmers and intellectuals and promotes their gradual fusion in the single collective of the working people of Communist society.

The party sets the following tasks:

(1) *In ... development of Communist consciousness.*

A. THE SHAPING OF A SCIENTIFIC WORLD OUTLOOK

Under socialism and at a time when a Communist society is being built, when spontaneous economic development has given way to the conscious organization of production and social life as a whole, ... the shaping of a scientific world outlook in all working people is of prime importance. The ideological basis of this world outlook is shaped as Marxism-Leninism, an integral and harmonious system of philosophical, economic and socio-political views. The party calls for the education of the population as a whole in the spirit of scientific communism and strives to insure that all working people ... take a correct view of international and domestic events and consciously build their life on Communist lines....

The party regards one of its most important duties to further elaborate Marxist-Leninist theory by studying and generalizing new phenomena in the life of Soviet society and the experience of the world revolutionary working-class and liberation movements, and creatively to combine the theory and the practice of Communist construction.

B. LABOR EDUCATION

The party sees the development of a Communist attitude to labor in all members of society as its chief educational task. Labor for the benefit of society is the sacred duty of all....

It is impossible for a man in Communist society not to work, for neither his social consciousness nor public opinion would permit it. Work according to one's ability will become a habit, a prime necessity of life, for every member of society.

C. THE AFFIRMATION OF COMMUNIST MORALITY

In the course of transition to communism, the moral principles of society become increasingly important, the sphere of action of the moral factor expands and the importance of the administrative control of human relations diminishes accordingly....

The Communists reject the class morality of the exploiters....

...Communist morality encompasses the fundamental norms of human morality which the masses of the people evolved in the course of millenniums as they fought against vice and social oppression. . . .

The party holds that the moral code of the builder of communism should comprise the following principles:

● Devotion to the Communist cause, love of the Socialist motherland and of the other Socialist countries.

● Conscientious labor for the good of society—he who does not work, neither shall he eat.

● Concern on the part of everyone for the preservation and growth of public wealth.

● A high sense of public duty, intolerance of actions harmful to the public interest.

● Collectivism and comradely mutual assistance between individuals—man is to man a friend, comrade and brother.

● Honesty and truthfulness, moral purity, modesty and guilelessness in social and private life.

● Mutual respect in the family, and concern for the upbringing of children.

● An uncompromising attitude to injustice, parasitism, dishonesty and careerism.

● Friendship and brotherhood among all peoples of the USSR, intolerance of national and racial hatred.

● An uncompromising attitude to the enemies of communism, peace and the freedom of nations.

● Fraternal solidarity with the working people of all countries, and with all peoples.

D. THE PROMOTION OF PROLETARIAN INTERNATIONALISM & SOCIALIST PATRIOTISM

...The party maintains that with the emergence of the world Socialist system the patriotism of the members of Socialist society is expressed in devotion and loyalty to their own country and to the entire comity of Socialist countries.

Socialist patriotism and Socialist internationalism necessarily imply proletarian solidarity with the working class and all working people of all countries. . . .

E. ALL-ROUND & HARMONIOUS DEVELOPMENT OF THE INDIVIDUAL

...All-round development of the individual has been made possible by historic social gains—freedom from exploitation, unemployment and poverty, from discrimination on account of sex, origin, nationality or race. . . . Relations of dependence and inequality between people in public affairs and in family life disappear. The personal dignity of each citizen is protected by society. Each is guaranteed an equal and free choice of occupation and profession with due regard to the interests of society. . . .

F. ELIMINATION OF THE SURVIVALS OF CAPITALISM IN THE MINDS & BEHAVIOR OF PEOPLE

...Comradely censure of antisocial behavior will gradually become the principal means of doing away with manifestations of bourgeois views, customs and habits. . . .

The party uses ideological media to educate people in the spirit of a scientific materialist world conception, to overcome religious prejudices without insulting the sentiments of believers. . . .

G. THE EXPOSURE OF BOURGEOIS IDEOLOGY

The peaceful coexistence of states with different social systems does not imply discontinuance of the ideological struggle. The Communist Party will go on exposing the anti-popular, reactionary nature of capitalism.... The party will steadfastly propagate the great advantages of socialism and communism over the declining capitalist system....

(2) *In ... public education.*

...The system of public education is so organized as to insure that the instruction and education of the rising generation are closely bound up with life and productive labor and that the adult population can combine work in the sphere of production with further training and education.... Public education along these lines will make for the molding of harmoniously developed members of Communist society and for the solution of a cardinal social problem, namely, the elimination of substantial distinctions between mental and physical labor.

The main tasks in the field of instruction and education are:

A. THE INTRODUCTION OF UNIVERSAL COMPULSORY SECONDARY EDUCATION

In the next decade compulsory secondary general and polytechnical 11-year education is to be introduced for all children of school age, and education of 9 classes of young people engaged in the national economy who have not had the appropriate schooling. In the subsequent decade everyone is to receive a complete secondary education....

Secondary education must furnish a solid knowledge of the fundamentals of the basic sciences, and understanding of the principles of the Communist world outlook, and a labor and polytechnical training in accordance with the rising level of science and engineering, with due regard to the needs of society and to the abilities and inclinations of the students....

B. THE PUBLIC UPBRINGING OF CHILDREN....

The Communist system of public education is based on the public upbringing of children. The educational influence which the family exerts on children must be brought into ever greater harmony with their public upbringing....

C. THE CREATION OF CONDITIONS FOR HIGH-STANDARD INSTRUCTION & EDUCATION OF THE RISING GENERATION

The party plans to carry out an extensive program for the construction of schools and cultural-education establishments to meet fully the needs of education and instruction.... Rural schools will also have their own farming plots, large factories will have production training shops for school children....

D. HIGHER & SECONDARY SPECIALIZED EDUCATION

...Higher and secondary specialized education, which must train highly skilled specialists with a broad theoretical and political background, will be expanded.

Shorter working hours and a considerable improvement in the standard of living of the entire population will provide everyone with an opportunity to receive a higher or secondary specialized education if he so desires....

(3) *In the field of science.*

...Scientific progress and the introduction of scientific achievements into the economy will remain an object of special concern to the party.

Most important are the following tasks:

A. DEVELOPMENT OF THEORETICAL INVESTIGATIONS

...A high level of development in mathematics, physics, chemistry and biology is a necessary condition for the advancement and the effectiveness of technical, medical, agricultural and other sciences.

Theoretical investigations will be promoted to the utmost, primarily in such decisive fields of technical progress as electrification of the whole country, comprehensive mechanization and automation of production, the application of chemistry to the leading branches of the national economy, industrial uses of atomic energy, transport and communications....

Big advances are to be made in the development of all the biological sciences in order successfully to solve medical problems and achieve further progress in agriculture....

There must be intensive development of research work in the social sciences, which constitute the scientific basis for the guidance of the development of society....

The task of economic science is to theoretically generalize new phenomena in the economic life of society, and to work out the national economic problems whose solution promotes successful Communist construction....

The investigation of the problems of the world history and contemporary world development must disclose the law-governed process of mankind's advance toward communism, the change in the balance of forces in favor of socialism, the aggravation of the general crisis of capitalism, the break-up of the colonial system of imperialism and its consequences, and the upsurge of the national-liberation movement....

The social sciences must continue to struggle with determination against bourgeois ideology, against Right Socialist theory and practice and against revisionism and dogmatism....

B. MERGER OF SCIENCE & PRODUCTION

...It is essential to extend and improve the network of research institutions, including those attached to the central bodies directing economic development and those attached to the economic councils, and the network of research laboratories and institutes at the major industrial plants and in farming areas, to develop research at higher educational establishments, to improve the geographical distribution of research institutions and higher educational establishments, and to insure the further development of science in all the union republics and major economic areas.

The research institutions must plan and coordinate their work in the most important trends of research in accordance with the plans of economic and cultural development....

It is a point of honor for Soviet scientists...to take a leading place in world science in all the key fields.

(4) *In the field of cultural development, literature and art.*

Cultural development during the fullscale construction of Communist society will constitute the closing stage of a great cultural revolution. At this stage, all the necessary ideological and cultural conditions will be created for the victory of communism....

Communist culture, which will have absorbed and will develop all the best that has been created by world culture, will be a new, higher stage in the cultural progress of mankind.... It will be the culture of a classless society, a culture of the entire people, of all mankind.

A. ALL-ROUND ADVANCEMENT OF THE CULTURAL LIFE OF SOCIETY

In the period of transition to communism, creative effort in all fields of culture...becomes accessible to all members of society.... The development and enrichment of the arts are based on a combination of mass amateur endeavor and professional art....

To provide the material basis for cultural development on a grand scale:

- Book publishing and the press will be vigorously developed, and the printing and paper industries will be expanded accordingly.
- There will be more libraries, lecture halls and reading rooms, theaters, clubs, houses of culture and cinemas.
- The countrywide radio diffusion network will be completed, television stations covering all industrial and agricultural areas will be built.
- People's universities, people's theatrical companies and other amateur cultural organizations will be widely developed.
- A large network of scientific and technical laboratories and of art and cinema studios will be provided for the use of all who have the inclination and ability....

B. ENHANCEMENT OF THE EDUCATIONAL ROLE OF LITERATURE & ART

Soviet literature and art, imbued with optimism and dynamic Communist ideas are great factors in ideological education....

The high-road of literature and art lies through the strengthening of links with the life of the people, through faithful and highly artistic depiction of the richness and versatility of Socialist reality, inspired and vivid portrayal of all that is new and genuinely Communist, and exposure of all that hinders the progress of society.

In the art of Socialist realism, which is based on the principles of partisanship and kinship with the people, bold pioneering in the artistic depiction of life goes hand in hand with the cultivation and development of the progressive traditions of world culture....

C. THE EXPANSION OF INTERNATIONAL CULTURAL RELATIONS

The party considers it necessary to expand the Soviet Union's cultural relations with the countries of the Socialist system and with all other countries for the purpose of pooling scientific and cultural achievements and of bringing about mutual understanding and friendship among the peoples.

6. *Communist Construction in the USSR and Cooperation of the Socialist Countries*

The fact that Socialist revolutions took place at different times, and that the economic and cultural levels of the countries concerned are dissimilar, predetermines the non-simultaneous completion of Socialist construction in those countries and their non-simultaneous entry into the period of the fullscale construction of communism....

The first country to advance to communism facilitates and accelerates the advance of the entire world Socialist system to communism....

The construction of communism in the USSR promotes the interests of every country of the Socialist community....

The Socialist system makes possible the abolition of the economic and cultural gap between countries—a legacy of capitalism—the more rapid development of the countries whose economy lagged behind under capitalism....

It is in the best interest of Socialist and Communist construction that each Socialist country combine the effort to strengthen and develop its national economy with the effort to expand economic cooperation of the Socialist camp as a whole....

The objective laws of the world Socialist system, the growth of the productive forces of Socialist society, and the vital interests of the peoples of the Socialist countries predetermine an increasing affinity of the various national economies, and the eventual unification in a single world Communist economy that Lenin foresaw.

The CPSU and the Communist parties of the other Socialist countries consider their tasks to be:

● In the political field, the utmost strengthening of the world Socialist system, ... political consolidation of the countries of the Socialist community in a joint struggle for universal peace and for the complete triumph of communism.

● In the economic field, ... development of the Socialist international division of labor, increasing coordination of long-range economic plans among the Socialist countries envisioning a maximum saving of social labor and an accelerated development of the world Socialist economy, the promotion of scientific and technical cooperation.

● In the cultural field, steady development of all forms of cultural cooperation and intercourse between the peoples of the Socialist countries, ... extensive measures to insure the mutual enrichment of national cultures and bring the mode of life and the spiritual cast of the Socialist nations closer together....

7. The Party in the Period of Fullscale Communist Construction

...The Communist Party of the working class has become the vanguard of the Soviet people, a party of the entire people, and extended its guiding influence to all spheres of social life.... It looks keenly into the future and shows the people scientifically motivated roads along which to advance, arouses titanic energy in the masses and leads them to the accomplishment of great tasks....

Unlike all the preceding socio-economic formations, Communist society does not develop sporadically, but as a result of conscious and purposeful efforts of the masses led by the Marxist-Leninist party....

There must be a new, higher stage in the development of the party itself and of its political, ideological and organizational work that is in conformity with the fullscale building of communism....

The cult of the individual and the violations of collectivism in leadership, of inner-party democracy and Socialist legality arising out of it are incompatible with the Leninist principles of party life....

In order to effect the Leninist principle of collective leadership consistently, to insure a greater influx of fresh party forces into the leading party organs, to properly combine old and young cadres, and to rule out the possibility of an excessive concentration of power in the hands of individual officials and prevent cases of their getting beyond the control of the collective, the party considers it necessary to carry out the following measures:

A. To introduce in practice a regular renewal... of the members of all elected party bodies—from primary organizations to the Central Committee, thus insuring continuity of leadership.

At all regular elections, not less than 1/4 of the members of the Central Committee of the CPSU and its Presidium shall be renewed. Presidium members shall, as a rule, be elected for not more than 3 successive terms. Particular party workers may, by virtue of their... abilities, be successively elected to the leading bodies for a longer period. In that case, the respective candidate is considered elected, provided not less than 3/4 of the votes are cast for him by secret ballot.

Members of the central committees of the Communist parties of union republics, of territorial and regional committees shall be renewed by not less than 1/3 at each regular election, and that of area, city and district committees, and the committees and bureaus of primary party organizations, shall be renewed by 1/2. Furthermore, members of the leading party bodies may be elected consecutively for not more than 3 years, and secretaries of the primary party organizations for not more than 2 consecutive terms.

A party organization may, in consideration of the political and professional qualities of a person, elect him to a leading body for a longer period. In that case a candidate is considered elected if not less than 3/4 of the Communists attending vote for him....

A decision on removal from the Central Committee of the CPSU and other leading organs shall be adopted solely by secret ballot and is valid when not less than 2/3 of the total membership of the body concerned vote in favor of the decision.

B. To extend the application of the elective principle and that of accountability in party organizations at all levels, including party organizations working under special conditions (army, navy).

C. To enhance the role of party meetings, conferences, congresses and plenary meetings of party committees and other collective bodies. To provide favorable conditions for a free and business-like discussion within the party of questions concerning its policy and practical activities for comradely discussions of controversial or insufficiently clear matters.

D. To reduce steadily the salaried party staffs, enlisting Communists more extensively as nonsalaried workers doing volunteer work.

E. To develop criticism and self-criticism to the utmost as a tried and tested method of work and a means of disclosing and rectifying errors and shortcomings and the proper education of cadres....

... The unshakable ideological and organizational unity of the party is the most important source of its invincibility, a guarantee for the successful solution of the great tasks of Communist construction.

The people are the decisive force in the building of communism. The party exists for the people, and it is in serving the people that it sees the purpose of its activity.... The party considers it its duty always to consult the working people on the major questions of home and foreign policy, to make these questions an object of nationwide discussion, and to attract the more extensive participation of non-members in all its work....

The CPSU is an integral part of the international Communist and working-class movement. The tried and tested Marxist-Leninist principles of proletarian internationalism will continue to be inviolable principles which the party will follow undeviatingly.

The Communist Party of the Soviet Union will continue to strengthen the unity of the international Communist movement, to develop fraternal ties with all the Communist and workers' parties and to coordinate its actions with the efforts of all the contingents of the world Communist movement....

When the Soviet people will enjoy the blessings of communism, new hundreds of millions of people on earth will say: "We are for communism." It is not through war with other countries but by the example of a more perfect organization of society by rapid progress in developing the productive forces, the creation of all conditions for the happiness and well-being of man, that the ideas of communism win the minds and hearts of the masses....

The party proceeds from the Marxist-Leninist proposition: the people are the maker of history, and communism is a creation of the people, of its energy and intelligence....

... The party calls on all Communists, on the entire Soviet people—all working men and women, *kolkhoz* farmers and workers by brain—to apply their energies to the successful fulfillment of the historic tasks set forth in this program....

The party solemnly proclaims: the present generation of Soviet people shall live under communism.

CP Rules Rewritten

The first recodification and revision of Soviet CP rules since 1952 was approved by the CP Central Committee June 19, published in Moscow newspapers Aug. 5 and adopted in revised form by the 22d CP Congress Oct. 31. The 1952 revision had been prepared by Khrushchev on Stalin's orders.

Like the new CPSU program, the new rules emphasized party democracy. "The CPSU bases its work on the unswerving adherence to the Leninist standards of party life—the principle of collective leadership, the promotion . . . of inner-party democracy, . . . criticism and self-criticism," the draft statute proclaimed. "Collectivism" was described as "the highest principle of party leadership." "The cult of the individual . . . must not be tolerated," the draft said. It denounced "all manifestations of revisionism and dogmatism" as "profoundly alien to revolutionary theory."

The draft statute reiterated "the principle of systematic renewal of the composition of party bodies" and set strict standards to avoid the perpetuation of officials in elective office—with some exceptions.

The draft asserted that "the guiding principle" of the CP's structure "is democratic centralism, which signifies: (a) election of all leading party bodies, from the lowest to the highest; (b) periodic reports of party bodies to their party organizations and to higher bodies; (c) strict party discipline and subordination of the minority to the majority; (d) that the decisions of higher bodies are obligatory for lower bodies." The draft said that "discussion of controversial or insufficiently clear issues may be held" at appropriate party levels when warranted.

Non-party organizations were to be subjected to party control, the draft indicated. It directed that when 3 or more party members found themselves in a non-party mass organization, they were to form party groups "for the purpose of strengthening the influence of the party in every way and carrying out party policy among non-party people. . . ."

Rules covered in the draft ranged from those for the acceptance of new members and the disciplining of those found remiss to the schedule of dues for members and candidate members (ranging from 10 kopeks monthly for those earning up to 50 rubles a month to 3% of earnings for those earning more than 300 rubles a month).

Party Structure Altered

The Congress concluded Oct. 31 with a secret session devoted to elections for the Central Committee, which in turn chose the 2 bodies responsible for running the party between Congresses—the policy-making Presidium and the Secretariat, responsible for day-to-day direction.

The election confirmed Khrushchev's continued party leadership as first secretary of the Central Committee and member of both the Presidium and Secretariat. It also confirmed the rise of Frol R. Kozlov to 2d place in the hierarchy. Kozlov's position was made clear by the listing of his name immediately after Khrushchev's, out of alphabetical order, in the official Central Committee roster.

The Central Committee was enlarged from 133 full and 122 candidate members to 175 full members and 156 candidates, the largest in history. (The election apparently was carried out in conformity with the party's new statute, which required replacement of at least 3/4 of the Central Committee at each Congress.)

The CP Presidium was reduced from 14 to 11 full members and from 9 to 5 candidates. These 4 full members were dropped: Culture Min. Yekaterina A. Furtseva, Nuritdin A. Mukhitdinov, Amb.-to-Poland Averky B. Aristov and Deputy Premier Nikolai G. Ignatov. One member—Gennadi I. Voronov—was added. 7 full members were reelected: Khrushchev, Kozlov, Soviet Pres. Brezhnev, First Deputy Premiers Mikoyan and Aleksei N. Kosygin, Russian Republican Premier Polyansky, Ukrainian CP First Secy. Podgorny, Central Committee secretaries Suslov and Kuusinen, and CP Control Committee Chrmn. Nikolai M. Shvernik.

The CP Presidium's 5 candidate members: First Secretaries Kirill T. Mazurov of the Byelorussian CP, Vasily P. Mzhavanadze of the Georgian CP and Sharaf R. Rashidov of the Uzbek CP, Ukrainian Premier Vladimir V. Shcherbitsky, and Victor V. Grishin, Soviet trade union chief. The 5 candidates dropped from the new Presidium: Latvian Pres. Janis E. Kalnberzins, Sverdlovsk CP Secy. Andrei P. Kirilenko, Ukrainian Pres. Demyan S. Korotchenko, Pyotr N. Pospelov, director of the Marx-Lenin Institute, and Amb.-to-East Germany Mikhail G. Pervukhin.

The Secretariat was increased from 5 to 9 members. 4 of the former members were retained (Khrushchev, Kozlov, Suslov and Kuusinen) and one (Mukhitdinov) was dismissed. The 5 new Secretariat members: Chrmn. Aleksandr N. Shelepin of the Soviet cabinet's State Security Committee, Secretaries Pyotr N. Demichev of the Moscow CP and Ivan V. Spiridonov of the Leningrad CP, Leonid Ilyichev of the Central Committee's Agitation-Propaganda Department, and Boris N. Ponomarev, head of its International Affairs Department.

The membership of the new Soviet CP Central Committee elected by the 22d party congress was made public Nov. 1. Almost 200 of the committee's 331 full and candidate members had not previously held positions on the body. Among the new full members were *Izvestia* editor Aleksei I. Adzhubei, Khrushchev's son-in-law, and a number of senior military officers. 4 members of the alleged anti-party plot were dropped from the committee: Voroshilov, Bulganin, Pervukhin, and Maxim Z. Saburov.

Moscow sources reported Nov. 11 that Molotov, Malenkov and Kaganovich had been expelled from the Soviet CP. Molotov, 71, chief of the permanent Soviet mission at the Vienna headquarters of the International Atomic Energy Agency, returned to Moscow from Vienna Nov. 12 with his wife. Voroshilov was turned away Nov. 7 when he sought to join Khrushchev and other Soviet leaders reviewing the annual military parade from atop the Lenin mausoleum in Red Square.

FOREIGN POLICY

Khrushchev for Coexistence & Liberation Wars

Soviet views on the need to promote revolutionary struggles against colonial and reactionary regimes without provoking world nuclear war were outlined in a speech delivered by Khrushchev Jan. 6 and published Jan. 18 by the Soviet CP theoretical journal *Kommunist*. Khrushchev, at a Kremlin meeting of members of the Higher Party School, the Academy of Social Sciences and the Institute of Marxism & Leninism, outlined these Soviet policies on war and revolution:

●The USSR would work to prevent the outbreak of general nuclear war because it would result in the deaths of hundreds of millions and in unprecedented destruction. It was opposed to "local wars" of the Suez or Indochina variety because they could develop into general nuclear conflict.

●"Liberation wars" such as those under way in Algeria and Cuba were "sacred" and would go on "as long as imperialism exists, as long as colonialism exists." "These uprisings are directed against decayed reactionary regimes, against the colonialists. Communists support such wars fully and without reservation and march in the van of the people fighting for liberation."

●"In present conditions, wars are most probable not between capitalist and imperialist countries, although such an eventuality should not be discounted. The imperialists are preparing war chiefly against the Socialist countries ... [and] the Soviet Union."

●Such war can be avoided by adherence to peaceful coexistence and by disarmament. The USSR's disarmament proposals were genuine and "not a tactical move." "We sincerely want disarmament" because it would help to prevent war and would aid "the fight against imperialism."

●The Dec. 6, 1960 Moscow manifesto issued by 81 Communist parties had "set our watches so that our mighty armies will keep in step and march confidently toward" a Communist world. This goal could be achieved best not by force but by communism's victory in an "intense economic, political and ideological struggle" carried out within the limits of peaceful coexistence.

At a Tiflis rally marking the 40th anniversary of the Georgian Communist Party, Khrushchev declared May 12 that Soviet progress would ensure the victory of communism without war. He said: "I repeat that we do not need a war to achieve domination of our ideas, the most progressive Marxist-Leninist ideas. War brings only harm.... We will create this victory because other peoples will follow ... our example." Denouncing Western contentions that the Soviet people lacked liberty, Khrushchev shouted: "They say we have no freedom! We Communists ... we are the freest of the free people in the world. We have freedom for those ... who work in mines, factories, laboratories.... But there is no freedom in the Soviet Union for those who robbed people [and] took profits."

Russia & the West

The first exchange of messages between the Soviet government and the incoming U.S. Administration of Pres. John F. Kennedy took place Jan. 20, immediately after Mr. Kennedy's inauguration. The exchange, carried out in notes between Khrushchev and Mr. Kennedy and in Moscow diplomatic conversations, expressed both nations' desire for a fresh attempt at negotiations on East-West problems. The first message, congratulating Mr. Kennedy on his inauguration, was cabled Jan. 20 by Khrushchev and Soviet Pres. Brezhnev. It expressed the hope "that by joint efforts we shall be able to attain a radical improvement of relations between our countries." It said Soviet leaders were confident that, "moving step by step, it is possible to remove the existing suspicion and mistrust" between the U.S. and USSR. It pledged that the USSR would "support any good initiatives in this direction ... for a lasting peace."

Khrushchev and Mr. Kennedy met in Vienna June 3-4 for a personal discussion of world problems. It was their first private meeting and the first major East-West confrontation to take place since the abortive May 1960 Paris summit conference. Their talks produced no substantive agreement on any of the problems discussed. The 2 leaders June 4, however, issued a joint communique affirming their support for a neutral Laos and their willingness to maintain contact on all differences between their governments.

A Soviet demand for Western participation in a conference on a World War II peace treaty with Germany and a settlement of central Europe's postwar frontiers was repeated in notes delivered to the U.S., Britain and France Aug. 4 and made public Aug. 5. The Soviet messages were in reply to Western notes transmitted to the USSR July 17 in response to the memo on Germany delivered by Soviet officials at the end of the meeting of Pres. Kennedy and Khrushchev.

The 3 parallel Soviet notes repeated the cardinal points of Russia's recent policies toward Germany: (1) To preserve peace, a settlement was necessary of the outstanding problems left by World War II in Berlin, Germany and central Europe. (2) The most feasible way to effect a settlement was by signing a German peace treaty under which West Berlin would be transformed into a demilitarized "free city" and negotiation of Germany's reunification would be left to the East and West German governments. (3) If the West refused to join the USSR in an international conference on such a treaty, the USSR would sign a separate treaty with East Germany. (4) This treaty would terminate Western occupation rights in West Berlin and would force the Western powers to renegotiate the guarantees of their Berlin position with the East German government. (5) The entire Soviet bloc was ready to support East Germany if the West refused to accept a peaceful transformation of its Berlin position. (6) The USSR was prepared to begin negotiations with the West either on (a) a German peace treaty, or (b) guarantees to assure the freedom of West Berlin and its contacts with the West under a "free city" statute.

Khrushchev said Sept. 7 that he was willing to meet Pres. Kennedy again in an effort "to find solutions for the major international issues now causing concern." "But the main thing is that such a meeting must be fruitful," Khrushchev declared. "And if Pres. Kennedy agrees to a meeting, ... it will be important that both sides display understanding of the need to resolve such important matters as the signing of a German peace treaty and the solution on this basis of the question of West Berlin as well as the problem of disarmament under strict international control." The Khrushchev statement was given to C. L. Sulzberger of the *N.Y. Times* to clarify views expressed by Khrushchev Sept. 5 in a lengthy interview with Sulzberger. The statement and excerpts from the interview were printed Sept. 8 in the *Times* along with an article in which Sulzberger reported his impression that Khrushchev (a) was "supremely confident that he can win the present test of iron wills without recourse to war" and (b) "sure that the Western world will ... accept his basis for a new Berlin formula." *Among views Khrushchev stated during the Sulzberger interview:*

Atomic tests—The USSR would not resume the moratorium on nuclear tests nor would it accept a U.S.-British proposal of a ban on nuclear tests in the atmosphere. The moratorium was proposed for the USSR, U.S. and Britain. "We already declared in the past that if France conducts tests, we shall also be compelled to start testing." The U.S. and Britain "want us to stop [testing]... while France is left complete freedom of action" to test—with U.S. and British aid—"not only for herself" but for NATO.

"A cessation of thermonuclear tests without a solution of the disarmament problem" would be useless "if the arms race continued and war industry went on... creating nuclear weapons.... The chief danger now facing mankind is the danger of thermonuclear war, and it would not be lifted as a result of a moratorium. Moreover,... this would... [lull] public opinion.... People would think something had been done to prevent war while, in effect, nothing was being done." The Anglo-U.S. proposal says nothing on a cessation of underground test explosions and on so-called explosions for peaceful purposes... [which] mean legalization of tests of atomic and hydrogen bomb devices."

The USSR was "lagging far behind" the U.S., Britain and France in the number of tests. "We... have a moral right to equal conditions as regards measures to assure our security.... We must assure ourselves of no lesser capability than [the Western 3]."

"We believe that... the main thing is disarmament and not a test ban. If an agreement on disarmament and control is reached, no man of reason will manufacture any nuclear weapons...."

A-weapons use—The USSR would not promise that it would not be the first nation to use nuclear weapons in a war. "Anyone who made such a statement could turn out to be untruthful even though, when making such a pledge, he would be sincere...." Even if both sides in a war promised "not to employ nuclear weapons while retaining their stockpiles," the side that thought it was losing "would undoubtedly use its nuclear bombs." "If atomic weapons are preserved and if war is unleashed, it will be a thermonuclear war."

"We already have" a bomb "equal in capacity to 100 million tons of TNT... and shall test the explosive device for it." "We will stop short of nothing if aggressors attack us.... Several such super bombs at our disposal will considerably increase the [USSR's] defensive capability.... The aggressors will think twice before attacking us.... [We] have repeatedly declared we have no intention of attacking anyone.... We are only creating means to defend our Socialist camp and secure peace."

A-weapons spread—The USSR had not given nuclear warheads or long-range missiles to Communist China or to any Warsaw Pact nation. No such Soviet weapons were stationed outside the USSR except "possibly in East Germany."

Anti-missile defense—Soviet scientists started work on means to combat intercontinental rockets at the same time as work was started to develop ICBMs. The USSR was "very satisfied with the work of those who produced the means of combating" ICBMs.

Berlin & Germany—"I believe in the common sense of the Western statesmen.... They will draw the conclusion that a peace treaty must be signed with...the 2 German states actually in existence, and they will give West Berlin the status of a free city.... It would be criminal to begin war over Berlin if West Berlin becomes a free city and if access to it is thereby insured not on the basis of the present occupation regime but on the basis of an agreement with...the German Democratic Republic. The substance, after all, remains unchanged—access to West Berlin will be insured for all peoples and all countries who want it.... [We] declare that the political system of West Berlin will not be encroached upon and...the Socialist countries will not interfere in the affairs of West Berlin."

Peaceful coexistence—"The concept 'peaceful coexistence' has wider meaning" than merely the absence of war. It assumes the existence of states whose economic and social systems have "antagonistic" differences. It requires the "rejection [by these states] of military interference in each other's affairs," rejection of interference in each other's domestic affairs, recognition of each other's sovereignty, "rejection of wars and the maintenance of peace" and rejection of "the export of both revolution and counter-revolution." It "presumes normal trade relations, development of cultural contacts, scientific exchanges, development of tourism and other links."

Liberation wars—"We do not recognize that any country has a right to fight a war for the liberation of another country.... We recognize a people's right to wage a struggle for its [own] liberation.... We are against...all sorts of wars...with the exception of wars waged by nations fighting for their own liberation.... We fully support such wars.... Our sympathies are with peoples fighting for their liberation, and we are prepared to help them in every way we can."

Yugoslavia—"We regard Yugoslavia as a Socialist country, and should she be attacked by an imperialist state and appeal to us for help, I think we . . . would come to her help. If any Socialist state is attacked and appeals to us for help, we shall of course help it."

Cuba—"As far as we know, [Fidel] Castro is not a member of the Communist Party. He is just a revolutionary and patriot of his country. . . . We have no treaties with Cuba, but if she appeals to us for help in case of aggression against her, we will . . . not leave such an appeal unanswered."

Proposals for a withdrawal of Soviet and Western armed forces from their borderline positions in Central Europe were reiterated Oct. 12 by Khrushchev. His renewal of the plan was contained in a letter written to British leftist Emanuel Shinwell and other Laborite MPs. The letter, made public Oct. 12, proposed this 5-point agreement for settling East-West differences on Germany: (1) "Disengagement of NATO and Warsaw Treaty armed forces"; (2) a ban on the supply of nuclear weapons to both East and West Germany; (3) an agreement on "guaranteed access" to Berlin; (4) recognition of the Oder-Neisse boundary between East Germany and Poland; (5) recognition of East and West Germany and their entry in the UN.

(A U.S.-Soviet agreement signed in Moscow Mar. 17 provided for the exchange of U.S. and Soviet scholars to lecture and do research in literature, history, economy, law and dramatic criticism, starting in September. The agreement was signed by Dr. Frederick Burkhardt, president of the American Council of Learned Societies, Dr. Philip Mosely, chairman of the Society of Scientific Research and of the Council on Foreign Relations, and Prof. Aleksandr N. Nesmeyanov, head of the Soviet Academy of Sciences.)

Troop Cut Halted, Armed Forces Buildup Ordered

Khrushchev announced July 8 that the USSR had suspended planned troop reductions and had ordered a 25% increase in defense expenditures for 1961. Khrushchev declared that the Soviet government had been "compelled" to take this decision by a Western military buildup resulting from the continuing East-West crisis over the future of Berlin and Germany. Disclosing the decision at a Kremlin meeting of military academy graduates, Khrushchev said:

"Comrades, the ... Soviet Union follows attentively the military measures taken of late by the United States ... and its NATO allies. We cannot disregard such facts as the building up of armed forces in the Western countries, the steps to increase considerably the number of strategic A-bombers which are constantly kept in the air. The forces of West Germany are being equipped with the latest weapons and increased numerically....
Mr. Kennedy proclaimed in his recent messages to Congress the so-called 'new course.' It provides for stepping up the program of developing rocket-missile strategic weapons, the raising of the military readiness of all services. For this purpose, Pres. Kennedy has proposed to increase military allocations ... by more than $3.5 billion. This means that the [U.S.'] military spendings in the fiscal year of 1961-1962 will exceed $53 billion."

"Taking into account the obtaining situation, the Soviet government was compelled to instruct the Defense Ministry to suspend, temporarily, pending special orders, the reduction of the armed forces planned for 1961. In view of the growing military budgets in the NATO countries, the Soviet government has passed a decision to increase defense spendings in the current year by 3.144 billion rubles ... raising the total ... in 1961 to 12.399 billion rubles."

A statement issued by the Soviet cabinet and the CP Central Committee Aug. 29 said that Marshal Rodion Y. Malinovsky, Soviet defense minister, had been ordered to halt the demobilization of all personnel scheduled for release "until the conclusion of a peace treaty with Germany" and the cessation of Western war threats.

A general build-up of Soviet-bloc armed forces was approved at a 2-day meeting of Warsaw Pact defense ministers and general staff chiefs in Warsaw Sept. 8-9. The decision was disclosed in a joint communique reported by Tass from Moscow Sept. 9. Thousands of Russian, Polish and Czech troops were reported entering East Germany Oct. 10 to take part in the largest joint military maneuvers in the history of the Warsaw Pact. West Berlin sources reported that at least 50,000 new Soviet troops and 10,000 Poles, mainly parachute, airborne and other combat units, already had arrived at East German maneuver areas. The new arrivals were said to have increased Russian forces in East Germany to 300,000. Plans for the maneuvers had been announced by the Warsaw Pact powers Sept. 25.

Khrushchev had declared Aug. 1 that the USSR had enough military power to repel any attack on the Soviet bloc. Speaking at a Kremlin luncheon in honor of Rumanian CP First Secy. Gheorghe Gheorghiu-Dej, Khrushchev said that "no provocations can change the course of history or are strong enough to divert the ... Socialist countries from the path they have chosen." He added: "We decisively warn all lovers of military adventures to behave wisely and remember that we have all the necessary means to cool off your heads."

Marshal Vasily D. Sokolovsky had asserted in a Tass interview Feb. 20 that the USSR's armed forces had completed their reorganization for missile warfare. Sokolovsky, retired chief of the Soviet General Staff, said: "The Soviet army and navy have completed their reorganization and re-equipment with qualitatively new weapons. The strategic rocket forces have been established as the principal arms of the armed forces of the USSR." The "power and military preparedness of the Soviet armed forces now are at a higher level than ever before" despite military manpower reductions which were being carried out in accordance with the demobilization ordered in 1960.

Malinovsky said in a speech delivered in Moscow July 6 and made public July 14: "All weapons of the [Soviet] armed forces are being converted to rocket equipment. Thus the rocket units ... are becoming basic fighting strength of all branches of the armed forces.... Under modern conditions we must learn to wage war in a new way. If the imperialists unleash a war, there will be no unbroken front lines. We shall have to act ... with exceptional speed.... The victory will often be won by small but bold detachments."

A record fiscal 1962 state budget that provided for defense expenditures of 13.4 billion rubles, a 44% increase over 1961, was presented to the Supreme Soviet by Finance Min. Vasily F. Garbuzov Dec. 6 and approved Dec. 8. Garbuzov said the defense outlay, representing 1/6 of the total budget, was necessitated by NATO's "increases in armed forces, perfecting armaments and open threats of war." U.S. Defense Department officials estimated that Soviet defense expenditures actually totaled 1/2 of the budget since much arms spending was concealed in nonmilitary categories. (The budget also provided for a 33 1/2% increase in capital investments in the consumer goods industry and an 18% increase in capital investments in heavy industry.)

Russia Resumes Nuclear Tests

The Soviet government announced Aug. 31 that it was breaking the 34-month-old voluntary moratorium on nuclear weapons tests. It said that it was forced to resume the testing of new nuclear weapons to defend the USSR against war threats from the U.S. and its Western allies. The Soviet announcement said the USSR had designed "super-powerful nuclear bombs" with a yield equivalent to up to 100 million tons of TNT. It asserted that "powerful rockets similar to those" used in Soviet manned orbital flights could deliver such bombs "to any point on the globe." Within 24 hours of its announcement the USSR detonated a nuclear device—the first it was known to have tested since Nov. 3, 1958—and it detonated a 2d Sept. 4, a 3d Sept. 5 and a 4th Sept. 6.

The 2 most powerful bombs ever tested—of 25 and 58 megatons intensity, respectively—were detonated by Soviet scientists Oct. 23 and 30 at the USSR's Novaya Zemlaya proving area in the Arctic. Khrushchev said Dec. 9 that the USSR had nuclear bombs more powerful that 100 megatons and would use them "against our enemies whenever they unleash war against the Socialist countries."

(The U.S. resumed nuclear tests Sept. 15.)

DOMESTIC DEVELOPMENTS

Economic Expansion Claimed

Soviet assertions that the USSR would overtake and surpass the U.S. in agricultural and industrial production were the subject of an exchange of statements by Khrushchev and U.S. Pres. Kennedy in June and July. The 2 leaders' major statements:

●Khrushchev, addressing an Alma-Ata rally marking the 40th anniversary of Soviet Kazakhstan, declared June 24 that "old Russia" had been an economically underdeveloped country but that "the Soviet Union has now outstripped all the developed capitalist countries and is already closely approaching, is about to touch the heels of the very leader of the capitalist world, the

U.S.A." He predicted that "it will not be long before we tell them: Make way, gentlemen. We are outstripping you and never again will you catch up to us." Khrushchev pledged a "tempestuous growth" in Soviet farm and factory output; he urged Kazakhs, however, to increase their production of horse meat, "a nutritious, tasty and cheap product."

●Khrushchev, in a speech broadcast from Alma-Ata June 25, reiterated that the USSR's economy would overtake the U.S.' by 1970. "This is our date," he declared. "We, the country which has existed for only 44 years... have come to occupy 2d place in the world. England... which had Africa and Asia—we left them behind us. We left France behind us too. Comrades! There is only America. And this country can be compared to a worn-out runner."

●Pres. Kennedy, at his news conference in Washington June 28, derided Khrushchev's claims but invited him to continue Soviet efforts to catch up to the U.S. Mr. Kennedy said: "Premier Khrushchev states that the Soviet Union is only 44 years old, but his country is far older than that; and it is an interesting fact that in 1913, according to the best calculations I can get... the Russian gross national product was 46% of the United States' gross national product. Interestingly,... in 1959 it was 47%." "If both countries sustain their present rate of growth, 3 1/2% in the United States and 6% in the Soviet Union, Soviet output will not reach 2/3 of ours by 1970.... Indeed if our gross rate is increased to even 4 1/2%, which is well within our capacity, it is my judgment that the Soviet Union will not out-produce the United States at any time in the 20th century."

●Khrushchev, in a Kremlin speech to Soviet military academy graduates, disagreed July 8 with the President's statistics and conclusions but said: "Let us, Mr. Kennedy, allow history to judge who gives the right prediction and who is in error." Khrushchev's analysis of the U.S. and USSR's comparative economic positions: "The... Soviet Union's industrial production accounted for 60% of the American output in 1960"; Soviet industrial growth had averaged 10.6% annually since World War II; if it continued at a rate of 10%, "in 1966 the Soviet Union will produce 106% of the present-day American output and in 1970, 156%." "But even if the Americans succeed in... an annual increment of 4.5%... we shall overtake them just the same in 1970." "If the Americans retain the rate of... 2%, which they averaged in the postwar years, the Soviet Union will outstrip America...in 1967. If American industrial output increases by 3% annually we shall leave them behind in 1968."

(The USSR's official report on the Soviet economy for 1960, published Jan. 25 by the Central Statistical Board, asserted that Soviet industrial production had risen by 10% during 1960 and by 22.1% in 1959-60, the first 2 years of the 7-year plan. The report estimated that Soviet national income had reached 144 billion new rubles in 1960, or 666 new rubles per capita, based on a mid-1960 population of 214,400,000.)

Khrushchev had declared May 30 that Soviet leaders "consider our heavy industry as built" and no longer were "going to give it priority." Speaking at a reception in honor of a British Trade Fair that had been opened in Moscow the previous day, Khrushchev declared that in the future the USSR's "light industry and heavy industry will develop at the same pace."

The 1962 economic expansion plan, submitted to the Supreme Soviet Dec. 6 by State Planning Chrmn. Vladimir N. Novikov and approved Dec. 8, provided for: (1) a 17% increase in consumer goods output compared with an 8.8% rise in capital goods production; (2) a steel output of 76,900,000 tons (1961: 71 million tons); (3) electric power output of 366 billion kilowatt hours (1961: 327 billion kilowatt hours).

(The Supreme Soviet Dec. 8 approved the establishment of a State Committee for Fuel Industries and a State Committee for Ferrous & Nonferrous Metallurgy in a move to restore centralized agencies to administer those industries. The government had decentralized most Soviet industries in 1957.)

Farm Officials Denounced, Reforms Ordered

A sweeping reorganization of the administration of Soviet agriculture had been demanded by Khrushchev and approved by the CP Central Committee at a plenary meeting held in the Kremlin Jan. 10-18. The committee adopted the reorganization plan after hearing Khrushchev charge that Soviet farm administrators had lied and cheated in claiming that they had achieved farm goals set by the 7-year plan. The reforms were apparently ordered to conform with Khrushchev's long-range plans to revitalize the Soviet peasantry by creating *agrogorods* ("agro-cities") in which it would be possible to integrate farms and industry, rural and urban society.

Izvestia Jan. 20 reported these major details of the reorganization:

●An all-union agency was to be created to serve as "an intermediary between the farms and industry." The new agency was to be in charge of supplying the farms with machinery, spare parts, fertilizer and other facilities. It was to be responsible for the "maintenance and utilization of machines in collective and state farms" (these functions had been given to the farms themselves after the dissolution in 1959 of the machine and tractor station system). The new agency, to be placed under the supervision of the Central Planning Board (Gosplan), was to establish and control a system of local industries serving collective and state farms.

●A "state procurement committee" was to be established to take charge of "all government purchases of farm products of every kind." The committee, also to be under Gosplan direction, was intended to improve the distribution of food and industrial crops delivered under state quotas. It was suggested that food produced above state quota levels be sold through a system of cooperatives rather than directly through city markets.

●The Agriculture Ministry was to be stripped of most administrative functions and become a center for the coordination and dissemination to farms of research information on the "rational organization of agriculture and training of cadres."

●Agricultural investments were to be increased over 7-year-plan goals for projects intended to "make agriculture independent of the whims of nature." These were to include (a) renewed large-scale irrigation projects, (b) increased fertilizer and machinery production, (c) increased production of corn for livestock use.

Khrushchev repeatedly denounced the reports presented at the plenum by regional leaders.

Interrupting Russian SFSR Premier Dmitri S. Polyansky as he was delivering his report Jan. 10, Khrushchev demanded that the party expel "figure jugglers" and others who tried to "hoodwink" the government on crop figures. He told Polyansky that officials who had failed in their tasks should resign. Khrushchev broke in as reports were being delivered by CP First Secretaries Nikolai V. Podgorny of the Ukraine and Dinmukhamed A. Kunayev of Kazakhstan Jan. 11. He accused regional leaders of "deceit" in farm production claims, and he told Podgorny that "the figures you give are only half the harvest...the other half was stolen in the fields." Informed Jan. 12 by Kirghiz CP First Secy. Iskhak R. Razzakov that Kirghiz farms had bought butter at retail markets to fulfill state quotas, Khrushchev demanded that lying officials be tried as criminals. The dismissal of Kirghiz Interior Min. Mukhambet Isayev was announced the same day.

Khrushchev told the Central Committee Jan. 13: "The days when leadership was hereditary are over. Now the rule is: If you work well, they welcome you. If you work badly they replace you. That is democracy."

In parts of his final plenum speech Jan. 17, Khrushchev attacked Ukrainian Premier Nikifor T. Kalchenko for agricultural mistakes and expressed wonder that he still was in office. Kalchenko was dismissed Feb. 28 as chairman of the Ukrainian Council of Ministers and was replaced by Vladimir V. Shcherbitsky, secretary of the Ukrainian CP Central Committee. Kalchenko, who had served as Ukrainian premier since 1954, was appointed chief of the State Procurement Ministry and made a Ukrainian deputy premier Mar. 3.

The first of the agricultural reforms was instituted Feb. 20: The government reorganized the Agriculture Ministry into a farm research agency and created an All-Union Agricultural Machinery Agency to encourage lagging farm production. Pavel S. Kuchumov was appointed head of the all-union agency Feb. 21.

The government Feb. 27 announced a plan to expand the economy of collective farms by reducing taxes on dairy products, providing more time to repay state loans and decreasing interest rates on loans.

A Central Committee communique Jan. 19 had said that Soviet grain production in 1960 had totaled 131 million metric tons, slighty more than in 1959 but less than the 141 million tons grown in 1958 and the 150 million tons planned. It reported that Soviet farms had produced 8.75 million metric tons of meat and 61.5 million metric tons of milk and dairy products, both quantities short of 7-year-plan quotas. The failure to increase meat production was attributed in part to the unexplained loss of 3 million sheep and goats in Kazakhstan in the winter. (The dismissal of Kazakhstan Agriculture Min. Mikhail Roznets was reported by Tass Mar. 3. He was replaced by Khaydar A. Arystanbekov, president of the Kazakhstan Academy of Agricultural Sciences. Among other replacements of republican agricultural officials: Abdurakhmen A. Abdullayevo was replaced by G. A. Aliev as agriculture minister of the Tadzhikistan SSR, the newspaper *Kommunist Tadzhikistan* reported Mar. 25. The newspaper *Sovetskaya Litva* reported Mar. 25 that Yan F. Vanag had replaced Aleksandr A. Nikonov as Latvian SSR agriculture minister. Nazirulla Mannanov, head of Soviet research in cotton growing, was appointed agriculture minister of the Uzbek republic Mar. 28; the ministry recently had been reorganized to concentrate on developing agriculture science and training specialists.)

Khrushchev warned at an agricultural conference in Moscow Dec. 14 that farm officials would be ousted from the CP unless they improved lagging farm production. Khrushchev was quoted by Soviet newspapers as saying that the failure to increase livestock output had caused a meat shortage in Soviet cities. The speech was one of several Khrushchev made in different parts of the USSR in November-December in an effort to spur falling farm output.

The Supreme Soviet Dec. 29 issued an edict providing 3-year prison terms for farmers who used equipment negligently.

Republic Officials Attacked & Ousted

Pravda reported Apr. 16 the dismissal of several Tadzhik SSR leaders on charges of "gross political errors." Those ousted (replacements in parentheses): Premier Nazarsho Dodkhudoyev (Abdulakhad K. Kakharov); CP First Secy. Tursunbai Uldzhabayev (Dzhabar R. Rasulov, ex-deputy minister of agriculture of the USSR); Deputy Premier Barat Dodabayev; Pyotr S. Obnosov, 2d secretary of the Central Committee (I. G. Koval); K. Usupov, the Economic Council's deputy chairman; Khalik Ibragimov, first secretary of the Leninabad regional party committee.

Formal charges against the ousted officials had been made in Stalinabad at an Apr. 11-12 Tadzhistan Central Committee meeting, which was addressed by Soviet Presidium Secy. Frol R. Kozlov. Dodkhudoyev and Uldzhabayev, who also were ousted from the Central Committee and dismissed from the CP, were accused of having reported for the past 3 years that the republic's cotton-output goals had been fulfilled ahead of schedule, whereas actually they had not even been met. Charges against all the ousted officials included protection of "swindlers and robbers who stole from the state and collective farms," poor supervision of farms and nepotism.

Pravda reported Apr. 19 the dismissal of Ivan P. Ganenko as first secretary of the Astrakhan Region's CP. He had been accused of personal "shortcomings and mistakes" in connection with lagging farm and industrial production. Ganenko was replaced by V. I. Antonov.

The *N.Y. Times* May 14 reported a government and CP shakeup in the Kirghiz SSR. Kazy D. Dikambaev was ousted as premier and dismissed from his CP post for "unsatisfactory direction of the... Council of Ministers and [for] permitting serious deficiencies in the national economy." He was replaced by Bolot Mambetov May 14. Iskhak R. Razzakov was ousted as the Kirghiz CP's first secretary and replaced by Turdakun Usubaliev.

(Government decrees published in *Pravda* July 23 established "commissions of state control" to supervise economic reports and data, the expenditure of state funds, procurement of materials, and the fulfillment of production goals. The commissions' main task was described as the elimination of fraud and irregularities from Soviet economic reports. The senior commission was to be headed by Khrushchev; subordinate commissions were to be responsible to the cabinets of the Soviet republics.)

Science Coordination Tightened

The formation of a State Committee for Coordinating Scientific Research was announced Apr. 11 by the Soviet CP and the Council of Ministers. The committee would control all scientific research in the USSR and direct all Soviet international scientific contacts. Ex-Aviation Min. Mikhail V. Khrunichev, 60, had been chosen committee chairman Apr. 8 with the rank of deputy premier. (But Khrunichev died in Moscow June 1 of a heart attack.) The announcement said the purpose of the committee was to eliminate duplication of research heretofore conducted by the Soviet Academy of Sciences and the Scientific Technical Committee. (The academy henceforth was to devote itself mainly to the development of the major physical and human sciences.) The new committee's principal functions would be to: (a) narrow the gap between research and production; (b) strengthen basic theoretical research that had economic value; (c) hasten the introduction of new scientific developments into the Soviet economy.

Chrmn. Konstantin N. Rudnev of the State Committee for Defense Technology was appointed June 10 as a Soviet deputy premier and chairman of the State Committee for Coordinating Scientific Research, a post in which he was to head the USSR's space and rocket drive. Leonid Smirnov replaced Rudnev in the defense post.

The Academy of Sciences May 19 had unanimously elected its vice president, Prof. Mstislav V. Keldysh, 50, as president. Keldysh, the USSR's leading expert in space and aerodynamics, replaced Prof. Aleksandr Nikolayevich Nesmeyanov, 62, who had resigned. The academy voted to retain Nesmeyanov as a member of its governing presidium. Nesmeyanov and the academy had been criticized for maintaining an outmoded organization, for duplicating work and for concentrating on theoretical problems.

Geographical De-Stalinization

Cities in the USSR and Eastern Europe continued to remove the appellation Stalin from their names. Most Stalin statutes were said to have been removed and many "Stalin" streets, factories and collective farms renamed. Stalingrad, site of the famed World War II victory, was renamed Volgograd Nov. 11. Stalino, in the Ukraine, was renamed Donetsk Nov. 8. Other newly named Soviet cities: Dushambe (formerly Stalinabad), Novokuznetsk (Stalinsk). The only open resistance to the effort to erase Stalin's name from Communist maps was in Georgia, where Stalin was born. First Secy. Vasily P. Mzhavanadze of the Georgian CP appealed to Georgians Nov. 18 not to hinder the campaign against the Stalin cult "just because Stalin was a Georgian."

In East Germany, the city of Stalinstadt was renamed Eisenhuettenstadt Nov. 14, and the Stalin Allee thoroughfare in East Berlin was renamed in 2 sections: Frankfurter Allee (its former name) and Karl Marx Allee. East Berlin's Stalin statue was removed, and factories and subway stations were renamed.

(Apparently encouraged by the de-Stalinization campaign, Mrs. Natalia Sedova Trotsky, widow of the murdered former Soviet leader Leon Trotsky, appealed Nov. 2 to the Soviet government and CP for the posthumous rehabilitation of her husband. Her letter, made public in Paris Nov. 4th by the Trotskyite 4th International, also demanded an investigation of the murder of Trotsky in Mexico in 1940 and the disappearance of her son, Serge Sedov, in the USSR in 1935.)

Other Developments

Vladimir Y. Semichastny, former Komsomol (Communist youth league) leader, was appointed Nov. 13 to succeed Shelepin as chairman of the Soviet cabinet's State Security Committee (KGB), ruling organ of the Soviet secret police. Shelepin, a member of the Soviet CP Central Committee, was released for full-time work within the committee's 9-member secretariat. Semichastny, a Central Committee alternate member, had succeeded Shelepin in the Komsomol post in 1958 and had served as 2d secretary of the Azerbaijan CP Central Committee since 1959.

The Soviet government announced Mar. 23 that it was ending prior censorship of news dispatches sent out of the USSR by foreign press, radio and TV correspondents. The announcement was made at a Moscow news conference by Mikhail A. Kharlamov, Soviet foreign ministry press chief. Foreign correspondents were told that they would continue to be held responsible for any outgoing news that Soviet authorities considered to be "incorrect rumors." (News coming into the USSR was still subject to strict government censorship.) Heretofore, correspondents had been required to submit their copy to the Central Telegraph Agency for Glavilit (censorship bureau) approval. Under the new ruling, news dispatches could be given to any telegraph office for transmission out of the Soviet Union.

The Presidium of the Supreme Soviet May 6 added the following crimes to the list of those punishable by death (execution by firing squad): embezzlement of state property; counterfeiting; especially dangerous habitual offenses; violence committed in places of confinement. The decree followed a CP Central Committee decision, made at a January plenary meeting, to strengthen the penal code.

A bimonthly literary review called *Sovietish Heimland* (*Soviet Homeland*) appeared in Moscow Aug. 22 and thus became the first Yiddish-language periodical published in the USSR in 13 years. (Stalin in 1948 had ordered the closing of

Yiddish publishing houses, newspapers and other Yiddish language institutions.) The magazine's editor, Yiddish poet Aaron Vergelis, said the decision to publish the review had been encouraged by Soviet Writers Union leaders, including Ilya Ehrenburg. The first issue totaled 25,000 copies.

The lay leader of the Jewish community in Leningrad and 2 lesser Jewish officials in that city were tried and convicted about Oct. 9-13 on charges of "criminal contact with the embassy [in the USSR] of one of the capitalist states." The leader of the community, Gedalia Rubinovich Pechersky, 60, reportedly arrested in June, was sentenced to 12 years in prison. The other 2 defendants—Y. S. Dynkin and N. A. Kaganov, both more than 70 years old—were sentenced to 7 years imprisonment. The Soviet newspaper *Leningradskaya Pravda* confirmed the trial and sentences Nov. 11. Tass charged Nov. 17 that the Western press had used the trial of the Leningrad Jews as a pretext for a campaign about "a wave of persecution of Jews in the Soviet Union." Tass said that the arrested Jews had "sold themselves" to Israeli intelligence agents.

A Leningrad court Nov. 17 sentenced 3 men to death for speculating in gold and foreign currency. 6 others received prison terms. According to the AP, all had Jewish names except one of the 6 given jail terms.

The Supreme Soviet Dec. 8 approved a new civil code modernizing Soviet laws. The code, effective May 1, 1962, dealt with: (1) property rights of public institutions and private citizens; (2) copyrights and patents; (3) rights of foreigners in the Soviet Union; (4) libel action procedures, which required newspapers to print retractions of libelous statements.

A law abolishing income taxes for workers whose monthly earnings did not exceed 60 rubles (about $65) went into effect Oct. 1. Taxes on incomes of 61 to 70 rubles were reduced 40%.

1962

U.S. Pres. Kennedy announced in October that the U.S. had verified that the USSR was building "offensive missile sites" in Cuba only 90 miles from the U.S. mainland. He demanded that the Russians remove the missiles. After nearly a week of war fears and feverish diplomatic activity, Soviet Premier Khrushchev yielded to the U.S. demand. Khrushchev's actions deepened the widening ideological rift between the USSR and Communist China. The USSR was also beset by domestic woes. Troubled with industrial and farm problems, Soviet authorities reorganized the country into 17 major economic regions in an effort to increase management efficiency. Khrushchev instituted a dual party/government system of administering the agricultural and industrial segments of the economy. Charging that the farm failures were due to "mismanagement," Khrushchev pushed through a fresh reorganization of Soviet agriculture in an effort to increase production. Western critics noted that in a crackdown on "economic crime," the widest publicity and severest penalties—including capital punishment—went to defendants who appeared easily identifiable as Jews.

CUBAN MISSILE CRISIS

One of the most threatening Soviet-U.S. confrontations of the cold war took place late in 1962 in the Caribbean. The U.S. disclosed that it had discovered aggressive Soviet missile bases under construction in Cuba—only 90 miles from Florida. Pres. Kennedy ordered the U.S. Navy to blockade the island, and he demanded that Russia remove the bases. For 6 days the world lived in fear of an armed clash between the 2 great powers. Then the Soviet government announced that it would dismantle the launching sites and withdraw its missiles. By the year's end, U.S. reconnaissance planes had verified Russia's removal of 42 medium-range missiles and 42 jet bombers.

U.S. Demands Russia Remove Missiles

The U.S. disclosure that the USSR was building "offensive missile sites" in Cuba was made by Pres. Kennedy in a nationwide radio-TV address Oct. 22 on the basis of "the closest [U.S. aerial] surveillance of the Soviet military buildup" there. He charged that "the purpose of these bases can be none other than to provide a nuclear strike capability against the Western Hemisphere." Mr. Kennedy announced that he had ordered Cuba blockaded to prevent further deliveries of offensive weapons to the island. He called on Khrushchev to dismantle the rocket sites, to remove Russian missiles from the island and to end this "provocative threat to world peace."

Mr. Kennedy asserted that this "urgent transformation of Cuba into an important strategic base by the presence of these large long-range and clearly offensive weapons . . . constitutes an explicit threat to the peace and security of all the Americas." The President expressed contempt for "the repeated assurances of Soviet spokesmen . . . that the arms buildup in Cuba would retain its original defensive character and that the Soviet Union had no need or desire to station strategic missiles on the territory of any other nation." He quoted from a Sept. 11 Soviet government statement in which the USSR had defended its Cuban arms deliveries and said: "That statement was false." He cited a similar avowal made to him personally by Soviet Foreign Min. Andrei A. Gromyko during a White House meeting Oct. 18—that Soviet assistance to Cuba " 'pursued solely the purpose of contributing to the defense capabilities of Cuba' "—and commented: "That statement also was false."

Mr. Kennedy held that the Soviet-Cuban action had upset the current nuclear balance between East and West. He said: "For many years both the Soviet Union and the United States... have deployed strategic nuclear weapons with great care, never upsetting the precarious *status quo* which insured that these weapons would not be used in the absence of some vital challenge." "But this secret, swift, extraordinary buildup of Communist missiles in an area known to have a special and historical relationship to the United States and the... Western Hemisphere... —this sudden, clandestine decision to station strategic weapons for the first time outside Soviet soil—is a deliberately provocative and unjustified change in the *status quo* which cannot be accepted by this country if our courage and our commitments are ever to be trusted again, by either friend or foe."

The U.S. President declared that "our unswerving objective... must be to prevent the use of these missiles against this or any other country; and to secure their withdrawal or elimination from the Western Hemisphere." He said he therefore had ordered the following "initial steps" be taken: "First, to halt this offensive buildup, a strict quarantine on all offensive military equipment under shipment to Cuba is being initiated. All ships of any kind bound for Cuba from whatever nation or port, will, if they are found to contain cargoes of offensive weapons, be turned back. This quarantine will be extended if needed to other types of cargo and carriers.... 2d, I have directed the continued and increased close surveillance of Cuba and its military buildup.... 3d, it shall be the policy of this nation to regard any nuclear missile launched from Cuba against any nation in the Western Hemisphere as an attack by the Soviet Union on the United States requiring a full retaliatory response upon the Soviet Union. 4th, as a necessary military precaution, I have reinforced our base at Guantanamo.... 5th, we are calling tonight for an immediate meeting of the Organ of Consultation under the Organization of American States to consider this threat to hemisphere security and to invoke Articles 6 and 8 of the Rio Treaty in support of all necessary action.... 6th, we are asking tonight that an emergency meeting of the [UN] Security

Council be convoked without delay to take action against this latest Soviet threat to world peace.

"Our resolution will call for the prompt dismantling and withdrawal of all offensive weapons in Cuba under the supervision of UN observers before the quarantine can be lifted. 7th, and finally, I call upon Chrmn. Khrushchev to halt and eliminate this clandestine, reckless and provocative threat to world peace and to stable relations between our 2 nations. I call upon him further to abandon this course of world domination and to join in an historic effort to end the perilous arms race and to transform the history of man."

The Soviet government rejected Pres. Kennedy's blockade warning and declared Oct. 23 that any aggressive American actions toward Cuba or its sea lanes to the Soviet bloc could result in thermonuclear war. The USSR's initial official reaction came in a government statement made public Oct. 23. The statement said: "The peoples of all countries must be clearly aware that, undertaking such a gamble [by blockading Cuba, the U.S.]...is taking a step along the road of unleashing a thermonuclear world war. Cynically flouting international standards,...the United States usurped the right...to attack ships of other states on the high seas—*i.e.,* to engage in piracy.... The Soviet government reaffirms that all weapons of the Soviet Union serve and will serve the purposes of defense against aggressors.... The Soviet Union will continue to discharge this mission with all firmness and consistence.... [The U.S.] accuses Cuba of allegedly creating a threat to the security of the United States. But who will believe that Cuba could create [such] a threat...? It is hypocrisy, to say the least, to allege that small Cuba can encroach on the security of the United States.... As to the Soviet Union's assistance to Cuba, it is aimed solely at enhancing Cuba's defense potential. As stated on Sept. 3 [in a joint Soviet-Cuban communique]...these arms and military equipment were designed exclusively for defensive purposes.... [The U.S.] demands that military equipment Cuba needs for self-defense should be removed from Cuban territory, a demand which...no state which values its independence can meet."

Latin Nations Back U.S.

The Council of the Organization of American States Oct. 23 approved a 4-point U.S.-sponsored resolution authorizing "the use of force" in carrying out the U.S. arms quarantine against Cuba. The resolution was adopted by a vote of 19-0 at an emergency meeting held in Washington. Uruguay abstained because its delegation had not received instructions from its government at the time of voting, but Uruguay approved the resolution Oct. 24 and made the OAS action unanimous.

The resolution: (1) Urged "the immediate dismantling and withdrawal from Cuba of all missiles and other weapons with any offensive capability"; (2) recommended that OAS states "take all measures, individually and collectively, including the use of armed force ... to ensure that ... Cuba cannot continue to receive from the Sino-Soviet powers military material ... which may threaten the peace and security of the continent and to prevent the missiles in Cuba with offensive capability from ever becoming an active threat to the [continent's] peace and security"; (3) announced the OAS Council's decision "to inform" the UN Security Council of this resolution in "the hope that the Security Council will ... dispatch UN observers to Cuba at the earliest moment"; (4) announced the OAS Council's plan "to continue to act provisionally as the Organ of Consultation and to urge member states to keep the Organ of Consultation duly informed of the measures adopted in accordance with Paragraph 2. . . ."

UN Takes Up Issue

The UN Security Council convened in New York Oct. 23. It was called into session by Soviet Amb.-to-UN Valerian A. Zorin, Council president for October, on the basis of requests received Oct. 22 from U.S. Amb.-to-UN Adlai E. Stevenson and Oct. 23 from Cuban Amb. Mario Garcia-Inchaustegui.

Stevenson, who was the first of the contending representatives to address the Council, charged that the USSR had sought to carry "the cold war into the heart of the Americas." Its success, he said, had brought the transformation of Castro's government into a "puppet" regime and the emplacement of Soviet missiles in Cuba. Stevenson declared that the USSR had turned Cuba into a Communist "bridgehead and staging area," into "a base for putting all of the Americas under the nuclear gun." Stevenson warned the Council: "Since the end of the 2d World War, there has been no threat...so profound.... The action we take may determine the future of civilization." A U.S. draft resolution submitted to the Council by Stevenson called for (1) "the immediate dismantling and withdrawal from Cuba of all missiles and other offensive weapons"; (2) the sending to Cuba of a UN "observer corps to assure and report on compliance with this resolution"; (3) "termination of the measures of quarantine...[on UN] certification of compliance"; (4) U.S.-Soviet talks "on measures to remove the existing threat to the security of Western Hemisphere and the peace of the world."

Garcia-Inchaustegui, who spoke immediately after Stevenson, devoted his address primarily to a denunciation of the quarantine. "The American blockade...is an act of war," he charged. "It is the use of force by a great power against the independence of our homes. It is a criminal act violating the [UN] Charter and the principles of our organization.... The reply of our people and of our government to the imminent armed attack of the United States has been general mobilization."

Zorin, following Garcia-Inchaustegui, reiterated the Soviet warning that "in embarking upon an open adventure of this kind,...[the U.S. was] making a step towards the unleashing of a world thermonuclear war." Zorin rejected Stevenson's version of postwar history and of recent events in Cuba. He declared: "The Soviet delegation...officially confirms the statement already made...in which it was said that the Soviet government has not directed and is not directing to Cuba any offensive armaments." A Soviet draft resolution presented by Zorin called for (1) condemnation of the U.S. action toward Cuba; (2) elimination of the blockade; (3) ending of U.S. "interference into the domestic affairs" of Cuba; (4) the U.S. and USSR "to establish contacts and enter into negotiations for the purpose of normalizing the situation and thereby removing the threat of war."

U.S. Ships Blockade Cuba

The U.S. blockade of Cuba was imposed Oct. 24 under a proclamation signed by Pres. Kennedy Oct. 23. In the proclamation, Mr. Kennedy ordered "the forces under my command...to interdict...the delivery of offensive weapons and associated material to Cuba." The proclamation listed "prohibited material" as "surface-to-surface missiles; bomber aircraft; bombs; air-to-surface rockets and guided missiles; warheads for any of the above weapons; mechanical or electronic equipment to support or operate the above items; and any other classes of material hereafter designated" by the Defense Secretary. The Defense Secretary was ordered "to prevent the delivery of prohibited material to Cuba, employing the [U.S.'] land, sea and air forces...in cooperation with any forces that may be made available by other American states." He was authorized to designate "prohibited or restricted zones" and "prescribed routes" "within a reasonable distance of Cuba" and to "issue such [other] directives as he deems necessary...."

The proclamation provided that: "Any vessel or craft which may be proceeding toward Cuba may be intercepted and may be directed to identify itself, its cargo, equipment and stores...to submit to visit and search, or to proceed as directed. Any vessel or craft which fails or refuses to respond to or comply with directions shall be subjected to being taken in custody. Any vessel or craft which it is believed is *en route* to Cuba and may be carrying prohibited material or may itself constitute such material shall...be directed to proceed to another destination of its own choice and shall be taken in custody if it fails or refuses to obey....Force shall not be used except in case of failure or refusal to comply with directions,...regulations or directives...after reasonable efforts have been made to communicate them to the vessel or craft, or in case of self-defense....Force shall be used only to the extent necessary."

No direct confrontation of U.S. and Soviet naval power took place off Cuba despite the U.S. blockade.

U.S. Defense Secy. Robert S. McNamara had reported Oct. 23 that as many as 25 Russian and Soviet-bloc vessels were *en route* to Cuba and would be subject to halt and search by the U.S.' naval blockade. Pentagon spokesmen reported Oct. 24, a few hours after the blockade took effect, that 12 of the Soviet ships had changed course but that the others were still steaming toward Cuba. The Pentagon officials expressed the view that the diverted vessels presumably had been carrying weapons or military supplies banned by the blockade proclamation.

The first contact between a Soviet vessel and the U.S. blockaders took place off Cuba early Oct. 25. The Defense Department reported that U.S. naval units had halted the Soviet tanker *Bucharest* but had permitted it to continue toward Havana without search after "the Navy satisfied itself that no prohibited material was aboard this particular ship." The 2d contact of the blockade was made Oct. 26 when U.S. vessels intercepted and boarded the Lebanese-registered freighter *Marucla,* bound from Riga, USSR to Havana under Soviet charter. The *Marucla*'s officers cooperated with the U.S. boarding party, and the vessel was permitted to continue to Havana after its cargo was checked.

In his first public statement since the start of the crisis, Soviet Premier Khrushchev Oct. 24 indorsed a proposal that he and Pres. Kennedy meet to seek a resolution of the crisis. His statement, made in reply to an appeal for such a meeting by Bertrand Russell, British philosopher and pacifist, came at a time when worldwide fears had been expressed that the crisis might result in war. Khrushchev, in a letter written to Russell and made public in Soviet broadcasts and press dispatches, said: "I understand your worry and anxiety" over U.S. "aggressive actions" "in pushing the world to the brink of war" by blockading Cuba; "I ... assure you that the Soviet government will not take any reckless decisions, will not let itself be provoked by the unwarranted [U.S.] actions ... and will do everything to eliminate the situation fraught with the irreparable consequences which has arisen in connection with the aggressive [U.S.] action"; if the U.S. continued its "piratic actions" the USSR "shall have to resort to means of defense against an aggressor to defend our rights and international rights"; "the question of war is so vital that we should consider useful a top-level meeting in order to discuss all the problems which have arisen, to do everything to remove the danger of the unleashing of a thermonuclear war."

Acting UN Secy. Gen. U Thant appealed to the U.S., Soviet and Cuban governments Oct. 24 to suspend all potentially aggressive actions and begin negotiations for a peaceful resolution of the crisis. Thant's plea was made in personal messages addressed by Thant to Pres. Kennedy and Khrushchev. Appearing before the Security Council later that day to report on his action, Thant said that his messages to Mr. Kennedy and Khrushchev had asked that "in the interest of international peace and security all ... refrain from any action which may aggravate the situation and bring with it the risk of war." "This involves on the one hand the voluntary suspension of all arms shipments to

Cuba, and also the voluntary suspension of the quarantine measures involving the searching of ships bound for Cuba." Khrushchev and Pres. Kennedy Oct. 25 sent conciliatory replies to U Thant's appeal. The responses differed, however, in that Khrushchev fully accepted the Thant proposal whereas Mr. Kennedy accepted the suggestion for preliminary talks without mentioning Thant's request for suspension of the blockade.

Khrushchev and Pres. Kennedy pledged Oct. 26 to take all steps to avoid a direct naval confrontation on the U.S.' blockade line around Cuba. Their pledges were made in responses to a 2d appeal from U Thant. Thant's new appeal, cabled to the U.S. and Soviet leaders Oct. 25, expressed his "grave concern that Soviet ships already on their way to Cuba might challenge the quarantine... and produce a confrontation at sea between Soviet ships and United States vessels, which could lead to an aggravation of the problem" and "destroy any possibility of the discussions I have suggested." Thant asked Khrushchev "to instruct the Soviet ships already on their way to Cuba to stay away from the interception area for a limited time only, in order to permit discussions...." He urged Mr. Kennedy to instruct U.S. vessels in the Caribbean "to do everything possible to avoid direct confrontation with Soviet ships in the next few days to minimize the risk of any untoward incident." Khrushchev and Mr. Kennedy Oct. 26 accepted Thant's appeal for caution in the Caribbean, but each strongly denounced the other for the continuation of aggressive policies in the Cuban situation.

Khrushchev warned: "If any conflict should arise on the approaches to Cuba—and this may become unavoidable as a result of the piratical measures taken by the United States—this would... seriously complicate the endeavors... to put an end, on the basis of negotiation, to the critical situation that has now been thrust on the world by the [U.S.'] aggressive actions.... We therefore accept your proposal and have ordered the... Soviet vessels bound for Cuba but not yet within the area of the American warships' piratical activities to stay [temporarily] out of the interception area." Mr. Kennedy said that "if the Soviet government accepts and abides by your request..., you may be assured that... [the U.S.] will accept and abide by your request that our vessels... 'avoid direct confrontation with Soviet ships'."

Khrushchev Proposes Cuba-Turkey Deal

Khrushchev offered Oct. 27 to withdraw all Soviet missiles and offensive weapons from Cuba if Pres. Kennedy would pledge the U.S. to a similar withdrawal from its bases in Turkey. Khrushchev's proposal, made in a letter, contained the admission that the USSR had sent to Cuba missiles and other weapons deemed offensive by the U.S. Khrushchev said: "You want to make your country safe. This is understandable, but Cuba, too, wants the same thing. All countries want to make themselves safe. But how are we, the Soviet Union,... to assess your actions which are expressed in the fact that you have surrounded with military bases the Soviet Union; surrounded with military bases our allies;... have stationed your rocket armament there.... You are worried by Cuba... because it is a distance of 90 miles by sea from the coast of America. But Turkey is next to us.... Do you... have the right to demand security for your own country and... not acknowledge the same right for us?" "I therefore make this proposal: We agree to remove those weapons from Cuba which you regard as offensive weapons. We agree to do this and to state in the United Nations this commitment. Your representatives will make a statement to the effect that the United States... will evacuate its analogous weapons from Turkey...."

A White House statement issued Oct. 27 in reply to the broadcast version of Khrushchev's Cuba-Turkey offer rejected any such *quid pro quo* as a basis for resolving the crisis. The statement, while it did not reject the specific terms mentioned by Khrushchev, declared that "the first imperative must be to deal with this immediate threat, under which no sensible negotiations can proceed." Asserting that "work on these offensive weapons is still proceeding at a rapid pace," the statement said that it was "the Western Hemisphere countries and they alone that are subject to the threat that has produced the current crisis."

U.S. Accepts Soviet Withdrawal Offer

Pres. Kennedy disclosed later Oct. 27 that a prior Khrushchev offer to settle the Cuban crisis would be accepted by the U.S. unless it had been superseded by the proposal for a Cuban-Turkey "deal." The President's disclosure was made in a message in which he replied to a hitherto-unreported letter that had been sent to him by Khrushchev Oct. 26. In this earlier letter, Mr. Kennedy said, Khrushchev had offered to remove the Soviet missiles from Cuba under UN supervision if the U.S. suspended its blockade and gave assurances that it would not invade the island. Mr. Kennedy's reply to Khrushchev said, in part: "As I read your letter, the key elements of your proposals—which seem generally acceptable as I understand them—are as follows: (1) You would agree to remove these weapons systems from Cuba under appropriate United Nations observation and supervision; and undertake, with suitable safeguards, to halt the further introduction of such weapons systems into Cuba. (2) We, on our part, would agree—upon the establishment of adequate arrangements through the United Nations, to insure the carrying out and continuation of these commitments—(a) to remove promptly the quarantine measures now in effect and (b) to give assurances against an invasion of Cuba. I am confident that other nations of the Western Hemisphere would be prepared to do likewise."

Khrushchev Orders Missiles Out

Khrushchev informed the U.S. Oct. 28 that he had ordered Soviet missiles withdrawn from Cuba and all offensive Soviet bases on the island dismantled under UN inspection. Khrushchev's decision was announced in a letter in which he replied to Pres. Kennedy and assured him that the USSR stood by its offer for a settlement. Khrushchev said: "In order to eliminate as rapidly as possible the conflict which endangers the cause of peace...the Soviet government, in addition to earlier instructions on the discontinuation of further work on weapons construction sites, has given a new order to dismantle the weapons, which you describe as offensive, and to return them to the Soviet Union.... The Soviet government decided to render assistance to Cuba with the means of defense against aggression, only with means for the purposes of defense. We have supplied the defense means which you describe as offensive means. We have supplied them to prevent an attack on Cuba.... I...trust the statement you made in your message on Oct. 27th, 1962, that there would be no attack, no invasion of Cuba, and not only on the part of the United States, but also on the part of other nations of the Western Hemisphere, as you have said in the same message of yours. Then the motives which induced us to render assistance of such a kind to Cuba disappear. As I had informed you in the letter of Oct. 27, we are prepared to reach agreement to enable [UN] representatives ... to verify the dismantling of these means...."

Pres. Kennedy declared Oct. 28 that Khrushchev's agreement to withdraw Soviet missiles from Cuba under UN verification was a "statesmanlike decision" and an "important and constructive contribution to peace."

Pres. Kennedy reported to Americans in a radio-TV address Nov. 2 that the USSR had begun dismantling the Cuban missile bases. Mr. Kennedy said, in part: "I want to ... report on the conclusions which this government has reached on the basis of yesterday's aerial photographs ... namely, that the Soviet missile bases in Cuba are being dismantled, their missiles and related equipment are being crated and the fixed installations at these sites are being destroyed."

U.S. and Soviet negotiators reached agreement on 2 forms of verification of the elimination of the Cuban missile threat. These agreements, produced by intensive U.S.-Soviet negotiations carried out at UN headquarters in New York, provided for (1) Red Cross inspection of Soviet vessels en route to Cuba, and (2) U.S. observation at sea of crated Russian missiles being shipped back from Cuban ports to the USSR. The agreement for inspection of Cuba-bound Soviet vessels was reported to have been reached Nov. 2. It was advanced by the USSR after the rejection by Castro of an earlier Soviet proposal for the V. of Red Cross-designated observers in mobile inspection teams, for on-site verification of the base dismantling and for dockside checks of the weapons being returned to the USSR. The 2d agreement, for U.S. observation at sea of missiles being removed, was reached at the UN Nov. 7. Chief participants in the UN negotiations were Thant, U.S. Amb.-to-UN Stevenson, John J. McCloy, named by Pres. Kennedy Oct. 29 to be chairman of a special coordinating committee on Cuban policy, Carlos M. Lechuga, who replaced Garcia-Inchaustegui Nov. 1 as Cuban delegate to the UN, Soviet Amb.-to-UN Zorin, Soviet Deputy Foreign Min. Vasily V. Kuznetsov, who had arrived in the U.S. Oct. 28 to act as Khrushchev's special envoy on the Cuban problem, and Soviet First Deputy Premier Anastas I. Mikoyan.

The removal of the Soviet missiles was announced by Khrushchev Nov. 7 at a Kremlin reception in observance of the 45th anniversary of the Bolshevik Revolution. In an impromptu toast to peace, Khrushchev asserted that the USSR had emplaced 40 missiles in Cuba but that "we have taken our rockets out and they probably are on the way." Khrushchev added that although the Cuban crisis was not yet ended, it no longer threatened the world with war. He declared that at the beginning of the crisis "we were very close—very, very close—to a thermonuclear war." He asserted that "if there had not been reason then we would not be here tonight and there might not have been elections in the United States."

The first inspection of Soviet ships removing missiles from Cuba was made by U.S. ships Nov. 8. Within 3 days, Soviet vessels carrying 42 MRBMs had passed through the U.S. blockade after submitting to a system of alongside scrutiny devised to assure the U.S. of the weapons' removal. None of the Soviet ships were boarded. The beginning of the shipboard missile count was announced by Asst. Defense Secy. Arthur Sylvester in Washington Nov. 9. According to Sylvester, the first Soviet ship contacted, the *Alapayevsk,* had proved to be carrying only missile support and earth moving equipment. The first 3 Russian ships intercepted Nov. 9—the freighters *Dvinogorsk, Votgoles* and *Labinsk*—were found to be carrying missiles on deck; they cooperated in the alongside inspection by pulling off tarpaulins to permit the rockets to be photographed and examined from circling U.S. destroyers and helicopters.

U.S. Wins Bomber Removal

The Kennedy Administration took steps early in November that ended in the withdrawal of the IL-28 jet medium bombers shipped to Cuba by the Soviet Union. Amb. Stevenson and John J. McCloy took up the question Nov. 4 at a UN meeting with Kuznetsov. They warned that refusal to withdraw the bombers would result in an intensification of the U.S. blockade. The Soviet representatives stressed that the planes were obsolete and no threat to the U.S., but they were said to have conceded that they constituted "offensive weapons" within the meaning of the Oct. 28 Khrushchev-Kennedy accords. Pres. Kennedy finally announced at a televised press conference Nov. 20 that

Khrushchev had agreed to withdraw the IL-28 bombers and that the U.S. would reciprocate by ending its naval blockade of Cuba. Mr. Kennedy disclosed that the accord had been worked out in his continuing exchange of secret letters with Khrushchev. He added: "The evidence to date indicates that all known offensive missile sites in Cuba have been dismantled. The missiles and their associated equipment have been loaded on Soviet ships. And our inspection at sea of these departing ships has confirmed that the number of missiles reported by the Soviet Union as having been brought into Cuba, which closely corresponded to our own information, has now been removed.... The Soviet government has stated that all nuclear weapons have been withdrawn from Cuba and no offensive weapons will be reintroduced." The U.S. naval quarantine of Cuba was ended Nov. 20.

42 Soviet IL-28 bombers left Cuba aboard Russian-bound ships Dec. 1-6. The bombers, dismantled and crated on the vessels' decks, were counted by observers aboard U.S. planes as they began the return trip to the USSR. The 42 planes were believed to be all of the Soviet bombers sent to Cuba.

Washington officials reported Dec. 6-7 that intelligence information received from anti-Castro sources in Cuba had described intensive work by Soviet military personnel on Cuban defenses. The information, said to have been dated Nov. 29, indicated that some Soviet military camps had been closed but that many Soviet military and technical units remained despite the departure of Russian missiles. The Russians were said to be concentrating their efforts on construction of bunker-type defenses, underground fuel and munitions depots, airstrips and fighter defense facilities and anti-invasion defenses.

Khrushchev called on the U.S. Dec. 12 to honor its agreement not to invade Cuba as the USSR had honored its promise to withdraw its missiles, jet bombers and other aggressive weapons from the island. Khrushchev's demand was made in a 2 1/2-hour speech before the Supreme Soviet. In the address he defended his Cuban policies on the ground that they had turned the recent crisis away from a nuclear war that would have destroyed the world. The USSR, Khrushchev declared, would continue to fulfill its share of the Cuban agreement "so long as the other side stands by this understanding." "But," he added, "if the commitments assumed are not observed by the other side, we shall be compelled to take... action." Khrushchev acknowledged that the

USSR had sent rockets to Cuba and had made them "ready for launching, ready for action." But he denied that these missiles had been intended to be used for an attack on the U.S. "Had we wanted to start war against the United States," he declared, "we would not have agreed to dismantle the rockets.... We would have brought them into play. But we did not do that because we had no such aims." Khrushchev's assertion that the Soviet withdrawal of weapons from Cuba had saved the world from potential destruction was cheered loudly by the 1,443 deputies present.

Chinese Oppose Missile Withdrawal

Reports from Moscow, Peking and other Soviet-bloc capitals in October indicated that Communist China had opposed the USSR's decision to withdraw its missiles from Cuba and dismantle its launching sites there. Chinese leaders criticized the Russian action as a "retreat" in the face of U.S. imperialism. The Chinese charges and the Russian defense against them were aired in government and press statements and in addresses delivered by representatives of both sides at a series of Communist party congresses held in the Soviet bloc and Western Europe. Although the language of the initial Chinese-Russian exchange was elliptical and rarely referred specifically to the matter—or the persons—in question, the series of strong Chinese attacks on policies identified personally with Khrushchev eventually forced the Russian leader to label China publicly as the opponent of his efforts to prevent nuclear war.

The Chinese opposition to the USSR's handling of the Cuban crisis first became apparent after Khrushchev Oct. 28 had agreed to Pres. Kennedy's demand for the withdrawal of Russian missiles from Cuba. The Chinese CP newspaper *Jenmin Jih Pao (Peoples Daily)* reported the Khrushchev-Kennedy agreement in a single paragraph on an inside page Oct. 29 but devoted the front page of the same edition to a Peking mass rally that pledged Cuba China's support until it achieved "final, complete and thorough victory" against the U.S. The newspaper Oct. 31 published editorials in which it was implied that Khrushchev had erred in accepting the Kennedy demands. It contrasted Russia's attitude with China's full support of Premier Fidel Castro's revolutionary regime.

Hundreds of thousands of Chinese marched to the Cuban embassy in Peking Nov. 3-5 to demonstrate support for Cuba. *Jenmin Jih Pao*, in a front-page editorial Nov. 5, condemned any "appeasement" of the U.S. in the Cuban situation. In an implied rebuke to Khrushchev, it declared: "To compromise with or meet the Kennedy government's truculent demands can only encourage the aggressor and will in no way insure world peace." Articles in the Chinese press denounced the Cuban position taken by the "modern revisionists," a term considered an allusion both to Khrushchev and Yugoslav Pres. Tito. They charged that these interests, frightened by the confrontation with U.S. power in the Caribbean, had betrayed Marxist principles by withdrawing Soviet missile power from Cuba. *Jenmin Jih Pao* declared in a front-page editorial Nov. 18 that it was "nonsense" to claim that "peace had been saved" only by the withdrawal from Cuba.

The USSR's alleged retreat in Cuba was attacked Nov. 8 by the Chinese chief delegate to the Bulgarian CP Congress in Sofia. Wu Hsiu-chuan, a member of the Chinese CP Central Committee, assailed the USSR for its Cuban failure and for its policies toward Yugoslavia and Albania.

Moscow dispatches made it clear Oct. 30-Nov. 10 that Khrushchev had turned to East European Communist leaders for support in his handling of the Cuban crisis and his rift with the Chinese. Nearly every East European Communist leader visited Moscow during that period, and all of them conferred secretly with Khrushchev on the Cuban problem. The Moscow visitors included Czechoslovak Pres. Antonin Novotny, who arrived Oct. 30, East German CP First Secy. Walter Ulbricht, who arrived Nov. 1, Rumanian CP First Secy. Gheorghe Gheorghiu-Dej, Bulgarian CP First Secy. Todor Zhivkov, Polish CP First Secy. Wladyslaw Gomulka, who arrived Nov. 3, and Hungarian Premier Janos Kadar, who was the last to visit Khrushchev and who left Moscow Nov. 10.

The traditional Kremlin address on the eve of the anniversary of the Bolshevik revolution, delivered Nov. 6 by Soviet First Deputy Premier Aleksei N. Kosygin, contained an explicit defense of the Soviet position in the Cuban crisis. Speaking to an audience of 8,000 Soviet and foreign dignitaries, Kosygin asked: "To whom is it not clear that if war had broken out it would have been a thermonuclear world war from the very outset?" Examining the question of "who made concessions to whom," Kosygin said: "We feel that there were concessions both from one and from the other side. They were concessions to sanity and peace. Some may ask whether it was worth making concessions. We feel that this compromise was in the interest of all nations, because on its basis it was possible to eliminate the threat of a thermonuclear world war."

The Soviet CP Nov. 18 denounced Communist critics of Khrushchev's Cuban policies for "pushing mankind toward thermonuclear war." CP Central Committee Secy. Boris N. Ponomarev, writing in *Pravda,* declared that Khrushchev's actions had been subjected to "unlimited slander" from critics within the Communist bloc. Ponomarev, considered a specialist in relations among the Communist parties, said that "neither bourgeois propagandists nor other falsifiers" could detract from Khrushchev's contribution to peace during the Cuban crisis. In a reference directed at Albanian leaders but presumed to apply to China, he charged that "they have undertaken an especially shameful and...provocative campaign in connection with the crisis in the Caribbean."

In a major foreign policy address broadcast Dec. 12 from the Supreme Soviet, Khrushchev defended his actions in the Cuban crisis. Khrushchev specifically identified China as the source of Communist-bloc charges that he had "appeased" imperialism by his settlement of the Cuban crisis. It was believed to be the first official confirmation to the Russian people of Chinese opposition to Khrushchev's foreign policies. Khrushchev made this rejoinder to a Chinese gibe that imperialism was a "paper tiger": Let them remember that the "paper tiger has nuclear teeth" and "may still use them and should not be treated lightly." Conceding that elements within the Communist bloc had opposed as a "retreat" his decision to accept U.S. demands for withdrawal of Soviet missiles and bombers from Cuba, Khrushchev declared: "In what way have we retreated, one may ask. Socialist Cuba exists. Cuba remains a beacon of Marxist-Leninist ideas in the Western Hemisphere. The impact of her revolutionary example will grow. The...United States has given a pledge not to invade Cuba. The threat of thermonuclear war has been averted. Is this a retreat?" Khrushchev added: "Will anybody censure the People's Republic of China because fragments of colonialism remain intact [in China]? It would be wrong to push China to any actions which she regards as untimely. If...China tolerates Macao and Hong

Kong there must be weighty reasons for this. It would be ridiculous to use this for an accusation that they are making a concession to the British and Portuguese colonialists, that this is appeasement."

During a visit to Moscow Yugoslav Pres. Tito addressed the Supreme Soviet Dec. 13 and praised Khrushchev's actions in the Cuban crisis. He said Khrushchev had acted "bravely at the most critical moment, taking into account the interests of all humanity and showing the farsightedness of a real statesman." Alluding to Albanian and Chinese criticism, Tito said: "Unfortunately there are strange views about this policy ... which are dangerous as they might lead certain circles to a false assessment of the motive for this wise and peace-loving action. I think that it is shortsightedness to consider these actions as a sign of weakness."

Earlier Developments

U.S. Pres. Kennedy had said at his news conference in Washington Aug. 22 that Cuba "definitely" was receiving "large quantities" of equipment and "an increased number of technicians" from the Soviet bloc. But he said there was no evidence to support Cuban exile reports that Soviet troops and military aid were pouring into the country. Mr. Kennedy's statement followed an Aug. 20 report by U.S. officials that about 3,000 to 5,000 Soviet-bloc technicians and supplies had arrived in Cuba between July 21 and 27 aboard 15 Soviet ships.

The *N.Y. Times* reported Sept. 7 that about 4,000 Soviet and other Communist-bloc troops in Cuba were functioning in separate units or in conjunction with Cuban forces. The *Times* account, written by Tad Szulc, was based on reports from: (a) persons who had recently arrived in Miami from Cuba; (b) foreign diplomats in Cuba; (c) Cuban underground groups. The report said: Soviet soldiers in civilian dress, described as "service troops," were in charge of Soviet equipment ranging from short-range missiles to communications and trucks; individual Soviet advisers were directly attached to Cuban air force bases, antiaircraft and coastal artillery units, radar and observation centers and training camps; the latest Soviet equipment and personnel had started to arrive in Cuba about July 25, but no new arrivals had been noticed since Aug. 20; the men and equipment had entered through at least 12 ports mainly on the north coast;

the Communist equipment, largely of battlefield variety, included ground-to-air missiles, radar and communications equipment, coastal torpedo and patrol craft; Soviet-bloc military aid to Cuba since mid-1960 included such equipment as light and medium tanks, antiaircraft, coastal, antitank and field artillery and truck-mounted rocket launchers.

A program of increased Soviet military and industrial assistance to Cuba had been announced in a joint Cuban-USSR communique issued in Moscow Sept. 2. The bilateral agreements were reached following talks that had started in Moscow Aug. 27 and whose major participants were Cuban Industry Min. Ernesto (Che) Guevara, Emilio Aragones Navarro, head of the Cuban militia, Khrushchev and other Soviet leaders. The amount or type of the Soviet military aid was not specified. The communique said only that "in view of the threats of aggressive imperialist quarters with regard to Cuba," the USSR had agreed to Cuba's "request for help by delivering armaments and sending technical specialists for training Cuban servicemen." The communique also announced that: (a) under an agreement signed Sept. 1, the USSR would help Cuba build a metallurgical factory and expand the output of 3 existing metallurgical factories from 110,000 to 350,000 tons a year; (b) both countries would "continue the exchange of experience" "in the sphere of agriculture by means of working out separate agricultural problems, by sending specialists to Cuba for work in the spheres of irrigation,... hydrotechnical construction and others"; (c) Soviet agricultural assistance to Cuba would include the sending of Cubans to the USSR for instruction in farm production.

The Soviet government warned the U.S. Sept. 11 that any U.S. attack on Cuba or on Soviet ships carrying supplies to Cuba would result in nuclear war. The Soviet statement said:

U.S. "imperialists have been alarmed by the failure of the...[U.S.'] economic blockade... to strangle the Cuban people, to make them their satellite, to wipe out the achievement of the [Cuban] revolution"; the USSR and other Communist nations "stretched out a hand of assistance to the Cuban people" to counteract "imperialist provocations and threats"; the U.S. was "so much frightened" of the Soviet revolution "that it seems to you some hordes are supposedly moving to Cuba when potatoes or oil, tractors... and other farming and industrial machinery" were shipped to Cuba; "we can say to these people that these are our ships, and what we carry in them is no business of theirs"; the USSR was shipping to Cuba on Cuban request "a certain amount of armaments" "designed exclusively for defensive purposes"; the USSR also was sending Cuba "military specialists and technicians" "because up-to-date weapons now call for high skill and much knowledge"; "the number of Soviet military specialists sent to Cuba is in no way to be compared to the number of workers in agriculture and industry sent there"; there was "no need for the Soviet Union to shift its weapons for the repulsion of aggression...to any other country, for instance Cuba," because "our nuclear weapons are so powerful" and the USSR "has so powerful rockets" to deliver them "that there is no need to search for sites for them" outside the USSR; "if the aggressor makes an attack on one state or another and this state asks for assistance, the Soviet Union has the possibility to render assistance to any peace-loving state and not only to Cuba"; "let no one doubt that the Soviet Union will render such assistance."

The signing of a Cuban-Soviet pact providing for trade valued at $700 million in 1962 (a $150 million increase over 1961) had been reported by Jan. 10. Cuba was to send the USSR sugar, alcohol, nickel, ores, rum, tobacco and other products for oil and petroleum products, ferrous and non-ferrous metals, fertilizers and other items. USSR-Cuban trade in 1961 totaled 529 million rubles, compared with 157 million rubles in 1960, Prof. Nikolai N. Lyubimov of the Institute of International Relations in Moscow reported July 13. Other figures cited by Lyubimov: Soviet foreign trade in 1961 had increased by almost 6% to 10.6 billion rubles, the level planned for 1965; the USSR had an export surplus of 150 million rubles in 1961 compared with a 60 million-ruble deficit in 1960; Britain led Western Europe in trade with the USSR in 1961 [total: 320 million, rubles], followed by West Germany, Finland, Italy and France. Tass reported Aug. 28, however, that in 1961 the USSR had sent Cuba 284 million rubles ($275,280,000) worth of goods, and Cuba had sent the USSR sugar and some fibres valued at 281 million rubles ($271,091,000). Tass said that, according to the Soviet Merchant Marine Ministry, Soviet cargoes to Cuba had increased to the point where ships under the flags of NATO nations had to be chartered. 5 ships of West German, Norwegian, Greek and Italian registry were then in Soviet ports loading industrial equipment, flour, paper and fertilizers for Cuba.

Cuban Premier Fidel Castro announced Sept. 25 that the USSR had agreed to help build a port in Havana Bay as headquarters for a Cuban-Soviet fishing fleet.

Castro, disclosing the plan after signing a fishing treaty with Soviet Fisheries Min. Aleksandr A. Ishkov, said: the port, to be built at a cost of 12 million pesos (unofficial free market value: about $1,920,000), would be used by the USSR under a 10-year contract, "which surely will continue much longer than 10 years"; the port would be built by Cuban labor with Cuban materials, operated by Cubans and owned by Cuba; Cuba would be compensated by additional Russian food shipments; Soviet credit would finance the purchase of $6 million worth of port machinery.

OTHER FOREIGN POLICY DEVELOPMENTS

Albanian/Chinese Communist Heresies Attacked

The ideological split between the USSR and Communist China widened during 1962. A declaration published Jan. 14 by the international Communist journal *Problems of Peace & Socialism* declared that Albania's leadership had "joined ranks with the enemies of the Communist movement" and no longer could be considered a member of the Socialist bloc. Such Soviet denunciations of Albania were generally known to be disguised attacks on Communist China. The declaration blamed Albania's deviation on "narrow nationalist egoistic interests" fostered by Albanian CP First Secy. Enver Hoxha and Premier Mehmet Shehu. It called on Albanians to "return their country to the Leninist path."

The Soviet Foreign Ministry publication *International Affairs* charged Jan. 30 that "in inculcating ... the idea that the outbreak of war is fatally inevitable, the Albanian leaders are ... fanning a war hysteria ... which cannot fail to lead to the aggravation of the situation in the Balkans." It declared that Hoxha and Shehu had installed a "regime of terror" in the Albanian party.

Soviet First Deputy Premier Anastas I. Mikoyan, in an Erivan address published Mar. 14 in *Izvestia*, declared that the USSR's program for general disarmament had been opposed by Soviet-bloc critics who took "alleged leftwing positions" against the USSR. These critics, "in particular... some Albanian 'theoreticians' who have a confused knowledge of Marxism," had opposed the USSR's "peaceful coexistence" policy on the ground it would harm national liberation movements in Asia, Africa, and Latin America.

Mikhail A. Suslov, a member of the Soviet CP Presidium and Secretariat, had said Jan. 30 that coexistence aimed at preventing war between the capitalist and Communist blocs but that an unrelenting "ideological struggle is unavoidable" between them. Suslov spoke at a Moscow meeting of Soviet social scientists. Denouncing Western "bourgeois ideology" as implacably anti-Soviet, he said: "Is any conciliation, any compromise, even temporary, possible with that ideology? It is impossible and unthinkable. It would be ideological disarmament of the Communists, it would be disarmament of the international workers' movement." (Suslov had been in charge of Soviet CP relations with the Chinese CP until his replacement by Lt. Gen. Aleksandr S. Panyushkin. Harrison E. Salisbury, reporting the change, wrote in the *N.Y. Times* Feb. 25 that the appointment of Panyushkin, who had served as Soviet ambassador to the Chiang Kai-shek regime in 1939-44 and then to the Communist regime in 1952 [until Stalin's death in 1953], was regarded as an affront to Chinese CP First Secy. Mao Tse-tung.)

An article in the Sept. 23 edition of the Soviet CP ideological journal *Kommunist* warned the Communist and other revolutionary parties of Asia, Africa and Latin America against "undue haste" in seeking to transform newly independent colonies into Communist states. Noting that few of the new nations had succeeded in "extricating themselves from the fetters of the economic system of world capitalism," *Kommunist* advised revolutionary parties in these nations to devote themselves to the creation of "national fronts" that could be used to free them from imperialist influence. It warned that "unjustified over-zeal" from Communist slogans might actually slow their advance toward communism. It cautioned them: "Neglect of general democratic problems and undue haste may narrow the popular basis of Socialist revolution and compromise the noble idea of socialism in the eyes of the masses."

A new version of an article written by Lenin in Mar. 1918, entitled *The Immediate Aims of the Soviet Regime,* was published by *Pravda* Sept. 28. It asserted that Russia must seek to conquer capitalism by economic, rather than political or military means. It said: "The very basis, the very essence of the Soviet regime, as well as the very essence of the transition from a capitalist to a Socialist society, lies in the fact that political tasks assume a subordinate role compared with economic tasks. Now, after the gains of the October Revolution, ... victory over the bourgeoisie can and must be understood as something much more lofty, even though more peaceable in form." *Pravda,* in an accompanying editorial, declared that "the ideas stated in this outstanding Leninist document also have tremendous significance in our time."

The U.S. State Department reported Dec. 9 that trade between the USSR and Communist China had declined by 45% to a total value of $919 million in 1961. The report said that China had been the USSR's leading trade partner in 1959 but had dropped to 4th place in Soviet foreign trade in 1961. The USSR's exports to all countries were reported to have totaled $6 billion in 1961, an increase of $436 million over 1960; its imports during 1961 were valued at $5.8 billion, an estimated increase of $203 million. The UN Food & Agriculture Organization reported in its October *Bulletin of Statistics* (appearing Nov. 17) that the value of Soviet farm commodity purchases from China had dropped from $406,260,000 in 1959 to only $37,740,000 in 1961. Soviet imports of Chinese eggs, wheat, edible oils and natural rubber were reported to have halted completely during 1961. The USSR's imports of Chinese rice (658,400 metric tons in 1958; 2,300 tons in 1961) and oilseeds were said to have been virtually ended.

Overtures to Yugoslavia

Soviet Pres. Leonid I. Brezhnev visited Yugoslavia Sept. 24-Oct. 4, on what was described officially as a mission to improve Soviet-Yugoslav cooperation in the causes of peace and of communism. Although the final joint communique issued Oct. 4 by Brezhnev and Yugoslav Pres. Tito proclaimed "the identity or proximity of views of both sides on pressing international problems and tendencies of world development," it was clear that

Brezhnev had not been able to win Tito's acquiescence for a more disciplined Yugoslav relationship with the USSR and the Soviet bloc. The communique, instead, explicitly reaffirmed Yugoslavia's right to continue on its own road toward communism. In the communique both countries pledged to refrain from interference in each other's affairs "for whatever reason, whether of an economic, political or ideological nature, because questions of internal organization, of different social systems and of different forms of Socialist development are solely the concern of individual countries."

Yugoslavia's Tanyug news agency disclosed Oct. 4 that a trade protocol signed during Brezhnev's visit provided for the exchange of $180 million worth of goods between the 2 countries in 1963. The USSR was to supply Yugoslavia with machinery, coal, naphtha, chemicals and pharmaceuticals; Yugoslavia was to ship machinery, lead, cables, chemicals and pharmaceuticals, textiles and furniture.

Tito visited the Soviet Union Dec. 3-20. His trip was described officially as a "holiday," but the Belgrade newspaper *Borba* said its purpose was to exchange views with Khrushchev "on pressing international issues, on mutual relations between the 2 countries and on questions of mutual interest." Tito was greeted at a Moscow railroad station Dec. 4 by Khrushchev, who said that "personal contacts" between Yugoslav and Soviet leaders would be "useful" and "help strengthen [Yugoslav-Soviet] friendship and cooperation." In an address to the Supreme Soviet Dec. 13, Tito said that "the obstacles to our [Soviet-Yugoslav] relations, artificially created in the past, have been gradually removed."

Nuclear Policy

The Soviet Union asserted July 13 that it was entitled to carry out the last nuclear test before tests were banned because the U.S. had conducted the first and had, with Britain, performed many more such tests than had the USSR. The Soviet claim was made in a statement issued by the Tass news agency in answer to recent U.S. State Department charges of Soviet responsibility for the 1961 renewal of nuclear testing. The Soviet statement said: The USSR's unilateral resumption of tests in 1961 had been "a great service to the consolidation of the defense potential of the USSR ... and to the cause of preserving peace"; the resumption had been necessary because of France's testing in contradiction to Western professions of peace; the U.S. had committed "a monstrous crime against mankind" by its nuclear bombings of Hiroshima and Nagasaki; "the interests of world peace ... demand that the Soviet Union would be the last to carry out nuclear tests."

Khrushchev asserted July 13 that the USSR had an anti-missile missile capable of hitting "a fly in outer space." He said the USSR thus was able to defend itself against missile attack whereas the U.S. was deluding itself in thinking that high-altitude nuclear explosions could produce the same protection. Khrushchev's claim was made during a Kremlin interview granted to 14 visiting U.S. newspapermen and editors. It was made public with the release of a transcript of the interview July 16. Khrushchev said that action films of the new anti-missile missile had been offered at a recent Moscow disarmament conference but had not been shown because they might have been misconstrued as a threatening gesture. He said: "Had people been shown this film they would have seen what kind of a machine it is. You can say our rocket hits a fly in outer space."

Khrushchev said that the USSR had "a global rocket that cannot be destroyed by any anti-rocket means, and I know, if anybody knows, what anti-rocket means are because we do have them."

Khrushchev also disclosed that the USSR planned another series of nuclear tests after a current U.S. series—unless the U.S. made a new Soviet series unnecessary by agreeing to Soviet disarmament and atomic-ban proposals. He said he hoped that after the next Soviet test series, the U.S. "will perhaps agree after all to sign a treaty on ending tests for all time." He added that "if, however, the Americans stopped their nuclear weapons test now, and agreement were reached on general and complete disarmament and destruction of nuclear weapons, there would be no need for us to hold our tests."

The Soviet Union announced July 22 that in response to the U.S.' continued nuclear tests, it had again been forced to order the resumption of Soviet testing. The USSR had not publicly exploded a nuclear device since Nov. 4, 1961. The Soviet announcement stressed that the decision to resume testing was "a forced step" that had been taken to preserve Soviet security in the face of U.S. efforts "to try to achieve a military supremacy." It put the blame for the step entirely on the U.S.: "On it [the U.S.], and on it alone, depended whether the tests to which the Soviet Union had had to resort in the fall of 1961 would be the last or whether our planet would be swept by a new wave of nuclear tests. And the... United States made its choice. The explosions of American nuclear bombs... have produced their echo—they have made reply-nuclear tests by the Soviet Union inevitable." The announcement concluded with a pledge to limit test-caused radiation and fallout to "the minimum," and a renewed expression of the USSR's hopes for a treaty permanently banning nuclear tests with "control over strict compliance... effected by the national means of detection." Russia resumed testing Aug. 5 with the detonation of a device 2d in power only to the 58-megaton device exploded by the USSR Oct. 30, 1961.

Soviet Deputy Foreign Min. Valerian A. Zorin announced July 19 that the USSR was prepared to sign a commitment that the nuclear powers withhold atomic arms or information from countries not possessing them.

The Soviet Defense Ministry newspaper *Krasnaya Zvezda (Red Star)* had said May 11, in a review of current Soviet military strategy, that any new world war inevitably would involve the use both of nuclear-armed missiles and of mass armies. It asserted that Soviet military planners based their work on 2 basic tenets: "First, if the imperialist aggressors succeed in unleashing a world war, it would inevitably become a rocket nuclear war. 2d, the use of nuclear weapons, which have unlimited capabilities when carried by rockets, creates opportunities for achieving decisive military results at any distance and over territories of tremendous size. In addition to concentrations of the armed forces of the enemy, his air force and rocket bases, industrial and vital centers, areas in which production and stockpiles of nuclear weapons are concentrated and communications centers would also become targets for devastating blows." *Krasnaya Zvezda* reiterated past Soviet claims that "the problem of destroying enemy rockets in flight has been successfully solved in the Soviet Union."

Tass had reported Feb. 14 that Andronik M. Petrosyants, 56, had replaced Vasily S. Yemelyanov, 61, as chairman of the USSR's atomic energy program.

(The USSR's armed forces draft registration age was lowered from 18 years to 17.)

Attack on European Common Market

During 1962 the USSR launched a major campaign against Western Europe's Common Market. It proposed a world conference to discuss establishing "an international trade agency to embrace all regions and countries of the world without any discrimination." In a speech at a friendship meeting in Moscow May 30 in honor of a Mali delegation headed by Pres. Modibo Keita, Khrushchev denounced the EEC (European Economic Community, or Common Market) as a new form of "colonialism" created to suppress the newly independent African nations. At this meeting Khrushchev made the USSR proposal of a UN-sponsored trade conference to counter the EEC's "aggressive policy."

Khrushchev, at a Moscow reception for Italian Trade Min. Luigi Preti June 7, denounced the Common Market as "a marriage against nature..., [which] will be broken because... these are not 2 sexes, male and female, but only 2 males." He urged Italy to withdraw from the EEC and trade with the USSR. Khrushchev, at a meeting June 29 with Austrian Chancellor Alfons Gorbach (who was in Moscow on a state visit), warned Austria against entering the EEC, "a community [that] disorganizes European trade, declares war on other countries and disrupts the independence and sovereignty of small states connected with it and their ability to determine national policy for themselves." Soviet talks with a French delegation on renewal of the Franco-Soviet commercial agreement had been opened in Moscow May 16 but were suspended by the USSR June 13 because of French rejection of Soviet demands for tariff concessions equal to those given France's EEC partners.

Khrushchev renewed his world trade conference proposal in a *Pravda* article Aug. 26. The restatement followed the newspaper's text of an analysis of the Common Market that had been prepared by the Institute of World Economics & International Relations of the Soviet Academy of Sciences. The analysis termed the EEC a "new phenomenon in the development of the economics of capitalism" and an attempt of "monopolistic capital to reconcile a private-enterprise economy with the productive forces that have outgrown national boundaries." In his article Khrushchev said "economic collaboration and peaceful economic competition" between the Western and Communist groups was possible. He added that the USSR was studying "objective tendencies in the internationalization of production now operating in the capitalist world" in order to formulate its own economic policy.

DOMESTIC DEVELOPMENTS

New Parliament; Government Posts Filled

The newly elected bicameral Supreme Soviet convened jointly in Moscow Apr. 23 for a 3-day session. The members of both legislative bodies—the House of Union and the House of Nationalities—had been elected in nationwide balloting held Mar. 18. In the voting, 99.43% of those who cast ballots approved the single list of "party and non-party candidates" for the House of Union; 99.14% approved the House of Nationalities candidates.

The opening session, postponed from Apr. 10, was devoted to the adoption of an agenda and the election of the heads of the 2 legislative bodies. Leningrad CP chief Ivan V. Spiridonov was elected Soviet of the Union chairman, replacing Pavel P. Lobanov; Latvian Premier Yan V. Peive was reelected Soviet of Nationalities chairman. (A CP communique announced Apr. 26 that Spiridonov had been relieved of his party post because of his election to the Soviet of the Union chairmanship; Peive's replacement as Latvian premier by Vitali P. Ruben, an ex-deputy premier, was announced in an Apr. 25 cabinet listing.)

Leonid I. Brezhnev was reelected Apr. 24 as chairman of the 33-man Supreme Soviet Presidium, which acted on behalf of the Supreme Soviet between regular sessions. Brezhnev's post was equivalent to president of the USSR. Among those retained on the Presidium: Marshal Kliment Y. Voroshilov, Frol R. Kozlov, Nikolai V. Podgorny and Kirill T. Mazurov. New presidium members: Pyotr N. Demichev; Sverdlovsk Province CP leader Andrei P. Kirilenko.

The Supreme Soviet Apr. 24 renamed Khrushchev as premier after he formally relinquished his post at the conclusion of his 4-year term. After his reappointment, Khrushchev was instructed to form a new Soviet Council of Ministers (cabinet). The Soviet of Nationalities Apr. 25 approved Khrushchev's cabinet appointments. Among those retained: Culture Min. Yekatrina A. Furtseva, whose dismissal had been expected because she had not been renamed a Supreme Soviet deputy in the Mar. 18 elections; Foreign Min. Andrei Gromyko; Finance Min. Vasily Garbuzov; Defense Min. Marshal Rodion Malinovsky; Higher Education Min. Vyacheslav P. Yelyutin; First Deputy Premiers Aleksei N. Kosygin and Anastas I. Mikoyan; Deputy Premiers Nikolai G. Ignatov, Vladimir N. Novikov, Konstantin N. Rudnev, Aleksandr F. Zasyadko and Dmitri F. Ustinov. (Ignatov, however, was removed Dec. 20 as a deputy premier and named chairman of the Presidium of the Supreme Soviet of the Russian Republic, a largely honorary position. Ignatov, 61, replaced ex-Presidium Chrmn. Nikolai N. Organov, 61.) Major changes in the Soviet Council of Ministers Apr. 25: Sergei K. Romanovsky replaced Georgi A. Zhukov as head of the Committee for Cultural Relations with Foreign Countries; First Deputy Agriculture Min. Konstantin G. Pysin, 52, was named agriculture minister, replacing Mikhail A. Olshansky, who had been appointed president of the Academy of Agricultural Sciences.

Khrushchev announced at the Apr. 25 session that he had established a Commission of the Presidium of the Council of Ministers for Foreign Economic Matters. The new agency, to coordinate the USSR's foreign trade and economic aid program, was headed by Mikhail A. Lesechko.

The Soviet of Nationalities reappointed Aleksandr F. Gorkin as Supreme Court president and appointed Vasily Kulikov and Lev N. Smirnov as vice presidents. It also appointed 13 regular judges and 45 lay judges.

The Soviet of Nationalities appointed a 96-member commission, headed by Khrushchev, to draft a new constitution. In a parliament address, Khrushchev said: A new constitution was needed to reflect the current ideological state of "full-fledged construction of a Communist society"; "the 1936 constitution has now outlived itself and does not reflect the changes that have occurred" since that time; the new constitution would provide "even more solid guarantees for the democratic rights and freedoms of the working people as well as guarantees of strict observance of Socialist legality."

The appointment of Veniamin E. Dymshits, 52, as State Planning Committee (Gosplan) chairman and as a deputy premier was announced by Tass July 18. Dymshits, who replaced Vladimir N. Novikov as Gosplan chairman, became the first Jew to hold a leading government position since the ouster of Lazar M. Kaganovich as a deputy premier in 1957. Dymshits had been first deputy chairman of Gosplan since 1959.

The establishment of a State Committee for Timber, Paper & Pulp & Woodworking, in a move to restore centralized agencies to administer those industries, had been disclosed Jan. 22. Georgi M. Orlov was named committee head.

Foreign Ministry press chief Mikhail A. Kharlamov was appointed chairman of the State Committee for Radio & TV (reported Feb. 13). He replaced Sergei V. Kaftanov.

The establishment of a committee to coordinate Soviet transport services was announced by Khrushchev May 10. The agency, under the cabinet Presidium's jurisdiction, was headed by Railways Min. Boris P. Beshchev. Khrushchev's announcement was made on the final day of a 3-day conference called in Moscow to discuss expansion and modernization of the country's rail system. In a speech to the 2,400 delegates, Khrushchev said that a nation that had sent a rocket to the moon and had launched manned spaceships should be able to provide better rail service.

USSR Divided into Economic Regions

It was reported in February that Soviet authorities had completed a reorganization of the USSR into 17 major economic regions. This economic division, which had been started in 1961, was designed to provide for more efficient management of the national economy. The 17 new regions replaced 13 planning areas used by the State Planning Committee for long-term development programs. The new regional organization consisted of 10 regions in the Russian Republic, 3 in the Ukraine and one each in Kazakhstan and in the Baltic, Transcaucasian and Central Asian Republics. The Moldavian and Byelorussian republics were placed under separate economic management, presumably because their economies had little in common with the other areas. Each economic region was to be directed by coordinating and planning councils that were to emphasize local economic interests. *Pravda* Feb. 23 identified 3 of the 17 deputy council chairmen: Y. K. Ragozin of the Central Region around Moscow; A. A. Kuznetsov of the Northwest region around Leningrad; I. P. Krasozov of the Ukraine's Dnieper-Donets region.

Soviet industrial production was 9.2% higher in 1961 than in 1960, according to the Central Statistical Board's annual economic report, published Jan. 22. The report said gross industrial production in the first 3 years of the 7-year plan had increased 33%, or 6% more than the projected figure. But 1961 production quotas were unfulfilled for pig iron, steel, rolled metal, chemical and oil equipment, newsprint and other items. The report estimated that Soviet national income had reached 153 billion rubles, or 7-1/2% more than in 1960. The USSR's factory and labor force was estimated to total 66 million in 1961. The USSR's population Jan. 1 totaled 220 million.

Dual Farm/Industry Controls Adopted

A sweeping reorganization of the party/government system, providing for a dual system of administering the agricultural and industrial segments of the economy, was announced by Khrushchev Nov. 19 at a CP Central Committee meeting.

Under the new system: (a) The single CP committees that had jurisdiction over all phases of the economy would be replaced by a dual hierarchy of industrial and agricultural committees; (b) the current regional *(oblast)* CP committees, previously the highest authority on the regional level, would be divided into 2 CP committees, one concerned with industrial affairs, the other with agriculture (there also were to be 2 regional governments); (c) the regional farm body would administer agricultural producer administrations, and the current rural districts within the administrations would be abolished; (d) the regional industrial body would directly administer cities, industrial zones within a rural area and large isolated industrial plants.

Khrushchev, in announcing the dual industry/agriculture scheme, said "radical measures" were required to bring the party structure into line with previous economic management reforms.

Among other reforms announced by Khrushchev: (a) Transformation of 100 industrial management regions into 40 larger units to discourage factionalism and regional shortcomings; (b) decentralization of economic planning; (c) centralization of industrial construction and design under specialized state committees that would have greater powers in planning, research and technical development; (d) creation of advisory workers' factory committees to confer with management on planning, work norms and other problems; (e) establishment of a joint Committee on Party & Government Control, which would, with the aid of volunteer public inspectors, see that party and government directives were carried out and would crack down on economic mismanagement, embezzlement and other malpractices.

CP Secretariat member Aleksandr N. Shelepin was appointed head of the new Committee on Party & Government Control Nov. 23. Shelepin was also named a deputy premier, as was Dmitri S. Polyansky, who was a full member of the party Presidium. Veniamin Dymshits, chairman of the State Planning Committee, was named head of the new Council of the National Economy Nov. 24. The council's powers included authority to implement annual economic plans and to decide on resources reallocation. The State Planning Committee, in its current form, was abolished.

Other changes announced Nov. 24:

● Mikhail A. Lesechko, 53, head of the State Committee for Foreign Economic Matters, was named a deputy premier in charge of foreign aid and trade. (Vladimir N. Novikov, replaced by Lesechko as deputy premier, was demoted to minister without portfolio. Novikov was Soviet representative to the Council of Mutual Economic Assistance, the Soviet bloc's economic coordinating agency.)

● Electric Power Station Construction Min. Ignati T. Novikov, 56, was named a deputy premier in charge of an enlarged State Construction Agency. He replaced Ivan A. Grishmanov. Pyotr S. Neporozhny succeeded Ignati Novikov as electric power station construction minister.

● The State Economic Council, headed by Pyotr F. Lomako, 58, was renamed and reorganized as the State Planning Committee. Its functions: to devise long-range plans and to coordinate the annual economic plans submitted by the republics within the framework of long-term development. (Lomako had been appointed a deputy premier Nov. 10 to head the Economic Council, a government agency charged with long-range planning and resources development. Lomako succeeded Aleksandr F. Zasyadko, who had resigned Nov. 9 because of ill health.

Lomako, a nonferrous metals expert, had served for some 20 years as minister in charge of USSR nonferrous industries. For the past year he had served on the Communist Party's Central Committee as deputy of the agency that managed the Russian Republic's industrial affairs.)

These 3 officials were reported Dec. 26 to have been appointed chairmen of the newly-formed committees to coordinate technical progress: Aleksandr I. Struyev, a deputy premier of the Russian Republic, to handle domestic commerce; Pyotr V. Naumenko, in charge of food products; Nikolai N. Tarasov, to coordinate consumer goods. Aleksandr A. Vezhevsky replaced Pavel S. Kuchumov as head of the agency directing the sales to farms of agricultural machinery, fertilizer and other implements.

At a December meeting of the Kazakhstan CP Central Committee, presided over by Soviet Deputy Premier Frol R. Kozlov, the Kazakhstan CP leadership was accused of "poor management of industry, transportation and especially agriculture" and of having filled important positions with party officials "who had not justified the confidence in them." The Central Committee Dec. 26 dismissed Dinmukhamed A. Kunayev as CP first secretary and Nikolai N. Rodionov as 2d secretary. Kunayev was appointed to the less important post of premier. He was replaced as first secretary by Ismail Y. Yusupov. Mikhail S. Solomentsev, ex-secretary of the Karaganda regional CP, replaced Rodionov as 2d secretary.

Farm Failures Conceded, New Reform Started

Conceding widespread failures in Soviet farm programs, Khrushchev Mar. 5 had urged the CP Central Committee to adopt another reorganization plan for Russian agriculture in an effort to spur lagging collective farm output. The Central Committee, meeting Mar. 5-9 in Moscow, adopted the plan after Khrushchev warned that, "as a result of agricultural mismanagement," the Soviet farm system was "in serious danger" of not fulfilling its 7-year-plan goals. Khrushchev's proposals were viewed as a return to more direct CP control of Soviet agriculture. They provided for the creation of these 2 types of agencies:

(1) Producer administrations, to function at the local (*okrug*) level, to plan and supervise the production of state and collective farms and the purchase of foodstuffs from them for

state delivery; the administrations would be staffed by local agricultural managers and party officials and apparently would have the power to appoint or dismiss local farm managers and officials.

(2) Agricultural management committees, to work at the level of the province, republic and nation, to plan and supervise the agricultural system as part of the Soviet economy; these committees would be run directly by high party officials, including regional party secretaries, and the national committee would be under a deputy premier responsible for planning farm machine output.

Khrushchev, speaking for 6 hours Mar. 5, told the Central Committee that Soviet farms had failed by 10% to meet their 1961 grain target and by 25% to achieve the 7-year-plan goals for milk and meat. "The fact is," he asserted, "there is simply not enough meat in the Soviet Union." He criticized the Russian SFSR, the Ukraine, Kazakhstan, Georgia and nearly every other Soviet farm area for production failures and mismanagement. Khrushchev declared that in order to fulfill 7-year-plan goals and the party's pledges to the Soviet people, "it is necessary to double or treble the output of the most important agricultural products within a short time." He cited statistics to show that increases of nearly 50% in meat output and 20% in milk and grain production would be needed to meet 1962 targets.

Khrushchev prefaced his speech with a defense of Soviet aims for material abundance. His remarks were viewed as an attack on the ascetic, revolutionary view of communism espoused by Red China. Khrushchev said: "Communism must not be regarded as a table set with empty plates around which sit high-minded and fully equal peoples. To ask people to join such communism would be like inviting them to eat milk with an awl. It would be a parody of communism." In his final address at the meeting Mar. 9, Khrushchev derided Western reports of his admission of Soviet farm failures. He said: "Let the imperialists yell about a crisis. We, comrades, know that there is no crisis in our agriculture." Khrushchev also asserted that the new farm reorganization would not entail a major shift of funds and resources allocated for industry and arms.

The Central Committee's decisions were published in a 9-point resolution made public in Soviet newspapers Mar. 11. The resolution confirmed the establishment of the agencies proposed by Khrushchev and (a) ordered the abandonment of the Stalin-era system under which 25% of Soviet farm lands were planted with low-yield grasses and hay to save on chemical fertilizer; (b) ordered incentive payment systems to reward high productivity by collective and state farmers; (c) called on the CP Presidium and government to draft plans for increasing farm machinery and fertilizer production.

The chairman and the guiding directorate of the central planning board for the new agricultural reforms were appointed Apr. 29. Deputy Premier Nikolai Ignatov, 60, was named as chairman of the 7-member national committee of the Union Committee on Agriculture, one of the agencies formed by the Central Committee (but he lost this job Dec. 20 when he was removed from his post as a first deputy premier). The Union Committee was composed of its national members and of management committees (headed by party first secretaries) established earlier in April at the republic and provincial levels. Their function was to plan and supervise the agricultural system as part of the Soviet economy.

Other members of the Union Committee: Vasily I. Polyakov, head of the Central Committee's agriculture department; Leonid R. Korniyets, first deputy chairman of the State Committee on Agricultural Purchases; Agriculture Min. Konstantin G. Pysin; Pavel S. Kuchumov, chairman of the farm machinery sales agency; Nikolai P. Gusev, deputy chairman of the State Planning Committee; Sergei M. Tikhomirov, deputy chairman of the State Economic Council.

Ivan D. Laptev and S. F. Demidov had been dismissed from the Soviet Academy of Agricultural Sciences during an academy session held Apr. 5-6 to discuss the Central Committee decisions on farm output. *Pravda* said Apr. 7 that Laptev and Demidov had been "subjected to sharp criticism for not having worked out any important scientific problems in the last few years and not having contributed anything useful to production." In his address to the Central Committee Mar. 5, Khrushchev had criticized them on similar grounds. The Agricultural Academy also accepted the resignation Apr. 5 of its president, Prof. Trofim D. Lysenko. Lysenko, who had resigned for "health reasons," was replaced by Agriculture Min. Mikhail A. Olshansky.

Khrushchev July 29 blamed the USSR's farm problems on Stalin's opposition to effective rural electrification. Speaking at the inauguration of the Kremenchug (Ukraine) Hydroelectric Station on the Dnieper River, Khrushchev said Stalin had not allowed farms to use the electric grid system, which would have permitted large plants to serve many farms. Soviet farms, therefore, built their own small power plants, which produced expensive power and thus resulted in costly farm output. "Stalin has been dead a long time," Khrushchev said, "... but his ideas are still ingrained ... and this inheritance will have to be rooted out, you see, if we are to untie the hand of farm production."

Food Prices Raised to Spur Farm Output

Increases of 30% in the price of meat and 25% in the price of butter—to encourage farm production and overcome lagging farm output—were announced by the Soviet government June 1. A Moscow broadcast, announcing the increases, said money could not be diverted from defense to meet farm requirements because "international reaction, with the U.S.A. in the lead, is conducting a frenzied drive for armaments and is hatching plans for a surprise nuclear and missile attack." The broadcast added: "The government has spent many billions of rubles to advance farming, but it can be seen from experience in developing stock farming, the investments have not been enough"; "in order to interest the collective farms materially in increasing livestock produce, there must be an increase [35%] in government purchasing prices for meat and butter"; "but this requires enormous funds"; despite the increased output of milk, meat, eggs, sugar and other foods in the past 8 years, "the level of production of livestock produce is still insufficient"; retail prices of sugar, staple fabrics and articles made from staple fabrics would be reduced; the meat and butter price increases were only temporary because "the expenses of producing livestock products will go down sharply and then there can be a reduction" in meat and butter prices.

Moscow shops June 1 were selling butter at 3.60 rubles ($4) a kilo (2.2 pounds) compared with 2.90 rubles ($3.22) May 31. Meat and meat products sold at up to about 4 rubles ($4.44) a kilo at the new price level. Examples [May 31 prices in brackets]: Lamb—1.90 rubles a kilo [1.40]; pork—1.90 rubles a kilo [1.60]; beef—2 rubles a kilo [1.50].

Khrushchev declared June 2 that the price increases were required to rectify a miscalculation in Soviet economic planning. Speaking at a Soviet-Cuban youth meeting in Moscow, Khrushchev said: The error had been in increasing wages and pensions quickly, thus giving people more money than ever before; farm production had not kept pace with a resultant rise in spending, and food shops could not meet consumer demands; the food price increases would help provide incentives for collective farmers and increase the production of fertilizer and machinery to encourage farm output; "in one or 2 years as a result of this decision agriculture will rise as if on yeast" and there would be an abundance of food; "the enemies of socialism" would have preferred that the USSR reduce defense spending to bolster lagging farm production; "this would create conditions for which our enemies have been waiting a long time," but "it will never be"; "it was very hard for me" to decide to raise prices, "but I know the people understand it in a correct way."

The *N.Y. Times* reported Oct. 8 that serious riots had occurred in several southern Soviet cities in June in protest against the food price increases, food shortages and work speed-ups. The *Times* said: The most serious outbreak took place in the industrial city of Novocherkassk, 20 miles southeast of Rostov, where an estimated 75-500 persons reportedly were killed by militiamen and army units attempting to halt rioting that followed several days of peaceful demonstrations by women, workers and students demanding an explanation for the price increases. The rioting began after militiamen fired into the air to disperse a crowd. The unrest spread to other parts of the city, where schools and government buildings were plundered. A city curfew imposed July 12 barred youths up to 16 from streets and public places after 8 p.m. in winter and after 9 p.m. in summer. Similar but less violent disorders occurred at about the same time in smaller cities near Rostov and in Voronezh, 300 miles to the north, in Krasnodar, 150 miles to the south and in Grozny, 400 miles to the southeast.

The UN Food & Agricultural Organization (FAO) reported in Rome Oct. 8 that in 1961-2 USSR farm output had increased about 2% but had fallen far short of goals. The FAO report said: The 1961-2 Soviet grain harvest rose to 137,300,000 tons (planned output: 154 million tons); "potato production failed to rise," other vegetable production dropped by 6%; sugar-beet production fell; cotton and oil seed output increased.

Other Economic Events

A fiscal 1963 state budget providing defense expenditures of 13.9 billion rubles was presented to the Supreme Soviet by Finance Min. Vasily G. Garbuzov Dec. 10 and approved Dec. 12. Defense expenditures for 1962 had been budgeted at 13.4 billion rubles. Other budget estimates: (1) 1963 revenues, a record 87.6 billion rubles, compared with 84.7 billion rubles in 1962; (2) expenditures, 86.1 billion rubles, compared with 82.7 billion rubles in 1962; (3) scientific development expenditures, 4.7 billion rubles, a 10% increase over 1962; (4) capital investment in agriculture, a record 4.1 billion rubles; (5) a 1.7 billion-ruble investment in the chemical industry, a 36% increase over 1962. The steel output goal for 1963 was set at 80 million metric tons, compared with 76,900,000 produced in 1962, but the goal represented a drastic cut in previous targets.

The Presidium of the Supreme Soviet Sept. 24 had canceled income tax reductions that were to go into effect Oct. 1. *Izvestia* reported that the proposed reductions were suspended "until further notice" because of "an increase in the aggressive schemes of imperialism." The projected cuts were part of a program, started in 1960, to abolish the income tax by 1965.

Economic Council Pres. Veniamin Dymshits assured the Supreme Soviet Dec. 10 that more washing machines, refrigerators, meat and other consumer goods would be available to the public in 1963.

Anti-Semitism & Anti-Crime Drive Linked

A widespread crack-down on such "economic crime" as currency speculation, blackmarketing and embezzlement continued throughout the USSR coupled with charges from Western sources that the anti-crime drive was blatantly anti-Semitic. Western critics pointed out that defendants with Jewish-sounding names frequently received the most publicity and the most severe penalties. Sir Barnett Janner, chairman of the Board of Deputies of British Jews, charged July 15 that the Soviet court proceedings "reveal a distinct anti-Jewish bias." He said that 28 of the 46 persons sentenced to death for economic crimes through June were Jews.

Izvestia reported July 21 that 4 persons (2 of them Jews) had been sentenced to death and other defendants sentenced to prison by the criminal division of the Soviet Supreme Court after a 4-month trial of 50 persons in Frunze, capital of the Soviet Republic of Kirghiz, on charges of embezzling government property, illegally manufacturing and retailing textiles and knitted goods, bribery and currency speculation. The newspaper *Sovetskaya Kirgiziya* reported July 24 that the number convicted in the case was 45 and the number given death sentences at least 9 (4 to 6 of them Jews). Those sentenced to death included Bekzhan Dyushaliyev, ex-chairman of the Kirghiz Republic's State Planning Committee.

An issue of the Uzbek newspaper *Pravda Vostoka (Truth of the East)* received in Moscow July 30 reported that Rauf Burhanov, an Uzbek slaughter-house superintendent, had been sentenced to death for a meat swindle that involved giving farms receipts for cattle they did not deliver. 16 CP and local officials were sentenced to "deprivation of liberty" for 10 years for taking bribes to let Burhanov continue the swindle.

2 men (one believed to be Jewish) were reported Aug. 1 to have been sentenced to death and 8 other defendants (several with Jewish names) given jail sentences of up to 15 years in Kaunas, Soviet Lithuanian Republic, for illegal currency speculation. 2 men with Jewish names were given death sentences and 4 others jail terms of up to 15 years in Khmelnitsky, Ukraine on charges of gold and currency speculation (reported Aug. 3).

The Moscow press Aug. 6 gave unusual publicity to the case of Ivan Kostrov, ex-knitted goods executive, who was sentenced by a Moscow court to 5 years in jail after he was unable to explain how he had spent more money for a private house (25,000 rubles) than his total legitimate earnings for the previous 10 years (14,200 rubles). (New regulations put into effect in the Soviet republics authorized local authorities to investigate the source of funds used to buy houses and to seize houses built with unearned money. Although the regulations were presumably enacted independently by each republic, the wording of all was identical. A Soviet government decree Aug. 7 ordered an end to the construction of one-family houses in urban areas and directed that the land be used instead for cooperative apartments.)

The Ukrainian Supreme Court in Chernovtsy sentenced 6 persons to death Oct. 20 for speculating in gold and foreign currency. 9 other defendants received prison sentences on the same charges. All 15 had indentifiable Jewish names. Sentenced to death: Alter Brohnstein, 81; Yefim L. Margoshes; Moishe-Meyer L. Cayats; Srul I. Zimilevich; Isaak B. Ronis; Feliks Y. Mester.

Decrees of the Presidium of the Supreme Soviet published Feb. 27 had added the following crimes to the list of those punishable by death (execution by firing squad): (a) receiving or extorting bribes by government officials with previous convictions (first offenders were liable to 3-year prison terms); (b) rape if it were committed by a group of persons, or by an "especially dangerous" person with a criminal record, or if it resulted "in especially serious consequences"; (c) attempts on the life of a policeman or a citizen-volunteer "under aggravating circumstances." (There had been recent reports of attacks by "hooligans" against policemen and police stations in the Moscow area.) Heretofore, convictions for bribery, rape and attacks against police had been punishable by maximum 15-year prison terms.

The Soviet trade union newspaper *Trud* Jan. 19 had accused Israeli diplomats in the USSR of spying and distributing anti-Soviet literature. *Trud* charged that Joshua Pratt, first secretary in the Israeli embassy in Moscow, had contacted 3 Leningrad Jews who later (in Oct. 1961) were jailed for passing to "members of an embassy of one of the capitalist states" information to be used against the USSR. *Trud* charged that Pratt, during his travels throughout the Soviet Union, had used synagogues to distribute anti-Soviet and Zionist literature to congregation members. *Trud* said the Leningrad trials had established that other Israeli diplomats had used Soviet synagogues "for meetings... for obtaining espionage and slanderous information." Israeli Foreign Office spokesman Abraham Kidron Jan. 21 denied the charges.

Charges of Soviet discrimination and persecutions of Jews were denied by Georgi M. Korniyenko, counselor of the Soviet embassy in Washington, in a letter sent Oct. 3 to Moses I. Socachevsky, president of the Jewish Nazi Victims Organization. The letter, made public by Socachevsky Oct. 10, said: Soviet Jews (2,268,000) comprised 1.1% of the total population but made up 3.2% of all undergraduates in institutions of higher learning; 15.7% of all Soviet doctors, 8.5% of all Soviet writers and journalists, 10.4% of all Soviet jurists and 7% of all Soviet citizens in the arts. Korniyenko's letter followed talks he had held with Socachevsky Aug. 27.

Other Developments

A decree made public Apr. 11 cancelled the award of medals given to a group of secret policemen in 1944 "for successful completion of a special assignment" in deporting the Chechen and Ingush peoples from their Caucausus homes. The minority groups had been "rehabilitated" and returned to their homes in 1957. Among those who had been honored for the deportation assignment: Interior Min. Lavrenti Beria (executed in 1953), ex-security chief Ivan A. Serov and ex-Interior Min. Sergei N. Kruglov.

Vasily Stepanov, ex-assistant editor of Pravda, was reported May 5 to have replaced Fedor Konstantinov as editor of *Kommunist,* the Communist Party's theoretical journal. Stepanov's appointment was made public in a communique announcing that he had been awarded the Order of Lenin.

Ex-Foreign Min. Vyacheslav M. Molotov, 71, disappeared from public view in February after conflicting reports that he was to resume his post as Soviet delegate to the International Atomic Energy Agency in Vienna. Molotov had returned to Moscow Nov. 12, 1961, ostensibly to defend himself against charges of participating in Stalin's purges and the "anti-party" plot against Khrushchev in 1957, and of opposing Khrushchev's peaceful coexistence policies. A Soviet Foreign Ministry statement Jan. 8 reported that Molotov (who had been reported ousted from the Vienna post and the CP) was returning to his IAEA post. The statement was retracted Jan. 9 after Molotov failed to arrive in Vienna. Molotov dropped out of sight Feb. 5 after returning to his Moscow home from hospitalization for influenza. The public denunciation of Molotov was resumed Jan. 17 in a *Pravda* article that said: "Molotov...in his dogmatic stubbornness stooped to statements that Lenin allegedly at no time and no place spoke about peaceful coexistence between states with different social systems."

Vasily Josevich Stalin, about 40-41, son of the late Josef V. Stalin, was reported Apr. 18 to have died recently of a heart ailment in Kazan, capital of the Tatar Autonomous Republic. A

Nov. 1961 AP dispatch had quoted Stalin's "friends" as saying that Vasily, generally known to be an alcoholic, had been demoted from lieutenant general to major in the Soviet Air Force. His death had previously been reported in 1955.

1963

As the Sino-Soviet dispute escalated in intensity, Soviet Premier Khrushchev solicited, and received, the support of non-Soviet Communist leaders in the ideological struggle. The USSR continued its removal of Soviet forces from Cuba during 1963, but some U.S. and Cuban exile sources said the Soviets were actually building up Cuba's military might. Khrushchev renewed his pledge to Castro—and warning to the U.S.—that the Soviet Union would help Cuba if the U.S. invaded the island. Soviet, U.S. and British representatives concluded an agreement to ban nuclear weapons tests in the atmosphere, space or under water; and the U.S. and USSR set up a "hot line" teletype link to assure quick communication between the 2 governments in any crisis. The lagging 7-year economic plan was dropped for its 2 final years (1964-5), and a new Supreme Council of National Economy was created to coordinate various areas of the Soviet economy. Agriculture was still in trouble; the grain harvest was so poor that the USSR had to buy tremendous quantities of wheat from Western countries. Charges of official anti-Semitism were renewed as Jews continued to face prosecution and severe sentences for alleged "economic crimes." Khrushchev warned writers and artists not to expect complete freedom of expression.

AFTERMATH OF CUBAN CRISIS

New Soviet Build-Up in Cuba?

Despite Khrushchev's agreement to remove Russian missiles from Cuba and to demolish the missile bases there, reports in the U.S. press early in 1963 asserted that the USSR had resumed shipments of arms to Cuba and that Soviet military men were helping the Castro regime integrate these arms into a highly sophisticated ground and air defense system. These reports, stemming largely from Cuban exile sources, persisted despite emphatic denials of their truth by Pres. Kennedy and other U.S. Administration officials. According to a *N.Y. Times* report Jan. 23: The number of Russians in Cuba during the missile crisis was estimated at 15,200. About 3,300 (presumably attached to the dismantled missile sites) had been withdrawn. But replacements brought the USSR's current force in Cuba to more than 12,000 men. An estimated 6,000 Soviet troops were manning 24 ground-to-air missile sites in all parts of Cuba. Soviet specialists were handling tactical battlefield rockets with a nuclear capacity and an over-the-horizon range of 15-25 miles.

The reports of aggressive Russian military activities in Cuba were denied by Khrushchev Feb. 9 during a 2-1/2-hour in the Kremlin with Roy H. Thomson, Canadian newspaper publisher. Thomson told Western newsmen in Moscow that he had informed Khrushchev of the U.S.' concern over the Soviet troops in Cuba and had asked whether there was any basis for this concern. Khrushchev, he said, had replied: "None at all." Khrushchev reportedly told Thomson that there were no Soviet nuclear weapons in Cuba. "All the atomic weapons are in our hands," Khrushchev was quoted as saying, "and we do not need to place them there [in Cuba]. We can reach anyone we want with our own weapons from our own territory. It is more reliable to have them on our own territory."

Khrushchev Warns U.S. Not to Invade Cuba

Khrushchev warned Feb. 27 that if U.S. "imperialists" invaded Cuba, the USSR would come to the aid of the Castro government "and strike a devastating blow at the aggressors."

Khrushchev's warning was made in a radio-TV election campaign speech in which he pledged similar Soviet assistance to Communist China, North Korea, North Vietnam, East Germany, "or indeed any Socialist country."

Khrushchev said: "... American imperialists have not apparently renounced the policy of aggression and provocations [against Cuba]. The most aggressive American circles, the 'wild men,' as they are called by the Americans, are urging the American government to invade Cuba on the pretext that she allegedly poses a threat to the United States ... [and] claiming that one cannot tolerate a differently minded neighbor.... If the United States undertook aggressive actions against Cuba and the Soviet Union against its different-minded neighbors, chaos would develop which would inevitably lead to war." The U.S. "cannot but understand that an invasion of Cuba ... would be incompatible with the commitments assumed during the [1962] crisis in the area of the Caribbean.... [Pres. Kennedy] pledged himself not to invade Cuba while we agreed to withdraw strategic missiles and IL-28 bombers from Cuba, and did withdraw them. But this does not mean that we have left ... Cuba at the mercy of the big shark of imperialism. We gave the Cuban people our word ... that the Soviet Union will come to Cuba's aid, and we shall not leave her in the hour of need."

USSR Reduces Forces in Cuba

Reductions of the number of Soviet troops in Cuba were made at various times throughout 1963.

The USSR had informed Pres. Kennedy Feb. 18 that "several thousand" of the Soviet troops in Cuba would be withdrawn by Mar. 15. The Soviet message, delivered by Amb.-to-U.S. Anatoly A. Dobrynin, was disclosed by Mr. Kennedy later Feb. 18 at a special White House meeting of Congressional leaders and top Administration officials. Mr. Kennedy reportedly said at the White House meeting that clamor in the U.S. over removal of the Soviet troops made it more difficult for Khrushchev to withdraw them because of his domestic political situation.

According to reports in the Soviet and Western press, about 3,700 to 3,800 Soviet troops left Cuba on 5 ships Feb. 5-Mar. 15. *Pravda,* discussing the departures, said Mar. 13 that the Soviet soldiers were leaving in accordance with a USSR-Cuban agreement. *Pravda* said: The Russian troops had completed the task of helping "their Cuban comrades to master fully the powerful modern Soviet military techniques which the revolutionary armed forces of ... Cuba now possessed, to protect their country from any intrigues of the imperialist aggressors"; the Soviet military specialists leaving the island had helped the Cubans "in the construction of defense fortifications and airfields where now are stationed airplanes of the Cuban Air Force."

Pres. Kennedy said at his news conference Apr. 3 that about 4,000 Soviet troops had left Cuba in March. Mr. Kennedy said this troop exit "still leaves some thousands on the island," and "we hope they are going to be withdrawn."

Pres. Kennedy said at his news conference Aug. 20 that since June there had been a further "decline" in the number of Soviet troops in Cuba. The President said "the primary emphasis of those [Soviet soldiers] who remain now is in training and not in concentrated military units." Asserting that it was "difficult" to estimate the number of troops withdrawn, Mr. Kennedy said, "On the information we have about outward movement and inward movement, it is the judgment of the intelligence community that there has been a reduction in the last 2-1/2 months." The June estimate of Soviet troops in Cuba: 12,500, of which 4,000-5,000 were believed members of combat units.

The *N.Y. Times* reported Nov. 10 that U.S. government officials currently estimated the number of Soviet troops in Cuba to be down to 5,000. The report said there were no longer any Russian combat units on the island. The estimates, based on U.S. aerial surveillance and other intelligence sources, indicated that Soviet troops had been leaving the island at the rate of 500 a week for the past 3 months.

Pledges to Castro Renewed

Cuban Premier Castro began a month-long visit to the Soviet Union Apr. 27. He returned to Havana June 3 after receiving renewed pledges of Soviet aid against military attack and, reportedly, assurances that arrangements would be made to free Cuban sugar for sale at rising world prices. Shortly after his arrival in Moscow Castro said in a speech in Red Square Apr. 28: "Comrade Khrushchev today expressed his confidence in the victory of the Cuban revolution, and we are confident that will be so"; "were it not for the Soviet Union, the imperialists would not hesitate to launch a direct military attack on our country"; "it precisely was the might of the Soviet Union and the entire Socialist camp that deterred an imperialist aggression against our homeland"; Soviet arms and economic aid had prevented the destruction of the "Socialist revolution in Cuba."

A joint communique issued by Khrushchev and Castro May 24 said: In the event of an attack "in violation of the commitments undertaken by the United States President not to invade Cuba," Khrushchev promised that the USSR would provide "the necessary help for the defense of . . . Cuba with all the means at its disposal"; Cuba had accepted a Moscow proposal to change the current Soviet-Cuban sugar agreement and to increase the price of Cuban raw sugar bought in 1963 to the world price level as "an effective role in strengthening the economic situation" in Cuba.

(Soviet First Deputy Foreign Trade Min. Sergei A. Borisov had reported Jan. 16 that 1962 Cuban-Soviet trade had totaled more than 500 million rubles [$550 million]. According to official Soviet publications, the 1962 Cuban-USSR trade goal had been $750 million.)

FOREIGN POLICY & DEFENSE

Foreign Communists Back USSR Vs. China

Russian-Chinese ideological and political differences were debated by Khrushchev and other high-ranking Communists Jan. 15-21 at a gathering in East Berlin of delegations from 70 national Communist parties. The meeting technically was the 6th Congress of the East German Socialist Unity (Communist) Party. But the guest delegations transformed the Congress into a forum for discussion of the Soviet-Chinese disagreement on international Communist policy. Nearly all Communist leaders attending backed Khrushchev against China and supported Khrushchev's appeal for a temporary truce in the ideological debate.

It had been apparent since Jan. 4, when it was announced that Khrushchev would head the Soviet delegation, that the East Berlin meeting would be used to demonstrate Soviet-bloc support for the USSR in its differences with China.

The East German CP newspaper *Neues Deutschland,* in its strongest attack to date on China's views, specifically condemned China Jan. 13 for supporting Albania in policies that were "a danger to the world Communist movement."

East German CP First Secy. Walter Ulbricht convened the meeting Jan. 15 with an address in which he attacked China for invading India. Ulbricht's address was followed by speeches by Khrushchev Jan. 16 and Polish CP First Secy. Wladyslaw Gomulka Jan. 17 and by Wu Hsiu-chuan, Chinese CP Central Committee member, who was jeered by the Congress Jan. 18 when he attempted to reply to Khrushchev.

In an address at a Kremlin meeting in honor of visiting Hungarian Premier Janos Kadar, Khrushchev July 19 denounced China's attack on his leadership and policies. Khrushchev charged that (a) China was attempting to supplant Russia's leadership of the Communist bloc to return it to the period of Stalinist rule-by-terror; (b) China's leaders had proclaimed their intention to provoke revolutionary wars to advance communism even if millions died in a nuclear conflict. Khrushchev said:

● "The attempts of those who want to change the leadership in our country and to defend all the abuses committed by Stalin are in vain. What do they want? To frighten our people, to bring them back to the order that existed before, when a man went to his job and did not know whether he would see his wife and his children again? Comrades, I receive letters.... [They say] it is good in our country now;... it is better now than it was, and... if Stalin had died 10 years earlier it would have been even better." "One of the lessons of the counterrevolutionary rebellion in Hungary, to be drawn by the world Communist movement, lay precisely in the fact that the personality cult leads to divorce from the masses, to gross violations of Socialist legality, and consequently created the ground for the activities of anti-popular forces."

● "A world war is necessary neither for the building of socialism or communism nor for the acceleration of the world revolution." "The question of the victory of socialism in any given country is decided by the people of that country...[not] by unleashing a world thermonuclear war." "Those who deny the possibility of victory of the working class' revolutionary forces in a class struggle under peaceful coexistence do not have faith in the revolutionary energy and determination of the working class." Some persons proclaimed their plans "to build a new society on the dead bodies and the ruin of the world." "Do these men know that if all the nuclear warheads were touched off, the world would be in such a state that the survivors would envy the dead?"

Treaty Curbs A-Tests

Soviet, U.S. and British negotiators in Moscow July 25 initialed a treaty prohibiting nuclear weapons tests in the earth's atmosphere, in space or under water, and the treaty was signed in Moscow Aug. 5 by the foreign ministers of the 3 negotiating countries. The 3-power talks that produced the treaty had been opened in Khrushchev's office in the Kremlin, and Khrushchev had taken personal (but temporary) leadership of the Soviet delegation for the opening phase of the negotiations.

The negotiations and the conclusion of the treaty were greeted by most nations—including the Communist states of Eastern Europe—with almost enthusiastic approval. Communist China, however, denounced the talks from their inception. The Chinese CP newspaper *Jenmin Jih Pao (People's Daily)* said July 20 that "such talks amount to saying that there is no alternative to capitulation in the face of imperialist nuclear blackmail." In a statement issued July 31, after the treaty was initialed, the Communist Chinese government denounced the treaty as a "dirty fraud" perpetrated by the U.S., Britain and USSR to "consolidate their nuclear monopoly and bind the hands of all peace-loving countries subjected to the nuclear treaty."

The discussion of further measures to lessen East-West tensions was carried forward by U.S. State Secy. Dean Rusk, Soviet Foreign Min. Andrei Gromyko and British Foreign Secy. Lord Home in a series of informal meetings begun in New York Sept. 28 in conjunction with the opening of the annual session of the UN General Assembly. The New York talks produced an agreement in principle on the banning of nuclear weapons from space and from orbiting earth satellites. The accord was announced Oct. 3.

U.S.-Soviet 'Hot Line' Arranged

The U.S. and USSR also agreed during 1963 to set up a direct Washington-Moscow teletype system that would assure rapid and private communication between the U.S. and Soviet governments in the event of a sudden crisis.

Proposals for such a link had been advanced repeatedly in past years, but they had received little impetus until a communications failure forced Pres. Kennedy and Khrushchev to publicly broadcast several of the diplomatic messages by which they settled the Cuban missile crisis. The proposals were turned over to the U. S. and Soviet delegations to the Geneva disarmament conference. Discussion of a possible treaty setting up the "hot line" was begun in April, and details were worked out during the next few months.

"A "Memorandum of Understanding" on the creation of a direct Washington-Moscow teletype system was signed in Geneva June 20. An annex detailed the procedures for its use in case of a grave international emergency requiring rapid and direct communication between the heads of the 2 governments.

The "hot line" between Washington and Moscow was declared operational Aug. 30. The system was to be kept open 24 hours a day but was to be used for emergency messages only.

Arms Budget Cut Called Peace Move

A reduction in the USSR's publicly reported military budget was announced by Khrushchev Dec. 13 in an address in which he linked the measure to Russia's disarmament proposals and its will to peace. The measure was introduced in the Supreme Soviet Dec. 16. Khrushchev's announcement was made in a speech at the close of a 5-day meeting of the CP Central Committee. His address, published Dec. 14 in *Izvestia,* coupled the planned cut in arms expenditures with proposals for a reduction in Soviet military manpower. The latter proposals, however, were not made part of the Dec. 16 budgetary proposals.

Khrushchev's announcement was accompanied by a new challenge to the West to match Soviet arms cuts. Khrushchev charged that the Western powers had rejected every major Russian suggestion for a lessening of the danger caused by the current East-West military confrontation in Europe. The USSR, he said, had proposed that foreign troops be returned to their respective countries or that foreign garrisons in East and West Germany be reduced by 1/3 or some other agreed amount. These proposals, he said, had been rejected on the ground that the USSR had an overwhelming superiority in conventional forces that would be enhanced by equal reductions of both sides' manpower. Khrushchev countered, however, that Western leaders, among them U.S. Defense Secy. McNamara, currently believed the West to have superiority in conventional manpower and armaments.

Khrushchev ended his comments on disarmament with the warning that despite the impending Russian military budget cut, "the Soviet Union has all that is necessary and more to curb any aggressor, to secure the security of our people and of the peoples of the Socialist countries."

In the 1964 state budget, submitted Dec. 16 by Finance Min. Vasily F. Garbuzov, the publicly announced allocation for defense was 13.3 billion rubles, a reduction of 600 million rubles from the expenditure budgeted for 1963. The military budget represented 14.6% of the total expenditures of 91.3 billion rubles foreseen in 1964.

Anti-Missile Rockets

4 rockets described as anti-missile missiles capable of destroying incoming enemy missiles were displayed for the first time in the USSR's traditional Nov. 7 military parade through Red Square in Moscow. The parade was part of ceremonies marking the 46th anniversary of the Bolshevik revolution. Although the Soviet press and radio commentators covering the parade did not use the phrase "anti-missile missile," it was clear from their reports that this was what the rockets were considered to be and was the main reason for their being placed on display. The Tass commentary on the parade said that the rockets had been tested successfully in recent maneuvers and had proved capable of destroying "any modern means of air-space attack." In a radio address delivered as part of the day's military observances, Marshal Sergei Semenovich Biryuzov, 58 (who in March had replaced Marshal Matvei V. Zakharov, 64, as chief of the USSR General Staff), said the rockets could destroy "the enemy's rockets in the air."

DOMESTIC DEVELOPMENTS

7-Year Plan Dropped for New Scheme

The discontinuation of the Soviet Union's 7-year economic plan and the establishment of a Supreme Council of National Economy were announced in Moscow Mar. 13. The decisions leading to this action had been taken at a joint meeting of the Communist Party's ruling Presidium and the governing Council of Ministers, presided over by Premier Khrushchev.

The 7-year plan, drawn up in 1958, had been rendered out of date by the new economic changes ordered by the CP's Central Committee in Nov. 1962. As a result, government agencies were ordered by the CP Presidium and the Council of Ministers to submit new proposals for the plan's last 2 years (1964-5). A new 5-year plan was to be drafted for 1965-70; its goals, according to a government statement, would be: (a) to surpass the U.S. in per capita production; (b) to create a "substantial" increase in the standard of living; (c) to fulfill housing needs "in the main"; (d) to convert all farms into "highly productive and profitable enterprises."

The new Supreme Council of National Economy was to be headed by Dimitri Ustinov, 54, as chairman. Ustinov, State Defense Industries Committee administrator, also was appointed a first deputy premier. Aleksandr M. Tarasov, 51, industry head of the Byelorussian Republic, was named council deputy chairman. Leonid V. Smirnov, 46, deputy administrator of the State Defense Industries Committee, succeeded Ustinov as full administrator. The Supreme Council was to coordinate the work of the Space Planning Committee, the Council of National Economy (which supervised industrial management), the State Construction Committee and specialized agencies. The council also was to have jurisdiction over electric power, natural gas production and geological surveys.

Nikolai K. Baibakov had replaced Viktor S. Fedorov as chairman of the State Committee of the Chemical Industry. Fedorov remained on the committee as first deputy chairman.

The government had established a joint economic region to manage industries and the unified construction agency of the 4 Central Asian republics of Uzbekistan, Kirghizia, Turkmenistan and Tadzhikistan. Stepan I. Kadyshev was named head of the region's industrial management agency (Sovnarkhoz). Valentin M. Gushchin, ex-deputy construction minister of the USSR, was named construction chief. Semyon M. Veselov, ex-Komsomol official, was appointed deputy chairman of the Central Asian Bureau (formed in 1962 to direct the overall affairs of the 4 republics).

Khrushchev Demands Farm Improvements

Khrushchev had declared that despite recent farm reforms aimed at increasing output, many local officials still "waste time in talk and red tape" instead of "skillfully" organizing production. His statement, published by Soviet newspapers Mar. 14, was made at a conference of Russian Republic agricultural officials Mar. 12. Khrushchev asserted that farm officials who aspired to higher positions would first have to demonstrate their ability to produce. "As an example," he introduced to the audience Ivan Platonovich Volovchenko, who had recently been appointed agriculture minister. (Volovchenko replaced Konstantin G. Pysin, who had been dismissed Mar. 8.) Volovchenko had headed the Petrovsky state farm in the Lipetsk region for the past 12 years.

Khrushchev, criticizing the current farm research system, pointed out that the so-called model farms outside Moscow, where the national and Russian Republic agriculture ministers had their offices, produced less than nearby farms.

Khrushchev made these proposals for improving the farm system:

● Abolish the 15 republics' agriculture ministries because they duplicated the work of the national agricultural ministry.

● Employes of the government's farm machine and supply agencies should be paid according to their farms' crop yields, livestock output and machine performance, rather than on a fixed salary basis.

● State farm workers should be barred from owning private livestock but be guaranteed enough meat and butter.

● The central government should not require grain deliveries from the Baltic republics and Byelorussia, whose natural resources were better adapted to livestock raising.

● The government should halt the reckless enlargement of state farms.

Khrushchev declared Sept. 27 that a poor grain harvest for the current year had put the Soviet Union in a "difficult position," making it vital that irrigation and the manufacture of fertilizer be increased to "guarantee us against all eventualities." In a speech (made public Sept. 30) to Ukrainian farm officials in Novaya Kakhovka, Khrushchev said: "We need grain now...and we must produce more of it every year. Because of bad weather this year we found ourselves in a difficult situation, and we must draw the necessary conclusions." Khrushchev disclosed that the USSR was "giving first priority to fertilizers [production] and only 2d priority to irrigation" "because a solution of both tasks simultaneously is beyond our capabilities." Khrushchev was touring southern Ukrainian farm areas to press for his goal of a "guaranteed" annual grain supply of 25-30 million tons from irrigated land and 35-55 million tons from dry-farming regions.

The Communist Party's Central Committee was reported Sept. 22 to have established a special commission to supervise construction of fertilizer factories. 5,000 "skilled construction workers," all members of Komsomol (the CP youth organization), were to be assigned to 59 projects scheduled to start operating by 1964.

Russians Buy Foreign Grain

Because of the poor grain crop, the USSR was forced to make huge purchases of grain from foreign producers.

Canada agreed Sept. 16 to sell the Soviets $500 million worth of wheat and flour by July 1964. This was the largest grain sale ever contracted for a one-year period. Under the agreement, the USSR was to buy 198 million bushels of wheat and 29.5 million bushels of flour. The agreement permitted the USSR to resell to Cuba 16.5 bushels of the Canadian wheat and flour. The USSR reportedly was acting as intermediary for the Castro government, which lacked dollars to buy the wheat directly. The USSR also agreed to buy 18.7 million bushels of Canadian wheat or flour in 1965.

The USSR's huge foreign grain purchases were disclosed to the Russian people Oct. 1 with the publication, by *Izvestia,* of a speech delivered by Khrushchev Sept. 26 in Krasnodar. Khrushchev, speaking of the USSR's need to improve grain production and its plans to expand fertilizer output and irrigation, said that Russia had been forced to buy 6.8 million tons of wheat from Canada and 1.8 million tons from Australia and had borrowed 400,000 tons of grain from Rumania. He said additional small amounts had been obtained from other countries, but he made no mention of a possible purchase of U.S. grain. The U.S.' agreement Oct. 9 to permit U.S. traders to sell the Soviet Union $250 million worth of U.S. wheat was reported in the USSR in a 2-sentence Tass news agency dispatch. (Pres. Kennedy informed the U.S. Congress in an Oct. 10 letter that other Western nations were also helping to fill Soviet-bloc grain needs, often with grain bought from the U.S.)

Science Management Revised

A major reorganization of the Soviet Academy of Sciences was announced May 16. The move was ordered by the government and the CP Central Committee to meet research needs in electronics, nuclear research and space exploration. According to *Pravda,* the academy, at a 2-day session earlier in the week, had adopted a charter that gave the academy authority over 14 local science academies in the Soviet republics. The charter also provided for the reorganization of the national academy into a larger number of specialized departments to replace the 8 broad departments that had directed work in such fields as biology, chemistry and history.

Details of the new science program were revealed in a speech by Academy of Sciences Pres. Mstislav V. Keldysh at a general session May 14. Keldysh disclosed a previously unpublished government and CP decree of Apr. 11 that had criticized the current system on the ground that there had not been effective coordination or economical use of the funds appropriated for scientific research. Local science academies were accused of duplicating research work performed by the national academy.

Keldysh said that under the new system: Academies in the republics would work on projects in which they had special interest or were advanced; the national academy would have complete direction over all basic research in the physical and social sciences; special state boards would be formed for each major industry to handle technical applications.

Citing research weaknesses of the past, Keldysh criticized the failure to introduce chemicals sufficiently into agriculture.

Republic Officials Purged

First Secy. Ismail Yusupov of the Kazakhstan CP reported at a party conference in Alma Ata Mar. 18 that 2,340 Kazakhstan Trade Ministry officials and more than 16,000 officials of other trade groups had been dismissed in 1962 for stealing, violating trade rules and committing other offenses. The report, published in *Kazakhstanskaya Pravda* Mar. 21, said: thefts in the Trade Ministry in 1962 totaled $1,440,000; state farms in the virgin lands had been operating at an increasing loss ($600 million in the past 3 years); 29 million sheep and goats had been lost in the past 10 years because of lack of care or mismanagement. Yusupov attributed the agricultural shortcomings to ill-qualified high officials who had been chosen from among a "narrow circle." He said many had engaged in drinking, gambling and embezzling and had shirked their duties. Yusupov suggested that government posts in the republic be filled by engineers and scientists as well as Communist youth.

Abdy Annaliyev was ousted as premier of Turkmenia in a widespread purge of the Central Asian republic's CP leadership, it was announced in Moscow Mar. 26. Others dismissed included Nurberdy Bairamov, president of the CP presidium, largely an honorary position, and the CP's 2d secretary. *Pravda,* reporting on a party conference held Mar. 25 in Ashkhabad, capital of Turkmenia, said: The republic's leaders had failed to indoctrinate "leading officials with a spirit of high responsibility for implementation of party and government directives. The presidium of the Turkmenian party lacks the necessary purposefulness, coordination and collective approach in its work."

The formation of a Trans-Caucasian Bureau of the CP Central Committee, in a move to tighten the central government's control over the republics of Armenia, Georgia and Azerbaijan was disclosed by Tass Mar. 22. The bureau was headed by Guri N. Bochkarev, an ex-CP official in Moscow. The new bureau was to implement directives issued by the central government and was to coordinate the 3 republics' activities.

Anti-Semitism Charged in Economic Trials

Western critics renewed their charges of Soviet anti-Semitism in the face of continued Soviet prosecution of alleged economic "criminals," many of whom appeared to be Jewish. As previously, extremely severe penalties often were imposed on Jewish defendants; several were sentenced to death.

Khrushchev Feb. 24 denounced the charges of official Soviet anti-Semitism as "a crude falsehood, a malicious calumny on the Soviet people and our country." Khrushchev's statement was made in reply to a letter he had received Feb. 23 in which the British philosopher Bertrand Russell had expressed concern over the execution of Soviet citizens, many of them Jews, for economic crimes. Khrushchev replied: "Among the persons punished by our courts for the so-called economic crimes . . . there are Russians, Jews, Georgians, Ukranians and Byelorussians and people of other nationalities. In short, these decisions of the courts are not directed against the people of a definite nationality, but against crimes and those who commit them."

Among reports of economic trials in the USSR:

● 6 persons, apparently all Jews, were sentenced to death by a Ukranian court for having engaged in illegal gold and currency transactions in Kharkov, *Ukraine Pravda* reported Jan. 7. 6 others received long prison terms. In another trial, reported by *Ukraine Pravda* Jan. 7, 3 officials of a curtain factory in Ivano-Frankovsk were sentenced to death for stealing factory goods; 2 others received jail sentences.

● The newspaper *Sovetskaya Rossiya* reported Jan. 10 that the head of an office that distributed supplies to geological parties had been sentenced to death in Gorki for accepting funds on many occasions in exchange for arranging quick delivery of autos. An alleged accomplice received a 15-year sentence.

● Moscow radio reported Jan. 10 that a Vladivostok official had been sentenced to 15 years' "deprivation of freedom" for accepting bribes for making arbitrary changes in lists of persons waiting for apartments. 36 others allegedly involved received lesser jail terms.

● A Kutaisi, Georgia court was reported Jan. 14 to have sentenced 3 persons to death and given jail terms to 39 others for misappropriating more than $300,000 worth of store goods. The defendants included store managers and salesmen, factory officials, police inspectors and prison officials.

● A Kiev court was reported Jan. 14 to have sentenced 62 persons to prison (5 of them for 15 years) in a 500,000-ruble embezzlement case involving a municipally operated chain fruit store. The defendants—managers, warehousemen and buyers—were accused of classifying high-grade fruit as low-grade, paying farms at the lower rate, selling the produce at high-grade prices and keeping the difference.

● N. Z. Babadzhanov, ex-mayor of Dushnanbe, capital of the Republic of Tadzhikistan, was reported Feb. 15 to have been sentenced to death on charges of bribery. 15 others received prison terms. Babadzhanov, who also had been first secretary of Dushambe's CP, had been accused with the other defendants of having taken or given bribes in the allotments of apartments and real estate plots. They also had been charged with changing waiting lists for autos.

● 6 officials of the Lvov industrial management council were reported Feb. 17 to have received sentences ranging from 5 to 15 years on charges of having allocated government-controlled textiles and other raw materials to persons engaged in private enterprise.

● *Trud* (the Soviet trade union newspaper) reported Feb. 24 that 7 Armenians had received 12-year jail sentences for buying and reselling at a profit 2,000 foreign and czarist gold coins worth 120,000 rubles.

● A Moscow court July 17 convicted 4 Jews on charges of selling illegally baked matzohs (unleavened bread used during Passover) for personal gain. 3 of the defendants were sentenced to 6 months in prison; a 4th was released because of old age and poor health. The first 3 had been imprisoned since their arrest in March. The 4 defendants had been seized shortly after Moscow chief rabbi, Yehuda-Leib Levin, had announced that no matzoh would be available from the city's government-operated bakeries.

● *Sovetskaya Rossiya* reported July 6 that 5 persons had been executed by firing squad as leaders of a 15-member ring that had profited from the illegal manufacture and sale of razors, fountain pens, buttons and rulers. The 5 had been convicted in Leningrad Feb. 21. The 10 other defendants received prison terms.

● The Rabbinical Council of America (representing 850 Orthodox rabbis) was reported Sept. 22 to have sent Soviet Amb.-to-U.S. Anatoly F. Dobrynin a letter protesting the death sentence imposed on a Soviet rabbi in August after his conviction on a charge of speculation in foreign gold currency. The letter, dated Sept. 6, was written by Rabbi Abraham N. AvRutick, council president. It charged that the sentence "leaves us with the feeling that a campaign is being waged against religious Jewry in Russia." Asserting that the council, for lack of information, would not comment on the nature of the charge against the convicted rabbi, AvRutick said, "We do feel that the penalty far exceeds the alleged crime." The Russian Republic newspaper *Sovietskaya Rossiya* had identified the rabbi Aug. 30 as B. Gavrilov and had said that he and 2 other persons had been sentenced to death after a 4-week trial in Pyatigorsk. At least 6 others received jail sentences.

World Jewish Congress Pres. Nahum Goldmann had charged Sept. 12 that Soviet authorities were applying "exceptional ferocity" against Jews convicted of economic crimes.

Khrushchev Bars 'Absolute Freedom' in Art

Khrushchev warned Mar. 8 that his de-Stalinization policies did not mean "the time had come to let things drift, that the reins of government had been relaxed...and that everyone is free to do and behave as he pleases." Khrushchev spoke on the 2d day of a closed 2-day meeting of high government and CP officials and cultural leaders. His speech was made public Mar. 10. Warning that the Soviet press, literature, fine arts, music, theater and cinema would be expected to conform to the strict party line, Khrushchev said: "There shall never be absolute freedom for the individual, not even under communism"; "under communism, too, the will of one man must be subordinated to the will of the collective."

Khrushchev denounced Stalin's abuses of power but defended Stalin's purges of "enemies of the revolution and Socialist construction," whom he described as "Troskyites, Zinovyevites, Bukharinites and bourgeois nationalists." Khrushchev said: "There would have been far more cases [of purges] if all those who worked with Stalin at that period [prior to his death in 1953] had agreed with him on everything." Stalin in those years "was a seriously sick man suffering from suspiciousness and persecution mania."

Referring to Stalin's arrest of thousands of "enemies of the people," Khrushchev said: "Did the leading people of the party know about the arrests...at that time? Yes, they knew. But did they know that completely innocent people were being arrested? No, that they did not know. They believed in Stalin and did not tolerate the thought that repressions were being used against honorable people.... We learned about the abuse of power by Stalin...only after his death and the exposure of Mr. [Lavrenti] Beria, this inveterate enemy of the party and people, this spy, and infamous provocateur." Beria and ex-Premier Georgi Malenkov had joined in making "a provocative proposal for liquidating the German Democratic Republic as a Socialist state," Khrushchev said. Khrushchev asserted that Beria and Malenkov also had recommended that the East German CP "abandon the slogan of struggle for building socialism." The CP's Central Committee, Khrushchev said, had "indignantly rejected these treacherous proposals."

Khrushchev singled out Ilya Ehrenburg and poet Yevgeny Yevtushenko in charging that some Soviet writers were ignoring the positive aspects of Stalin's regime while dwelling too much on the late dictator's "instances of lawlessness, arbitrariness and abuse of power." Khrushchev said that Ehrenburg may be "slipping into an anti-Communist position" by advocating "peaceful co-existence" in the arts with the West. (Ehrenburg was said to have been among a number of intellectuals who had signed and sent to the CP Central Committee a letter making such a suggestion. A party official said that the letter, disclosed Dec. 17, 1962 by Leonid F. Ilyichev, the party's ideological spokesman, had been retracted by the intellectuals "after careful consideration.") Khrushchev held that Ehrenburg's defense of modernist tendencies in art was a "gross ideological error."

In his criticism of Yevtushenko, Khrushchev said the poet "didn't show political maturity and demonstrated ignorance of historic facts" in his poem *Babi Yar*. The poem dealt with the World War II slaying of Jews by German soldiers in the Babi Yar ravine in Kiev and with Russian anti-Semitism. Khrushchev said Yevtushenko should have stressed in his poem that Ukranians and people of other nationalities, as well as Jews, had been massacred in Babi Yar. Khrushchev said the poem should also have brought out that Russian workers were opposed to czarist persecutions of Jews.

Ilyichev, at the Mar. 7 session, criticized Ehrenburg's "theory of silence" as the code of conduct during the days of Stalin's purges. In his memoirs, serialized in the literary journal *Novy Mir (New World)*, Ehrenburg had written that many Russians knew Stalin's purge victims were innocent but kept quiet. The Soviet official view was that the widespread extent of the purges did not become known until after Stalin's death. *Novy Mir,* under attack by government newspapers, continued to publish Ehrenburg's controversial memoirs. The March issue included both Ehrenburg's description of the USSR at the end of World War II and Khrushchev's Mar. 8 criticism of Ehrenburg.

Yevtushenko was severely criticized at the national Union of Writers conference in Moscow Mar. 26-28 for allowing the Paris weekly *L'Express* to publish selections from his *Precocious Autobiography.* Yevtushenko admitted that publishing abroad without clearance from Soviet censors was a "major mistake." He said *L'Express* had distorted the work through cutting and "sensational headlines." (His defense was carried only by Tass' English-language service.) The Soviet press Apr. 2 printed demands that writers not be allowed to travel abroad until they "mature politically," and Yevtushenko canceled a visit to Italy and a lecture tour of American universities, purportedly because of illness.

Composer Dmitri Shostakovich's new *13th Symphony,* which had had its premiere in Moscow's Tchaikovsky Hall Dec. 18, 1962, had been ignored by the press and was withdrawn from a Soviet music festival to be held in London in September. Shostakovich had offered his work in spite of criticisms of it made to him Dec. 17, 1962 by Khrushchev and other members of the Presidium. They had objected to verses, sung in the symphony by a choir, that were taken from Yevtushenko's *Babi Yar.*

In a speech delivered at an industrial conference in Moscow Apr. 24 and published in the Soviet press Apr. 26 Khrushchev expressed confidence that hitherto nonconforming writers and artists would "look at life from a new angle" and reaffirm Communist goals as a result of "healthy criticism." He asked writers themselves to join in such criticism.

African Students Protest Bias

About 500 African students clashed with Moscow police Dec. 18 in a mass demonstration in Red Square. The students were intercepted by police as they were marching on the Kremlin to deliver to Soviet authorities a petition protesting the recent death of a Ghanaian student and alleged racial discrimination against African students in the Soviet Union. The demonstrators, joined by African students from Leningrad and other Soviet cities, had started their march from the Ghanaian embassy. They dispersed after an official emerged from the Kremlin and announced that Higher Education Min. Vyacheslav P. Yelyutin would meet a student delegation to discuss their grievances. Yelyutin met with a group of 100 students, who demanded an investigation of the Ghanaian student's death. The students, who had complained of attacks by Soviet policemen, also told Yelyutin that their "physical safety was threatened."

The dead Ghanaian student was Edmond Assare-Addo, 29, whose body had been found Dec. 13 at Khovrino, 10 miles northwest of Moscow. The African students charged that Assare-Addo, who was returning from Moscow to his studies at the Medical Institute of Kalinin, had been beaten to death, possibly to prevent his scheduled marriage to a Russian girl Dec. 14. A Soviet autopsy made public Dec. 20 by Tass said Assare-Addo's death had been caused "by exposure to cold [12 degrees below zero] in a state of alcoholic intoxication." A Ghanaian student who had attended the autopsy said Dec. 18 that the body bore bruises and a wound.

Asserting that foreign students were expected "to respect and observe Soviet laws," Tass said Dec. 20 that "anyone who does not like our laws and rules . . . is free to leave our country at any time."

1964

Nikita S. Khrushchev, who had ruled the USSR for a decade, was deposed peacefully by his colleagues in mid-Oct. 1964. Leonid I. Brezhnev replaced him as CP first secretary, the most powerful position in the USSR, and Aleksei N. Kosygin succeeded Khrushchev as premier. Most foreign Communist parties accepted the change although they generally expressed uneasiness and pressed Russia's new rulers for an acceptable explanation of their actions. Communist China expressed enthusiastic approval of Khrushchev's downfall; shortly thereafter, however, it resumed its ideological dispute with the Kremlin but with the focus of its denunciations shifted to the new Soviet leaders. Prior to his ouster, Khrushchev had begun new attempts to restore unity to the world Communist movement, and he visited the United Arab Republic in a move to demonstrate Soviet support for the Arab nations in their quarrels with the West and Israel. Khrushchev, however, persisted in his policy of peaceful coexistence with the capitalist world. He also maintained his pressure for agricultural reforms. Evidence of continued persecution of Jews in the USSR provoked renewed foreign attacks on Soviet anti-Semitism. Anastas I. Mikoyan was named Soviet president on Khrushchev's nomination just 3 months before Mikoyan assisted in deposing Khrushchev.

EVENTS PRECEDING KHRUSHCHEV'S OUSTER

International Communist Unity Sought

Khrushchev asserted Feb. 14 that the Communist Party of the Soviet Union was working to restore "the monolithic unity of the world Socialist system" on the basis of the declaration adopted by 81 Communist parties at their 1960 meeting in Moscow. Speaking at a plenary meeting of the Soviet CP Central Committee, Khrushchev said that the Soviet party would continue its fight against the "newly baked Trotskyites" who were undermining Communist unity in the guise of promoting revolutionary anti-imperialist policies. Khrushchev's remarks, made at the end of a lengthy speech on Soviet chemical and agricultural production, were aimed at Communist China's recently-avowed intention of organizing a new Communist bloc directed from Peking. His statement defended Russian domestic and foreign policies as essential to the strength of the Soviet bloc and to the ultimate spread of communism throughout the world.

Khrushchev said:

By creating the material and technical basis of communism in the Soviet Union...our party and the Soviet people are strengthening the world Socialist system...and national-liberation movements. In this way our party and the Soviet people are fulfilling their international duty....

It is impossible to deny the paramount importance of economic construction in the Socialist countries and to oppose it to class struggle against imperialism...

For countries in which the people...are building socialism and communism, the main policy...is an economic policy which can prove in actual fact that a Socialist and Communist economy is superior in...improving the life of the masses, is superior over capitalist economy in the development of the productive forces of society. In the last analysis, this is the crux of the main dispute between the new world and the old world, the competition which paves the way to socialism for the whole of mankind....

Our Leninist party is working for the monolithic unity of the world Socialist system, the international Communist...movement, the national-liberation movement of the peoples, and all peace-loving forces....

Our party and people see it as their internationalist duty to uphold the cause of world peace.... Our party is guided by Lenin's teaching that the only real way to safeguard peace in a world with 2 opposing systems—Socialist and capitalist—is the policy of peaceful co-existence between states with different social systems.... The principle of peaceful coexistence meets the aspirations of the peoples of the Socialist countries and the interests of all mankind.

One key paragraph carried in an early Tass summary of the Khrushchev speech was deleted from an otherwise identical Novosti summary and the versions of the Tass text published by the Soviet press. These remarks were deleted: "We have fought and will continue to fight against revisionists and dogmatists, the newly baked Trotskyites who, while making high-sounding revolutionary phrases about the struggle against imperialism, undermine in fact the unity of the world Communist movement with their splitting activities."

Khrushchev went to Budapest Mar. 31 to participate in celebrations of the 19th anniversary of Hungary's World War II liberation by the Red Army from Nazi occupation. Speaking at a rally of workers at a Budapest electrical equipment factory Apr. 1, Khrushchev expressed scorn of those Communists—presumably the Chinese—who preferred "revolution" to "goulash." "There are people," he said, "... who call themselves Marxists-Leninists and at the same time say there is no need to strive for a better life. According to them only one thing is important—revolution. What kind of Marxism is this?" Lenin had known that it was necessary to promise the people more than just revolution, he declared. "Prosperity is the only thing worth while struggling for." "The important thing is that we should have more to eat—good goulash—schools, housing and ballet.... It is worth fighting and working for these things." Khrushchev said only one thing could "insure the victory of communism": increased "productivity of labor in the Socialist countries."

In a speech at a gala meeting Apr. 3 in the Budapest national opera house, Khrushchev denounced Chinese leaders for following "disruptive tactics" that endangered the unity and success of the world Communist movement. He said, however, that the Chinese actions were bound to generate a reaction: "The Communist parties will close their ranks more and more." Khrushchev asserted that "new organizational forms" must be found to assure Soviet-bloc unity, particularly in the sphere of foreign policy.

In Miskolc, Hungary Apr. 5, Khrushchev declared that he aimed to assure that those living under communism could "begin to live like human beings." "To satisfy man's needs—that is re-birth. How crazy it is to look on that as degenerate." The Chinese, he said, had asserted they would rely on themselves alone for their country's economic development. "Only a complete idiot could pretend to prove that it is easier to build socialism alone than by using the... support of... peoples who had previously taken the road," he said. Khrushchev held that China's policies were formed by men "who want to bring Stalin's corpse back to life, who do not rely on the ideas of Marxism-Leninism, who want to rely on the axe and the knife."

Communist China's willingness to see the world slip into a nuclear war was assailed by Khrushchev Apr. 6 in a speech to factory workers in Kazincbarcika, near Miskolc. His address included laudatory remarks about U.S. cooperation to keep the peace. Khrushchev, emphasizing that Soviet leaders were for peace and against war, asserted that the same could not be said of Peking's leaders. "The Chinese leaders tell us: If there is a war— so what? Suppose 1/2 of mankind will be destroyed. The other 1/2 will remain. Time will pass, women will again bear children and mankind will be the same number as before. In my opinion, it is not from an excess of brains but from an absence of them that people say such things." referring to Chinese charges that he was "afraid" of a war to advance Communist aims, Khrushchev said: "I would say that only a child and an idiot do not fear war—the child because he cannot yet understand, and the idiot because he has been deprived by God of this possibility." The U.S., Khrushchev said, despite its "predatory" imperialist policies, was not so "deprived of common sense" that it would resort to war. "When it is a question of their own lives, they [U.S. leaders] take things very seriously." Khrushchev said that the last speeches of the late Pres. Kennedy as well as those made subsequently by Pres. Lyndon B. Johnson, State Secy. Dean Rusk and Sen. J.W. Fulbright were "very reasonable." "They did not make these speeches because they feel sympathetic toward communism but from a feeling of realism," he said.

Aid & Friendship for Arabs

Khrushchev again found occasion to show Soviet support of Arab nations against the West and Israel.

Khrushchev visited the United Arab Republic May 9-25 in connection with celebrations marking the completion of the first stage of the Soviet-aided Aswan High Dam project. Addressing the UAR National Assembly May 11, Khrushchev expressed total support for the Arab states in their dispute with the "imperialist" powers and with Israel, which he termed a "stooge of the imperialists." He denounced Israel for its projected diversion of Jordan River waters to irrigate the Negev Desert; he said the project had "robbed Arabs of their own sources of water." He added that the USSR supported the "just demands of the Arab countries that Israel should implement the United Nations resolutions on Palestine." He demanded that Britain withdraw its troops and military bases from the Middle East, but he emphasized that "our [Soviet] armaments will always be available to those struggling for independence and liberty." Khrushchev, visiting a Soviet-built pharmaceutical plant near Cairo May 12, declared: "In the name of the Soviet Union, we shall not be neutral [in disputes between Arabs and imperialist nations]." He added that the USSR had not been neutral when British ex-Prime Min. Anthony Eden had informed him that Britain would "fight by every means to preserve its oil interests" in the Middle East. Imperialism was not invincible, he declared: "You in Egypt were able to twist the British lion's tail."

Khrushchev visited Aswan May 13-16 to inspect the dam project and the surrounding area. Khrushchev and UAR Pres. Gamal Abdel Nasser May 14 set off an explosive charge to open a diversionary channel for the Nile River; this completed the first stage of the $1 billion project, about 2/5 of which was being financed by the USSR. In a speech at a gathering of 5,000 government officials, diplomats and construction workers, Khrushchev called the project a "symbol of peaceful cooperation" in which "the Russian experts worked here hand-in-hand with 30,000 Egyptians." Khrushchev declared in a speech in Aswan May 16 that Arab leaders were overemphasizing "Arab unity and nationalism" instead of stressing "unity with workers of all nations." "To me," Khrushchev said, "an Arab worker is closer than a capitalist in Russia. . . . You speak only of Arab unity. Does that mean we Russians should go home? We are not Arabs."

Soviet agreement to lend the UAR $277 million was announced by Nasser at a farewell dinner for Khrushchev in Cairo May 24. The funds would finance about 10% of the UAR's 2d 5-year plan, starting in 1965. According to Khrushchev, the USSR also planned to give the UAR a steel plant (capacity: one million tons annually) and a 10,000-acre model farm for desert reclamation.

In a joint communique signed by Khrushchev and Nasser May 24, Nasser supported Moscow's stand on "peaceful coexistence," and Khrushchev again supported the Arab states in their dispute with Israel.

Khrushchev had left for the UAR immediately after concluding a series of talks with Algerian Pres. Ahmed Ben Bella, a visitor to the USSR Apr. 25-May 7. On his arrival at Moscow Apr. 25, Ben Bella had expressed gratitude for Soviet aid, particularly a $100 million credit granted by the USSR in 1963. The Soviet government newspaper *Izvestia* reported Apr. 27 that the 2 leaders had reached a complete identity of views on "all problems" discussed by them. Ben Bella accompanied Khrushchev to the Crimea, where the 2 leaders ended their talks May 5. A Soviet-Algerian communique issued in Yalta that day disclosed that the USSR had granted Algeria new long-term credits totaling 115 million rubles for technical assistance in the expansion of its economy. (The projects envisaged included construction of a large metallurgical complex and a technical school with a capacity of 2,000 students. Algerian sources told newsmen in Moscow May 5 that the USSR also had pledged to supply Algeria with small arms.)

Khrushchev Woos Scandinavians

Khrushchev toured Denmark June 16-21, Sweden June 22-27 and Norway June 29-July 4 during a trip that he later described as a useful exercise in "peaceful coexistence" and a stimulus for more trade between the Soviet Union and Scandinavia.

In a speech in Copenhagen, Denmark June 18, Khrushchev predicted major Soviet agricultural advances in the next 7 years and warned that Denmark could not depend much longer on the Soviet Union as a market for farm products. He recommended East Germany and Czechoslovakia as more "permanent stable markets" for agricultural products. He stressed that East Germany was sure to flourish. He said of projected moon flights: "The Americans want to get there first. Let them try. We will benefit from their experience."

Khrushchev asserted at a dinner in his honor at the Stockholm city hall June 23 that the once independent states of Estonia, Lithuania and Latvia were better off as republics of the Soviet Union. He called them nothing but "agricultural and raw-material appendages of the developed capitalist countries" before 1940, when they were incorporated into the Soviet Union. He insisted that industrial production in the 3 republics was 15 times greater currently than in 1940 and that they were progressing faster economically than the rest of the Soviet Union.

Khrushchev Demands Agricultural Improvement

Khrushchev again demanded that Soviet agriculture adopt more efficient methods. He urged the use of techniques such as those used in the U.S., West Germany and other capitalist countries. His demand, made in a memo to the CP Presidium, covered 3 of the 6 pages of the Apr. 23 edition of *Izvestia.* Khrushchev criticized Soviet agriculture as primitive. He said "Agriculture is no place for amateurs who do not know their business," and he urged that unqualified farm administrators be discharged. He conceded that Soviet agricultural research had failed to advance any worthwhile ideas and that the government had no choice but to learn progressive farming methods from capitalistic countries. Khrushchev stressed that the Soviet Union had 39 billion rubles invested in agriculture.

The CP announced Apr. 23 that a commission had been formed to implement Khrushchev's demands. Nikolai V. Podgorny was named commission chairman. Also named to the commission were Pres. Leonid I. Brezhnev, 5 other Presidium members, 7 ministers in charge of farm planning and management, and party and government leaders of the 15 republics. The commission was authorized to recommend improvements in the organization of specialized farms for egg and broiler production, the fattening of hogs and milk production and to organize a nationwide farm education program on modern techniques.

Khrushchev announced Aug. 4, during a visit to wheat farms near the Volga valley town of Yershov, that a meeting of the CP Central Committee had been called for November to take up the USSR's farm problems. Khrushchev suggested that farmers improve their methods of handling various crops. He proposed that farmers be assigned specific plots of land on which they would be responsible for everything. He called such a system a means of spurring farmers' interest in growing larger crops and thereby increasing their pay.

Pravda reported Sept. 15 that the Soviet government had already collected more grain from the 1964 harvest than from the entire harvest of 1963, when there was an exceptionally poor crop. Edwin A. Jaenke, associate administrator of the U.S. Agriculture Department's Stabilization & Conservation Service, confirmed the report on the basis of a 6,000-mile tour he had made of Soviet farm areas as head of a U.S. agricultural team. Jaenke called it unlikely the USSR would need any wheat imports.

Promotion of Atheism Pressed

Pravda reported Mar. 3 that the CP Central Committee had started a nationwide program to promote the abolition of religion in Soviet life and to encourage atheism. The CP's Ideological Commission had arranged for the setting up of an Institute of Scientific Atheism that was to operate within the party's Academy of Social Sciences. Starting in the 1964-5 school year, the institute was to promote the study of atheism in universities and teachers' colleges and in training schools for officials of the CP, Young Communist League and the government. Similar indoctrination programs were to be geared for school children, teachers, doctors, journalists and other education and mass communications workers. The plan envisaged the establishment of atheist action groups in cities with strong religious movements.

Anti-Semitism Attacked

The Soviet CP's Ideological Commission Apr. 4 denounced an anti-religious book ridiculing the Jews. The 193-page paperback volume, *Judaism Without Embellishment,* written in Ukrainian by Trofim K. Kichko, was published in Kiev Oct. 12, 1963 under the auspices of the Academy of Sciences of the Soviet Republic of the Ukraine. It stressed participation by Jews in black marketing and other economic crimes. Cartoons depicted Russian Jews as unpatriotic and morally inferior to other Soviet citizens. The commission's statement, published in *Pravda,* said: The book "may insult the feelings of believers and be interpreted in a spirit of anti-Semitism.... [The book] contradicted the party's Leninist policy on religious and nationality questions and merely feeds anti-Soviet insinuations of our ideological foes, who are trying at all costs to create a so-called Jewish question." Tass, the USSR's official press agency, had criticized the book in a review Mar. 28. The book had been condemned by many foreign groups, including the Communist parties in the U.S., Britain and France.

500 leaders of 24 U.S. Jewish organizations held an emergency conference in Washington Apr. 5-6 to voice their concern at Soviet efforts "to crush the spirit of Soviet Jews and sever their ties" with Judaism. Sen. Jacob K. Javits (R., N.Y.), addressing the conference Apr. 6, called Soviet anti-Semitism a threat to "all religious minorities in the Soviet Union." Supreme Court Justice Arthur J. Goldberg had opened the conference Apr. 5 with a speech charging that Soviet mistreatment of Jews violated worldwide concepts of human rights and dignity, "transgresses the UN Charter, to which the Soviet Union is a party, and violates the Universal Declaration of Human Rights, which is morally binding upon all member states of the United Nations." A fact sheet presented to the delegates Apr. 5 documented among Soviet discriminatory practices against the estimated 3 million Jews in Russia: (1) The closing of 396 of the country's 500 synagogues in the past 7 years, (2) the banning of the publication of Jewish prayer books, bibles and calendars of Jewish religious holidays and (3) the prohibition on emigration.

The International Commission of Jurists in Geneva July 8 condemned the USSR for anti-Semitism. It urged that the Russians reconsider their position. A 45-page study compiled by the commission's staff, helped by "a number of people familiar with conditions in the USSR," expressed hope that "the Soviet authorities" realized "the real and grave injustices which must result" from their anti-Semitic policies. Referring to the trials of Jews in the Soviet Union for economic crimes, the report charged: "Over and over again, the Jews are depicted as the initiators and master minds of the criminal gangs, the non-Jews primarily as the recipients of bribes and as accomplices of Jewish ringleaders." The report speculated that anti-Semitism was "being used by the Soviet authorities as a weapon to render unpopular economic offenses which appear to be rampant." The Jews "have been made the scapegoat for the transgression of those whose guilt it would be dangerous to make public," the study said.

Molotov Faction Expelled from CP

It was confirmed in Moscow Apr. 3 that ex-Foreign Min. Vyacheslav M. Molotov, ex-Premier Georgi M. Malenkov and ex-Deputy Premier Lazar M. Kaganovich had been expelled from the Soviet CP. The expulsions, long reported, were disclosed with the publication by *Pravda* of a speech in which CP Secy. Mikhail A. Suslov had assailed the 3 for their leadership of the 1957 "anti-party plot" against Khrushchev and for their involvement in Stalin's purges of the 1930s. Suslov, whose address was delivered Feb. 14 at a meeting of the CP Central Committee, disclosed the expulsions in a phrase in which he referred to China's efforts to restore the "inhuman practices" of which the 3 were guilty. Why, Suslov asked, did the Chinese party "show such sympathy for people who have been expelled from our party?"

Better Living Standards Planned

Khrushchev recommended, in a 3-1/2-hour speech to the Supreme Soviet July 13, a number of measures to raise Soviet living standards. He announced that the nation's 30 million collective farmers would be eligible for pensions starting in 1965 and that 18 million public service workers, including physicians and teachers, would receive pay raises of as much as 40%. He announced plans for a grain reserve sufficient to cover national needs. He indicated that the 1962 Cuban missile crisis had postponed the entire program for 2 years by forcing the USSR "to strengthen our defenses and to increase expenditures for this purpose." He stressed that the development of the economy and improvement of living standards of the masses were the "most important and most interesting" aims of the government. Khrushchev said that the Chinese Communists, who condemned Soviet policy as a "bourgeois deviation from Marxist ideology, did not know what they were talking about."

Mikoyan Named President

First Deputy Premier Anastas I. Mikoyan, 68, was elected July 15 as chairman of the Presidium of the USSR Supreme Soviet, the equivalent of president of the Soviet Union. Mikoyan succeeded Leonid I. Brezhnev, 58, who relinquished the post to devote himself to his duties as a member of the Secretariat of the CP Central Committee. Brezhnev was considered Khrushchev's chief aide in the Central Committee Secretariat. Mikoyan, a close associate of Khrushchev's in the Soviet government, became the 6th Soviet president.

The nomination was offered by Khrushchev at the concluding meeting of the current session of the Supreme Soviet. In proposing Mikoyan for the post, Khrushchev made it clear that Brezhnev was being freed to concentrate on his party work as a Central Committee secretary. Mikoyan's election was by acclamation of the 1,443 deputies of the Supreme Soviet. The shift was then believed to have enhanced Khrushchev's power by placing his 2 closest associates, Mikoyan and Brezhnev, in the key posts of head of state and deputy party leader.

KHRUSHCHEV'S DOWNFALL

Khrushchev Replaced by Brezhnev & Kosygin

Soviet Premier Nikita S. Khrushchev, 70, was stripped of his leadership roles in both the Soviet government and Soviet Communist Party by the CP Central Committee Oct. 14-15. Khrushchev's unexpected ouster took place with no open disruption of Soviet life. His removal was announced to the outside world in a communique dated Oct. 15 and issued shortly after midnight. His dual role as leader of both the party and the government was divided between 2 successors. Leonid Ilich Brezhnev, 57, was named Oct. 14 as first secretary of the party, the most important post in the Soviet hierarchy. Aleksei Nikolayevich Kosygin, 60, succeeded Khrushchev Oct. 15 as chairman of the Council of Ministers (cabinet), the Soviet equivalent to premier.

During his decade of rule, Khrushchev had been credited with liquidating the system of political terror and forced labor created by the Stalin regime, with orienting the Soviet government toward greater respect for the rights of its citizens, with successful encouragement of Soviet technological progress and with replacing Stalin's cold-war policies with an often-contradictory program based on "peaceful coexistence" with the West.

The new Soviet leadership gave quick assurances that it would continue Khrushchev's domestic and foreign policies. It said, however, that the USSR had returned to "collective rule" and that it would be able to pursue its goals more soberly and with greater stability than was possible under the rule of a single, often emotional, leader.

The announcement of Khrushchev's removal gave no political reasons for the change. It said only that he had asked to be relieved of his party and government responsibilities because of his "advanced age and deterioration of health." The full text of the Soviet announcement:

A plenary meeting of the Central Committee of the CPSU [Communist Party of the Soviet Union] was held on Oct. 14, 1964.

The plenary meeting of the CPSU Central Committee granted Nikita S. Khrushchev's request to be relieved of his duties as the first secretary of the CPSU Central Committee, member of the Presidium of the CPSU Central Committee, and chairman of the Council of Ministers of the USSR in view of his advanced age and deterioration of his health.

The plenum of the CPSU Central Committee elected Leonid I. Brezhnev first secretary of the CPSU Central Committee.

* * *

The Presidium of the USSR Supreme Soviet met on Oct. 15 this year with Comrade Anastas I. Mikoyan, president of the Presidium of the USSR Supreme Soviet, in the chair.

The Presidium of the USSR Supreme Soviet discussed the question of chairman of the USSR Council of Ministers.

The Presidium of the USSR Supreme Soviet granted the request of Nikita Sergeyevich Khrushchev that he be relieved of the duties of chairman of the USSR Council of Ministers in view of his advanced age and deterioration of health.

The Presidium of the USSR Supreme Soviet appointed Comrade Aleksei Nikolayevich Kosygin as chairman of the USSR Council of Ministers, releasing him from his duties of first vice Chairman of the USSR Council of Ministers.

The decrees by the Presidium of the USSR Supreme Soviet on the relief of Comrade Nikita S. Khrushchev of his duties as chairman of the USSR Council of Ministers and on the appointment of Comrade Aleksei N. Kosygin as chairman of the USSR Council of Ministers were adopted unanimously by the members of the Presidium of the USSR Supreme Soviet.

The members of the Presidium of the USSR Supreme Soviet warmly congratulated Comrade Aleksei N. Kosygin on his appointment to the post of chairman of the USSR Council of Ministers.

Comrade Aleksei N. Kosygin heartily thanked the Central Committee of the Communist Party of the Soviet Union and the Presidium of the USSR Supreme Soviet for the confidence shown him and gave the assurance that he would do his utmost to discharge his duties.

New Regime States Aims

The first public statement of the new regime's aims—and the first public indication of the reasons for Khrushchev's removal—were given in an editorial published Oct. 17 in the CP newspaper *Pravda*. Without mentioning Khrushchev by name, it attacked him for "harebrained scheming" and "hasty decisions." It indicated that the USSR would both continue to seek peace with the West and begin to work for the reconstruction of Soviet-bloc ideological and political unity. The references to Soviet-bloc unity were thought to imply that new efforts would be made, particularly at a world Communist Congress scheduled for 1965, to heal the split with Communist China. The editorial described the new regime as a return to "collective leadership... the greatest political asset of our party." The *Pravda* editorial said:

The general line of the party in the sphere of foreign policy is the struggle for peace and international security, the application of the principle of peaceful coexistence between states with a differing social order, advanced by V. I. Lenin....

Our party regards it as its duty to do its utmost to safeguard the peaceful labor of the people, to avert a world thermonuclear war, to set a course towards a solution of international disputes through negotiations, to improve and develop the relations with all countries in the interests of peace, to develop international cooperation in the sphere of the economy, science and technology....

The world Socialist system, the community of equal and sovereign peoples, advancing along the road of socialism and communism, are the greatest achievement of the international revolutionary movement. The CPSU and the entire Soviet people regard as their duty the development of fraternal relations with the Socialist countries, extensive cooperation in all spheres of economic, sociopolitical and cultural life....

Our party, as hitherto, will pursue an active line for the convocation of an international meeting of all Communist parties to discuss problems of the struggle for peace, democracy, national independence and socialism, for the consolidation of the unity of proletarian internationalism....

The monolithic unity of the party and its unflinching loyalty to Lenin's behests were demonstrated with new force by the plenary meeting of the Central Committee of the CPSU held on Oct. 14....

The Leninist party is an enemy of subjectivism and drifting in Communist construction, harebrained scheming, immature conclusions and hasty decisions and actions divorced from reality. Bragging and phrase-mongering, commandism, unwillingness to take into account the achievements of science and practical experience are alien to it....

The life and activity of the party are determined by the principles and standards which were worked out by V. I. Lenin, tested, confirmed and enriched by the historical experience of many decades. Collective leadership is one of the most important of these principles, a well tried weapon, the greatest political asset of our party....

It is only on the basis of the Leninist principle of collective leadership that it is possible to direct and develop the growing creative initiative of the party and all people. It is only on the basis of this principle that it is possible to analyze the situation correctly, to evaluate the successes achieved soberly, objectively, without conceit, to see the shortcomings and eliminate them in time and completely....

In a speech in honor of 3 Soviet cosmonauts at a Red Square rally Oct. 19, Brezhnev emphasized collective leadership, peace and Soviet-bloc unity as the central policies of the USSR's new rulers. The leading members of the new Soviet administration appeared together publicly for the first time at the rally for the cosmonauts, who had orbited the earth in a spaceship Oct. 12-13. Standing in a row on the reviewing balcony atop Lenin's Tomb were Brezhnev, Kosygin, Anastas I. Mikoyan, Mikhail A. Suslov and Nikolai V. Podgorny, members of the Soviet CP Presidium who were believed to have played key roles in Khrushchev's ouster. Although the principal address at the rally was delivered by Brezhnev, the theme of the rally was "collective leadership." Innumerable banners proclaimed the collective achievements of the Soviet people and its CP; none referred to a single leader. Portraits of the 5 prominent members of the new regime, however, were displayed throughout the city, and Brezhnev's portrait consistently preceded those of the other 4. In his speech at the rally Brezhnev said:

Comrades, among the crew of the *Voskhod* spaceship were a Communist, a Komsomol [Communist Youth League member] and a nonparty man. This was like a small cell of our society in outer space. They have cooperated closely and purposefully. That is how our entire people live and work, united in a single multi-million collective behind the Communist Party and the Soviet government. And therein lies the strength of our society, the mainspring of all its victories....

The foreign policy of the Soviet Union is predicated on the Leninist principles of the peaceful coexistence of states with different social systems, tireless struggle for the consolidation of peace, for friendship and cooperation among nations, for the further relaxation of international tension....

Our party will strive for the strengthening of the unity of the great community of the fraternal Socialist countries on a fully equal footing and on the basis of correct combination of the common interests of the Socialist community with the interests of the people of each country, the development of an all-sided cooperation between the Socialist states, in our common struggle for peace and socialism....

Johnson Discusses Leadership Shift

U.S. Pres. Lyndon B. Johnson sought to explain to the American people in a nationwide TV-radio address Oct. 18 the meaning of the shift of power in the Kremlin. Acknowledging that "we do not know exactly what happened to Nikita Khrushchev," Mr. Johnson said: "We do know that he has been forced out of power by his former friends and colleagues. 5 days ago he had only praise in Moscow. Today we learn only of his faults." The President said Khrushchev had been "guilty of dangerous adventure[s]" in foreign affairs. But the former Soviet leader, Mr. Johnson pointed out, had "learned from his mistakes," and "in the last 2 years his government had shown itself aware of the need for sanity in the nuclear age." As examples of Russian actions favoring peace, Mr. Johnson mentioned Soviet agreements on the nuclear test-ban treaty, the Moscow-Washington "hot-line" pact and the fact that space had been kept free of nuclear weapons. "We do not think" that "it was these actions that led to his removal," the President declared.

Mr. Johnson said that to Americans the Soviet government upheaval "means at least 4 things: "First, . . . the men in the Kremlin remain dedicated Communists. A time of trouble among Communists requires steady vigilance among free men—and most of all among Americans. . . . 2d, there will be turmoil in the Communist world. . . . 3d, this great change will not stop the forces in Eastern Europe that are working for greater independence. Those forces will continue to have our sympathy. . . . 4th, our own course must continue to prove that we . . . are ready to get on with the work of peace."

The President said that at a meeting in the White House Oct. 17 with Soviet Amb. Anatole Dobrynin, the Soviet government had "officially informed" him "that it plans no change in basic foreign policy."

(In assessing the Soviet power shift, ex-Pres. Dwight D. Eisenhower said in Gettysburg Oct. 20 that Soviet economic failures was a possible reason for Khrushchev's downfall. "The lack of consumer goods," he said, "and the fact that they had to buy . . . from the free world a lot of wheat, that may have had something to do with this.")

How Khrushchev Was Overthrown

Western sources in Moscow reported that Khrushchev's ouster appeared to have been meticulously prepared but that the final move against him apparently had not been undertaken until Oct. 12, while the then-premier vacationed at his villa outside Gagra, near Sochi, on the USSR's Black Sea coast.

Khrushchev had gone to Gagra Sept. 30 for what he apparently had intended to be a brief and routine respite from his official duties. While there, he received visitors and continued to participate in Soviet public affairs. The day the coup was believed to have been launched—Oct. 12—Khrushchev was televised as he spoke by radio with the 3 Soviet cosmonauts sent into orbit earlier that day. He was seen by millions as he congratulated the cosmonauts and promised to welcome them on their return to Moscow. Soviet Pres. Mikoyan was with him and was introduced to the cosmonauts by Khrushchev with the prophetic quip: "Here is Comrade Mikoyan. He is literally pulling the telephone from my hands...."

All the members of the Presidium of the CP Central Committee with the exception of Khrushchev and Mikoyan were in Moscow that day (Oct. 12). Brezhnev had returned Oct. 11 from a visit to East Germany. Other Presidium members had also converged on Moscow, Podgorny came back from Moldavia, and Nikolai M. Shvernik showed up after an absence of 3 months. The Presidium reportedly began discussion that day of proposals that Khrushchev be replaced. According to the *N.Y. Times,* by early Oct. 13 it had reached a firm decision to remove him. Mikoyan, who had left Gagra shortly after his televised conversation with Khrushchev and the cosmonauts, reportedly returned to Moscow late Oct. 12 or early Oct. 13 and was given an ultimatum to cooperate. He agreed and became the group's spokesman in its ouster of Khruschev. The Presidium called a meeting of the CP Central Committee for Oct. 13 to ratify its decision.

Khrushchev, still apparently unaware of the moves against him, was scheduled to spend Oct. 13 in Gagra conferring with Gaston Palewski, visiting French state minister for atomic and space research. Palewski met with Khrushchev, but their talks were cut short when Khrushchev received a message and excused himself, saying that he had to return to Moscow to deal with a matter involving the USSR's new cosmonauts. Khrushchev immediately flew to Moscow, arriving in the capital the afternoon of Oct. 13. (According to some rumors, Khrushchev already was under guard and returned to Moscow in the company of 5 secret policemen.) He was said to have gone directly to the Kremlin, where he was met by the other members of the Presidium and informed of their action against him.

The key confrontation between Khrushchev and his opponents was reported to have taken place at the Central Committee meeting begun later Oct. 13. The session, at which Khrushchev presided, was said to have been opened with a 5-hour denunciation of Khrushchev by Mikhail A. Suslov, considered the party's chief ideologist. Although Suslov was reported to have devoted himself to Khrushchev's alleged mishandling of foreign and Soviet-bloc affairs, particularly in the widening rift with Communist China, he was also said to have attacked Khrushchev personally, charging him with nepotism and the creation of a new type of "personality cult." Khrushchev defended himself against the charges. Speaking immediately after Suslov, probably early Oct. 14, he was said to have denounced his attackers in abusive language. Some reports described Khrushchev as insulting virtually the entire membership of the Central Committee, and the violence of his speech was reported to have hardened the opposition to him. Khrushchev's address was said to have been followed by one in which Dmitri S. Polyansky attacked him for his failure to solve the USSR's economic and agricultural problems.

The Central Committee vote depriving Khrushchev of his post of first secretary and his membership on the Presidium was reported to have been taken early Oct. 14. Khrushchev was said to have accepted the outcome. His associates then, by unanimous vote, elected Brezhnev his successor as party first secretary.

The Presidium of the Supreme Soviet was convened the following day, Oct. 15, to complete the shift by removing Khrushchev from his governmental duties. With Mikoyan presiding, the Presidium ratified the ouster of Khrushchev as premier and the election of Kosygin to succeed him.

It was reported from Moscow Oct. 16-19 that Khrushchev apparently was under house arrest.

Some of Khrushchev's close personal aides, particularly those responsible for publicity and propaganda, were removed from office with him. Aleksei I. Adzhubei, 40, Khrushchev's son-in-law, was dismissed Oct. 16 as editor of the Soviet government newspaper *Izvestia*. Vladimir I. Stepakov was named to replace him. (*Izvestia*'s regular evening edition had failed to appear Oct. 15, and this had been taken as a clue that a major Soviet government announcement was forthcoming. *Izvestia* occasionally had been delayed so that events of major importance would be announced simultaneously by it and the CP organ, *Pravda,* a morning newspaper.) Mikhail A. Kharlamov was dismissed Oct. 17 as chairman of the USSR State Committee for Radio & Television. He was replaced by Nikolai N. Mesyatsev. 3 members of Khrushchev's personal staff were reported to have been dismissed Oct. 16: Oleg A. Troyanovsky, son of a former Soviet ambassador to the U.S., Khrushchev's English translator and informal expert on American affairs; Vladimir S. Lebedev, chief of Khrushchev's personal secretariat; Aleksandr Shuisky, his personal adviser on agricultural affairs.

Communists Deny Existence of 'Indictment'

Foreign Communist correspondents in Moscow Oct. 31 denied reports that an official listing of the charges against Khrushchev had been circulated in Soviet government and Communist Party circles. The purported document, whose existence had been reported by Western correspondents the previous day, had been described as a 29-point "indictment" of Khrushchev for violating Soviet practices while he ruled the USSR. Western newsmen reported that the document had been distributed to Soviet officials responsible for explaining Khrushchev's dismissal to party and government groups and to the foreign Communist delegations that had come to Moscow to seek clarification of the events leading to his ouster. The document was said to have been based on the accusatory speeches made against Khrushchev by Suslov and Polyansky at the CP Central Committee meeting at which Khrushchev had been deposed.

Despite the denials of the document's existence, it appeared that a written summary of the charges against Khrushchev had been distributed in Communist circles. The foreign Communist newsmen who denied that such a "document" existed admitted that a written listing of about 29 major reasons for Khrushchev's ouster had been circulated to Soviet ideological workers. One of the Communist correspondents in Moscow, Augusto Pancaldi of the Italian CP newspaper *L'Unita,* reported Oct. 31 that the "document" mentioned by Western newsmen had been compiled from oral explanations given CP organizations on the Khrushchev ouster.

All accounts of the charges listed against Khrushchev agreed, however, that he had been accused of these major errors in his rule of the USSR and his conduct of Communist policy:

(1) He had been guilty of undignified behavior, creation of a new "cult of personality" and nepotism, especially in his advancement of his son-in-law, former *Izvestia* editor Adzhubei. (Khrushchev was rumored to have been rebuffed by the Central Committee in an attempt to elevate Adzhubei to the CP Secretariat.)

(2) He had violated Soviet norms of collective leadership, ruling capriciously and often making major policy pledges for the USSR without consulting the Presidium.

(3) He had disorganized Soviet industry by ignoring scientific facts, formulating unrealistic plans and imposing contradictory measures for centralization and decentralization.

(4) He had disorganized Soviet agriculture by pressing the virgin lands development scheme in Siberia and then demanding intensive farming of cultivated areas.

(5) He had made serious errors in Soviet foreign policy, particularly with respect to Cuba and the 1956 Suez crisis.

(6) He had permitted the USSR's ideological differences with Communist China to divide the 2 countries, split the Soviet bloc and degenerate into a personal feud with Chinese leaders.

Foreign Communists Vary in Views on Ouster

World Communist reaction to the Kremlin shake-up ranged from outright approval by Communist China, Bulgaria and Albania to reserve and skepticism and to praise for Khrushchev by Communist leaders and parties in East and West Europe.

The leaders of Communist China, long engaged in an ideological dispute with Khrushchev's leadership, sent to the USSR's new rulers Oct. 16 a message extending "warm greetings." The message, signed by CP Chrmn. Mao Tse-tung, Pres. Liu Shao-chi, Marshal Chu Teh and Premier Chou En-lai, called it "our sincere wish that" the new Soviet leaders "will achieve new successes... in all fields and in the struggle for the defense of world peace." The Bulgarian CP's Central Committee Oct. 18 officially approved the Soviet government change-over. It was the only East European CP to do so.

Albania hailed Khrushchev's loss of power as "a heavy blow" to U.S. imperialists and to "the modern revisionists who are faithfully serving their purposes." Albania, a close ally of Communist China in the ideological dispute, had opposed

Khrushchev and had accused him of plotting to overthrow its regime. Yugoslav Pres. Tito Oct. 17 congratulated the new Soviet CP leader, Brezhnev, and expressed the hope that "friendly...relations...between our parties and countries will continue and develop in the common interest." The Yugoslav CP newspaper *Borba* Oct. 17 reprinted *Pravda*'s Oct. 16 editorial report on Khrushchev but deleted a reference to Khrushchev as a "harebrained" schemer and braggart.

Polish CP leader Wladyslaw Gomulka and Hungarian Premier Janos Kadar, who was visiting Warsaw, proposed Oct. 17 that a world Communist meeting be convened to restore Communist unity. Gomulka lauded Khrushchev for his "immense achievements" in building Soviet power and in the "struggle for peace." Asserting that there were "many reasons" for the Soviet power shift, Gomulka said it had a "purely internal character." Kadar said Oct. 18 that Khrushchev had "very great merits in the fight against Stalin's personality cult and in the maintenance of peace." The Hungarian people, who had welcomed Khrushchev on a recent visit to their country "as the tireless fighter for peace," "did well in so doing and need have no afterthoughts about it," Kadar declared.

A statement drawn up by the East German Politburo Oct. 17 and released Oct. 18 said: "The news of the release of...Khrushchev['s] functions has caused deep emotion within our party and our peoples." The statement urged Moscow's new leadership to press "for the honorable fulfillment" of the Soviet-East German friendship pact signed June 12.

Italian CP Secy. Gen. Luigi Longo declared in a speech in Milan Oct. 18 that "the manner in which this change at the summit of the Soviet party and state occurred leaves us preoccupied and critical." He said the shift indicated "that the process toward...free debate inside the Communist movement is still slow and uncertain." Pietro Ingras, regarded as Longo's rival for leadership of the Italian CP, said in a Venice speech Oct. 18: "We ask to know the political debate that led to the substitution of Khrushchev."

A statement by the Czechoslovak CP Oct. 18 said it had learned of Khrushchev's ouster "with surprise and emotion." It expressed approval of Khrushchev's "struggle to accomplish the policy of peaceful coexistence" and his "disclosure of the erroneous methods in the period of the cult of personality."

U.S. CP leader Gus Hall said in New York Oct. 18 that Khrushchev may have been deposed for his "methods of work and certain personality traits" and "certain quick decisions." Hall commended Khrushchev for his "historic contribution for world peace."

Asserting that Khrushchev had played a "big, positive part" in the quest for peace and peaceful coexistence, the British CP said Oct. 20 that the "explanation of the [Soviet] changes so far given does not remove the natural concern felt by Communists abroad about this development."

The French CP's Politburo Oct. 21 demanded "more complete information and necessary explanations concerning the conditions and the methods under which the changes decided by the Central Committee of the Communist Party of the Soviet Union were carried out." But the French Communists expressed satisfaction with the new Soviet leadership's reaffirmation of the "Leninist policy of peaceful co-existence..., the consolidation of world peace, of friendship between peoples and strengthening of unity and cohesion in the international Communist movement."

While the world's Communist parties accepted Khrushchev's ouster, many of them, especially the European ones, were critical of the method of transition and of what seemed to be excessive secrecy surrounding its details. The reaction of the foreign parties was believed to reflect disquiet at the sudden shift and at the new leadership's repeated assertions of its intentions to restore Soviet-bloc unity. Khrushchev had been credited with ending the USSR's Stalin-era domination of foreign Communist groups.

The new Soviet regime Oct. 24 made its first major move to deal with foreign Communist disquiet over the ousters. Tass announced that Kosygin and Brezhnev had gone to the Belovezhskaya Forest district of northeastern Poland in "the last few days" to confer with Polish CP First Secy. Gomulka, in the past one of Khrushchev's main supporters among the USSR's East European satellite leaders. Also attending the Belovezhskaya meeting were Polish Premier Jozef Cyrankiewicz and Yuri V. Andropov, Soviet CP Central Committee secretary responsible for relations with foreign Communist parties. Gomulka announced Oct. 28 that his meetings with Kosygin and Brezhnev had "convinced" him that there were "justified grounds" for Khrushchev's ouster and that the Soviet leadership changes "took place according to Leninist principles of internal party democracy." Gomulka's statement, backing the new Soviet CP leadership, was made in Warsaw at a Mongolian-Polish friendship rally in honor of visiting Mongolian CP First Secy. Yumzhagin Tsedenbal. Gomulka confirmed at the rally that Khrushchev had presided at the Soviet CP Central Committee meeting at which he had been deposed. The discussions held by the Soviet and Polish CP leaders had disclosed "full unanimity" of views between the 2 parties, Gomulka declared. He expressed "full satisfaction" with the Soviet assurances "that the general line of the Soviet party as defined by the 20th and 22d Soviet party congresses will be upheld, and that it fully agrees with our [the Polish] party, our government, our country."

In an apparent confirmation that the Soviet-Chinese rift was a major cause of Krushchev's downfall, Gomulka urged the leaders of the Soviet and Chinese Communist parties to "undertake the needed and necessary steps" to reestablish international Communist "unity." "Only imperialism...utilizes the rift," he asserted, and "the biggest responsibility" for reestablishing unity "lies with the Soviet Union and China."

Reports from Moscow said Oct. 27 that the new Soviet leaders were planning to meet with Hungarian CP First Secy. Kadar, who had stated his misgivings at Khrushchev's abrupt dismissal. A statement published Oct. 25 by the Hungarian Central Committee had expressed "understanding" of the need for Khrushchev's ouster but had repeated Kadar's praise of Khrushchev as a leader of "significant merit in his fight for peace and his fight for international security."

Several Western European Communist parties sent delegations to Moscow to demand that the new Soviet leaders explain their action against Khrushchev. The first of the Western groups, a delegation sent by the French CP, arrived in Moscow Oct. 24 and began talks with Soviet officials the following day. The orders given the French group by its leaders were specific; according to a statement published by the French CP Oct. 21, the delegation was to seek "necessary explanations" on the "conditions and methods" of the dismissal of Khrushchev and his replacement by Brezhnev and Kosygin. French CP Secy. Georges Marchais, a member of the delegation, said Nov. 8 that French CP leaders were satisfied that Khrushchev had been removed primarily because he refused to consult with his colleagues and made hasty decisions that resulted in failures.

An Italian CP delegation returned to Rome Nov. 3 and said it had not been satisfied by the reasons it had received for Khrushchev's ouster. The leader of the delegation, Enrico Berlinguer, declared that the explanation given the delegates "did not seem to us sufficient to make us abandon the reservations that our party has expressed concerning the method followed in informing public opinion" of Khrushchev's ouster. He said Brezhnev had given satisfactory assurances that the USSR would retain its policies of peaceful coexistence. "But," he added, "on the forms and methods of development of the democratic life and political debate in Soviet society, our previous evaluations and Togliatti's memorandum showed that, on various aspects, our positions do not coincide with those of the Soviet comrades." The "Togliatti memorandum" referred to by Berlinguer on his return from Moscow had been published by the Italian CP Sept. 4, after the death of Palmiro Togliatti, who had been the Italian CP's first secretary. It had excited widespread debate in Soviet and Western circles by its outspoken criticism of the the USSR for its clumsy handling of world problems, especially the growing Soviet split with Red China, its efforts to prevent the growth of freedom in Soviet-bloc and Western Communist Parties and its continued toleration of Stalinist practices in Soviet life.

The 4,500-word memo declared that every Communist party should be free "to act in an autonomous manner" relevant to its national problems and without submission to central control. It criticized then-Premier Khrushchev's plans for a December Moscow conference of 26 Communist parties, called to prepare joint action against Communist China's ideological dissidence. It made clear, however, that the Italian CP rejected the "unbridled and shameful campaign" conducted by Peking.

U Thant Asks for Public Accounting of Ouster

UN Secy. Gen. U Thant Oct. 22 added his voice to those demanding an explanation of the circumstances of the shift in Soviet leadership. Speaking at a UN news conference, Thant, after praising Khrushchev's contributions to world stability, said: "I think that it would be helpful and even desirable if Mr. Khrushchev were able or inclined to make a public statement on the circumstances leading to his exit." Thant said that his "personal assessment" of Khrushchev was public knowledge. "I still believe," he said, "that he will be long remembered as a man who tried his best to implement the principle of peaceful co-existence and ... did so with some success in that he had been able to convince a considerable segment of public opinion in the West of his sincerity."

Thant said that he had met both Brezhnev and Kosygin and considered them capable and respected Soviet leaders. "Both Mr. Brezhnev and Mr. Kosygin," he said, "have a realistic appraisal of the world situation, and it is unlikely that they will reverse the course of history by taking the Soviet Union back to the pre-1953 [Stalin] era." Thant said that Soviet Amb.-to-UN Nikolai T. Fedorenko had assured him formally Oct. 16 of the continuity of Soviet foreign policy.

AFTERMATH OF KHRUSHCHEV'S OUSTER

Brezhnev Outlines Aims

Delegations representing every Communist state except Albania began arriving in Moscow en masse Nov. 5 to attend celebrations of the 47th anniversary Nov. 7 of the Bolshevik Revolution. Among the visiting Red leaders was Communist Chinese Premier Chou En-lai. Chou and the other Communist dignitaries conferred separately with Brezhnev, Kosygin and their associates.

The foreign Communist delegations joined Soviet leaders in a Kremlin meeting Nov. 6. The principal address of the evening, a strong restatement of the new Soviet government's hope for political and ideological unity among the Communist nations, was delivered by Brezhnev.

Brezhnev reviewed domestic Soviet problems, dwelling particularly on the need to reorganize the economy and stimulate farm and industrial output to fulfill the state's promise of constant betterment of living standards. "We know," he said, "that the quality of many goods we manufacture is below the level of the best and that the supply of goods and services for the people is far from satisfactory." In a presumed reference to Khrushchev, he said: "Experience has shown ... that wherever the scientific approach is replaced by subjectivism and arbitrary decisions, failure is certain and mistakes inevitable." The Soviet government and CP "regard it as their duty to carry out certain measures to improve economic management, and they are doing it cautiously and without any fuss or hurry."

Indicating the nature of the changes under study for Soviet industry and agriculture, Brezhnev added: "Today, as never before, there is an obvious need to apply extensively economic incentives for the development of production. Economic stimuli must encourage enterprises to make better use of their production funds, to use raw materials and semi-manufactured goods economically, to get new machinery running more quickly, to improve the goods produced and to raise the productivity of labor at every factory. The country's requirements in foodstuffs and raw materials are steadily increasing. This growth insistently suggests to us the task of overcoming the lag in agricultural production. We shall continue stepping up capital investments in agriculture and in the industries that supply it with machines and fertilizers. Fuller use of the principle of the material incentive of collective farms and collective farmers acquires special importance. It is necessary ... to provide collective farms and state farms with greater rights in organizing and planning their work."

Brezhnev disclosed that Soviet CP leaders planned to reverse Khrushchev's policies of full farm collectivization and intended to concentrate more on private farming and private ownership of livestock. "Farm production still falls short of the growing requirements of our society," Brezhnev said. "It would be wrong to disregard the potential of private plots cultivated by collective farmers, industrial workers and office employes to satisfy their personal requirements. Unwarranted limitations have been imposed in this sphere in recent years, despite the fact that economic conditions have not been ripe for such a step. These limitations have now been removed." Brezhnev cited the high productivity of private producers of potatoes (more than 60% of national output), vegetables (45%) and animal products (41% of the USSR's meat, 47% of its milk). Small private garden plots (comprising perhaps 3% of the USSR's cultivated land) produced 33% of gross agricultural output, including almost half of the total output of livestock products.

Even before Brezhnev's speech, a decree issued in the Ukraine had restored private holdings that were allowed until 1956, when Khrushchev began a campaign to encourage collective farms over private ones. A decree in Estonia annulled limitations on the size of private plots and on livestock holdings.

(The Communist Youth League newspaper *Komsomolskaya Pravda* Nov. 19 accused leaders of the Academy of Agricultural Sciences and officials of the Agriculture Ministry of trying to build a "Lysenko cult" around biologist Trofim D. Lysenko's theories of agricultural genetics. *Literaturnaya Gazeta,* organ of the Union of Soviet Writers, charged Lysenko Nov. 24 with having been responsible for "colossal harm" to Soviet agriculture.)

CP Hierarchy Reorganized

Major changes in the composition of the Soviet Communist Party Presidium and in the CP's organization at the regional and district levels were announced in Moscow Nov. 17. The changes had been debated and approved by the CP Central Committee Nov. 16 at its first meeting since the session at which it had deposed Khrushchev. The shifts in CP leadership and organization were part of the reshaping of the Soviet hierarchy begun by Brezhnev and Kosygin following Khrushchev's ouster.

The Moscow announcement reported that the Central Committee had elected 2 full members and one alternate member to fill 3 vacancies existing in the 18-man (12 members, 6 alternates) CP Presidium, the Central Committee's policy-making body. The first vacancy had been caused by the death May 17 of Presidium member Otto V. Kuusinen; the 2d resulted from Khrushchev's departure from the Presidium Oct. 14, and the 3d resulted from the resignation Nov. 16, for health reasons, of Frol R. Kozlov. Partly paralyzed by a stroke in 1963, Kozlov also resigned Nov. 16 as a Central Committee secretary.

Named full members of the CP Presidium were: Aleksandr N. Shelepin, 46, a deputy premier, Central Committee secretary and chairman of the CP's Committee on Party & State Control; Pyotr Y. Shelest, 56, first secretary of the Ukrainian CP and an alternate member of the Presidium since Dec. 1963. The Presidium's new alternate member was Pyotr N. Demichev, 46, a Central Committee secretary and former first secretary of the

Moscow city CP organization. (Shelepin's was regarded as the most significant of the 3 promotions; the former chairman of the USSR's cabinet-level Committee on State Security [controlling body of the Soviet secret police], Shelepin was said to have played a key role in the moves to oust Khrushchev.)

The regional and district-level reorganization of the CP decreed by the Central Committee Nov. 16 abolished the dual system of party organs created by Khrushchev in 1962, when separate local organizations were set up to deal with agriculture and industry.

The Moscow announcement said that the Central Committee had decided: (1) "To restore in regions and territories, where party organizations were divided into industrial and rural ones, single regional and territorial party organizations, uniting all Communists of a region or territory, employed both in industry and in agricultural production." (2) To "reorganize the party committees of... collective-farm and state-farm directorates into district party committees, vesting them with the leadership of all party organizations... of the given district." (3) "To hold, in Dec. 1964, in all territories and regions where single... party committees are to be restored, party conferences for the election of corresponding party bodies."

Vasily I. Polyakov, who had been chairman of the Central Committee's Bureau of Agriculture and was considered to have been one of Khrushchev's chief advisers on farm problems, was dismissed as a Central Committee secretary.

Western observers in Moscow reported Nov. 17 that CP Presidium member Podgorny apparently had been given chief responsibility for carrying out the planned reorganization and restaffing of subsidiary CP organizations. It was reported that this would make Podgorny the unquestioned superior of Premier Kosygin and 2d only to Brezhnev in the new Soviet leadership. Podgorny's new duties were those that had been performed by Brezhnev when he served as Khrushchev's chief aide in the Central Committee. They had then been performed by Kozlov until he suffered his stroke.

Pavel A. Satyukov, editor of the Soviet CP newspaper *Pravda* since 1956, was relieved of his post Nov. 13 and replaced by Aleksei M. Rumyantsev, 59, a political economist.

An editorial in the Dec. 6 issue of *Pravda* said the party's future role in Soviet affairs would be limited to "political guidance." In obvious criticism of Khrushchev's direct control of government agencies, the editorial declared: "This not only ... opens the way for errors and one-sided decisions, but it paralyzes the work of officials who are fully empowered and competent to solve concrete questions." It urged the "correct selection, promotion and disposition" of factory managers who could set production goals, wages and prices with guidance from central planners. High party and government leaders, it held, should be restricted largely to dealing with key political problems.

The Supreme Soviet Dec. 11 formally and unanimously ratified a resolution, presented by Brezhnev, approving the Supreme Soviet Presidium's Oct. 15 ouster of Khrushchev as premier and the naming of Kosygin to the post. The resolution "allowed" Khrushchev's "release" for "reason of advancing age and deteriorating health." The Supreme Soviet Dec. 13 unanimously named Brezhnev president of the drafting committee for a new constitution, Khrushchev's last remaining government post. (The AP had reported Oct. 29 that Khrushchev was living on pension in a 4-room apartment located only a block from his former Kremlin office. The building, at 3 Granovsky St., also was the official residence of Premier Kosygin, ex-Foreign Min. Vyacheslav M. Molotov and ex-Defense Min. Georgi Zhukov. Khrushchev was said to be receiving a 1,000-ruble monthly pension.)

(Tass reported Nov. 28 that Marshal Matvei V. Zakharov, 66, who had been dismissed by Khrushchev in Mar. 1963 as armed forces chief of staff, had been restored to that post, the 3d-ranking one in the Russian military hierarchy; he replaced Marshal Sergei S. Biryuzov, killed in a plane crash near Belgrade Oct. 19. Dinmukhamed A. Kunayev, who had been ousted by Khrushchev Dec. 26, 1962 as first secretary of the Kazakhstan Republic CP, was restored to that post Dec. 7. Konstantin G. Pysin, 54, whom Khrushchev had dismissed Mar. 8, 1963 as Soviet agriculture minister, was named Dec. 19 as first deputy premier of the Russian Republic; he replaced Leonid I. Maksimov.)

Budget & Economic Goals Disclosed

The 1965 budget and an accompanying economic plan to benefit consumers were presented to the Supreme Soviet Dec. 9, and both were approved unanimously by the 1,443 delegates. The budget, introduced by Finance Min. Vasily F. Garbuzov, called for expenditures of 99.4 billion rubles and estimated revenues of 99.6 billion rubles. Expenditures of 91.3 billion rubles had been budgeted for 1964, but actual 1964 expenditures were estimated at 92.8 billion rubles and revenues at 93.8 billion. Military expenditures were reduced by 500 million rubles to 12.8 billion rubles in the 1965 budget, as compared with 1964's 13.3 billion rubles. The cut had been 600 million rubles between the 1963 and 1964 budgets. Kosygin told the Supreme Soviet Dec. 9 that the military budget had been cut after U. S. officials had promised that the U.S. also would reduce its military budget.

Kosygin, discussing the budget and economic plan in a speech before the Supreme Soviet Dec. 9, pledged higher wages, lower prices, more consumer goods in stores and a continued narrowing of the growth gap between heavy industry and consumer-oriented production. He emphasized the people's welfare as of "paramount importance" for the next 5 years. Kosygin predicted changes in planning and economic management under which production would respond to market demand rather than to orders from planning authorities. He called for expansion in the Soviet market for Western goods and increased production and export of Soviet goods. Kosygin said the government was planning a 7.3% rise in real incomes, compared with a 3.9% rise in 1964. The growth rate of consumer goods was planned at 7.7% and of heavy industry at 8.2%. Kosygin deplored the fact that the overall growth rate for 1964 was only 7.8%, the lowest rate since the postwar switch to peacetime industry.

Kosygin pledged that: (a) 78% of the budget's 6.6 billion-ruble increase in expenditures would be used to improve comsumer goods and services; (b) consumer and public services would be increased by as much as 50%; (c) the government would build a record volume of housing (84 million square meters); (d) prices would be reduced on surplus shoes and clothing; (e) consumers would be treated more courteously; (f) industrial managers would be asked to produce better consumer goods; (g) housewives would receive more refrigerators; (h) salesmen would receive commissions; (i) collective farmers would be given more authority over individual crops; more money would be allotted for agricultural expansion; (j) taxes on collective farmers would be reduced.

A government decree published in early December in *Trud,* the labor union newspaper, had directed agencies to improve designs and require better construction for cooperative apartments and ordered local agencies to provide more land for cooperative apartments and to make payment terms easier. Another government decree, designed to base the production of consumer goods on market demand, provided for special cut-price stores in a move to cut down on inventories of low-quality, over-priced or outmoded consumer goods.

Sino-Soviet Dispute Renewed

Communist Chinese attacks on Soviet leadership, suspended following Khrushchev's ouster, were resumed Nov. 20, just a week after a Chinese delegation visited the new USSR leaders in Moscow. *Hung Chi,* the ideological journal of the Chinese CP's Central Committee, renewed the polemical exchange in an editorial charging that Soviet foreign and ideological policies remained a "revisionist" deviation despite Khrushchev's removal. Hailing Khrushchev's ouster as a victory for Peking's policies, the newspaper warned against those who promote "Khrushchevism without Khrushchev." It again criticized the USSR's "peaceful coexistence" policy with the West. It assailed the French and Italian Communist parties for having supported Khrushchev's thesis that power could be attained without violent revolution. *Hung Chi* also attacked CP leaders Wladyslaw Gomulka of Poland, Janos Kadar of Hungary and Walter Ulbricht of East Germany for having praised Khrushchev's programs. *Hung Chi* challenged Moscow's Oct. 16 communique, which had attributed Khrushchev's removal to reasons of health and age. Characterizing Khrushchev as a "buffoon on the contemporary political stage," the editorial said his "downfall is the result of a revisionist general line and the many erroneous policies he pursued at home and abroad."

Hsinhua, the Communist Chinese press agency, published Dec. 2 a Chinese report denouncing Soviet delegation action in Prague at a Nov. 14-17 meeting of the Executive Committee of the International Union of Students. Chinese delegation head Li

Shu-cheng assailed a Soviet foreign resolution for failing to stress that the principal task was "to concentrate all forces to oppose the main enemy, United States imperialism." The Soviet draft resolution, Li charged, had "wrongly defined the road to world peace as through peaceful coexistence and general and complete disarmament."

Khrushchev's coexistence policies had been reaffirmed by Kosygin and Brezhnev. In a meeting with a group of U.S. businessmen in Moscow Nov. 19, Kosygin said that peace remained the USSR's "immutable policy." In an address in the Soviet Central Asian city of Tashkent, Brezhnev declared Nov. 20: "In our relations with capitalist countries we consistently advocate the principle of peaceful coexistence. Those who wish to live in friendship with us will always meet our friendship."

Pravda Dec. 6 rebuffed a Nov. 21 article by *Hung Chi* that had criticized Moscow's concept of "the state of the whole people," the form of government under which the Soviet Union claimed that it ruled. In its reply, *Pravda* charged that China had favored one-man dictatorship for Communist nations. *Pravda* said that Peking's theory conflicted with conditions in the Soviet Union, which no longer was a "dictatorship of the proletariat," and that the Soviet CP had evolved "from a party of the working class...into a party of the whole people." The "state of the whole people" concept, in effect since 1961, was based on the contention that since social classes in the Soviet Union had been eliminated, the proletariat could no longer dictate policy. The *Pravda* article said: "Champions of the personality cult" "did not like our party's activities aimed at...the strengthening of the state of the whole people. But they did not dare attack openly and therefore they try to interpret the dictatorship of the proletariat in a way that suits them so as to make it a banner under which it would be possible to turn the countries of socialism to the ideology and practice of the personality cult."

DATE DUE

ILL 3/24/95	